# THE CANADIAN FAMILY TREE

# THE CANADIAN FAMILY TREE

## CANADA'S PEOPLES

Multiculturalism Directorate
Department of the Secretary of State

1450 Don Mills Road
Don Mills, Ontario M3B 2X7

© Minister of Supply and Services Canada, 1979

Published by Corpus Information Services Limited in co-operation with the Multiculturalism Directorate, Department of the Secretary of State, and the Canadian Government Publishing Centre, Supply and Services Canada.

ISBN 0-919217-13-3 Hardbound
ISBN 0-919217-14-1 Softbound

Government Catalogue Number:
CI95-7-1979

Printed and bound in Canada

DESIGN: Artplus Limited/Brant Cowie
TYPESETTING: Howarth & Smith Limited
PRINTING AND BINDING: John Deyell Company

---

**CANADIAN CATALOGUING IN PUBLICATION DATA**

Canada. Multiculturalism Directorate.
    The Canadian family tree

Previous ed. prepared by the Canadian Citizenship Branch, Dept. of the Secretary of State. Includes index.

ISBN 0-919217-13-3 bd. ISBN 0-919217-14-1 pa.

1. Canada — Population — Ethnic groups.* I. Title.

FC104.C35               971'.004          C79-094617-3
F1035.A1C35

---

# Table of Contents

# Foreword

EXCEPT FOR THE INDIGENOUS peoples of this country, all of us who live in Canada are immigrants or descendants of immigrants. Whether our settlement here can be traced back hundreds of years or one generation, we are all members of one or another ethnocultural group. This book is an account of the various ethnocultural groups that have come to Canada and the contributions each has made to the social, cultural, physical and economic development of this country.

The present volume constitutes the revised and updated version of the 1967 edition of *The Canadian Family Tree*, which itself was a revision of a 1960 edition, *Notes on the Canadian Family Tree*. The new edition takes into account the information recorded in the 1971 Canadian census and, in some instances, figures are given up to 1976.

In compiling this book, every effort has been made to include all ethnocultural groups, large and small, which have a distinct identity within Canadian society. For the purposes of this book, "identity" was understood as "one's sense of belonging to a group, and the group's collective will to exist", as defined in Book IV of the *Report of the Royal Commission on Bilingualism and Biculturalism*. Some other aspects of group identity which were taken into consideration include language, geographic origin, historical continuity and religion.

Every effort has been made to include in this summary all the groups and countries which have played, and are still playing, a part in Canadian immigration and the development of the country. Some groups and communities which are relatively small and unorganized have been included for purposes of information and comparison. However, some smaller groups could not be included because basic information was lacking or unreliable. In all cases, information included in this book has been checked with representatives of the communities concerned or with persons familiar with the groups.

In order to give as complete a description as possible, within space limitations, of the organizational components of groups, background information on countries of origin has been kept to a minimum. Readers wishing to learn more about this aspect of immigration history are advised to consult encyclopedias and other reference works.

Readers wishing further information on the groups listed can consult the bibliography at the end of this volume.

# Acknowledgments

IN RESEARCHING, writing and completing this project, acknowledgments are made to numerous individuals and associations for their kind cooperation. For compiling and writing the basic information on many of the ethnocultural groups, grateful thanks are expressed to Jan Andrews, Dr. Jan Fedorowicz, Nesta Hankey, Valerie Knowles, Dr. Tomoko Makabe, Fouad Shaker, Lennard Sillanpaa and Gregory Sucharczuk.

Thanks are expressed to many individuals who have contributed and verified a substantial amount or all of the information on specific ethnocultural groups; in particular, Dr. W. Murray Hogben, Dr. C. Jaenen, Wilson Ruiz, George Bonavia, Dr. T.A. Meininger, Dr. J.A. Boutilier and Dr. E.R. Appathurai.

Grateful thanks are also expressed to the many people and organizations who have contributed substantially to the contents of this volume through providing information, advice or editorial assistance. Every section has been reviewed by a member of the respective ethnocultural group or by individuals who are familiar with these groups.

Thanks are due to the members of the Canadian Ethnic Studies Advisory Committee, the Ethnic History Advisory Panel and the authors of the Ethnic History Project for their comments and advice. The contributions of the officers of the Multicultural Directorate are also gratefully acknowledged and appreciated, especially Myron Momryk who coordinated this project from its inception.

Comments and suggestions from the Historical Division, Department of External Affairs and from the Native Council of Canada are gratefully acknowledged and appreciated.

Special acknowledgment is made to John A. Roberts who edited the various drafts of the manuscript. Thanks are also due to the officers of the Communications Branch, Department of the Secretary of State, and to editor Ingrid Philipp Cook for preparing the manuscript for publication.

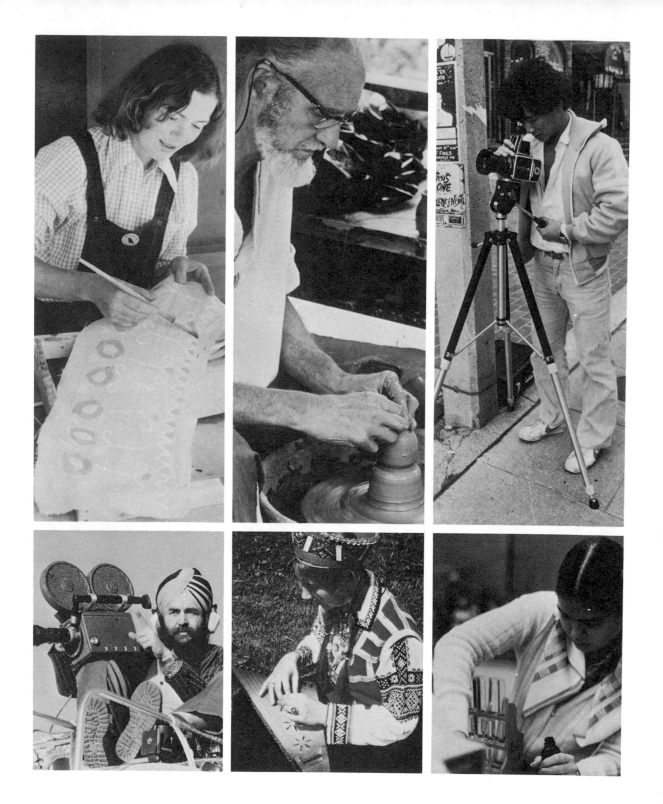

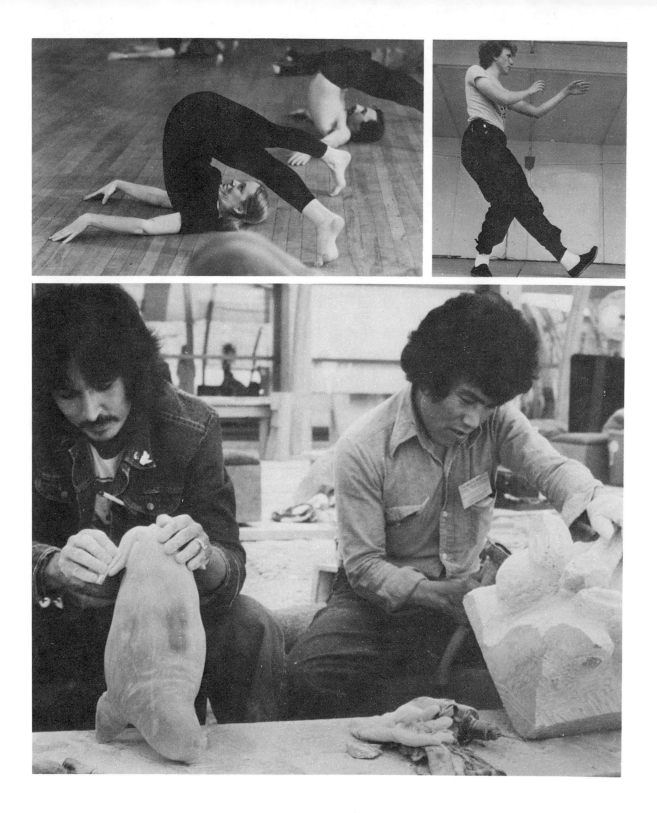

# Immigration: Key to Canadian History

*Samuel Raj, Ph.D. Ottawa, Ontario*

CANADIANS ARE A NATION of immigrants or descendants of immigrants. Even the native peoples of Canada descended from the immigrants of prehistoric times. While the precise time of arrival of the ancestors of the Amerindians and Inuit is hidden in the mist of prehistory, the arrival of the more recent Canadians began during the period of European expansion and colonization.

During the period of exploration and colonization the French were the first Europeans to immigrate in large numbers to Canada. Nearly all the six million French Canadians of the present day descend from the ten thousand immigrants who crossed the Atlantic during the years of French colonial rule in North America. Many of these immigrants established settlements in what was then known as Acadia, but the vast majority found homes along the St. Lawrence River from the Gaspé peninsula to the Island of Montreal.

The French government, like other contemporary colonial powers, subordinated the interest of the colonies to that of the mother country. When the government of France believed that a large populous colony would be advantageous to its interest, it actively sponsored emigration, but the moment it thought that the interests of France would be better served by increasing its own population, it dismissed its emigration scheme. Despite the French government's reluctance "to populate Canada by depopulating France", it sent large numbers of soldiers for the defence of the colony, many of whom later remained in Canada as settlers. During the great part of the French colonial rule, non-Catholics were prohibited from entering Canada; the French government did not want its domestic enemies to become a nuisance in New France. A small number of Blacks, English, Germans, Irish, Italians, Portuguese, Scots and Spanish were able to find their way into Canada during the French era.

The French colonial government did not have any consistent cultural and social policy towards its non-French subjects. At one time it hoped to assimilate the Amerindians and other non-French immigrants, but later it preferred a policy of laissez-faire. The various groups that lived in New France intermingled and intermarriage among the members of all these groups was not uncommon.

The British conquest of New France brought an end to French rule and opened a new chapter in the history of Canadian immigration. In the period immediately after 1760, British merchants and soldiers settled in the urban centres of Quebec, but there was no large wave of British immigration until the arrival of the United Empire Loyalists after the American Revolution. Between the years 1783 and 1785, nearly 35,000 Loyalists came to Canada from the eastern part of the United States of America. The vast majority of them took up settlements near Halifax, around the Bay of Fundy, along the Saint John River and on the shores of Cape Breton. Some of them found homes in L'Isle St. Jean (Prince Edward Island), and a few settled in more distant areas such as Newfoundland and the Chaleur Bay area in the Gaspé. About the same time there was also another exodus of about 10,000 Loyalists from western New York and Pennsylvania into Canada. They found homes along the upper St. Lawrence and the northern shore of Lake Ontario, in the Niagara Peninsula, and along the Detroit River. Some Loyalists also founded a settlement at Sorel, east of Montreal.

The United Empire Loyalists, it must be pointed out, were not the first British settlers in Canada. That proud claim belongs to some much-less-known settlers in Newfoundland. From the earliest days of European colonization, Newfoundland had had some British settlements. However significant these settlements might have been in Canadian history, they represented the labour of the earliest British settlers in Canada.

In addition to the United Empire Loyalists, there were also others who came from south of the border to seek homes in Canada. In the 1790s there was a stream of settlers flowing from northern Vermont into what came to be known as the Eastern Townships. By the time Canadians found themselves at war with the Americans in 1812, some 9,000 Americans had already well established themselves in that part of the country. They were to become the nucleus of an English-speaking population in the Eastern Townships.

Meanwhile there was also a steady flow of American settlers into what was then known as Upper Canada (now Ontario). Many of these immigrants were given the dubious title of "Late Loyalists". Whatever their real motives, land or loyalty to the Crown or both, they helped to swell the pioneer population. Out of the 94,000 people who resided in Upper Canada at the time of the outbreak of the war with the Americans, over 50,000 of them belonged to this wave of American immigration.

The Anglo-American war of 1812 put a temporary end to American large-scale immigration, but fortunately for the growth of Canada, the end of the Napoleonic Wars in Europe inaugurated a new period in the history of emigration from the British Isles. Prior to the end of the Napoleonic Wars in Europe, emigration from Britain was light. Apart from the Scottish settlers of Pictou and Antigonish in Nova Scotia, Point Prim in Prince Edward Island, and the Red River in Manitoba, relatively few had come from Britain. However, beginning with the end of the Napoleonic Wars and throughout the nineteenth century, there was a steady flow of immigrants from the British Isles to British North America.

Starting with a small number of arrivals in the late 1810s the flow of immigration rose to an annual average of over 15,000 in the late 1820s, reaching its peak in 1832, when 66,000 immigrants entered British North America. This tremendous increase became possible because cheap fares were available with the expansion of the timber trade between Britain and British North America in the 1820s. The vessels returning from Britain needed cargo on their voyage to Canada, and the immigrants came to meet the real need. Also during this period, several American Atlantic states began to impose a tax on immigration, and that had the effect of directing many of the poorer immigrants to Canada.

After the peak in 1832, there was a drop in the number of immigrants arriving in Canada. It was partly due to the cholera epidemic in Britain and partly due to the rebellions in Upper and Lower Canada. However, at the turn of the decade the immigration figure began to rise and it reached its climax in 1847 when nearly 90,000 immigrants, many of whom were Irish famine victims, landed in British North America. The annual immigration flow in the 1840s and 1850s averaged between 25,000 and 40,000. The flow slackened somewhat in the late 1850s. It is estimated that perhaps over a million immigrants entered British North America during the period between the Conquest and Confederation.

Despite the fact that such a large number of immigrants entered British North America, the governments of the day had no specific and defined immigration policy. As long as the British government was in charge of immigration, it simply allowed circumstances to dictate the course of its immigration policy. For example, after the American Revolution, Britain was glad to have its northern possessions as a place to send some of the refugees from former colonies. In the same way, after the end of the Napoleonic Wars, Britain sent some of its poor and unemployed to its American colonies as a solution to its own social, political, and economic problems. Even when the colonies, in 1848, assumed the responsibility for immigration, there was no real change in this attitude. Except for the prohibition against the landing of the criminal, the diseased, and the destitute, the governments of the various colonies continued to maintain an attitude of laissez-faire on immigration matters.

This attitude of laissez-faire came to an end with Confederation. In 1869, the new federal government in Ottawa enacted Canada's first immigration act. The Act provided the mechanism for securing and settling immigrants. It made provision for federal-provincial division of responsibilities, establishment of immigration agencies, quarantine stations and other necessary institutions related to the welfare of the immigrant. In the following two decades, the federal government established immigration agencies in London, Dublin, Belfast and Antwerp and spent large sums of money on promotion campaigns in the United Kingdom, Germany, France, Belgium and Switzerland. Prospective immigrants were promised free grants of land as well as a travel subsidy.

The result of the government's aggressive campaign was reflected in the immigration statistics of the period. After a brief slump in the late 1850s and in the 1860s, the immigration figures began to climb and averaged about 33,000 a year in the 1870s, 85,000 in the 1880s and 37,000 in the 1890s. The year 1883 holds the record for the nineteenth century. In that year, 133,624 immigrants entered Canada. It is estimated that about one and a half million people came to Canada during the years between Confederation and the end of the nineteenth century.

Not all these immigrants, however, remained in Canada. To many of them, the United States of America was still the "land of promise", and within a brief period of their entry into Canada, they simply crossed the border and went south. Throughout the nineteenth century more people emigrated from Canada to the United States than immigrated into Canada. As long as free or cheap good lands were available in the American midwest and as long as the border remained open, Canada found it difficult to hold either its own settlers or the immigrants who landed on its shores.

The decades of the 1870s and 1880s that saw the active campaign for immigrants also witnessed the development of restrictive regulations. In 1872, the Immigration Act was amended to prohibit the landing of criminals and other "vicious classes". In 1879, an Order in Council was passed to exclude paupers and destitutes. The year 1885 marked a new trend that was to characterize Canadian immigration for years to come. In that year, in response to demands from British Columbia, the federal government in Ottawa imposed a stiff head tax of fifty dollars on every Chinese immigrant. Never before had a Canadian government tried to restrict the entry of an immigrant on account of his racial or ethnic origin. This regulation against the Chinese immigrant however merely reflected the spirit of the time. A sense of racial superiority and a spirit of exclusion characterized the attitude of many people during that period both in western Europe and in North America.

The same decades also witnessed the westward expansion of Canada. The acquisition of the Hudson's Bay Company's territories in 1870 opened up a vast tract of land for agricultural settlement. Free and cheap lands once again became available in Canada, this time in the Prairies. In 1871, Canada's westward march reached the Pacific coast when the young crown colony of British Columbia joined the Confederation. The next few decades saw the construction of the transcontinental railway as well as of many branch lines both in the Prairies and in British Columbia. These railways not only helped to open up the country, but also facilitated the establishment and growth of many settlements, towns and cities.

The period between 1897 and 1914 was a watershed in the history of Canadian immigration. Within those eighteen brief years more immigrants entered Canada than in her entire previous history. During this period, over three million immigrants entered Canada; about 1,250,000 came from the British Isles, 1,000,000 from the United States, 800,000 from Continental Europe and 20,000 from the Orient including India. The year 1913 holds the record for the largest number of immigrants ever to enter Canada. Over 400,000 people found homes in Canada that year.

Although the Prairies underwent a phenomenal growth during this period, they received less than half of the immigrants of these years. About one half of the immigrants of this momentous period (as in all periods) went to central Canada, a smaller percentage proceeded to the Maritimes as well as to British Columbia, and the rest moved to the Prairies. The immigrants from Asia stayed on the west coast and did not cross the Rockies. Many of the immigrants to the Prairies became farmers but others found employment on railroads and in mines, lumber camps and factories in different parts of the country.

There were two major reasons for the great influx of immigrants during this period. First, the Laurier government launched an unprecedented campaign to attract agricultural settlers from the British Isles, the United States and Continental Europe. Not only were the immigrants given free land on certain conditions, but also many were promised several religious and cultural considerations. Many steamship companies and their agents were also actively involved in recruiting immigrants to Canada. Their eagerness to find passengers for their vessels led them to carry their campaign beyond Europe to include China and India. Second, by the 1880s, the American agricultural frontier in the midwest had become exhausted, and those who sought free or cheap land had no choice but go to the last frontier in the North American continent, the Canadian Prairies. The completion of the trans-continental railway across the country and the construction of other lines in the west and also the developments in dry land farming techniques encouraged many to settle in the Prairies.

This crucial period in the history of Canadian immigration also witnessed the second series of attempts to restrict the entry of Chinese and other Asian immigrants. In 1900, the head tax on Chinese immigrants was raised to one hundred dollars and three years later it was raised to five hundred dollars. In the following year (1904), Canada and Japan signed a gentleman's agreement limiting the number of Japanese immigrants to Canada to four hundred per year. Canada also tried to enter into a somewhat similar agreement with the British colonial government of India but without success. Therefore, in 1908, an Order-in-Council was issued to prevent the coming of East Indians. The order, which came to be known as the Continuous Voyage Regulation, required every prospective Asian immigrant to come to Canada directly without any change of vessel from the land of his birth and citizenship in order to be eligible for admission into Canada. Since there was no direct steam service from India to Canada in those days, it was an indirect but most effective way of preventing East Indians from coming to Canada. The same order was applied to prevent the landing of the Japanese coming from the Hawaiian islands. Sometime later the Canadian government stipulated that all Asian immigrants, except Japanese and Chinese, had to be in possession of two hundred dollars in order to be eligible to enter Canada. All of these restrictions, including some newly imposed restrictive measures on British and European immigrants, were incor-

porated into the Immigration Act of 1910.

These restrictive regulations reflected at least to a certain extent the growing concern of long-time Canadians towards the changing nature of their society. At the time of Confederation, non-French and non-British Canadians constituted only about 8 per cent of the total population of Canada, but by 1911, they had come to constitute over 15 per cent of the Canadian population. Where a new group become conspicuous, it fell victim to the resentment of more established Canadians. In the Prairies, protests were made against the presence of continental European immigrants, but on the west coast objections were raised against the Asian immigrants.

World War I brought a sudden halt to this era of unprecedented immigration and the next wave of immigration did not begin till the end of the war. The new wave of immigration of the interwar period did not last long. The Depression and political changes in Europe effectively reduced immigration to a trickle. From a high of 107,698 in 1919, the immigration figure went down to 27,530 in 1931. It fell even further as the Depression deepened and as Canada later entered the Second World War. Between the end of World War I and the beginning of the Great Depression, 1,476,724 immigrants arrived in Canada, but between the beginning of the Depression (1931) and the end of World War II (1945) only 219,494 entered Canada.

The interwar period witnessed the legislation of the most exclusive and restrictive immigration regulations in the history of Canada. The Chinese were completely excluded by the Chinese Immigration Act of 1923. Resident East Indians were allowed to bring their wives and minor children but all others from India were excluded. The Japanese were permitted to enter Canada on the basis of an agreed number. Eastern and southern Europeans no longer enjoyed the virtual free entry privilege they had had prior to the war. It was thought that Canada's national interest would be best served by excluding the "lesser breeds", and restricting the "lower orders", and confining her immigrant recruits primarily to the people of the British Isles and continental Western Europe. During this period a similar wave of xenophobia swept the United States as well. This attitude remained as one of the guiding principles of Canada's immigration policy until the end of the Second World War when racism and racial myths came under attack and became discredited.

The postwar period witnessed a radical alteration to the exclusive and restrictive basis of immigration. Although Prime Minister Mackenzie King's major policy statement of 1947 was still restrictive in content, the Prime Minister promised to remove "objectional discrimination" from the "existing legislation" and laboured hard to defend Canada's right to adopt a policy that seemed appropriate for her national interest. "Immigration is a matter of domestic policy," the Prime Minister declared, and "Canada is perfectly within her rights in selecting the immigrants she wants." The Prime Minister also defended the limitations on certain groups on the grounds that "the people of Canada do not wish to make a fundamental alteration in the character of their population through mass immigration." However, he added that the Canadian government was "ready to negotiate special agreements with other countries for the control of immigration based on complete equality and reciprocity."

In accordance with the Prime Minister's pronouncements, the Chinese Immigration Act of 1923, which had excluded the Chinese completely from Canada, was repealed. The discriminatory stipulation of landing money of $200.00 and the Continuous Voyage Restriction were also abolished. A selective system was introduced for East Indian, Pakistani and Ceylonese immigrants. The immigration policy towards Asians was no longer one of exclusion but one of selective restriction.

Among the other immigrants, preference was still given to the British, Irish, French and Americans. The determination of the admissibility of others was left to the judgment of the Minister of Citizenship and Immigration, who was to consider the prospective immigrant's suitability "to climatic, educational, social, industrial labour and other conditions and requirements in Canada." The Minister might also declare a prospective immigrant undesirable because of his "peculiar customs, habits, modes of life, methods of holding property" or his general inability to assimilate.

In the 1950s, despite the preference given to the immigrants from the British Isles, the United States and northwestern Europe, prospective immigrants from southern and eastern European countries who had once been declared "non-preferred" were reclassified as coming from "traditional sources". Furthermore, about the same time, several countries in the Middle East, including Egypt, Israel, Lebanon, and Turkey, came to be considered as "Europeans" for immigration purposes. Under pressure from the newly emerging Commonwealth countries, Canada also continued to loosen its restrictive policy towards specified categories of non-European immigrants.

The postwar immigration policies also reflected a greater concern for international refugees. Immediately after the war thousands of political refugees and displaced persons were allowed to enter Canada on a very liberal basis. Since then thousands of Slovaks,

Hungarians, Armenians, North African and Roumanian Jews, Congo Belgians, Czechs, Ugandan Asians, Chileans and most recently Vietnamese have been admitted into Canada as refugees. Almost every tenth immigrant in the postwar period has been a political refugee.

Throughout this period, the general immigration policy has been to relate the inflow of immigrants to Canada's "absorptive capacity". The flow of immigration was to vary from year to year depending upon the nation's economic condition. It was also thought that Canada should encourage immigration for reasons of security and improvement in the standard of living. Prime Minister Mackenzie King stated in 1947 that it would be difficult for a small population to contain "so great a heritage as ours" and also that a larger population would assist in developing Canada's resources and in enlarging its domestic markets. The general considerations have had the effect of modifying otherwise rather selective and restrictive immigration policies and making them more progressive.

The White Paper of 1966 and the Regulations of the following year marked the beginning of the latest phase in the evolution of Canada's immigration policies. All forms of discrimination based on race, colour, religion, national origin or sex were declared to be abolished. The basis of admission for all immigrants was to be Canada's manpower needs. The earlier postwar aims were again repeated —population growth, expansion of domestic markets, and lower per capita cost of governments and services. Cultural enrichment was added as part of the objectives of immigration. The older cultural and racial preference was replaced by educational and technical criteria which were to be assessed by certain number of merit points. Furthermore, the White Paper as well as the Regulations reaffirmed Canada's responsibility to take into consideration international refugee problems in admitting immigrants.

Since 1967, the immigration policies have remained substantially the same. Some modifications have been made in the procedures, and also some attempts have been made to define somewhat loosely Canada's "absorptive capacity". In 1972, the option of applying for landed immigrant status was taken away from students and visitors. The "absorptive capacity" is still closely related to manpower needs. With regard to objectives as well as in underlying principles, the 1976 Act is substantially the same as the 1967 Regulations.

As the result of these expansionary and progressive immigration policies, Canada has received nearly four and a half million immigrants in the last three decades. These immigrants represent a cross section of the society, and they have come from every part of the world. Today, the Canadian family consists of over eighty ethnocultural groups, and practically every major race, creed, and culture is represented in it.

Canadians of British origin still form the single largest group but they no longer are the majority. At the time of Confederation, they represented more than 61 per cent of the Canadian family. Canadians of French origin constituted about 31 per cent of the people of Canada at Confederation and today they represent about 30 per cent of Canadians. Throughout the post-Confederation period, the French Canadians' ratio in the Canadian mosaic has remained remarkably constant. Unlike these two groups, the British and the French, the proportion of Canadians of other origins has steadily increased, particularly since the end of the Second World War. It went up from about 15 per cent in 1911 to about 19 per cent in 1941. Today, Canadians of non-British and non-French origin constitute a little over 28 per cent of Canada's population.

Through the 1960s, the government as well as all major political parties came to recognize the pluralistic nature of Canadian society and to formulate policies and take measures to enable Canadians of diverse origins to feel at home and make their maximum contribution to Canada's social and cultural life. The Bilingualism and Biculturalism Commission Report, Dunton-Laurendeau Commission (Book IV), gave further stimulus to the ethnocultural groups' demand for recognition. Finally, in 1971, with the warm approval of all the political parties in Parliament, the government of Canada declared multiculturalism within the framework of bilingualism to be its official state policy.

# Albanians

ONE OF THE SMALLEST ethnic groups in Canada, but also one of the proudest, is the Albanians—or *Shqipetarë* (Sons of the Eagle), as they call themselves. Numbering between 7,000 and 10,000 persons in Canada, this ancient Balkan people traces its history back to the Illyrians, the oldest inhabitants of southeastern Europe. Waves of Greeks, Celts, Romans, Huns and Slavs forced these warrior clans into the mountains and the coastal plain of the Adriatic where they proceeded to maintain their linguistic and cultural identity with considerable success. They were divided into feudal clans, the largest being the Ghegs of the north and the Tosks of the south, and

these allegiances have not disappeared. After a subsequent long war of resistance to the spread of the Ottoman Empire, under the military leadership of Gjerj Kastrioti (or Skanderbeg), the Albanians underwent a period of Turkish domination from the late fifteenth to the early twentieth centuries. During that period most of the population became Sunni (orthodox) Muslims or Bektashi sectarians. Those groups currently total about 70 per cent, while the remainder are still 20 per cent Orthodox and 10 per cent Roman Catholic Christians. Under the Turks, the Albanians continued their martial tradition by providing generations of skilled irregulars for the Turkish forces and a series of leading administrators for the Turkish Empire, including Mehet Ali, the early nineteenth century founder of modern Egypt.

After the last century's wave of nationalism, the Albanians revolted against their Turkish overlords in 1911, and succeeded in winning their independence in November, 1912. However, their independence has been under constant threat ever since, and the state of Albania excludes at least one-third of its heirs who are minorities centred in neighbouring states. Aside from these losses, Albania was twice dominated by Italy in the First and Second World Wars, and by the Nazis until 1944. However, after a bloody guerrilla war, the current Albanian People's Republic emerged in 1946, only to become enmeshed in communist bloc politics and alliances.

As for the Albanians in Canada, the first probably arrived between 1904 and 1906 during the prewar nationalist revolutionary period, although others had emigrated to the United States in the late nineteenth century. In the post-revolutionary period, almost all Albanian immigrants to Canada were males who worked in factories, on railways and in restaurants, or wherever they could, to support themselves and their families in Albania. Their numbers remained small, centred on "Konaks" or inns, boarding houses which became the urban centres of Albanian cultural existence, aside from their religious organizations and nationalist clubs.

In the decade after the Second World War this handful of Albanians was joined by an influx of wives and families for the first time, as emigration from war-torn and newly revolutionized Albania became essential for many. In the subsequent two decades a small but steady trickle has continued to follow them. During the period 1947–60, 332 Albanians arrived in Canada. A total of 208 Albanians arrived in the period 1961–75. Most of these immigrants chose Ontario as their destination, with a smaller number arriving in Quebec. Many Albanians, however, entered Canada from other countries such as Greece, Yugoslavia, southern Italy, Egypt and Turkey. These immigrants entered the country on the national passports of their former country of residence.

The Albanian community has remained centred in the larger urban areas, especially Toronto and Montreal, and also in centres such as Peterborough, Ontario, and Calgary, Alberta. Their clan and religious affiliations deserve further study as do their various political affiliations, all reflecting their Albanian roots, dates of departure and social positions. Currently, the Albanians in Toronto are of all three religious groups, while in Montreal they seem predominantly Christian. It appears that these religious groupings do not stand in the way of political allegiances. As for their press, there are no Canadian Albanian newspapers, but *Dielli* (The Sun) is readily available to them, being published in Boston, Massachusetts, since 1909, largely in the Albanian language but with some English inserts. The *Liria* (Liberty), founded in 1941, is also published in Boston.

The Albanian social condition in Canada has been the result of at least as painful a progress as has been experienced by any European ethnocultural minority. The first immigrants were often considered "Turks" and hence discriminated against by some Canadians, and they have had to make the usual difficult decisions regarding employment, marriage, and language and religion retention in the face of a dominant culture. "Canadian" names were often given to children in order to protect them from very real discrimination, and many other adjustments had to be made. However, the expanding Canadian economy found various places for the Albanians. Many Albanians are in skilled and semi-skilled trades, and there is also a small but growing number of Canadian-born and educated Albanians who are in various professions. They remain largely a proud, traditional and independent people, still closely attached to their various affiliations. With time to make the necessary continuing adjustments, they will integrate further into the mainstream of Canadian life, as the younger generations are doing now.

# Americans

*See also Blacks*

FOR CENTURIES, people have moved from old homes to new. But possibly the greatest movement of immigrants of all time occurred after Columbus discovered America. Spain, France, Holland, Portugal, Sweden and Russia all claimed shares in America at one time, until the English finally established the American colonies. Thirteen of the Anglo-American colonies became the United States of America on July 4, 1776, when they adopted the Declaration of Independence, and in 1783 the articles of the Treaty of Paris were signed, ending the American Revolution and granting the new country independence from Great Britain.

The history of the western United States began with the movement of settlers beyond the Appalachian Mountains, and after the War of 1812 settlement in the west increased. With the gold rush to California and the westward spread of the railways, by the time the nation was a hundred years old American settlements spanned the continent.

Americans have always played an important role in the history of Canadian society. Immigration of large numbers of Americans to Canada began as early as 1760 with English traders and merchants coming to Quebec City and Montreal from New York and other trading centres in the Thirteen Colonies. Between 1946 and 1973, to bring our information closer to the present, 384,137 people who gave their last permanent address as the United States entered Canada as landed immigrants. In both 1971 and 1972, the United States stood as the leading source country for Canadian immigration. In 1974, when more than 22,000 American immigrants gained landed immigrant status, the United States was second only to Great Britain as a source country. These Canadians of American origin have integrated well into all levels of Canadian society.

Since sections of Canada and the United States are regions with a shared heritage, hold many customs in common, and are predominantly English-speaking, it is not surprising that the mainstream of American immigration has been made up of those for whom total integration has appeared as a natural and easy step, and who have not maintained a particular group identity in Canada. Exceptions to this include the American Mormons, who established pioneer settlements in southern Alberta, American Blacks, Swiss-origin Mennonites from Pennsylvania and Hutterites from the Dakotas. These groups have distinct histories as communities within the larger trends of American immigration.

In over two hundred years of history, American immigration into Canada has been a stimulus for both political and economic activity. The most important early political movement was that of the Loyalists during and especially after the American Revolution. About one in three of the people in the rebelling colonies who had been opposed to the revolution, and many of those opposed to the new government, chose to leave after the American victory in 1782. They were called the Loyalists. There is no doubt that their concern for the maintenance of British traditions, institutions and authority was of prime significance during the British North America's formative years, particularly in the history of the Maritimes.

The Loyalists numbered between forty and fifty thousand persons, the main body of whom settled in what are now Nova Scotia, Prince Edward Island and New Brunswick. They represented every socio-economic group of the colonial population, and many had the common experience of suffering the loss of most of their material possessions. Their settlement led to the establishment of the Province of New Brunswick separate from the Province of Nova Scotia, the New Brunswick group being composed mainly of new immigrants on the north shore of the Bay of Fundy, while the Nova Scotia Loyalists attached themselves to the established community around Halifax. They came to outnumber the earlier settlers in these two colonies by almost two to one.

There was also some Loyalist movement into what is now Quebec, and significant settlement in what is now Ontario. Other early political migrations included those of the Pennsylvania Mennonites and Amish into what is now Ontario after these religious groups had assumed the unpopular stance of conscientious objectors, and the migration of some 15,000 pro-Confederates and "skeddadlers", or those who chose not to serve during the American Civil War of 1861–65, along with refugees from the northern states who came to British North America to escape the ravages of war. Most of these deserters are thought to have returned to the United States when a general amnesty was granted at the end of the war.

The primary attraction to American immigrants from the earliest period to the early twentieth century was land. It was the quest for land that led thousands of New Englanders between 1760 and 1763 to accept the invitation of the Governor of Nova Scotia to repopulate areas left empty after the forced evacuation of the Acadians. When the Revolutionary War started, these "neutral Yankees" represented at least two-thirds of Nova Scotia's 18,000 non-native population figure.

It was also the search for land that led men like Philemon Wright, founder of the present city of Hull, Quebec, to follow the Loyalists north between 1785 and 1812. It is believed that about 70,000 Americans crossed the border between these years. The majority moved into what is now Ontario, but the migration into what is now Quebec by some 10,000 Americans caused a radical administrative change in the area. With their background of English land tenure and common

law, they were entirely unwilling to accept the seigneurial land tenure and French legal system maintained in the colony after the Conquest. Nor were they willing to accept a non-elected government. As a result, in 1791 the British Parliament passed the Constitutional Act, which solved most of the problems of the new situation. The old colony of Quebec was split into a largely French-Canadian eastern section to be known as Lower Canada, and a formerly almost uninhabited western section, called Upper Canada, which was largely immigrant Loyalist and English-speaking.

The last great land movement followed the passage of the Dominion Land Act in 1872. This Act officially opened the Prairies for settlement, and a few land-hungry American farmers began to go north in a movement which would bring large numbers to that area by the turn of the century.

In 1873, a total of 8,971 persons were listed as "immigrants from the United States", a number which rose to 14,110 in the following year and sagged back again in 1875 to 8,139. The value of settlers' effects in 1875 was put at $434,054. This same source of information adds that "other immigrants may have arrived from the United States without having made entries of settlers' goods; of whom, therefore, no record can be obtained." Included in the figure for the year 1875 was a "special Mennonite immigration, which numbered 3,285 souls." They came to Canada by way of the United States, although they did not live there.

The Mennonites were not the only religious group which came to Canada *en masse*. In 1886–87 a sizeable group of Mormons from Utah and Idaho, who were engaged in a political controversy with the federal authorities of the United States over the question of polygamy, decided to immigrate to the southwest corner of the present province of Alberta. They took up land on the site of the town of Cardston, where they gradually prospered. Within three years of the migration, the Mormon Church officially discontinued polygamy. These original settlers were joined at the turn of the century by another influx of Mormon settlers who were credited with the introduction of irrigation methods to the Canadian West and the early development of the sugar beet industry, centred in the region of Raymond, Alberta. Today there are thousands of descendants of the original forty-one settlers and subsequent groups scattered throughout Canada.

Completion of the Canadian Pacific Railway in 1885 and the introduction of a vigorous program to encourage immigration in 1896 by Clifford Sifton, Minister of the Interior, coupled with changing world economic conditions and improved agricultural technology, brought large numbers of settlers to the West. These events, along with improving economic conditions in Canada and the disappearance of land for settlement in the American midwest, combined to attract large numbers of Americans to the Prairies between 1896 and 1914. In general, the Americans were among the most widely sought-after immigrants during those years.

Between 1896 and 1915, nearly one million immigrants were admitted to Canada from the United States. In fact, during the years from 1907 to 1915, about 40 per cent of all homestead entries filed by immigrants were registered by Americans. Many were experienced in prairie farming, all were familiar with the North American lifestyle, many had capital, and many were able to bring livestock and machinery. They were able to establish themselves in their new surroundings quickly and

effectively. The peak year for admission from the United States was 1912, when over 120,000 persons came to Canada as immigrants.

The outbreak of the First World War brought about a substantial drop in American immigration, to some 24,000 in 1915. Although by 1917 the number had risen again to more than 65,000 for the year, never again did the flow of people from south of our border reach the proportions of prewar years. Growing prosperity undoubtedly kept many Americans at home, and the rapid expansion of industry provided many job opportunities which were not available in Canada. By 1924, admissions from the United States had dropped to about 16,000 for the year. Although there was a gradual increase over the next six years, the worldwide economic depression of the 1930s again reduced the flow.

The Depression, followed by the outbreak of the Second World War in 1939, kept immigration at a low level for a decade. Between 1936 and 1945, the total number of immigrants to Canada from all countries was 133,238 persons, of whom 56,043, or over 42 per cent, came from the United States. But while the Second World War had a negative effect on immigration, it had a marked effect on Canadian industrial and commercial development. As a result of the war, Canada emerged as a major industrial nation. The rapid and continuing expansion of industry and trade after 1945 brought many Americans to Canada who possessed an impressive array of experience and skills that were required in the economic and industrial development of the country. They came in large numbers to take advantage of the opportunities offered in Canada; between 1946 and 1973, over 384,137 persons whose last permanent residence was the United States immigrated to Canada.

Land and industrial opportunity were not

the only features of Canada that Americans found economically attractive. At various times natural resources were also a significant attraction to Americans. The British Columbia and Klondike gold rushes of the nineteenth century attracted thousands. American men and money were engaged in Cape Breton coal mining during the American Civil War, American interest in the mining potential of northern Ontario became evident in the years around 1900, and American involvement in the development of British Columbia mines and paper mills was extensive at both the managerial and technical levels. At present, 58 per cent of the oil and gas industry and 53 per cent of all mining and smelting in Canada are owned by companies with headquarters in the United States. Many of the technical workers engaged in drilling operations in western Canada have gained their experience in the oilfields of Texas, Oklahoma and elsewhere. With the expansion of Canadian universities in the 1960s, many teachers, researchers and other educators were recruited from the United States to staff new departments and faculties.

In more recent times, because of events surrounding American involvement in the Vietnam war, large numbers of young American men chose to refuse military service, leave that country and assume virtual refugee status in Canada. These men were often followed by wives and families, and by a substantial number of others who were dissatisfied with social and political conditions in the United States. After the cessation of the draft and the final conclusion of the war, the U.S. government pardoned or discharged various kinds of war resisters, but many of the "refugees" chose to remain in Canada. There was no general amnesty. It is not possible to determine exactly the size of this exile community, although in 1971 a minimum figure of 40,000 and a maximum of 100,000 persons was estimated.

There are other ways in which the American presence in Canada is being felt. Americans have played a prominent role in the development of professional sports including baseball and football in this country. Many outstanding coaches and players have been recruited in the United States, and a number have elected to remain in Canada after their playing days were over, some as coaches, others in professional or business fields related to sports. Americans have also been involved with Canadian radio and television from its beginnings, and the three major Canadian networks air numerous American shows, while radio stations rely on American music to a great extent. American tourists form an important part of the Canadian tourism industry.

Most Americans have never demonstrated a desire or a need to establish their own social structure in the communities in which they settle. In some of the larger centres, American clubs did appear which were entirely social in their aims and which provided members with the opportunity of meeting other Americans. Many of these clubs have gradually disappeared, however, since the close parallel between the modes of living, social customs and economic standards of Canada and the United States has resulted in most Americans rapidly becoming part of the Canadian scene, with little if anything to distinguish them from their Anglophone Canadian neighbours.

# Amerindians

*See also Métis*

CANADIAN INDIANS are descendants of the original immigrants to the continents of America. Archeological evidence seems to indicate that these original settlers likely came across the Bering Strait from Asia about 40,000 years ago, and that successive waves of immigration lasted until about 3,000 BC. The last of these waves is thought to have contained the ancestors of the early Inuit.

The term "Indian" is European in origin. It was apparently coined by Columbus, who hoped that he had reached some part of Asia when he arrived in the West Indies. Only in comparatively recent times has the name achieved general acceptance among the Indians themselves. Scholars now prefer the term "Amerindians."

At the moment of European contact in the fifteenth and sixteenth centuries, it is thought that there were about 200,000 Indians living in the area which constitutes present-day Canada. Their population declined drastically in the following centuries as a result of both the introduction of European diseases and the widespread changes and disruption in their lives. Only about 100,000 individuals registered as Indians were living in Canada at the turn of the twentieth century, but since then steady population increases have occurred.

There are now over 276,000 people registered as Indians in Canada according to the terms of the Indian Act. Consideration must be given to the fact that this Act allows non-Indian women who marry registered Indian men to be registered themselves, and causes to be "struck from the register" Indian women marrying non-registered men as well as those who, by choice, give up their Indian status. Deregistration is irreversible and applies to all descendants, giving rise to a group of Canadians who regard themselves as Indians but do not have the legal status of Indians. Exactly how many people fall into this category is not currently known. The Native Council of Canada, which is the national association of non-status Indians and Métis, currently claims to represent some 750,000 such people.

The history of Indian development in Canada is lengthy. It would appear, from archeological evidence gleaned thus far, that by the fifteenth century at least ten overall linguistic groupings had emerged in what is now Canada (five of which were among the Indians of British Columbia), and that possibly six overall cultural groups, each effective for a number of tribes, were then in existence.

The various cultural groups were quite distinct, and the differences in lifestyle and heritage were marked. The west coast Indians and the Six Nations Iroquois Confederacy lived relatively settled lives. Less structured than either of these groups were the Algonkian peoples of the eastern woodlands. The peoples of the plains were also nomadic. Other groupings included the tribes of interior British Columbia and those of the Yukon and Mackenzie basin.

As far as the Indian peoples are concerned, native involvement in Canadian history has been characterized by two main phases, independence and dependence. The first lasted until about 1812 in eastern Canada and somewhat longer in British Columbia and on the Prairies. Throughout this first phase, Indians maintained a position of relative equality and played an essential role in the events shaping Canadian history.

The early European settlers were outsiders who needed Indian knowledge and skills. Also, the new settlers were few in number and were sparsely scattered, and were threatened by their own internal rivalries. The French had never displaced any native peoples from their lands in North America in order to establish their own agriculture and towns. Indeed, they remained dependent upon the Indians for military support, the exploitation of the fur trade and the supply of their hinterland posts. Indian allies were, therefore, a significant factor in the military history of Canada's colonial period.

The original Indian Department, established by the British in 1755, was a branch of the military formed to win Indian support at first against the French and later against the Americans. The French, in the years prior to 1763, used trade agreements and alliances with various tribes to gain loose hegemony from the Gaspé to Lake Winnipeg; the British welcomed the assistance of Chief Thayendanegea (Joseph Brant) and his Mohawks during the American Revolution, and eventually settled them in Upper Canada as Loyalists.

During the second phase the balance of power changed irrevocably. The most important single factor in this phase was the question of numbers. The Indian population was declining, as European diseases and violent involvement in trade and international rivalries began to take their toll. White settlers were entering the country at an ever-increasing rate. As European miners moved into British Columbia and agricultural settlers moved onto the prairies, the attitudes towards Indians changed. Not only were the native peoples rapidly outnumbered, but also the food

resources on which they depended—fish in the Fraser valley and buffalo on the plains—were threatened. Throughout the course of previous dealings between Indians and Europeans there had been some European disregard for Indian achievements, values, customs and beliefs, unless these were perceived as being useful to the encouragement of trade and military support. Now, as the non-Indian population grew, and as the importance of the fur trade declined and was replaced by a desire for land, the Indians were pushed off their traditional homelands.

Reluctantly, the Indians gave up their lands and entered into treaties with the Europeans in most parts of Canada. Under these treaties, the Crown undertook to set aside reserved lands and to provide such benefits as cash payments, annuities and educational facilities in return for the tribes' relinquishing their claimed territories. A branch of the government was formed to administer these reserves and benefits; it is known today as the Indian Affairs Branch of the Department of Indian Affairs and Northern Development. Government regulations regarding Indians were first consolidated in the Indian Act of 1876. This Act was revised and amended over the years, was rewritten in 1951, and is currently under study for revision once again.

The Indian Affairs Branch is encouraging Indians to take an increasing role in the management of their community self-government. Indians on reserves may elect band councils consisting of a chief and councillors. The chief and one councillor for every hundred members of the band are elected for a two-year term. About two out of every three bands follow this elective system, and most of the remaining bands have modified their customs to correspond with it. The band council is the officially recognized body with which the Indian Affairs Branch deals. The councils may pass by-laws regarding local matters and they have acquired a certain amount of control regarding the expenditure of band funds and the management of property. Welfare assistance, community planning, economic development and school administration may also be managed in varying degrees by the band councils.

Eight regional advisory councils have been established in order to increase the participation of Indians in the management of their affairs. Each council is composed of eight to twelve Indians selected by the bands in the region in addition to the representatives of Indian organizations. A consultation procedure is used to interpret federal policies and to obtain Indian views on matters of policy, proposed legislation, federal-provincial arrangements, new programs and suggested changes in old programs. A National Indian Advisory Board, formed to bring together Indians from all regions, includes eighteen representatives named by the regional councils. The number of representatives from each council is based on population.

Status Indians are at present divided into 565 bands, each affected by the cultural heritage of its own tribal grouping. There are about 2,274 reserves of varying sizes, and about 70 per cent of status peoples live either on these reserves or on Crown land. A substantial migration of Indians to the cities has been evident in recent years, however. The reserves have not grown in size, although their natural resources are being developed. In many areas employment opportunities are insufficient or even non-existent. For these reasons, many Indians have chosen to leave the reserves. Yet their previous experience, tribal concepts and education or training has not prepared them for employment in the larger Canadian soci-

ety. Many face bewilderment and loneliness in transferring from a tribal and insular way of life to an industrialized urban society.

Even though Indians remain subject to considerable social and economic disadvantages, there have been some improvements in some areas due to increased public sensitivity and, more importantly, to determined efforts on the part of the Indians both to be heard and to regain the major voice in the management of their affairs. Important to these efforts was the presentation by the federal government in 1969 of a White Paper, which set forth a proposal for a new Indian policy. Opposition to it proved a powerful unifying force.

Some Indians have managed to achieve the transfer from their traditional lives to the urban economy with conspicuous success, resulting in an increasing number of Indian lawyers, medical doctors and other professionals. Many Indians are attracting attention in the arts. Rapidly accelerating educational programs and facilities, an increasing use of provincial schools, scholarships for university courses and financial assistance to Indian students are helping to develop the potential and the capabilities of the Indians.

On the more isolated reserves, many people still pursue the traditional occupations of hunting, trapping and fishing and, where conditions are favourable, agriculture and cattle raising. To supplement their income, some Indians are able to find casual employment in construction work, lumbering and railway work in areas adjacent to their reserves.

Indian handicrafts provide a means of income for those skilled in their production. Beaded and furred moccasins and jackets, snowshoes, lacrosse sticks and articles for the tourist trade all bring in a considerable annual income. For the most part, these craft industries have been initiated by the Indian people themselves.

As more co-operatives are formed and more retail outlets become available, both on and off reserves, craft work is becoming a reliable source of income for status Indians. An example of this can be seen on the Cape Croker reserve in Ontario, where members of a co-operative produce and market rustic furniture. Fish processing and freezing co-operatives are operated by Indians in Manitoba and Saskatchewan. Other commercial enterprises include La Ronge Industries in northern Saskatchewan and the Prince Rupert cultural and handicraft project sponsored by the Native Brotherhood of British Columbia.

In almost all of the larger centres where a number of Indian people live, Indian clubs or associations, such as the North American Indian Club of Toronto and the Nickle Belt Indian Club of Sudbury, have been formed. These clubs attempt to provide social, recreational and cultural activities for their members. Both men and women members often visit Indian patients in local hospitals. They understand, as few others can, the predicament of Indians new to the city. The members of such clubs have at times been the real impetus behind the establishment of a growing number of Friendship Centres.

There was and still is a need for readily accessible meeting places where Indian people may find a welcome in a pleasant, non-institutional atmosphere, where they can also find counselling for immediate problems of finding employment and accommodation. The first Indian and Métis Friendship Centre opened its doors in Winnipeg in 1959, and was soon followed by about twenty similar centres in towns and cities in many parts of Canada. These centres are meant to provide a bridge from one way of life to another for Indian

people. Both Indians and non-Indians work together in the centres, both as staff members and as volunteers. In addition to offering counselling services, they provide a referral service which directs individuals to other agencies most able to help with specific problems.

Most of the centres attempt to provide facilities for studying Indian cultural subjects, and for short educational or orientation courses. Many also provide accommodation for regular meetings of Indian clubs, pow-pow or Indian dance groups and social gatherings. Some centres provide retail outlets for Indian craft work from reserves, and many employ one or two court workers to assist Indians in dealings with the law.

In most Canadian provinces, Indians have organized themselves into associations such as the Native Brotherhood of British Columbia, the Alberta Indian Association, the Federation of Saskatchewan Indians, the Manitoba Brotherhood of Indians, the Union of Ontario Indians, the Association of Iroquois and Allied Indians, the Grand Councils of Treaties Numbers 3 and 9, and the Confederation of Indians of Quebec. These organizations concern themselves with promoting the welfare and interests of reserve Indians in their respective provinces.

In 1961 the National Indian Council was organized by William Wuttunee, a Cree lawyer then living in Calgary. It was the first all-Indian organization that attempted to deal with matters of concern to Indians on a national basis. In 1969, a national status-Indian body, the Indian Brotherhood, representative of all of the provincial associations, was officially founded. Each association works through programs designed to improve the cultural, social and economic well-being of its members. Lobbying, political negotiation and policy-making are nonetheless the most important aspects of their endeavours. In this field, the National Indian Brotherhood has, among other things, made representations to the federal government on all major issues, including matters relating to the Mackenzie valley pipeline, the James Bay project, and the Indian Act revision.

One of the most active organizations concerned with the welfare and progress of Indian people is the Canadian Association in Support of Native People, which has a large number of both Indian and non-Indian members across the country. Indian women on reserves, like women in other Canadian communities, are often active members in homemakers' clubs and home and school associations. A number are members of the National Native Women's Association and its related associations.

Like other ethnocultural groups, Indians have seen a need for their own newspapers, periodicals and communications systems. Thus, publications such as the Alberta-based *Kainai News*, the *Indian Voice* of British Columbia, the *Micmac News* of the Union of Nova Scotia Indians, and the *Saskatchewan Indian* of the Federation of Saskatchewan Indians, to name but a few, have arisen. Groups such as the Friendship Centres have instituted their own regular publications: the Native Canadian Centre of Toronto, for instance, produces the *Toronto Native Times*, and the Ontario Federation of Indian Friendship Centres publishes *Ontario Native Experience*.

Communications societies have been formed to utilize the potential of television, radio and film. Societies such as the Alberta Native Communications Society exist in various parts of the country. The Alberta group provides programming to radio stations, produces a weekly television show, makes films, has a weekly newspaper, and co-operates

in a training program. CBC Radio produces a weekly native program called "Our Native Land", which features both native news and native broadcasters and performers.

There has been an upsurge in the number of Indian pageants and annual pow-wows in recent years, and in the number of Indian people who attend these events. Generally speaking, the western and plains Indians hold pow-wows with everyone present participating in spontaneous singing and dancing. In Ontario and eastern Canada it is usual for a group of performers to present a planned program, which the other Indians enjoy as spectators.

The annual Sioux pow-wow at Fort Qu'Appelle, Saskatchewan, attracts thousands of Indians from all over Canada and the northeastern United States. Non-Indians may attend and watch this colourful gathering, but it is designed primarily as a religious and cultural event in which all Indians in attendance take part. Between fifteen and twenty drumming and singing groups from various plains Indian reserves provide the music for thousands of costumed dancers circling about a huge tent on the Standing Buffalo reserve near Fort Qu'Appelle. Sun dances held at various points in the three Prairie Provinces are solemn festivities, with a religious connotation. Often a sun dance may be followed with a pow-wow.

A different but equally interesting annual pageant is presented by the Six Nations on their reserve at Osweken, Ontario. Held in a natural outdoor theatre, the pageant presents dramatizations of major events and personalities from the past of the Six Nations people. The Wikwemikong Pow-wow on Manitoulin Island is another annual festival of Indian music and dancing, attended by Indians from many parts of Canada.

In the annual Calgary stampede, Indians participate in various events, make up a colourful section of the parade and erect a village of teepees within the stampede grounds. Indian men and boys compete in various rodeo competitions. Banff Indian Days is another annual event attended mainly by the Stony (Assiniboine) Indians from Morely Reserve near Banff. Many Indian bands were active in preparing special celebrations for Canada's Centennial, participated in Indian Day at Expo 67, and took part in the closing ceremonies for the Montreal Olympics.

The contributions of Indians to Canadian national life are almost incalculable. From the very beginning, Indians gave freely of their skills and knowledge. Wherever explorers went in the unknown land, Indians guided them and helped them survive. From that time forward, Indians aided in the defence of the country, discovered remedies that gave rise to modern drugs, and have contributed a unique art form, among other things, that has formed an important facet of Canadian culture. Indian culture is again a dominant force in many aspects of Canadian society.

# Arabs (General)

*See also Egyptians, Iranians, Lebanese, Syrians*

THIS SECTION DESCRIBES the Arab community in Canada and, more particularly, the Arabs who have emigrated to Canada from the Arabian Peninsula. The Arabian Peninsula is divided into a number of political units, including Saudi Arabia, Yemen Arab Republic, Peoples Republic of Yemen, Kuwait, Qatar, Bahrain, Oman, and the United Arab Emirates (a federal state that embraces seven emirates), Iraq and Jordan.

There are many reasons for Arab emigration to Canada. Different reasons apply to different countries, but in the main they include economic opportunity, educational opportunity, a better future, and a better standard of living. Immigration first began in the period 1901–10, when 447 Arabs, an average of 45 yearly, came to Canada. Between 1911 and 1950, only 149 Arabs immigrated, with a further 591 between 1951 and 1961. The period of most significant immigration, 1961–75, saw 4,837 Arabs immigrate to Canada, an average of 322 yearly.

According to official statistics, between 1966 and 1975, 268 (or 6.6 per cent) came from Saudi Arabia, 703 (17.2 per cent) from Kuwait, 863 (21.1 per cent) from Iraq, 2,004 (48.9 per cent) from Jordan and 257 (6.4 per cent) from the remainder of the Gulf states and the two Yemens, for a total of 4,095 individuals. Until the beginning of the 1970s, nearly all Arab immigration to Canada came from Arab countries other than those located on the Arabian Peninsula. Between 1946 and 1975 there were 18,047 immigrants from Egypt, 15,618 from Lebanon, 3,079 from Syria, and between 5,000 and 6,000 from other Arab countries.

The largest Arab community in Canada is located in Montreal, with a smaller group in Toronto. Most Arab Canadians reside in the metropolitan areas. From a total of 1,438 Arab immigrants to Canada from countries in the Arabian Peninsula area between 1973 and 1975, 184 (12.8 per cent) chose Quebec as their destination while 995 (69.2 per cent) went to Ontario. Of the remainder, 103 (7.1 per cent) settled in Alberta and 92 (6.4 per cent) chose British Columbia. Only 64 persons (4.5 per cent) chose the other provinces.

There exist among the Arabs scattered associations that have more of political, national and religious goals than other cultural organizations. The Canadian Arab Federation (CAF) comprises thirteen associations in nine Canadian cities, including Montreal, Toronto, London, Windsor, Quebec City, Sudbury, Calgary, Edmonton and Hamilton. The Arab communities in these cities have formed social, cultural and religious associations, clubs and societies which are under the CAF umbrella.

The Arab Canadian Professionals in Ottawa was formed to foster communication among professionals sharing a common interest in the development of Arab culture in Canada, and the Islamic centres of Montreal, Ottawa and Vancouver have recently been organized to promote cultural exchange.

The Montreal newspapers, both monthly and bi-monthly, which include *The Canadian Middle East Journal*, *Arab World Review*, and *ARC*, are published respectively by a Lebanese, a Syrian and an Egyptian, but are directed toward the entire Arab community. *Fedayin* and *Al Fagr Al-Arabi* (Arab Dawn) are published in Montreal and *Asda'a Maaraka* in Toronto. Other publications include *Al-Maorid* (The Source) in Edmonton, which merged with the *Palestinian Voice* in 1977; *An-Nahda* in Ottawa; *CAFA* in Vancouver, and *Sarkhat Al Haq* in Ottawa.

While the Arabs are still few in number, their presence in Canada is being felt, especially in the business and professional fields. Their organizations aim to improve relations and understanding between the Arab groups and other Canadians, and their efforts have thus far proven successful.

# Argentinians

AFTER ARGENTINA ACHIEVED independence from Spain in 1810, immigration to that country from European nations other than Spain became significant. Her development as an immigrant country is also reflected in Argentine figures for immigration to Canada. Of the 8,612 Canadians who claimed Argentina as their last permanent residence between 1949 and 1973, only 5,100 had Argentine citizenship and only 4,609 gave Argentina as their country of birth. Notable in this regard is an early recorded group movement from Argentina to Canada, which took place in 1901 and involved the migration of Welsh colonists from Patagonia to Saskatchewan. It can reasonably be assumed that many Argentine immigrants ally themselves with others of their own ethnocultural group in Canada.

Argentina currently has a large population of refugees from various parts of South America. Many of the Chileans who came to Canada under the Special Chilean Movement had come from Argentine points of departure. In July, 1976, the Canadian government agreed to accept another one thousand Latin American refugees, all of whom were channelled through Argentine facilities.

Argentine immigration to Canada is marked by the same increase in volume as has recently become prevalent from Latin America in general. Thus, between 1946 and 1970, Argentinian-born immigrants arrived at the rate of just over 200 yearly, while in 1973, 948 immigrants of Argentinian birth were recorded. A further 1,088 arrived in 1974 and

674 in 1975.

Recent political, social and economic disruptions in Argentina have been regarded as significant factors in the decision of many Argentinians to leave their country. It is believed that while some have come to Canada for economic and social advancement, others are motivated by more political considerations. Little has been done, however, regarding the gathering of information on this group in Canada. It would appear that most Argentine Canadians came from urban areas and that, while the majority are skilled or semi-skilled workers, there is also a fairly high percentage of white-collar workers and professionals. As commonly occurs among immigrants seeking to become established, a large number of Argentinians are forced to take work outside their previous area of experience upon arrival.

There is, at the moment, little evidence of the presence in Canada of a distinct Argentine community, although there are known to be Argentinians in Toronto, Montreal and Sudbury, as well as in western centres such as Edmonton, Calgary and Winnipeg. Argentinians have worked with other Latin Americans in those cities where overall Latin American associations have been formed, such as the Centre for Spanish-speaking Peoples in Toronto and the Latin Association de Sud Americanos in Montreal. As their numbers increase and their community becomes established, their presence will be felt in the broader Canadian society.

# Armenians

ARMENIANS WERE AMONG the first people to adopt Christianity in the fourth century, prior to its adoption by the Roman Empire. Their country has had a long and difficult history and in 1921, a treaty between the Soviet Union and Turkey limited Armenia to the previous province of Yerevan. In 1922, Armenia formed part of the Transcaucasian Federation of Soviet Socialist Republics, but in 1936 it became a separate Soviet Socialist Republic.

The first Armenians are believed to have arrived in Canada in the 1880s, but they were few in number, and it is not known whether or not they stayed and settled permanently in Canada. More came during the 1890s, many by way of the United States, and worked in factories and on the railroads. Between 1900 and 1914, 1,853 Armenians came to Canada, with a peak of 882 between 1906 and 1908. A further 1,066 entered the country between 1920 and 1925.

There was a long interlude between 1926 and 1945, in which only 213 Armenians immigrated to Canada during the 20-year period. The years 1946 to 1955 witnessed a further 491 Armenian immigrants. The years of significant Armenian immigration were between 1956 and 1961, when 4,572 Armenians immigrated to Canada.

Between 1946 and 1961, after which time no official statistics on Armenian immigration were kept, 1,192 Armenians settled in Canada. Of this number, 726 (60.9 per cent) chose Quebec as their destination, 436 (36.6 per cent) went to Ontario, while only 30 Armenians (2.5 per cent) chose all the other provinces combined. Most settled in the metropolitan areas. The rates of distribution after 1961 are not believed to show a significant difference. A substantial number of Armenians came from different Arab states such as Lebanon, Syria, Iraq and particularly Egypt after 1961. These people were recorded officially, not as Armenians, but rather as part of the emigration from their country of provenance.

It is possible to estimate the Armenian presence in Canada at approximately 29,000 persons, with the largest number in Montreal (18,500), 8,000 in Toronto, 400 in Ottawa, 300 in Vancouver, 600 in Hamilton, 400 in St. Catharines, and 300 in other Canadian cities.

The Armenian community is served by four monthly newspapers and one weekly. *Lrakagh*, a monthly, is published in Montreal by Sourp Hagop Armenian Apostolic Church. *Artzagank* is a monthly published in Toronto by the Armenian Community Centre. *Pourasdan*, a Montreal monthly newsletter, is published by St. Gregory the Illuminator Cathedral, and *Keghart* is put out by the Armenian Cultural Association "MEG" in Montreal. *Abaka* is a weekly published in Montreal by the Armenian Cultural Association, Tekeyan. Various churches also publish newsletters, and many Armenian Canadians read *Ararat*, *Hayrenik* and *Baykar*, Armenian periodicals published in the United States.

Armenians in Canada lead a very active religious life. The majority of them follow the Armenian Gregorian (monophysite) form of Eastern Christianity, with smaller numbers of Roman Catholics and Protestants. The rites of worship are often in the classical Armenian tongue, despite the fact that the parishes, around which many cultural and recreational activities revolve, are widely scattered. There are five Armenian churches in Montreal, of which two are Apostolic, two Protestant and one Roman Catholic, and three in Toronto, one for each of the above-mentioned denominations. There are also rented Armenian churches in Ottawa, Vancouver, Brantford, Cambridge, London, St. Catharines and Hamilton.

There is a distinct tendency for Armenian Canadians to organize, and one of their most important organizations is the Armenian National Committee (ANC), formed in 1902. ANC has branches in Montreal, Toronto, Hamilton, Ottawa, St. Catharines, Vancouver and Windsor. It is the official spokesman for the Armenian Revolutionary Federation (ARF), the leading nationalist party of the Diaspora. The ANC embraces the Armenian Cultural Association, "Hamazkain" (Pan-National), the Armenian Youth Federation (AYF), the Armenian Relief Society, and "Homenetmen," the Armenian Sports and Scouts Organization.

The "Hamazkain" Armenian Cultural Association of Canada was founded with the purpose of maintaining Armenian culture. Its active and auxiliary membership of nine hundred is involved with folk dancing, theatre, library, seminars, academic research and cultural promotion, including exhibitions for artistic works displaying Armenian heritage, architecture and miniature arts. Since 1969, the group in Montreal has operated a weekly half-hour radio program "Hamazkain", the Armenian Radio Hour. Centres in Toronto, Hamilton and Cambridge promote similar activities. The branches have promoted Armenian day schools, a nursery and an Armenian-language school operated on Saturdays.

The Armenian Youth Federation has branches in Montreal, Toronto, Hamilton,

Cambridge, St. Catharines, Brantford and Vancouver. There are 550 members in this federation.

"Homenetmen" is an organization with two main divisions, scouting and sports. The Homenetmen Boy Scouts and Girl Guides are affiliated with the Canadian scouting movement. In sports "Homenetmen" has various teams in soccer, basketball, volleyball, ping pong and track and field sports. It is active in four cities: Montreal, Toronto, Cambridge and Hamilton.

There are Armenian schools and nurseries in Montreal and Toronto, operated by the respective Armenian Community Centers. Saturday schools in Armenian language and history are also in operation in Montreal, Toronto, Cambridge, Hamilton, St. Catharines and Ottawa.

The Armenian Relief Society has branches in Montreal, Hamilton, Toronto and St. Catharines to assist Armenian immigrants and needy families.

The Armenians are well integrated into Canadian life, but are conscious of their cultural heritage and tend to preserve it with pride.

# Australians

THE SMALLEST CONTINENT, Australia is also the world's largest island, a dry land bounded by the Great Barrier Reef to the east. The first recorded landing by European explorers was in 1606 when a Dutch ship put in on the west coast of northern Queensland. In 1788, Great Britain established a penal colony in Australia, in the area where the city of Sydney now

stands. Sheep raising was introduced early and became an integral part of the economy. A gold strike in New South Wales in 1851 and the development of wheat farming formed the base of the Australian economy. By the mid-nineteenth century, a systematic, permanent colony had completely replaced the old penal settlements. Federation came in 1901, when the colonies of New South Wales, Victoria, Queensland, South Australia, Western Australia and Tasmania were united.

Although Australians come to Canada in significant numbers each year, very little is known about them as members of an Australian national group. The Canadian census does not provide information on the characteristics of Australians as "ethnic" group members, nor does it provide data on the characteristics of any "national" Australian group. Thus even the most basic data on the size and composition of this population are not yet available.

Australians share with many Canadians, especially those of British origin, an ethnic background, cultural heritage and language. In many respects the way of life of Canadians of Australian origin is very similar to that of other English-speaking Canadians; they do not constitute a close knit "ethnic" group. As for those Australians of non-British background, they may choose to become members of their original ethnocultural communities. Moreover, because Australians are widely dispersed throughout Canada and because they merge quickly into the Canadian way of life, they are not easily identifiable. For these reasons, it seems almost irrelevant to make a distinction between Canadians and Australian immigrants to Canada in areas such as ethnic identity, language and religion.

Australian immigration has steadily risen in the postwar decades, but it is impossible to analyze the prewar period, since no separate immigration figures were kept for Australians. According to *Canadian Immigration Statistics*, between 1946 and 1965, 30,092 people from Australia were admitted to Canada, although not all were citizens of that country at the time of their arrival. From 1966 to 1975, 24,479 Australian citizens immigrated to this country. Some Australian citizens came via other countries, mainly from England and the United States. The possible return migration of immigrants from Canada to Australia, England or the United States notwithstanding, the number of Canadians of Australian origin can be considered significant.

The personal backgrounds of Australians who have entered Canada during the past ten years covered by immigration statistics are almost identical to the backgrounds of the other recently arrived immigrants from Asia. Australian immigrants tend to be young (25–40 years old), and in their prime productive years; they tend to settle in English-speaking parts of Canada; and they tend to be highly educated and well qualified in their chosen fields. Of the 18,691 immigrants from Australia who entered Canada between 1966 and 1975 and who were seeking employment, 8,850 (47.4 per cent) of them reported that they intended to enter the professional or managerial fields; 20 per cent were in some manual or service job category. Like the highly qualified immigrants from other countries, they left their homeland for strictly economic reasons; to obtain better income, job satisfaction and career mobility.

It is estimated that the largest percentage of Australian immigrants settled in Ontario, followed by British Columbia and Alberta. The larger urban centres in the English-speaking sections of Canada are the most popular areas for settlement, regardless of the province. Thus, Toronto and Vancouver are the two cities in which most Australians have settled. In addition, several thousand Australians have settled in Ottawa, Montreal, Calgary, Edmonton and Winnipeg. Even in the areas in which they most commonly settle, however, Canadians of Australian origin are widely dispersed throughout the cities and the surrounding suburbs.

Because their background is almost identical to that of many other Canadians, and because the majority of the Australian immigrants are well suited to white-collar positions, they generally have little difficulty in integrating into Canadian society. Australians in Canada do not seem to stick together in closely knit groups to form a distinct community.

Nevertheless, there are three social clubs formed by Australians in conjunction with New Zealanders in Canada, two of which are found in Vancouver and one in Toronto. The Australia-New Zealand Association in Vancouver, formed in 1935, is a social club pursuing the objectives of fostering friendly relations between Canadians and Australians and New Zealanders, of promoting good fellowship among Australians and New Zealanders residing in British Columbia, and of promoting social activities for members and their friends. The club's activities are strictly social and recreational.

The two other associations formed by Australians and New Zealanders, TRANZAC in Toronto and the Southern Cross International Association in Vancouver, are very similar to the Australia-New Zealand Association in nature. They are non-profit, non-political and non-sectarian organizations.

All of these clubs publish monthly newsletters, offer charter travel facilities and regularly organize social events for their members. Apart from a few staff members hired to operate the clubs, all work is done by club executives and volunteer members.

While little is known of the Australian presence as a group in Canada, immigration statistics indicate that Canadians of Australian origin deserve further study. Australia, like Canada, is considered a middle power in world affairs, and also in a manner similar to Canada's, immigration is actively encouraged. Australian-born Canadians continue to make a contribution to the economics and management of Canadian business, and their efforts in Canadian sports, especially in swimming and sailing, are evident.

# Austrians

THE DESIGNATION "AUSTRIAN" historically has had a number of geographical and political meanings. In its narrowest sense it has referred to Upper and Lower Austria, including Vienna; in its widest sense, to the multilingual Hapsburg Empire which stretched from Galicia to the Adriatic, and held together Slavs, Germans (known as Austrians), Magyars, Jews and other ethnic groups, all of whom formed an uneasy association. In its present meaning, the term refers to the Republic of Austria, which came into being in 1918.

It is not always possible to establish exactly what nineteenth and early twentieth century observers meant when they referred to "Austrian" immigrants. "Austrian Origin" in the 1901 Canadian census, for example, included "Bohemian, Bukovinian and Slavic". The first immigrants from Austria-Hungary to settle in Canada in any numbers were German-speaking people from Galicia, a region which was once part of the Kingdom of Poland, and which is now divided between Poland and Ukraine. These German-speaking peoples started coming to the Prairies in the 1880s in response to the promise of free land and in reaction to worsening economic conditions in their homeland, where a shortage of agricultural land and a dearth of industry contributed to mounting unemployment. Added to these factors was a deteriorating political climate, in which attempts were made to eliminate the separate school system of the German minority and to suppress their language. So they came to Canada, settling near Langenburg, Lemberg, Regina, Melville and Kendal in Saskatchewan and near Edmonton, Josephsburg, Spruce Grove, Golden Spike and Stony Plain in Alberta. Nearly all of this group were of the Lutheran faith.

Similar economic and political conditions also convinced German-speaking settlers from the Banat, an area now divided between Yugoslavia and Roumania, but then part of Hungary, that they should settle on the Canadian Prairies. They came to Saskatchewan between 1897 and 1914 and established themselves near Regina, Qu'Appelle, Indian Head, Kendal, Swift Current and other centres, usually joining German-speaking Catholic settlers. German-speaking immigrants from Bukovinia, a region now divided between Roumania and the Ukraine, started arriving in 1890. Belonging for the most part to the evangelical denominations, they settled on farms near such centres as Edenwold, Vibrank, Spring Valley and Sifton, Saskatchewan.

Most of the immigrants who came from Austria-Hungary during the late years of the nineteenth and early part of the twentieth centuries were of agricultural background. It should be mentioned that a large percentage of the "Austrian" immigrants prior to the First World War were Ukrainian peasants who were described as "Ruthenians, Galicians and Bukovenians." The fact that there were large numbers of people and little land in their homelands turned their thoughts to Canada. Initially, they were wooed by Clifford Sifton, who during his tenure as Minister of the Interior (1896–1905) went to great lengths to populate the Prairies with "sturdy" farmers. To attract the type of immigrant in whom he had unbounded faith, Sifton shifted Canadian immigration publicity to regions in central Europe such as the Austro-Hungarian Empire and arranged for a group of booking agents in Hamburg, Germany, to attract "agriculturalists and peasants" to Canada.

Although few of these immigrants from the Austro-Hungarian Empire had experienced the singular conditions of the Canadian Prairies, they had the ingenuity and courage which are marks of the successful pioneer. Along with newcomers with the same qualities from other parts of the globe, they opened up some of the most fertile, some of the most arid, and some of the most isolated parts of the West.

Migration to Canada was a symptom of the gradual dissolution and final dismemberment of the Hapsburg Empire which produced what was primarily a migration of individuals from the farming class. They appeared in Canada especially in the period 1920–21. Upon their settlement in Canada, they usually asserted their unique and distinctive cultural identities as Czechs, Serbs, Croatians, Ukrainians, Jews, Magyars, Roumanians and others.

The factors that had been at work before the First World War were intensified as a result of the war. In spite of immigration restrictions, some 5,000 immigrants from the new Austria arrived in Canada between 1926 and 1933. Large-scale immigration did not resume until the late 1920s. By this time the Dual Monarchy had collapsed (1918), to be replaced by several succession states and the Republic of Austria. Life had been particularly difficult in Austria after the First World War, with the country reduced to a fraction of its former size. The time was ripe for emigration.

The new state of Austria was a small, landlocked country with a population of seven million that was overwhelmingly German-speaking and Roman Catholic. In three states of the federal republic—Carinthia, Styria and Burgenland—there were small Slovene and Croatian minorities.

To escape the turbulent political situation of the 1920s and 1930s, many Austrians left for other countries. From 1926 to 1933, substantial numbers of Austrians emigrated to Canada. With the occupation of Austria by Germany in 1938, these earlier arrivals were joined by thousands of political refugees, mainly from the educated, business and professional classes.

For ten years after the Second World War, Austria was occupied by the forces of Great Britain, France, the United States and the USSR. During this time, the country was again faced with tremendous economic problems, this time because of damage to housing, industry and communications during the war, and because of the interference with economic life in the Soviet occupation zone. Emigration during these years was heavy. In fact, over 18,000 Austrians came to Canada between 1946 and 1955. Between 1956 and 1967, the number exceeded 13,000. In all, between 1946 and 1973, some 67,000 persons who gave their place of last permanent residence as Austria emigrated to Canada, Austria being the tenth leading source country of immigrants in 1960 and seventh in 1968.

But Austrian immigration to Canada has since fallen off dramatically, reflecting the country's economic prosperity and extremely low rate of unemployment. In 1970, for example, only 431 Austrians came to Canada.

In 1971, the Canadian census recorded 42,120 Canadians of Austrian origin, of whom the largest number (15,765) were living in Ontario. British Columbia and Alberta followed with 9,845 and 6,310 respectively, Saskatchewan with 3,845, Manitoba with 3,200 and Quebec with approximately 2,500. Fewer than 500 Canadians of Austrian origin were living in the Maritimes in 1971.

The majority of Austrians, over 82 per cent, were shown by the census as living in cities and towns. In Metro Toronto alone there were about 7,800. Many more settled in Ontario's smaller cities and towns. The more than 2,100 Canadians of Austrian origin in Metro Montreal represented close to 84 per cent of the total number in the Province of Quebec. Other large concentrations were shown by the census to be in Vancouver (over 5,000), and in and around the cities of Edmonton (over 2,400), Winnipeg (1,900), Calgary (1,700) and Regina (1,100).

Before the Second World War, German ethnic societies served German-speaking Canadians with a wide variety of origins. There was a tendancy, however, to establish societies called *Landsmannschaften* for German-speaking people who traced their origins to a particular country or region of a country. Thus Canadians of Austrian origin preferred organizations where other immigrants from Austria predominated, while Bavarians usually opted for Austrian groups because they had more in common with Austrians than with other German-speaking peoples.

With the outbreak of war in 1939, Austrians who had arrived in Canada immediately previous to this time, among whom were a number of prominent political leaders, began to press for Austrian independence. With the assistance of a group of Canadians who sympathized with their aims, the Austrians formed an organization called The Canadian Friends of Austria. This group remained active throughout the war. A German-language monthly called *Donau Echo* and a short-lived English-language publication, *Voice of Austria*, appeared during this period. With the cessation of hostilities and the re-establishment of the Austrian Republic, the activities of The Canadian Friends of Austria came to a close.

In many of the larger Canadian cities, there is at least one Austrian club or organization, in some communities, there are several. Most of these organizations are of a social or benevolent nature, formed to help meet the needs of the more recent immigrants. They also serve as a point of contact for other Canadians interested in the cultural life and heritage of Austria.

Among the more prominent clubs are those located in Vancouver, Edmonton, Toronto, Kingston and Montreal. The Austria Club of Vancouver was formed in 1971 by a group of young Austrian-Canadian soccer players. It has since expanded its activities to include dances and festivals, cruises and sports contests. It also sponsors its own professional singing group, the Tyrolean Mountain Boys, and publishes a monthly news bulletin, *Austrian Echo*, aimed at Canadians of Austrian origin living in British Columbia.

The Austrian Club of Edmonton is noted for its annual Vienna Opera Ball and a "Heurigen," or wine-tasting party. Both events are attended by a wide cross-section of the population. The club also maintains a scholarship fund to send gifted Albertans to study in Austria.

The Edelweiss Club of Toronto, founded in 1950, has many culturally oriented activities. It places particular emphasis on music, and has its own Edelweiss Children's Choir and children's instrumental group. The Austrian International Club of Kingston, on the other hand, features folksinging and dancing. Its singing group, The Boys From The Austrian Alps, is well known throughout the area.

One of the highlights of the Montreal social season is the Austrian Ball, staged by the Austrian Society of Montreal. This society was founded in 1958, and with funds collected from its various activities, the club, like most other Austrian organizations, supports welfare projects and provides scholarships for students to study in Austria. The Montreal club is a benevolent organization dedicated to helping persons of Austrian origin and to forming a contact point for Canadians interested in the cultural life and heritage of Austria.

There is no Austrian newspaper as such, but news about Austrian Canadians and articles by them appear frequently in the German-language press.

Most of the pioneer immigrants from Austria were farmers and artisans who played an active role in the early development of Canada, particularly in the opening of the Canadian Prairies. Today, individual Canadians of Austrian origin have made important contributions in the field of music, in the decorative arts, and in the field of recreation. The growth of their clubs indicates their desire to maintain cultural contacts with the old country while becoming an active part of Canadian life.

# Barbadians

*See also West Indians*

BARBADOS IS A SMALL ISLAND in the Caribbean with a very high population density, and a population predominantly of African descent. In the absence of comprehensive data on Barbadian immigration to Canada, it is impossible to account for the exact or even approximate numbers of Barbadians in this country. Department of Immigration statistics account for 9,518 Barbadians who immigrated to Canada between 1946 and the first quarter of 1976, and whose last country of permanent residence was Barbados. There is reason to believe that many Barbadians now residing in Canada may have re-emigrated from England or from other countries. The peak years of immigration occurred during the latter half of the 1960s and early 1970s, mainly because of overpopulation in the mother country and the opportunity for advancement in Canada.

There is at least one Barbadian association in each of the major Canadian cities, each of which is well organized and has been thriving for many years. The oldest of these organizations is the Barbados ex-Police Association, which was started during the early years of Barbadian immigration to Canada when most of the immigrants were former police officers. The ex-Police and other Barbadian associations are active in maintaining liaison with the High Commissioner on matters of a consular nature as well as organizing Independence Day celebrations. These organizations also serve the social and recreational needs of the communities.

*BAM*, a quarterly publication of the Barbados Association of Montreal, is the only publication in Canada which is specifically Barbadian. *Contrast* is another publication of the Black community.

The Barbadians, a small group in Canada, are finding opportunities in Canada that they could only hope to achieve through emigration. They are keeping their cultural heritage alive through their organizations and publications in this country.

# Belgians

BELGIAN IMMIGRANTS come from a small, heavily industrialized country which is composed of two distinct groups, the Flemings, a Germanic people who live in the northern and eastern provinces and speak Dutch or Flemish, and the Walloons, a primarily Celtic people who live in the southern and eastern provinces of Belgium and speak French and local dialects to a great extent. There is also a small German-speaking minority in the eastern districts of Eupen and Malmedy. The vast majority of both the Flemings and Walloons are Roman Catholic, although the Flemings have traditionally been more conservative and strict in their religious observances.

The first immigrants to Canada from the region that would become the Kingdom of Belgium (1830) came as indentured servants, artisans, soldiers and missionaries during the seventeenth and early eighteenth centuries. A Walloon, for example, helped construct the first presbytery at Quebec. Also, Walloon brickmasters and Flemish quarrymen arrived at Louisbourg in 1752 to assist in the rebuilding of the fortress.

A number of those who came during the French Régime and whose names have been preserved belonged to the persecuted Walloon Protestant community which found refuge in the Anglo-American colonies, Holland and England. In 1669, for example, a "Belgian" Protestant, Pierre Huré, abjured his religion at Quebec; in 1709 another compatriot and co-religionist was taken prisoner during a raid on New England and settled in New France; and forty years later, the first "Belgian" woman came to the French colony as a captive, married a habitant and raised a large Canadian family. In the decade immediately preceding the British conquest of Canada, several more Walloon Protestants appear in official records.

During the French Régime, a few members of the Catholic clergy came from Wallonia. Much of the trickle of Belgian emigration to Canada in the years following Confederation also went to the Province of Quebec. Between 1871 and 1900, 2,221 Belgian immigrants registered with a Montreal agency and 2,806 with a Quebec agency. These figures represented 2.7 per cent of all immigrants registered at the two centres. Since immigration fell under shared federal and provincial jurisdiction, both Ottawa and Quebec appointed immigration agents in Belgium, whose government at the time was still favourable to emigration from certain overpopulated or economically depressed regions. E. Simays was appointed federal agent in Antwerp in 1869 and Edouard Barnard as Quebec agent in 1871. The former, however, was alloted only 1.9 per cent of the federal appropriation designated for European immigration agents. The latter went to Belgium with the abbé P. J. Verbist in 1872 to recruit construction workers for the North Shore Railway and the Grenville canal. About 600 Belgians came to Quebec in a two-year period, to the satisfaction of the provincial Minister of Public Works. However, recruitment soon dropped off sharply. One reason for this decline in immigration may have been reports concerning an earlier agricultural colonization scheme at Namur, Quebec, which had had disastrous results. Most of the original settlers in the forested region had had to find work in the Ottawa area. In the ensuing years the supposedly model Belgian colony fell prey to bad crops, bad publicity and Protestant proselytism.

In 1887 the Société d'Immigration Française included Belgium in its fields of activities. The curé Labelle visited Europe in 1890 and influenced Louis Hacault, a journalist of note in Brussels, to visit Canada. Hacault directed most of the Belgian immigrants thereafter to Manitoba, where he himself settled. However, immigration agents began encountering opposition from competitive booking agents from railway and steamship lines and from Belgian legislation prohibiting or strictly regulating the emigration propaganda. A ministerial memorandum of September 1890 had required all sub-agents to register with the Belgian government; by 1894 all except those of the Red Star Line had done so, but the authorities remained suspicious of activities of sub-agents and individuals, including clergy, which tended to lure Belgians into Canada without safeguards of gainful employment once they arrived in their adopted country.

Also, the appeals henceforth were directed more to the Flemish farmers than to the Walloon constituency. The Belgians who came to the Prairies were lured by the promise of free land and the hope of making a rapid fortune. They came mostly as individuals, although a pattern of village transplantation is also discernible. These family units, it must be added, were often part of a larger Catholic colonization effort. There was also a flurry of colonization schemes in the late 1880s.

Enthusiasm cooled considerably with the eruption of the Manitoba schools question in the 1890s, and this was reflected in the official reports of Belgian consuls and travellers as well as in the correspondence of recruiting agents. Furthermore, in several parishes of French, Flemish and English-speaking settlers, the clergy were unable to satisfy all the linguistic groups and the Flemish-speakers were most often discriminated against by the predominantly French-Canadian clergy and hierarchy. There was also some concern about the liberal, social and slightly anti-clerical views expressed by some European Catholic immigrants, especially French and Walloons. On the other hand, a number of Belgian priests served in western Canada by helping other ethnic groups to establish schools and parishes which would perpetuate particular cultures and heritages.

The year 1890 saw a reduction in British immigration to Canada, and an increase in the numbers of other nationalities that settled here, including the Belgians. A government immigration agent was appointed to Belgium and France, and he reported that as a class the immigrants were usually "quite well off," some even having "considerable wealth." In 1898 a Canadian of Belgian descent from Quebec, Treau de Coeli, was appointed the official government agent to Belgium and Holland, with headquarters in Antwerp. When he took his posting, de Coeli was chagrined to learn that very little was known about Canada in that part of the world, particularly in the Flemish-speaking provinces. He therefore concentrated on recruiting Flemish immigrants from the densely populated northern provinces, a practice which was to continue and to result in the Flemings becoming more numerous than the Walloons in Canada.

Manitoba attracted the largest number of early Belgian immigrants, and Belgian communities grew up around Winnipeg and St. Boniface, and in the southwest part of the province around such areas as Bruxelles, St. Alphonse, Deloraine, Mariapolis and Swan Lake. Most of these settlers came chiefly from overpopulated villages in Belgium, and upon their arrival in Canada they tended to become farmers. Farming and construction work have remained two of the principal occupations which Belgians have held.

Between 1899 and 1919, 1,016 homesteads were taken by Belgians in the four western provinces. To the approximately 9,500 Belgians in Canada in 1910, another 7,000 were added before the invasion of Belgium and the outbreak of the First World War in 1914. A sizeable contingent of these immigrants, mostly Walloons from the Mons and Charleroi regions, went to the coal mines of Cape Breton and other parts of Nova Scotia. Not until the 1920s could immigration resume, and in that postwar decade about 13,000 Belgians seeking a new life in a peaceful land came to Canada. The 1921 census recorded 20,234 Canadians of Belgian origin, a number of whom came after the war either as war brides or in an effort to improve their fortunes as a result of the economic crisis in their homeland brought on by the conflict. Since Canada was once again actively promoting the immigration of agriculturalists, many of the Belgian settlers who arrived after the war were farmers. Instead of going west, however, as others had before them, many settled in southwestern Ontario, where they achieved a great deal of success in tobacco and sugar beet farming. The Dominion Sugar Company, for example,

carried out its own recruitment in Belgium and tried to attract up to 500 workers from West Flanders each year. This company had first drawn Belgian workers to Chatham, Wallaceburg and Kitchener, Ontario, from the United States. Soon Belgian agriculturalists were recruited directly in Belgium for the sugar beet industry at Raymond, Alberta.

The population of Belgians in Canada remained fairly stable throughout the 1930s and early 1940s. The 1931 census recorded 27,585 Canadians of Belgian descent, and the 1941 census recorded 29,711. Disturbed economic conditions after the Second World War prompted another large exodus of Belgians to Canada. Between 1946 and 1955, approximately 12,000 of them emigrated to this country, and between 1956 and 1967, another 13,000 came. In 1951, Belgium was the eighth largest source country for immigrants to Canada. Since then, Belgian immigration has fallen off sharply, reflecting the country's improved economic situation.

According to the 1971 census, there were 51,135 Canadians of Belgian origin in Canada. This figure compares with 61,382 recorded in the 1961 census, the difference in the two figures resulting from the fact that most third and fourth generation immigrants of Belgian descent consider themselves Canadians. Today there are more people of Belgian origin in Ontario than in any other single province (19,955 in 1971). Most of them live in the southwestern counties, in particular Essex, Kent and Norfolk. They are concentrated in towns such as Chatham, Delhi, Wallaceburg, Blenheim and Langton, a predominantly Belgian village which each year stages a two-day Belgian fair.

In 1971, 8,220 Canadians of Belgian origin lived in Quebec, many thousands of whom resided in Montreal. Others operate market gardens outside the city. There are also small groups in Joliette County in the Richelieu valley, where a colony of Walloon and Flemish dairymen has prospered, in Labelle County and in Ungava, where the development of mineral resources has attracted Belgian miners who were formerly employed in Nova Scotia mines.

The Belgian population in the Maritimes has remained small, with about 1,200 Canadians of Belgian descent spread throughout all the Maritime Provinces. The majority live in Nova Scotia (665 in 1971), where a fairly large settlement grew up around the turn of the century in and about the coal mining town of Inverness on Cape Breton Island. Next to Manitoba, which had 9,055 people of Belgian origin, British Columbia has the largest Belgian-Canadian community in the western provinces, with 4,840 Belgian Canadians in 1971.

Belgian Canadians tend to form social clubs of a local nature rather than large national organizations. At Wallaceburg, Ontario, for example, there is the Belgian-Dutch Social Club which concentrates on helping new immigrants. At Delhi, Ontario, the 1,500 member Belgian Club stages social activities of all kinds in a community hall which it built for this purpose in 1948. In Manitoba, Le Club Belge, which is located in Winnipeg, was formally incorporated in 1905 to provide a place where the Belgians who were arriving in large numbers every month could gather to discuss their problems and engage in recreational activities; to consider and discuss questions affecting the interests of Belgians in Manitoba; and to render voluntary aid to any member of the club or any Belgian residing in Manitoba. It soon became the focus of social and recreational activities for Manitoban Belgians and the focal point of Belgian

ethnic consciousness in the province. As part of its mandate to build and preserve a sense of identity among Belgian Canadians, the club has consistently endeavoured to maintain some liaison not only with other Belgian communities in Manitoba, but also with communities elsewhere in the country and in the United States.

In the Province of Quebec, the Association Belgique Canada, located in Montreal, promotes cultural relations between Belgium and Canada. A much larger organization is the Belgian National Union, founded in 1939 as a mutual benefit society for the promotion of welfare and recreation. Its activities include celebrations to mark July 21, Belgian Independence Day, the date in 1831 when Prince Leopold of Saxe-Coburg was proclaimed King of Belgium following that country's declaration of independence from the Netherlands. In Montreal the event is commemorated with a parade, in which many of the participants wear national dress, and a religious service in Notre Dame Cathedral. Belgian Independence Day is also celebrated in Quebec City, where Le Comité des amitiés belgo-canadiennes stages a gala event. In the Richelieu valley, Belgian Canadians have formed an association called The Club Belgo-Canada which, in addition to celebrating the feast of St. Nicholas in the traditional manner, organizes dances and other festivities for its members.

These organizations, along with a few others which are active in Quebec, are financed by the proceeds of a bequest left to them by Jean Biermans, a Belgian immigrant who made a major contribution to the Quebec economy.

Belgians have probably made their greatest contribution to Canada in the field of agriculture. They have specialized regionally—tobacco culture in southern Ontario, beet growing in Alberta and Ontario, dairying in Manitoba, small fruit growing in British Columbia and market gardening in Quebec.

In Ontario and Quebec, Canadians of Belgian origin have put their experience in building dykes and reclaiming land to good use. At Grand Bend, Ontario, for example, a 1,000-acre marsh was drained by a group of settlers from Belgium and Holland who had been brought over by an enterprising Delhi tobacco farmer and recent Belgian immigrant, Gerhard Vanden Bussche. After it was drained, the marsh was used to grow top-grade vegetables for markets in Ontario and the United States. Belgian Canadians have also made contributions in such diverse fields as diamond cutting, business, the academic world and the arts.

As a group, Belgians have readily adapted to their new homeland. The Walloons have tended to merge with the French-speaking population, and the Flemings with the English-speaking groups. As a result, many Canadians are unaware of their fellow citizens of Belgian origin, and consequently of the role played by Belgian Canadians in the development of this country.

# Blacks

THE BLACK PRESENCE in Canada began in 1629, when it was recorded that a six-year-old slave boy was brought with the English Kirke expedition to New France from Madagascar. Slaves continued to be imported into New France as domestic servants, and an act of 1790 permitted free importation of all "Negroes, household furniture, utensils of husbandry, or clothing." They continued to be used as domestic servants by wealthy families. By the mid-eighteenth century, there were about 1,200 Black slaves in Quebec. Slavery was continued in British North America until 1833, when all slaves in the British Empire were freed.

The first significant movement of Blacks from the American colonies into Canada occurred during and after the Revolutionary War (1755–83). Some entered as the "property" of whites who were not only migrant Loyalists but also slave owners. These slaves usually remained with their owners after settlement, since slavery was at that time still legal in all parts of Canada. They became a feature of almost all Loyalist communities, but since the majority of the Loyalists were engaged in agriculture, and since their holdings were not sufficiently productive to support a large group of slaves, within twenty years of their arrival the Loyalists had all but ended the practice of slavery.

Over 3,000 American Blacks arrived in Canada as free men. Many had been encouraged to desert from their American owners in a British attempt to undermine the American economy. The British also offered the slaves their freedom if they would fight for the British in the Revolutionary War, and after the fighting had ended, these Blacks came to Canada. Their number included an entire army corps, the Black Pioneers. Free Blacks considered themselves Loyalists and expected to be treated as such, with land grants, rations, and seed for three years.

The majority of Blacks went to Nova Scotia. Among the American-born Blacks and their Nova Scotian children, disenchantment followed their settlement, and in 1792 over 1,000 participated in a "back to Africa" movement, with Sierra Leone as their destination.

The Maroons, a group which had come from Jamaica, were equally disenchanted and followed them to Sierra Leone in 1800. Those who decided not to leave took up residence, their settlement from the first being arranged in segregated communities, including those in Annapolis County, in Clements, on McNutt's Island, in Shelburne Township, in Tracadie, in Sydney (now Guysborough) County, in Birchtown, in Preston Township in Halifax County, and in other areas. Most settlements were unsuccessful due to the inadequacy of many land grants and the infertility of the soil. Ultimately, therefore, some moved on, particularly to the towns of Preston, Tracadie, and to the city of Halifax. A similar pattern of events took place along the Nerepis River, at Milkish, and at Oroquaco in New Brunswick.

A second immigration of Blacks from the United States took place during the War of 1812. Again, this was the result of British encouragement, and again, the main destination was Nova Scotia. The British ships that burned Washington brought many Black refugees to Nova Scotia, and free transport was given to any United States citizen who wanted to settle in British territory. Some runaway slaves took advantage of this offer, with the result that 2,000 American Blacks became Nova Scotia immigrants at this time. Most settled in the Halifax region, although some did go to Amherst and Truro, and to the Loch Lomond and Lake Otnabog areas of New Brunswick.

Initially, problems arose because the Nova Scotia government was not afforded sufficient time to prepare for this influx of settlers. Delays in aid and grants occurred. Subsequently, there was a deterioration of the general economic situation and of agricultural conditions. The immediate, and indeed long term, result was a situation of deprivation for almost all involved.

On May 21, 1793, Lieutenant-Governor John Graves Simcoe introduced a bill preventing the introduction of further slaves into Upper Canada, and in 1829 the Executive Council of the Legislature of Lower Canada declared that "the state of slavery is not recognized by the laws of Canada. . . ." Four years later, slavery officially ceased to exist in Canada. Yet even as early as 1820, and for the next forty years, fugitive Black slaves were crossing the United States-Canadian border into what is now Ontario. Although accurate figures on the numbers involved are not available, it is believed that by 1860 the Black population of Upper Canada stood at 60,000, most of whom were fugitives or their children who had come to Canada by way of the Underground Railway.

Most of the escapees came alone, and in the early years of the Underground Railway they entered mainly at Detroit and Niagara and settled first near the border. Black communities sprang up at such places as Welland, St. Catharines, Colchester, Windsor, Amherstburg, London, Chatham and Dresden, where their descendants still live. Later, especially after 1850 when the passage of the Fugitive Slave Act in the United States made life more uncertain for fugitives in the northern states, they also crossed the lower St. Lawrence and headed for Coburg, Kingston and Toronto. In time, Black communities grew up in Hamilton and Montreal as well. Some came in groups organized for the establishment of communal settlements. Projects of this nature were attempted, for example, at Dawn, Wilberforce, and Elgin. Some of the descendants of the original settlers are still to be found in North Buxton, near Chatham, Ontario.

These early settlers in Upper Canada

excelled in the building trades, service enterprises, cash crops and fruit farming, and the like. They built their own houses, schools and churches, many of which are still in good condition after more than 150 years.

The individual migration was, in general, far more successful than the group settlement. Farms were established and businesses opened. Two newspapers, *The Voice of the Fugitive* and *The Provincial Freeman*, published and edited by Blacks, gave expression to the problems and accomplishments of the southwestern Ontario Black community.

For many, a measure of prosperity was achieved. A number of the Blacks who entered Canada during this period returned to the United States to fight for the North during the American Civil War. Others returned to the United States after the war had won freedom for all Blacks. It is thought that only about one-third of the original Black immigrants made Canada their permanent home.

Suppression of skills and denial of economic opportunity through the exercise of rigid discrimination and segregation was one of the prime reasons for the exodus back to the United States between 1870 and 1920. The churches of the Amherstburg Baptist Association of Ontario, however, reached a peak of their membership at various times between 1870 and 1920. The First Baptist Church of Windsor, Ontario, built its present structure in 1915 at a cost of over $15,000 when it had an active membership roll of about 300 persons. The church property today is valued in excess of $250,000, while membership has levelled off at about 120 to 150. The membership of other Black churches in Ontario has likewise declined over the last half century.

A certain amount of American Black settlement took place in various parts of western Canada. In the 1850s, the laws of California began to limit the rights of freed Blacks, and in 1858 Blacks began to arrive in Victoria from California. Records indicate that about 600 Blacks came at this time, and formed a settlement which still exists. Many of the heads of families were small businessmen; almost all were skilled workers and soon thriving barber shops, bakeries, restaurants, tailoring establishments and other businesses were set up. Within two years, taxable property valued at $50,000 was owned by Blacks. Families and small groups of Blacks later moved to other parts of British Columbia. Pioneer farming was undertaken at Saltspring Island and at Nanaimo.

American Blacks came to the Prairies, largely from Oklahoma, during the land rush period of 1890–1914. They participated in the founding of settlements at Maidstone and Wilkie in Saskatchewan, and at Junkins, Breton, Clyde and Amber Valley in Alberta. Many Blacks helped with the construction of the railroads at that time. Of these communities, Amber Valley is the only one to have survived as a predominantly Black community. The Black movement into the West would quite definitely have been more extensive had it not been for the passage of an immigration act in 1910 which allowed for the selection of immigrants along racial lines.

During the 1920s, Black Americans were also attracted to Canada by opportunities offered in connection with the railroads. Black communities were founded or enlarged at major railway centres such as Montreal, Winnipeg, Calgary, Vancouver and Toronto. In Montreal, descendants of those who lived in the St. Antoine Street area form the nucleus of the so-called "old families", many of whom are still employed on the railroad.

With the passage of time, communities of Blacks in Canada who have resided here for several generations have achieved a degree of permanency. Like other immigrants, they regard themselves as Canadians, although at no point in their history has their position in Canadian society been genuinely satisfactory. As early as 1784, a race riot broke out over the settlement of Shelburne, Nova Scotia; in almost every community of settlement in Canada, Blacks were accepted as long as they did not appear in substantial numbers; the 1910 immigration act was an attempt to prevent further immigration by those of non-white origin; in the First World War, Blacks were discouraged from enlisting in the armed forces because it was thought that whites would refuse to serve with them. There are many other examples.

Black Canadians have, therefore, continually been faced with external barriers and with the internal problems resulting from these external barriers. Even though at all times numbers of Blacks, both collectively and individually, have managed to succeed in many different ways, a large percentage have become caught in patterns of living resulting from social disadvantage. What this has meant in human terms can be illustrated by the situation in Halifax in 1960. The proportion of the Black population holding jobs in that city was only half as great as the proportion of the white population holding jobs; only 6 per cent of Blacks had graduated from high school; and of the 134 Black families living on two "Black" streets, 85 per cent lived in inadequate housing.

The aims of the most influential Black Canadian organizations now in existence reflect a clear awareness of the realities of Black problems and Black development in Canada. Several are now grappling with the community's problems and are accelerating its cultural, social and economic integration into the mainstream of Canadian development.

Among the better known organizations composed principally of Blacks of longstanding Canadian ancestry are the Black United Front of Nova Scotia, and the New Brunswick and Nova Scotia Associations for the Advancement of Coloured People. In other regions, the influence of more recent West Indian and African immigrants who possess overall commonality of interest and goals has been strongly felt. Such groups as the Côte des Neiges Black Community Development Project of Montreal and the Toronto Black Community Centre Project are reflective of a more varied popular composition. In 1969 the National Black Coalition of Canada was founded. The Coalition is an umbrella organization which strives to serve and speak for all elements of the Black community. The main news voice for the Black community is the Toronto-based weekly, *Contrast.* The Black United Front also publishes a monthly paper, *Grasp.*

From the time of slavery onwards, Blacks from the United States have been coming to Canada in small numbers. Although they have always represented less than 4 per cent of the total population, their influence has not been negligible. They have participated in the development of the Atlantic Provinces, the West and Upper Canada, contributed to the growth and expansion of agriculture, mining and railroad building, and have added their cultural heritage to the expanding Canadian society.

# Bulgarians

CANADIANS OF BULGARIAN descent comprise one of the smallest branches of this country's family tree. Prior to 1944 and the creation of a socialist Bulgaria, most Bulgarian immigrants were peasants and labourers who had left their homeland in the troubled years surrounding the Balkan Wars (1912–13). Immigration records suggest that a second major wave of Bulgarian immigrants arrived during the years of the Depression. Most of the Bulgarian immigrants who came to this country before the Second World War were young, single and poor, and they were without any advanced education. In Canada they began working as unskilled labourers on highways and railroads and in general construction. They settled mainly in Ontario, in particular in Toronto, Hamilton and the Niagara region. A number of these Bulgarian immigrants displayed entrepreneurial and other talents which they were soon contributing to the society of which they became an active part.

Census returns indicate that there were 1,765 Canadians of Bulgarian origin in 1921, 3,160 in 1931 and 3,260 in 1941. The 1941 census is the last in which Bulgarians appear as a separate group.

After the Second World War, the social profile of the immigrant from Bulgaria began to change. The Bulgarian immigrant now often tended to be a person with advanced education who had been a professional or a skilled worker in Bulgaria. Furthermore, the immigrant was often a political refugee, fleeing a homeland that had become a Marxist state.

Some of these immigrants came directly to Canada, while others came by way of the United States, Germany, Austria, Greece and other countries. According to immigration statistics, between 1946 and 1966 at least 1,269 individuals of Bulgarian origin arrived in Canada.

It is difficult to estimate the present number of Canadians of Bulgarian origin. Both before and after the Second World War, Bulgarian immigrants to Canada included a very high number of single men. In the early years, a single man might write back to Bulgaria to find a spouse, who would then come to join him. More typically, however, the immigrant would find a spouse among members of a kindred or related immigrant community. Religious affinity played a major role in this regard. In all these cases, to classify members of families, in particular children, as being of Bulgarian origin can only be an arbitrary decision. According to the estimates of community leaders, the Bulgarian ethnocultural group includes no fewer than 10,000 persons. Most Canadians of Bulgarian origin live in Toronto, but Montreal also has a large Bulgarian community composed of from 1,000 to 1,500 persons.

From the very beginning, the Orthodox religion and church have played an extremely important role in the community life of Bulgarians in Canada. Circumstance dictated the establishment of joint churches or congregations wherein Bulgarians came together with Macedonians, Greeks and others. The first such church in Toronto, known as the Saints Cyril and Methody Macedonian Bulgarian Orthodox Cathedral, was established and led by the Orthodox Archimandrite Theophilact, the late Dr. D. M. Malin.

Saints Cyril and Methody Cathedral remained for a long period a centre of cultural and social life for Bulgarians in Toronto. In 1915, a Bulgarian-language school was established by the cultural and educational society "Prosveta" ("Enlightenment"), working in collaboration with the church. In 1917, the society "Balkanski Tunak" ("Balkan Hero"), also working closely with the church, formed a Bulgarian school for adults. Many activities took place in the parish hall of the church: drama, concerts, lectures, *khoros* or round dances, and many others.

Following the growth of the Bulgarian community in Toronto, two other Bulgaro-Macedonian churches have been established: St. George's Macedono-Bulgarian Eastern Orthodox Church and Holy Trinity Greek Orthodox Church. Both churches conduct Bulgarian-language schools, and are important meeting places for the Bulgarian community in Toronto. In other communities, Bulgarians participate in the activities of other Orthodox churches, be they Ukrainian Orthodox, Greek Orthodox, Russian Orthodox, or some other.

A major secular organization of the Bulgarian immigrant community in Canada has been the Bulgarian National Front, which has had chapters in a number of communities. As a non-profit organization, the Bulgarian National Front has sought to promote the idea of a Bulgaria without communism. At the same time, the Front has attempted to aid Bulgarian immigrants in their integration into Canadian society. The Bulgarian National Front has published a monthly entitled *Borba* (Struggle). A more recent (1976) Bulgarian-language publication bears the title *Budno Oko* (The Alert Eye) and depicts itself as an anti-communist publication. Another newspaper, *Novo Vreme*, now presents a positive view of Bulgaria's communist government and system.

The Bulgarian Canadian Society of Toronto has been primarily interested in cultural and social activities. It has stressed the preservation of the Bulgarian heritage by organizing gatherings on Bulgarian national days and church holidays.

The Bulgarian immigrant community has succeeded in becoming an integral part of Canadian society. As individuals, Canadians of Bulgarian descent have made a mark in numerous different walks of life. At the same time, however, many of these Canadians have not lost sight of their roots. In their cultural and other activities, and indeed in their general political outlook, these Canadians have continued to display a vital interest both in their rich ethnic heritage and in the fate of Bulgaria itself.

# Byelorussians

BYELORUSSIANS, together with Ukrainians and Russians, belong to the eastern branch of the Slavic nations, forming a distinct linguistic and cultural group within this family. The present territorial limits of Byelorussia, with its capital at Minsk, include an area of 80,134 square miles (207,547 km$^2$), and a population of nine million. It is situated in the eastern lowlands of Europe, and is bordered to the south by the Ukraine, to the east by Russia, to the north by Lithuania and Latvia, and to the west by Poland. It is one of the constituent republics of the Soviet Union, and was a founding member of the United Nations.

The word "byelo" in the Byelorussian language means "white", and the Byelorussians have therefore been called "White Russians" at times. The origin of the term "white" in connection with the name of the country has never been established beyond question, but the term should not be confused with the "white" (as opposed to the "red") Russians who fought for the restoration of the Tsarist regime after the revolution of 1917.

In the latter years of the eighteenth century, Byelorussia became part of the Russian Empire. The nineteenth century saw a revival of national consciousness among Byelorussians, and this consciousness crystallized into a definite desire for separate statehood. Taking advantage of the outbreak of the Russian Revolution, the Byelorussian National Council (Rada) ultimately proclaimed the independence of Byelorussia on March 25, 1918. Less than a year later, however, Soviet troops overthrew the Byelorussian state and set up the Byelorussian Soviet Socialist Republic as part of the Soviet Union.

The major difficulty encountered when attempting to reconstruct the history of Byelorussian immigration into Canada is the fact that Byelorussians were not listed as separate from other ethnic groups until the 1971 census. Before that time, those who had entered Canada before the First World War were classified as Russians, while those who immigrated between the wars, when western Byelorussia was under Polish rule, were classified as Poles.

With a few exceptions, the first Byelorussian immigrants arrived in Canada at the beginning of the twentieth century. Although most came from an agricultural background, these early immigrants tended to seek employment in the lumber and construction industries, with the majority settling in major cities such as Montreal and Toronto, as well as in the industrial urban centres of Ontario such as Sudbury and Timmins. Several large groups of these first Byelorussian settlers went to the Prairies.

Between the two world wars, Byelorussia was divided, with the eastern section remaining under Soviet rule, and the western section coming under Polish administration. Byelorussian immigration from the Soviet-occupied regions ceased entirely at this time, while a steady flow of Byelorussians from the western territories entered Canada. Because the Byelorussian immigrants of this period were classified as Poles, it is virtually impossible to estimate the numbers of Byelorussians involved.

During the Second World War, Byelorussia was occupied by the Nazis, and as a result many Byelorussians were deported to Germany as forced labour. Finding themselves in zones controlled by the western Allies at the end of the war, those Byelorussians decided to remain in Western Europe rather than return to their homeland. Furthermore, many Byelorussians had served in the Polish army, which had made its way to Western Europe during the early stages of the war. They embarked on a search for a new home and fresh opportunities after demobilization.

As a result, Canada experienced an influx of Byelorussian immigrants immediately after the Second World War. Some came on contract from Italy and Great Britain to work as farm labourers for a stipulated number of years. The majority were displaced persons who represented a cross-section of the Byelorussian population, including both educated professional people and unskilled workers.

The 1971 census of Canada recorded 2,280 persons who claimed Byelorussian ancestry. This must be regarded as a minimum number, inasmuch as many persons of Byelorussian descent are certainly included among the Polish, Russian and Ukrainian groups, as in previous enumerations. Of the number listed in the census, about half (1,135) resided in

Ontario. The remainder of the Byelorussian-Canadian population was distributed mainly throughout the western provinces, with 400 in British Columbia, 255 in Alberta, 175 in Manitoba and 50 in Saskatchewan. There were also 195 Byelorussians living in Quebec, mostly in Montreal. Undoubtedly the largest centre of Byelorussian population in Canada is Toronto, although other Ontario cities such as Windsor, Sudbury and Timmins also contain Byelorussian communities.

The majority of the Byelorussian people are of the Greek Orthodox faith, although a substantial number of Roman Catholics can be found in the group. There are two Byelorussian-language Greek Orthodox churches in Canada, both in Toronto. The first, the Church of St. Cyril of Turau, is under the jurisdiction of the Byelorussian Autocephalic Orthodox Church, and thus forms part of an independent Byelorussian ecclesiastical organization. It was organized as a parish in 1954 by the Byelorussian Canadian Alliance. The second Byelorussian church in Toronto is dedicated to St. Euphrasinia of Polatsk. It is under the jurisdiction of the Ecumenical Patriarch of Constantinople, and it also follows the Greek Orthodox rite. It was founded by the Byelorussian National Association after the creation of the latter organization in 1952.

The first Canada-wide Byelorussian organization was created in 1949, when a general convention of the Byelorussian Alliance in Canada was held in Toronto. Later renamed the Byelorussian Canadian Alliance, this organization has its headquarters in Toronto with branches in Sudbury, Ottawa and London. Dedicated to the promotion of the Byelorussian national and cultural heritage, this organization also provides moral and financial support for its members, including the Byelorussian (Toronto) Credit Union Ltd.

which was founded in 1953, and the establishment of the parish of St. Cyril of Turau in 1954. Furthermore, the Alliance has operated a Byelorussian community centre in Toronto, and among its other activities has initiated biennial conventions of North Americans of Byelorussian origin which still continue. The Alliance was also involved in various publishing activities, and a member of the Alliance conducted classes in Byelorussian language and culture at the University of Toronto between 1950 and 1952.

As a result of differing political opinions within the original Byelorussian Alliance in Canada, a new group, the Byelorussian National Association, was formed in 1952. With objectives similar to those of the Alliance, the National Association established the parish of St. Euphrasinia of Polatsk, and organized a Byelorussian-language Saturday school and a dance group. It has a community centre in Toronto. The Byelorussian National Association has also participated in conventions with Byelorussian organizations in the United States.

The need to co-ordinate activities within the community became apparent and by 1966 the Byelorussian Canadian Co-ordinating Committee was established, not only to act as a liaison between the major Byelorussian organizations, but also to represent the community in its dealings with the Canadian government and with other ethnic groups. Furthermore, it organizes the celebrations of Byelorussian Independence Day, March 25, and the Byelorussian Memorial Day, November 28, the latter in commemoration of the anti-Soviet Slutsak uprising of 1920. The Committee consists of five member organizations. The founding members are the Byelorussian Canadian Alliance, the Byelorussian National Association, and the Byelorussian

Relief Association. Two other organizations joined the Committee in 1970, the Byelorussian Institute of Arts and Sciences, Canada, and the Byelorussian Canadian Youth Association.

The Byelorussian Relief Organization was founded originally as a mutual benefit society with the intention of helping Byelorussian immigrants integrate into Canadian society. It now conducts a number of social activities. The Byelorussian Institute of Arts and Sciences, Canada, was founded in 1967. This institute is primarily interested in promoting scholarly studies and exhibitions on Byelorussian themes and subjects.

Another relatively new organization within the Byelorussian community is the Byelorussian Canadian Youth Association, founded in Toronto in 1970. Associated with a similar body in the United States, the Canadian organization promotes a number of activities of interest to the young, and has participated in Toronto's 'Caravan' ever since the Association's founding. The Association is a member of the Folk Arts Council of Toronto and generally contributes dance groups and other entertainment to the events staged by other Byelorussian organizations.

Another interesting organization is the Byelorussian Women's Association, which specializes in organizing poetry reading and artistic exhibitions.

The earliest publication regularly appearing in Canada in the Byelorussian language was *Byelorussian Emigrant* (Byelaruski Emihrant), published by the Byelorussian Canadian Alliance until the end of 1953. Its place has been taken by the *Byelorussian Voice* (Byelaruski Holas), a monthly published in Toronto. This publication is the official organ of the Federation of Byelorussian Free Journalists. Associated with the newspaper is a literary magazine, *Bayavaya Uskalos.*

In the period between 1963 and 1969, the Byelorussian Canadian Alliance cooperated with the Byelorussian American Association in the publication of a monthly newspaper, *Byelarus*, which carried two pages of news from Canada. Since then, Byelorussian-Canadian activities have been covered in *Byelarus* and *Byelorussian Times*, both of which originate in the United States.

In addition to the annual celebrations of Byelorussian Independence Day, Byelorussian Memorial Day, Christmas and Easter, the Byelorussian community in recent years has participated in several important cultural events. In September, 1967, the 450th anniversary of Byelorussian printing was commemorated in Canada, the event marking both the Canadian Centennial and the work of Francisak Skaryna, who translated and in 1517 printed the first Byelorussian version of the Bible. In 1967, the Byelorussian community acquired the property "Slutsak" near Parry Sound, Ontario, as a Centennial project. The property serves as a summer resort and a meeting place for Canadians and Americans of Byelorussian origin. Another important event for the Byelorussian community was the tenth Biennial Convention of Byelorussians of North America, held in Toronto in September of 1972. A Byelorussian Study Week was organized at the University of Ottawa in April, 1975, by the Byelorussian Institute of Arts and Sciences in conjunction with the Department of Slavic Studies of the University of Ottawa and the National Museum of Man. A similar conference was first organized in Kingston in 1971.

The members of the Byelorussian community participate in the cultural and political life of Canada through their active involvement in political and cultural conferences and meetings. They contribute to Canadian life and culture as members of various occupations and professions and as individual artists, writers and scholars.

# Chileans

CHILE IS A NARROW COUNTRY stretching from Peru down the western coast of southern South America. The population is predominantly European in origin, with a large *mestizo* (mixed Indian-European) element and a small number of South American Indians. Like so much of South America, Chile was once part of the Spanish Empire. As a result, the official language of the country is Spanish, and the Chilean culture is based on the Spanish, although the influence of nineteenth-century German immigration is apparent in certain areas, particularly in the south, where German is spoken and German customs are evident. Eighty-nine per cent of the Chilean population is Roman Catholic.

The vast majority of Chileans in Canada are political refugees who were forced to leave their country after the 1973 overthrow of the Allende government, and the establishment in its place of a military junta. Refugees have been arriving in Canada since 1974, and often come by way of Argentina. Prior to 1974, Chilean immigration was very light; only 318 persons are recorded as having emigrated from Chile to Canada in the five years between 1963 and 1967, and an additional 1,817 between 1968 and 1973. The majority of this pre-1974 group consists of a small number of Chileans of the Jewish faith who came to Toronto around 1970, and other small groups that settled in Winnipeg and Vancouver. Subsequent to 1974, the Department of Manpower and Immigration had begun to record the arrival of a small but significant number of Chileans as regular landed immigrants.

Initially, the refugees from the overthrow of Allende came to Canada in two small groups, both of whom had sought asylum in Canadian institutions in Chile during the *coup d'état*. The Canadian government then implemented the Special Chilean Movement, in which up to 5,000 registered refugees were to be accepted into Canada and helped to settle. The Movement had, by November, 1976, brought 4,600 Chileans to Canada, of whom 100 were part of the One Hundred Prisoner List, a program established as a cooperative effort through the action of the Inter-Church Committee on Chile. These people came, with their families, directly from internment as political prisoners.

Normal immigration regulations and procedures were relaxed somewhat for the Special Chilean Movement. The Movement also attempted to direct participants to destinations in Canada where they would most easily find employment, and the first Chileans to arrive under the program were directed to Montreal, Vancouver and Toronto, as well as to other areas in Ontario such as Sudbury. More recently, they have been sent almost exclusively to the Prairie Provinces, and there are now Chilean communities in Winnipeg, Saskatoon, Regina, Calgary, Edmonton and other western cities.

Chileans have demonstrated a high level of individual community organization. This is due in part to the special circumstances of their migration; in part to the high percentage of professionals, civil servants and highly skilled workers among their numbers; and in part to the fact that all had been in some way organizers or community leaders in Chile. Therefore, in most Chilean communities associations have quickly been formed and committees established. The Winnipeg Chilean Association, for example, has four committees—for education and culture, for finance, for women, and for social welfare. In Edmonton, the Chileans have organized a housing co-operative of two projects with twenty houses each. At the same time, Canadians of Chilean origin have made a particularly active contribution to those overall Latin American associations which would appear to be becoming an increasingly important feature of the Canadian-Latin American community.

Like most political refugees, Chileans begin by looking very much towards their country of origin. They hope for a swift change in the political situation, a change which will enable them to return. As time passes, however, many begin to realize that events may not take place quickly, and with this realization comes an increasing involvement in and commitment to life in Canada.

# Chinese

THE CHINESE ARE ONE OF the oldest ethnocultural groups in Canada. In 1958, when British Columbia was observing the centennial of its founding as a Crown colony, the Chinese were celebrating the 100th anniversary of their arrival in Canada. According to some reports, the Chinese were in Canada even before 1858, for it is conjectured that there were Chinese with the early British explorers, such as Captain John Meares, who sailed to the west coast of Canada from China. There are no records, however, of any Chinese settlement being established on Canadian shores as a result of these expeditions.

Chinese first came to Canada in significant numbers during the Cariboo gold rush. Gold was discovered on the Fraser River in British Columbia in 1858, and a large number of people, many from California, converged on the scene within a few months. Several thousand Chinese were among them. They had originally emigrated from China to the California gold fields in 1849. By 1866 most of the mines in British Columbia were exhausted, and many Chinese left the country for their homeland or returned to the western United States. Of those who remained, some continued to search for gold, but the majority turned to other ways of making a living, such as domestic service, operating laundries and market gardening.

Until recently, practically all Chinese in Canada came from a few counties in the Province of Kwangtung, which lies southeast of Canton. A large majority of the Chinese from this area were of peasant stock and came from a single county in the region, T'ai-shan. Poverty and overpopulation were the main causes of emigration. At first they came to Canada by way of the United States, but after 1860 they sailed directly from Hong Kong to Victoria. Most of the early immigrants had not planned to stay in Canada permanently, but hoped to go back to China and retire as soon as they had earned enough money.

Very few Chinese emigrated to Canada in the twenty years between 1860 and 1880. Then, in 1881, construction began on the Canadian Pacific Railway, and from 1882 to 1885 approximately 15,000 Chinese men were imported into the region under contract to build the British Columbia section of the line.

After disembarking from sailing vessel or steamer at Esquimalt, the Chinese labourers were transferred to river boats which took them to Yale, Boston Bar, China Bar and other places in the Fraser Canyon, where they were put to work clearing ground and laying tracks. For very low wages they worked a twelve-hour day. They helped make it possible to complete the huge construction project within five years.

When the transcontinental railway was completed in November of 1885, large numbers of Chinese were thrown out of work. Many returned to China or the United States, while others made their way to the Prairie Provinces and eastern Canada. The majority, however, remained in British Columbia. Both there and in other western provinces they tended to settle in cities and towns, many operating laundries, restaurants and grocery stores. A few had contracted for the food and supplies of Chinese railway workers and became the founders of the original Chinese businesses on the lower mainland of British Columbia and Vancouver Island.

From the beginning, the Chinese in British Columbia were considered little more than a cheap labour reserve which could be exploited for particular projects. Many Canadians believed that the Chinese should never become a permanent part of the Canadian population. The situation was made more difficult for the Chinese because they also lacked external support from the government of their homeland. There was not even consular representation between China and Canada until 1909. And because of the transient nature of the Chinese immigrants, they were also lacking in leadership and organization. Unable to present a strong united front within Canada, and without a strong home government to take their case to Ottawa, the Chinese were an easy

target for discrimination, a situation which proved to be not only severe but also prolonged.

Numerous special regulations were introduced by the federal and provincial governments to restrict Chinese entry in the late nineteenth century, restrictions which continued into the early twentieth century and included the imposition of a head tax which increased from fifty dollars in 1885 to five hundred dollars in 1903. In 1907, anti-Asian sentiment in British Columbia reached the boiling point, culminating in a violent attack on Vancouver's Chinatown, during the course of which part of the community was destroyed, although few people were injured and no one was killed. This incident was part of a larger web of anti-Chinese sentiment which eventually led to the Chinese Immigration Act of 1923. Under this Act, with few exceptions no Chinese were allowed to enter Canada, and the legislation was so effective that in the 25 years it remained in force, only 44 Chinese immigrants entered the country. It was impossible for Chinese men to bring their families to Canada. It had such a profound effect upon the nature of the Chinese community before the Second World War that, in fact, the number of Chinese residing in Canada decreased from 46,519 in 1931 to 34,627 in 1941. The large majority of these Chinese residents were men, and most of them lived in British Columbia.

In the meantime, the Chinese community became organized and firmly established. The Barkerville Lodge of the Chinese Freemasons, one of the first Chinese associations in Canada, was founded in the 1860s. The Freemasons served as the main protector, arbiter and organizer in each Chinese community until the advent of the Chinese Benevolent Association (CBA). From the 1880s to the 1950s, the

Freemasons' role was assumed by the CBA in British Columbia and the rest of Canada. The original purpose of these associations was one of mutual assistance and protection for the Chinese who, as immigrants and individuals, found it difficult to cope with the problems they faced in their early years in Canada. As a result, the Chinese in Canada seldom, if ever, depended on public or private charity. They always looked to their own people in times of sickness and unemployment, or when there were legal or financial difficulties. The CBA also provided direction within communities across the country and served as their spokesman in dealing with the government. It also sought to promote fair immigration laws.

When the Sino-Japanese War broke out in 1937, the plight of China drew the Chinese in Canada together in raising money and contributing toward the National Salvation League in support of the government in Chungking. The Kuomintang (Chinese Nationalist Party) had become organized among the overseas Chinese after 1911, and during this war it increased its support and influence considerably. As the war enlarged to include Canada in 1939 and the United States in 1941, the Chinese became an ally. Four hundred Chinese volunteers from British Columbia served in the Armed Forces, and Chinese community leaders took an active part in raising war loans and organizing the community for other war causes. At the same time, relations with non-Chinese Canadians improved somewhat, and as a result the end of the war brought a repeal of the Chinese Immigration Act. Eligible Chinese were granted the full rights of citizenship for the first time since 1898. Also for the first time, Chinese who became citizens were given the right of other citizens to send for their families who had been living outside Canada. More than 22,000 Chinese residents now became naturalized citizens, and many of them brought their families to this country.

With the repeal of the exclusion act, the whole character of Chinese life in Canada changed, as the families of Canadians of Chinese origin began to immigrate in increasing numbers. Between 1946 and 1965 it was reported that 36,370 Chinese entered Canada, most of whom were families and relatives of Chinese already settled in Canada. The Chinatowns of the large cities suddenly began to come to life, and adventurous new immigrants moved into many cities where previously there had been few or no Chinese.

The ascendancy into power of the People's Republic of China in 1949 caused many of the older generation to reconsider their original intention to return to China and confirmed their identity as permanent residents of Canada. Taking advantage of the educational opportunities which were presented to them in the new country, many of the second and subsequent generations of Chinese became well-educated and entered a profession. This, in turn, enabled the Chinese to improve their economic position substantially. A 1959 study reported that among all ethnic classifications, the Chinese ranked fifth in the country in absolute numbers of professional personnel.

Since the new immigration act of 1962 was introduced, the Chinese community has gone through yet another drastic change in its composition. The system of sponsorship that was in force from 1947 to 1962 permitted only close relatives of Chinese Canadians to enter Canada. Under the present point system, Chinese may now immigrate even if they have no relatives in Canada. Consequently, the change in the law brought a total of 47,759 Chinese into Canada between 1963 and 1970, thereby almost doubling the Chinese population during the 1961-71 period.

The most recent immigrants are much more varied in their places of origin, in the language they speak, and in their occupations and socio-economic status. Many of them are highly educated technical and professional people or business people. Their arrival has significantly affected the structure of the Chinese community in Canada.

The 1971 census reported a total Chinese population of 118,815 in Canada, of whom more than one-third were born here. Chinese live in every province and every territory of the country, although the largest number (44,315) still live in British Columbia. The City of Vancouver alone, with its 30,640 Canadians of Chinese origin, comprises the largest single community in Canada, and its Chinatown is the third largest in North America, after New York and San Francisco. Ontario has the second largest and growing Chinese group (39,325), followed by Alberta with 12,905 and Quebec with 11,905. The vast majority live in urban areas; in fact, nearly 90 per cent live in cities with populations of 100,000 or more. New Chinese immigrants in Toronto, for example, are making a successful adjustment to their new environment, perhaps because of their higher educational level and their prior experience of urban living in cosmopolitan centres such as Hong Kong, Singapore, Taipei, or even in Shanghai, Peking or Canton in mainland China.

As the Chinese rise on the social and economic scale, there is a strong trend away from the old neighbourhood of Chinatown. By 1961, half the Chinese population of Vancouver had undergone outward and upward residential mobility. In Toronto, one-third of the Chinese immigrants live in a Chinatown area of the city. Integration among the young Chinese, both residentially and

socially, has been very rapid. University graduates in particular socialize more frequently with Canadians of European descent and, as a result, are intermarrying on an increasing scale. Active participation of Chinese Canadians in the political sphere, especially in British Columbia, is also noteworthy.

The Chinese community has never ceased its active life. Societies, clubs and associations, with their business and social meetings, festive occasions and ceremonial functions play a large part in the lives of many Chinese in Canada. Some are national in scope, with branches in the various cities and towns across Canada where Chinese communities have developed.

Chinese associations fall into several categories. The large umbrella association with which many independent organizations are affiliated is the Chinese Benevolent Association, or the Chinese Community Centre as it is known in Toronto. In addition, there is the national Freemasons Association and district and family or clan associations, trade and professional associations, and a variety of others. The Chinese have perhaps more formal organizations than any other ethnocultural group of comparable size.

Another Chinese-Canadian organization is the district association, to which those coming from the same district in China automatically belong. Among these are the Hoy San Ning Yung (for T'ai-shan), the Hoy Ping Association (K'ai-p'ing), the Kong Chow Society (Chung-shan), and a number of others. The purpose of these societies is centred around mutual aid and social activity, although in earlier days they also provided protection and arranged for the shipment of bones back to the village of origin of the deceased.

Clan associations are important among the Chinese. The idea behind such associations is that all persons sharing a family name have descended from the same ancestor and are therefore bound together by links of clanship. Altogether there are about twenty clan associations among the Chinese in Canada. Branches are found in those Chinese communities where there are sufficient members of one clan to form a group in relation to other clans. The clan associations, like the district associations, provide welfare, mutual aid, and protection for their members, although these functions are far less important today. The largest clan association, the Wong Kung Har Tong, runs a Chinese-language school in Vancouver, the Mon Keong School.

Of the numerous associations, the trade and professional groups such as the Chinese Merchant's Association, the Chinese Chamber of Commerce, the Chinese Trade Workers' Association, and the British Columbia Lower Mainland Grocers' Co-operative have always been active. A variety of social-recreational clubs and societies have also been organized along sex and generational lines, and the growth in the numbers of associations among Chinese in the postwar period is quite impressive. New associations have recently been formed, such as the Mon Sheong Foundation in Toronto, the Sien Lok Society in Calgary and the Manitoba Chinese Fellowship in Winnipeg. Many of the new associations are supported by English-speaking Chinese Canadians who wish to become involved in the Chinese community, as well as by new immigrants who are not related to the older Chinese Canadians.

There are a number of Chinese-language schools across the country, in Vancouver, Calgary, Edmonton, Winnipeg and Toronto, together with a number of classes offered within the public school system. These community schools are all self-supporting. The

Chinese traditional culture of Confucian philosophy and the way of living associated with the extended family tradition have been at least partly maintained through the language schools. The younger generation finds it difficult to maintain the language in the more flexible and open conditions which have prevailed in the past twenty years. Nonetheless, many of the children of mixed marriages, as well as non-Chinese, are interested in learning the language. Many universities are now teaching Chinese (Mandarin) and are aiding in language retention.

The Chinese press in Canada comprises six daily newspapers, three of which are in Vancouver and three in Toronto. The oldest of these papers is *The Chinese Times*, published in Vancouver since 1907. There are also a number of magazines or small journals which are written both in Chinese and English.

The religious traditions brought from China were strongly influenced by Confucianism. Religious institutions have a presence among the Chinese community, but they play a far less important role than do voluntary associations in community life. Christian groups have been playing more important and active roles in the religious and social functions of the Chinese of late, and the proportion of Christians among the Chinese is growing due to the larger number of Christians among the most recent immigrants. Several of the major Canadian churches that have established missions in the Chinese communities are now established congregations.

The Chinese have brought to Canada a number of traditional festivals, including the Chinese New Year's Day, which usually falls in February, the Festival of Ching Ming which is observed in the spring, the Dragon Boat Festival in early summer, and the mid-autumn festival. Some Chinese also commemorate national days on October 1 and 10.

In 1971, 64 per cent of the Canadians of Chinese origin were still first generation immigrants. However, as the old prewar immigrant generation gradually declines, the community will keep changing its shape and structure, and there is every reason to believe that its contributions will be both more varied and more recognizable for years to come.

# Croatians

CROATIA CONSTITUTES, along with Slovenia, Bosnia-Herzegovina, Serbia, Montenegro and Macedonia, one of the component republics of Yugoslavia. Together with the Serbs, Slovenes, Macedonians, Montenegrins and Bulgarians, the Croatians formed the southern branch of the Slavic family of nations.

It is very difficult to estimate the exact extent of Croatian immigration to Canada. Croatians were never given a separate entry in immigration statistics, but were classified together with the Austrians and Hungarians before 1918. After the formal establishment of the state of Yugoslavia in 1929, they were classified as Yugoslavs. However, according to some scholarly estimates, more than 65 per cent of the emigrants from what is now the modern state of Yugoslavia have been Croatians.

On the basis of this assumption it was estimated that the number of Croatians residing in Canada in the mid-1960s was 45,000. If this assumption is correct, the present number of Croatians and their descendants in Canada is over 80,000 on the basis of the official 1971 census. According to this census, however, only

23,380 persons formally reported Croatian as their ethnocultural group. It would appear from this that there were some Croatians, especially in the second and third generations, who perceived themselves as English Canadians, or were described by the census takers as Yugoslavs rather than as Croatians. According to the census statistics of 1971 there were 23,380 Croatians living in Canada of whom 16,800 were in Ontario, 3,120 in British Columbia, 1,130 in Alberta, 1,100 in Quebec, and smaller numbers in the other provinces. At present, almost 80 Croatian communities exist, the largest being in Toronto, Montreal and Hamilton, with other smaller communities scattered across the country.

The Croatians came to Canada at a number of distinct periods. The first may be indicated as a period of pre-mass migration, when few and occasional contacts were made with Canada. The second period was that brought about by mass migration to the United States, when Croatians, for social, economic and political reasons, left in the hundreds of thousands for the New World. This period of migration lasted from 1900–14, and was interrupted by the First World War, when Croatian immigration to Canada was ended because of that country's position within the Austro-Hungarian empire. Emigration from Croatia was generally curtailed until 1923.

The next major phase in Croatian immigration to Canada was the inter-war phase of 1923–39, when some 12,000 immigrants arrived, 10,000 of whom came between 1925 and 1930. This group consisted mainly of unskilled labourers seeking occupations in farming, forestry and fishing during the Depression years. The fourth and last phase of migration occurred during the postwar period, which brought wartime and postwar refugees from Yugoslavia, including skilled workers, technicians and professionals, all destined for Canada's rapidly growing metropolitan areas.

The Croatians did have limited contact with Canada prior to 1900, especially in the maritime, military and mining fields. The first Croatians to arrive in Canada may have been two Dalmatian sailors recruited for the Cartier expedition of 1542–43 by Sieur de Roberval. The second contact was likely a "Sclavonian" miner named Jacques, who accompanied Champlain in 1605–6 on his voyages to Acadia. Other Croatians served as soldiers in the Austrian military units sent by the French government to defend New France in 1758–59. Others came with the fur trade to the interior and to the Pacific coast, and with the gold rushes of the late 1850s and the Yukon rush of 1898. However, this was a transitory population, and few remained in Canada.

The first permanent Croatian communities were established along the Pacific coast. Some Croatian fishermen came to British Columbia in the 1880s and stayed to settle, and in 1890 several families migrated from Losinj to Vancouver. Soon after their arrival, these families moved to Ladner (formerly Port Guichon), where they settled. In 1898, several Croatian miners from Zumberak came via the United States to Ladysmith, seeking better wages. They were soon followed by another group of miners who settled in Ladysmith, Cumberland, Nanaimo, Wellington and Britannia in the early 1900s. Several hundred Croatians came to British Columbia between 1911 and 1914, and of the twenty-nine Croatian settlements established in Canada before the First World War, fourteen were in British Columbia.

Other Croatian immigrants moved to the new provinces of Saskatchewan and Alberta. A group arrived in Saskatchewan in 1905 and settled at Bladworth, Hanley and Kenaston. At the same time, settlers came to Leask and Duck Lake near Prince Albert, but several returned to Michigan after considerable hardship during their first year of homesteading. Settlements west of Edmonton in the Peace River and Coal Branch districts were established before the war. Most of these Saskatchewan and Alberta settlers had come from the province of Lika in Croatia, or from Severin in the adjacent Pokuplje region.

Other agricultural and industrial settlements were established in Ontario, primarily by former residents of Dalmatia, Primorje, Zumberak and Zagorje. In southern Ontario, the first settlement of industrial workers and their families was founded in Welland in 1907, and in Hamilton in 1910. Settlements were also established in Sault Ste. Marie, Port Arthur and Schumacher, composed mainly of steelworkers, miners, railway workers and lumberjacks.

In the years immediately after the First World War, Croatian immigration to Canada was limited. Only 60 Croatians came to Canada from 1919 to 1921, and the total number of Canadians of Croatian descent in 1921 was less than 4,000. A heavy period of Croatian immigration suddenly began in 1924 and lasted until 1929, during which approximately 10,000 Croatians entered Canada. The Depression limited immigration after 1929, so that between that date and 1931, only 2,100 Croatian immigrants came to Canada.

During the 1920s, numerous settlements were established; at one time it was estimated that there were as many as 171 settlements. Most of these obviously comprised a small number of settlers and were of short duration, for many of them disappeared during the Depression. Among the settlements established during this period were those at Ford City near Windsor in 1923; Creighton Mine and Levack in Ontario, in 1924; Arvida and Montreal in Quebec, and Toronto, in 1925; New Waterford, Reserve Mines, Stellarton and Sydney in Nova Scotia in 1926; Schumacher–Timmins, Carson Mine, Kapuskasing and Kirkland Lake in Ontario, in 1926; and Taber and Wayne in Alberta, in 1927.

A relatively small number of Croatians, some 2,100 persons, did immigrate to Canada between March 1931 and March 1941. Most of these immigrants were the wives of earlier arrivals; indeed, this decade was the only time in which the number of male Croatian immigrants was surpassed by the number of females. The increase in the total number of immigrants over the previous decade was negligible; in 1941 there were only 12,728 Croatians in Canada.

The immigrants who came to Canada between the world wars differed from the prewar immigrants in several respects. The more recent immigrants were better educated and generally sought employment in the industrial cities and towns of central Canada. Although they were initially destined for Winnipeg, the centre for farm labour, the news of unemployment in the west which they received en route often compelled them to remain in Ontario and Quebec and to find employment in the industries and mines.

During the Second World War, Canadians of Croatian descent bought thousands of dollars of war bonds and many served in the Canadian Armed Forces. The Croatians in Hamilton, for example, presented the Canadian Red Cross with an ambulance. After the Second World War, thousands of Croatian immigrants came to Canada. Many of them, in addition to having the traditional economic motives for migration, came as political refugees who wished to leave their homeland rather than live under the communist regime established in postwar Yugoslavia. This group of Croatians was better educated than any previous group and included many educators and other professionals, skilled tradesmen, businessmen and industrialists. In addition to these refugees, many young Croatians also left their country to join their relatives and friends in Canada. By far the greatest number of this postwar migration settled in Canada's major cities, as well as the mining towns in both northern Ontario and Quebec.

An interesting addition to the Canadian cultural scene has been the Croatian folklore, which has been brought to the attention of the general Canadian audience by numerous Croatian choirs, Kolo Dancers in their colourful native costumes, and tamburitza players who play a thirteen-century-old native stringed instrument similar to the mandolin. Croatian folklore groups participate annually in many Canadian festivals and celebrations such as the Festival of Neo-Canadians, Canadian-Croatian Folklore Festival, Vancouver Croatian Day, the St-Jean-Baptiste Day festivities in Montreal, and the Canada Day celebrations in Ottawa.

Croatians are predominantly Roman Catholic, and use the Latin script. The first Croatian Catholic Parish was established in Windsor in 1950. In 1955 an old church was purchased by the Croatian community of Toronto. This church was destroyed by fire in 1962, but an impressive new structure was built in its place in 1965; the new church, Our Lady Queen of Croatia Church, is one of Canada's well-established parishes. Other Croatian Catholic parishes and missions are located in most Canadian cities including Hamilton, Sault Ste. Marie, Winnipeg, Calgary, and Vancouver. Two new churches are currently under construction in Mississauga and Montreal. The Croatian Catholic priests and Croatian Dominican Sisters direct a number of humanitarian and cultural institutions. The Croatian Islamic Centre was founded in Toronto in 1973 to serve the Islamic members of the group.

The first branch of the Croatian Peasant Society was founded in Toronto in 1930. Its aim was to enable Canadians of Croatian origin to express their democratic feelings and love of liberty, to unite all Croatians in their loyalty to Canada, to foster understanding of Canadian laws and institutions, and to further cultural and educational work among Croatians. For these reasons, the Society has built seventeen Croatian homes or halls as centres of social, cultural and recreational activity, and has established numerous chapters to serve various clubs associated with some of the chapters. The Croatian Peasant Society publishes *Kalendar (Almanac)* and its own weekly newspaper *Hrvatski Glas (Croatian Voice)*. The newspaper was first established in Winnipeg in 1929 as *Kanadski Glas (Canadian Voice)* by journalist Peter Stankovic, who remained its editor until 1973. *Hrvatski Glas* is currently published in Acton (Halton Hills), Ontario.

In addition to the Croatian Peasant Society, there are other Croatian societies in Canada. The Croatian Fraternal Union, which established its first lodge in Nanaimo in 1903, is a fraternal insurance organization with headquarters in Pittsburgh, Pa., which had about 10,000 members and 66 lodges in Canada in 1970, most of which had youth and sport sections. Another fraternal insurance society is the Croatian Catholic Union, which in 1970 had 34 lodges and 1,548 members in Canada.

In the past two decades several new Croatian organizations have been created in Canada. The United Croats of Canada has sixteen branches in a number of communities and its own publication, *Nezavisna Država Hrvatska (The Independent State of Croatia)* in Toronto. A monthly newspaper *Hrvatski Put (Croatian Way)*, formerly *Nas Put (Our Way)*, is also published in Toronto by the Hrvatski Republikanci (Croatian Republicans). *Jadran (The Adriatic)* is published by the Montreal chapter of Savez Hrvatskih Drustava u Kanadi (The Federation of Croatian Societies in Canada). One of the newest and fastest growing organizations is Hrvatsko Narodno Vijeće (Croatian National Congress) with 21 branches from Montreal to Victoria. The Croatian Movement of Canada and the Croatian National Resistance also have a number of organizations across Canada.

The Croatians have made significant contributions to Canadian economic life within each generation of migration. They began with helping in the construction of two transcontinental railroads, and by taking an important part in the mining, forestry, agriculture, and especially fishing occupations. The second generation of immigrants, those who came during the inter-war period, for the most part became industrial workers in Canadian industry. The third generation has been building their careers in the service, industrial, private and professional sectors of Canadian urban society. At the same time, Croatians born in Canada exhibit the upward mobility of many hard-working ethnocultural groups into the professional and managerial sectors of the economy.

The contribution of Croatian individuals from each generation to the social, cultural and intellectual life of our country has been substantial. Croatians have been active in the fields of art and sculpture, poetry, popular culture and sports. The popularity of chess and soccer, particularly among the more recent post-war immigrants, is evident in the proliferation of chess and soccer clubs in each major city of Canada where Croatians live. They have won at least two provincial chess championships, several provincial and national soccer cups, and most recently the North American Soccer League championship, won by Toronto Metros-Croatia in 1976. In 1979, the soccer team was renamed Toronto Blizzard.

# Czechs

THE CZECHS AND SLOVAKS, who belong to the same western group of the Slav family, have a common ancestry in the Great Moravian empire which was destroyed by the Magyars in the tenth century. At that time the two groups spoke closely related dialects, but since then their historical development has been different. The Czechs remained within the Holy Roman Empire and later, under Austrian domination, in the Kingdom of Bohemia and the crown lands of Moravia and Silesia. The Slovaks lived within the framework of the Kingdom of Hungary.

When their national aspirations failed in the eighteenth and nineteenth centuries, at the time of the Slav national awakening, the Czechs and Slovaks hoped to separate from the Hapsburg monarchy. Their ideal was not fulfilled until 1918, however, when the Czechoslovak Republic was proclaimed. In March of 1939, the Czech lands, Bohemia and Moravia, were incorporated into Germany as "autonomous protectorates," and the Slovak Diet proclaimed the Slovak state. Since the end of the Second World War, the Czechs and

Slovaks have lived within Czechoslovakia.

Of great significance in Canadian history were the activities of the Moravian Brethren, a religious group which had emerged in Bohemia in 1727 as a continuation of the old Hussite Czech Brethren, who were suppressed by the Hapsburgs. They began their missionary work in the 1730s by sending clergymen to Greenland, Labrador and the American Colonies. Moravians from the United States, who had fallen into disfavour because of their pacifism during the American Revolution, settled in Canada after 1791 in Moraviantown, near Chatham, Ontario. The name of their community bore witness to their Czech origins. Their mission was united with the Methodists in 1903.

Substantial Czech immigration to North America did not begin until after 1860, and in its initial phases was motivated to a great extent by political discontent over the fate of the Czech nation within the Austrian Empire. At this early time, Czech immigration to Canada was minimal, individual, and highly selective, those who did come being skilled workers and artisans. During the 1860s, most Czechs leaving Bohemia went to the United States rather than to Canada, though many from this group later settled in Canada when opportunities to the south diminished.

The first recorded Czech immigrants to Canada were four families who settled in Kolin, Saskatchewan, in 1884. Further Czech agricultural immigration did not come from the Czech lands proper, but from Volhynia (now part of Ukraine) where Czech settlers had been farming for quite some time previously. Finding conditions in Volhynia difficult, they migrated to Canada, where they settled in and around Gerald, Saskatchewan.

The first Canadian of Czech origin to settle in Ontario was John Nenicka, who came to

Kenora in 1896. In Alberta, Czechs founded the town of Prague, near Viking, Alberta, while a group at Glenside, Saskatchewan, erected a church to commemorate Jan Hus. Czech Moravian Brethren settled in southern Manitoba amid the Mennonite community there.

The first large, urban settlements to receive Czech immigrants were Edmonton, Kingston and Windsor. Toronto had only a small and transient Czech group, while the largest Czech group eventually formed in Winnipeg, where Czechs were to be found working as artisans, businessmen, construction workers and rail-waymen. The first Czech organization in Canada, the Czecho-Slav Benefit Association, was formed in Winnipeg in 1913.

The Canadian census of 1911 listed approximately 1,800 Czechs in Canada, which suggests the hitherto sporadic nature of their immigration into this country. After 1921, however, the number of Canadians of Czech and Slovak origin jumped rapidly as a result of the introduction of the quota system for immigration into the United States. With immigration to the south severely curtailed, Czechs turned in increasing numbers to Canada. The 1921 Canadian census reported 8,840 people declared themselves of Czech and Slovak background, while the figures jumped to 30,401 in 1931, 42,912 in 1941, 63,959 in 1951, and 73,061 in 1961, decreasing to 57,840 in the 1971 census.

A small percentage of the Czechs who began coming to Canada around 1921 were farmers who specialized in sugar beet production, and they eventually established extensive operations near Lethbridge, Alberta, and Chatham, Ontario. Most of the Czechs who immigrated at this time, however, were drawn to the cities, particularly to Montreal, which replaced Winnipeg as the largest area of Czech

concentration after 1921, and remained in that position until the Second World War. The onset of the Great Depression put a temporary halt to the steady flow of Czech immigration to Canada, but after the Nazi occupation of the Czechoslovak state in 1938, many refugees fled the country, and many of these settled in Canada. After a Communist government took over the reins of power after the war, Czech immigration again increased, although it became very difficult to leave the country after 1948. Between 1946 and 1950, however, 6,888 immigrants who gave their last permanent residence as Czechoslovakia came to Canada, and between 1947 and 1958, 5,787 Czech and Slovak refugees were admitted to the country. Many Czechs who came to Canada after the Second World War settled in Ontario, particularly in Toronto, which now contains the largest Czech- and Slovak-Canadian community in the country.

As a result of the Soviet invasion of Czechoslovakia in the summer of 1968, many Czechs and Slovaks fled the country. Among other countries, Canada decided to help these refugees, and a special Czechoslovakian Refugee Program was established for the duration of the crisis to assist Czechs and Slovaks who wished to immigrate. In the period between September of 1968 and January, 1969, over 9,000 Czechs and Slovaks were admitted to Canada under relaxed immigration procedures, assisted passage, and special language-training programs. Some 12,000 Czechs and Slovaks eventually settled in Canada as a result of the 1968 crisis, and the most recent report of the Department of Manpower and Immigration suggests that their economic and social integration has been largely successful. Since 1971, however, immigration to Canada from Czechoslovakia has slowed to a mere trickle, with only about 150

Czechs and Slovaks entering annually.

The 1971 census of Canada reported 57,840 Canadians of Czech origin, of whom some 27,780 (48.0 per cent) actually spoke the Czech language. By far the largest concentration of the Czechs was in Ontario, where some 25,765 (44.5 percent) individuals of Czech descent resided. Other provinces with sizable Czech communities included Alberta (10,320), British Columbia (8,560), Quebec (4,420), Saskatchewan (4,200) and Manitoba (3,715). The majority of the Ontario Czechs resided in Toronto. Some 9,975 Canadians of Czech and Slovak origin were listed as residing in Toronto, while Vancouver (4,460), Montreal (3,970), Edmonton (2,630), Winnipeg (2,275), Calgary (2,405) and Hamilton (2,140) were also important Czech centres. At present, over 60 per cent of Canadians of Czech and Slovak origin reside in Canada's largest urban centres, and this percentage is growing.

Although the majority of Czechs are Roman Catholic (some 60 per cent), the sporadic nature of their initial immigration to Canada made the organization of religious institutions difficult. Above all, there was a lack of Czech-speaking priests, and such communities as were large enough to warrant it depended upon Czech-speaking priests from the United States to visit their churches periodically. It was not until larger settlements of Czech and Slovak Canadians developed that separate Czech-language churches were established, the first such church being built at Chatham, Ontario, where a regular American-based priest visited after 1928 in the parish of SS. Cyril and Methody. It was not until 1948, however, that the first Czech priest settled there permanently.

A Czech parish was organized in Toronto in 1951, St. Wenceslaus, and a new church building was consecrated there in 1963.

Another Czech church was established at Batawa, Ontario, for the benefit of those employees of the Bata shoe firm who fled Nazi-occupied Czechoslovakia in 1939. The number of Czechs gradually declined in this area, however, after the church was built. The Jesuit order now maintains a Czech House in Montreal, for the training of Czech-speaking priests, so the availability of priests who can say Mass in the language is becoming less of a problem.

Significant, although less numerous, is the Czech Baptist group, the majority of whom are descended from the Hussite-influenced Czech Brethren. The first Baptist group came to Canada from Volhynia, settling at Minitonas, Manitoba, where a congregation was organized in 1929 and a church was built in 1932. Other Czech Baptist congregations have been formed in Windsor, Ontario, where a church was built in 1960; in Glenside, Saskatchewan, where the Hus chapel was erected; in Winnipeg, where the Bethlehem chapel was built in 1930; and in Toronto, where a Baptist congregation has been functioning since 1942.

The first secular Czech organization to be founded in Canada was the Czecho-Slav Benevolent Association of Winnipeg, established in 1913 as a voluntary mutual aid society. Its membership was by no means limited exclusively to persons with a Czech background, and with the political union of the Czechs and the Slovaks after 1918, the Association changed its name to the Czechoslovak Benevolent Association in order to reflect the new political reality in the homeland. As a centre for patriotic action, the Association participated in the formation of the 'Bohemian' detachment of the 223rd Battalion during the First World War. In 1919, the Association acquired a hall and a Czech-language library in Winnipeg, while at about the same time a women's auxiliary and a youth group were formed in conjunction with the Association. The Association's activities later extended to include sports and education, and in 1963 it celebrated its fiftieth anniversary by issuing a commemorative book.

Another early Czech organization was formed in Montreal in 1924 under the name of the Czechoslovak Mutual Benefit Society. Although it established a branch in Toronto in 1927, it eventually ceased operation.

A much more successful organization has been the Czechoslovak National Alliance in Canada. Before the Second World War, there was no body which co-ordinated the activities of Czechs and Slovaks throughout Canada. A branch of the Czechoslovak National Council in America was founded in Winnipeg, but the dismemberment of the Czechoslovak state by the Nazis provided the impetus for the creation of a new central organization with definite political goals. In May of 1939, representatives of the Czechs, along with some Slovak and Ruthenian groups, met in Toronto to form a new umbrella organization; shortly thereafter, some 46 local branches, representing most Czech and some Slovak organizations in Canada, had been formed. By 1942, the Czechoslovak National Alliance in Canada had 86 branches and some 6,500 members across Canada.

Dedicated to the ideals of T. G. Masaryk, the first president of a united Czechoslovak state, the Alliance administered a war charities fund, promoted the interests of Czechs in Canada, worked on behalf of Czechoslovak independence, and when peace came to Europe, contributed to the reconstruction of the homeland. With the Communist coup of 1948, many Czech and Slovak refugees came to Canada, and the activities of the Alliance became centred around the promotion of Czechoslovak independence from Communist

rule. By 1960 the Alliance had been granted a federal charter, and its name was officially changed to the Czechoslovak National Association in Canada, with headquarters currently in Toronto. Some sixteen branches of the Association remain active today, and because other Czech local organizations remain affiliated with it, the actual number of Czechoslovakian Canadians which it represents is quite substantial.

A Czech social and cultural organization of importance is the Sokol movement ("sokol" meaning "falcon" in Czech), which is patterned on the athletic and patriotic organizations which sprang up in Czech lands during the nineteenth century. The first Canadian Sokol seems to have been established as early as 1912 at Frank, Alberta, although it was not until 1929 that the movement spread to larger centres such as Regina, Winnipeg and Montreal. Affiliated with the 100,000-member-strong international Czechoslovak Sokol Abroad, the Sokol Gymnastic Association of Canada underwent organizational vicissitudes in the 1950s and early 1960s until internal differences were settled. At present, the organization has numerous branches across Canada, including those in Toronto, Kitchener, Windsor, Rouyn-Noranda and Ottawa.

An important Czech social and cultural centre was the Masaryk Memorial Hall, which was founded in Toronto in 1945. Affiliated with the Hall were the Masaryktown Recreational Centre, located in Scarborough, the Czech-language newspaper *Novy Domov (New Homeland)*, a library, schools teaching in both Czech and English, as well as dramatic and folklore groups.

There are numerous other Czech organizations operating in Canada, including the Women's Council of the Czechoslovak National Association, and the Czechoslovak

Society of Arts and Sciences, among others. As well, there is a Czechoslovak branch of the Royal Canadian Legion (Ontario Branch 601), active in Toronto.

Several Czech-language publications have existed in Canada at various times. At present, three are noteworthy. *Novy Domov* (*New Homeland*), printed largely in Czech but containing some English-language articles as well, was founded in 1919 as the successor to the Montreal-based *Nova Vlast* (*New Homeland*). It is the largest Czech-language newspaper in Canada. The weekly *Nase Hlasy* (*Our Voices*) was founded in Toronto in 1954, and for a time was affiliated with the Czechoslovak National Association of Canada. In 1970 it passed into independent hands, and since that time has assumed a strongly anti-Communist stand. There is also a Toronto-based monthly, *Hlas Novych* (*Voice of Newcomers*) which represents the interests of recent Czech immigrants to Canada.

A survey conducted by the Department of Manpower and Immigration in the early 1970s concluded that in the three-year period under study, the unemployment rate of newly arrived Czech immigrants and refugees remained below 10 per cent, while over half of this group acquired jobs in their intended fields. Language skills have improved dramatically as a result of language training programs, and most recent arrivals become fluent very quickly in one of the official languages. Relatively few Canadians of Czech or Slovak origin become members of service clubs, suggesting a high degree of self-reliance. On the whole, the Czechs have expressed general satisfaction with Canada and the way in which they have become members of Canadian society.

# Danes

THE FIRST KNOWN DANISH contact with Canada came as the result of the voyage of Captain Jens Munk in the early seventeenth century. Munk was sent by King Christian IV of Denmark to find the Northwest Passage. On September 7, 1619, Munk landed at the mouth of what is today the Churchill River, which he named Munk's Bay. His party stayed there for the winter, and he claimed the land for Denmark, calling it "Nova Dania" (New Denmark). Only three of the original crew of sixty-six survived the winter, and in June of 1620, Munk and his two companions left for Denmark on the small ship *Lamprenen*, and arrived in Norway on September 21, 1620.

Although Danish emigration to North America never reached the proportions that were seen in other Scandinavian and European countries during the nineteenth century, a few individuals such as Danish sailors migrated and there are early accounts of Danes working as trappers in Canada, although there are few traces of their experiences. Yet in the mid-nineteenth century, migration began in earnest, despite the fact that economic conditions in Denmark were not as harsh as they were in other countries in Europe. The general population increase swept the country much as it had other parts of Europe, but Denmark was able to absorb much of the increase. The Danish soil was fertile, land was plentiful, and crops were abundant.

The Prussian-Austrian invasion of 1864 acted as the initial stimulus for Danish emigration to North America. In addition, hundreds of thousands of Europeans were moving to America and the Danes followed suit, more for the lure of the continent than because of any specific cause at home. Once there, they were joined by relatives who were also bitten by the "American fever" of the earlier arrivals.

Another factor influencing Danish emigration to North America was the greater religious tolerance in the New World. In the nineteenth century a fierce religious cleavage had developed within the Evangelical Lutheran Church of Denmark between the conservative Inner Mission led by Wilhelm Beck, who advocated a literal reading of the Bible, and the followers of N. F. S. Grundtvig, who believed in a more liberal attitude towards the Bible and the church. Many Danes involved in this controversy felt that they could practise their religion more freely in the United States.

The Danes first settled in the United States, but as the land filled up and became too expensive, they moved on to Canada, where there was still plenty of good, free land for homesteaders. This significant movement of settlers out of the midwestern United States into Canada influenced many of the emigrating Danes to come directly to Canada. One of the earliest Danish settlements in Canada, the town of New Denmark in New Brunswick, was begun on June 19, 1872.

Seven families and six single men were recruited in Denmark and accompanied to Canada by a Captain Heller, an agent working for the New Brunswick government. The final leg of the long journey was by land boat, a wooden platform on skids, drawn by a team of horses. Their destination was a site in a region of Victoria County between the Saint John and Salmon rivers. The Government of New Brunswick had agreed to set aside one

hundred acres of good farming land for each male immigrant and would provide suitable temporary dwellings and employment until the immigrants could get settled. The families lived in the government-constructed Emigrant House until they were established.

Another small party followed in August, 1872, and a further 75 people came the following year. These latter two groups were also brought over by Captain Heller, who had negotiated the original agreement with the New Brunswick government. Other Danes continued to arrive as a result of their own efforts.

Danes were not accustomed to the large forests of Canada, and it took them many years to clear the forests and develop mixed farming. By 1892 a cheese factory had been built, which was later expanded to make butter. For about twenty-five years, cheese making, operated on a co-operative basis, changed New Denmark into a promising dairy district. Only gradually did cheese making give way to potato farming. Although English has long since replaced Danish as the main language of New Denmark, the various communities now comprising the settlement are proud of their heritage. On June 17–19, 1972, New Denmark celebrated the centenary of its founding.

Prior to the twentieth century, two Danish communities were also founded in Ontario. In 1893, London was the site of an early Danish settlement, and the Danes also settled at Pass Lake near Thunder Bay near the turn of the century.

Most of the original Danish settlers on the Prairies did not come directly from Denmark, but instead from the United States, especially from the midwest and northwest, where they had originally migrated. Around the turn of the century, Canadian land and mining policies began to change, coinciding with land restrictions in the United States. Suddenly there was not enough land available to immigrant farmers in the United States. Into this vacuum of expectations moved the CPR land agents, along with a vigorous advertising campaign by the Dominion government. These new land policies received wide publicity in the United States, where many Danish farmers were faced with mounting debts and few new opportunities for expansion. The Canadian Prairies offered them fresh possibilities for making a living.

Dickson, Alberta, is the oldest Danish community in the Prairie Provinces. It was founded in 1902 by a group of settlers who had first left Denmark for Omaha, Nebraska, before they began to explore the possibility of homesteading in Canada. They arrived in Dickson in 1902 and completed a Lutheran church in 1908.

Markerville, Alberta, was never a Danish community, although it was close to Dickson. It was settled by Icelanders, but was named after a Dane, C. P. Marker, and the most important commercial enterprise in the community, a creamery, was founded by Danish-born Dan Morkeberg. In 1910, Danish immigrants from the Kimballton-Elkhorn, Iowa, area settled in Standard, Alberta. They were attracted there by the CPR, which had set aside a 17,000-acre (27,713 km²) tract of land to be developed into a Danish colony. A Danish Lutheran congregation was established in 1911, and by 1917 a church was erected. Dalum, Alberta, was settled in 1918 under the auspices of the Dansk Folkesamfund (Danish Folk Society). Other Danish settlements in Alberta were located at Olds, Viking and Ponoka.

Small Danish settlements in Manitoba were established at Moosehorn, Goodlands,

Sperling and Ostenfeld. In Saskatchewan, early Danish settlements were located at Alida and Redvers, and smaller settlements were founded at Canora, Borden, Lloydminster and near Regina and Saskatoon.

All of the early Danish communities on the Prairies were founded by immigrants who had originally come from the United States, and they had at least a working knowledge of English. They were also semi-accustomed to the American way of life, and some had lived in relatively large cities, where they had intermingled with other groups. The use of the Danish language had begun to decline, and continued to do so quite rapidly after the settlers came to Canada. No new Danish residents came to these communities on the Prairies after 1930, and the children of many Danish immigrant farmers left in search of greater opportunity in the cities.

Most of the Danes who settled in British Columbia went to urban centres such as Vancouver, or to the various mining areas. A Danish pioneer settlement at Cape Scott on the western tip of Vancouver Island was established in 1896, and later at Fishermen's Bay. Some also settled along the Atlantic coast, trying to earn a living from the sea.

A second period of immigration occurred in the 1920s, when Danes left their homeland in significant numbers and made Canada their main destination, especially since immigration to the United States was severely curtailed after 1924. Many Danes who came at this time settled in the rural areas of Ontario, British Columbia and the Prairies, while a significant number settled in the larger urban areas.

In the decade of the 1950s, there was a massive migration of Danes to Canada. In the years 1946–50, the census reveals that 2,673 Canadians who gave their last permanent residence as Denmark settled in this country, while that number jumped to 22,250 between 1951 and 1957. These Danish immigrants were well-educated, their numbers including many professionals and skilled workers who were attracted by the economic prosperity that Canada offered following the war. Most of the immigrants during this period headed for the cities of British Columbia, Alberta and Ontario. In the complete decade of 1951–60, a total of 27,750 Danish immigrants entered Canada, with the peak year being 1957, when 7,790 entered, the majority of whom went to Toronto.

Of the 75,725 Canadians of Danish origin in 1971, British Columbia had 21,205 Danes, Alberta 20,120, and Ontario 19,075. There were also 5,220 Canadians of Danish origin in Saskatchewan, 4,120 in Manitoba, and 2,630 in Quebec. Danes have also been attracted to the Maritimes in relatively large numbers, with 1,675 living in New Brunswick and 1,055 in Nova Scotia.

Since the Lutheran Church is in the state church of Denmark, it was natural that most Danish immigrants would turn to some form of Lutheranism in Canada. The 1931 census showed that of the Danish-born in Canada, some 78 per cent were Lutheran. In 1971, 92.5 per cent of Canadians of Danish origin reported Lutheran affiliation.

The first attempt to establish a Danish Lutheran church in Canada took place in 1875 when Niels M. Hansen came to New Denmark as a lay missionary under the auspices of the Inner Mission of the Danish Lutheran Church. Because he encountered financial difficulties, yet remained determined to pursue his Christian calling, Hansen became an Anglican minister in 1877. In 1884, St. Ansgar's Church was completed in New Denmark, probably the only Anglican Church to be named after Ansgar, the missionary who brought Christianity to much of Scandinavia.

St. Peter's Lutheran Church was first started in New Denmark in 1905, and organized as a parish of the United Danish Evangelical Lutheran Church. Later on, another Lutheran Church was built in this area. Other Danish Lutheran churches in eastern Canada are located in New Brunswick at Saint John and Wallace, and in Toronto and Montreal.

The Lutheran Church played a major role in most of the early Danish communities on the Canadian Prairies, for as soon as a Danish church was established in a Danish prairie community, it would claim practically all the members of the settlement. These churches were direct offshoots of Danish Lutheran churches in the United States, and most of the original pastors had served in the United States before coming to Canada.

As Danes settled in certain areas in large numbers, there developed a demand for Danish-language periodicals and newspapers. Most Danes could speak enough English to meet their daily needs, since English is taught in Danish grammar schools and many had learned the language in the United States. However, they still preferred to use Danish in their family and social life.

Several factors combined to lessen Danish language retention beyond the first generation. Danish communities in Canada were scattered, small, and few in number; many of the settlers had been acculturated in the United States; and many Canadians of Danish origin intermarried with members of other ethnocultural groups.

Nevertheless, a number of periodicals sprang up in an attempt to meet the needs of those who still wished to read in their native language. The first, *Danebrog*, was a small sheet that ceased publication during the First World War. The Norwegian-language newspaper

*Norrona*, published in Winnipeg, tried to attract Danish readers in 1918 by including articles by Hans A. Brodhal. There were a couple of attempts to start Danish papers in Winnipeg during the 1920s when immigration increased, but these were short-lived.

Danes published the only Scandinavian-language newspaper in the Maritimes, the *Danish Herald*. This weekly was published at Brooklyn Farm near Kentville, Nova Scotia, between 1931 and 1941. During the Second World War, the *Scandinavian News* was published in Toronto. The paper was printed in English to inform Canadians of conditions in Scandinavia during the war. It ceased publication in 1947. The only Danish-language newspaper today is the semi-monthly *Modersmaalet* (*Mother Tongue*), originally published in Toronto but now based in Oakville. It contains articles extracted from Danish papers, and has little information on Danish-Canadian activities. The Danish Lutheran Church published *Kirken og Hjemmet* (*Church and Home*) for its members. It began in 1930, but was discontinued in the late 1950s when most of the church members spoke English as a first language.

There have been a number of Danish-language publications which have served regional and specific needs. However, the Danes in Canada have never had a Danish-language periodical that established itself as the Danish community spokesman for any length of time.

While many Danish-born Canadians have felt a need for social and cultural activities in their mother tongue, there has never been a national organization to co-ordinate the social activities of Danes in Canada. Social activities were originally centred around the church, but there are at present many local clubs across the country, particularly in Ontario and eastern Canada. There are Danish-Canadian clubs in New Brunswick at Saint John and Salmonhurst, in Montreal, in Toronto and many other communities in Ontario, in Winnipeg, Calgary, Edmonton, Red Deer and Innisfail. Danish clubs in Edmonton sponsor sports activities, and Danes have organized a senior citizens' home in Puslinch, Ontario.

Within British Columbia, the cities of Victoria, Vancouver and Burnaby have Danish social groups. One distinctive Danish organization is the Royal Danish Guards Association, which sponsors activities in Vancouver, Calgary and Kingston for those who have served in the Royal Danish Guards in their homeland.

The Danish Brotherhood in America started its Canadian activities in Winnipeg as a sick-benefit society. It also sponsored a number of social activities. During the Second World War, branches of the Danish Brotherhood co-operated with other Danish groups in collecting funds for assisting Danes in the homeland. The only branch of this organization remaining in Canada is in Vancouver.

Danes also promote their cultural heritage in co-operation with other Scandinavian groups in Canada. The most notable are the Scandinavian Centre Association in Edmonton and the Scandinavian Centre in Calgary, both of which are incorporated as co-operatives. They promote social activities, language instruction, and folk dancing, and commemorate the national days of the respective Scandinavian countries. In Saskatchewan, Danes work with other Nordic groups to support Scandinavian clubs in Saskatoon, Moose Jaw and Birch Hills. There are also Scandinavian clubs in Montreal and Toronto, and a Nordic Society in Ottawa.

Canadians of Danish descent have made some distinctive contributions to Canada, but in general Danes have adapted so quickly to

Canadian society that their achievements are usually a part of the Canadian setting rather than a contribution by a particular, distinctive group. They have made significant contributions in the development of Canadian dairy farming, in the understanding of the Canadian Arctic, and in medicine. Danes have also been influential in design by importing Danish styles of products into Canada.

The Danish community is rapidly being absorbed into the larger Canadian society, at least partly because of the readiness on the part of individual Danes to integrate. Furthermore, most Danes have come to Canada with the particular skills which have assisted them to fit readily into Canadian labour, industry and educational institutions.

# Dutch

THE DUTCH, MAINLY DUE to the location and size of their country, have been world traders for centuries. Their contacts in many lands resulted in widespread settlement, and their national characteristics, shaped by struggles at home and abroad, made the Netherlanders readily adaptable to foreign environments.

The coming of the American Revolution in the United States brought about an exodus of those who had supported the British crown. Dutch United Empire Loyalists joined the thousands of other refugees who sought a new beginning in Canada. Settling in Nova Scotia, New Brunswick and Upper Canada, they lost all contact with the old communities in New York, Delaware and Pennsylvania. Without the traditional support of their Reformed churches, they rapidly integrated into the Methodist and other Protestant churches, and ceased to have a separate cultural identity. Active in the public and social life of their community, they simply regarded themselves as an integral part of the Canadian society.

Unlike the British Isles, the Netherlands did not suffer those political, social and economic problems which encouraged mass emigration until the mid-nineteenth century. At this time, the movement came to be directed towards the agricultural frontier and growing urban areas of the United States. By the end of the century, Dutch settlements were to be found from the east to the west coast, with heavy concentrations in Michigan, Illinois and Iowa. Not until the American agricultural frontier was filled in the 1890s did the Canadian West hold any importance for Dutch emigrants, but by that time the number of potential emigrants had been greatly depleted in the rush to America.

The Canadian West, with its millions of acres of free or cheap land, attracted the Dutch and Dutch Americans alike. Individuals and families of Dutch origin from the United States began to take up homesteads on the Prairies and make their appearance in western urban areas such as Winnipeg. The first significant group immigration took place in 1892 when a contingent of single men arrived in Winnipeg and obtained temporary jobs on the railways, in the city, and on surrounding farms in order to accumulate settlement capital. In the following year the Christian Emigration Society in Holland facilitated the emigration of 103 persons to Winnipeg and Yorkton, Saskatchewan, in reaction to the agricultural unemployment prevailing in the Dutch countryside. From these small beginnings was to develop a steady movement of Dutch agriculturalists to Canada.

Persistent problems in Dutch society such as the lack of arable land and a rapidly increasing population combined with mechanization and high intensity production left large numbers of agriculturalists with little opportunity to take up their trade. Rather than be absorbed in the developing industrial sector of the economy, they sought future independence on the Canadian frontier. This agricultural orientation accounts for the predominance of settlement west of Winnipeg. The West, as opposed to the more settled regions of the East, offered a surfeit of free or cheap land and readily available jobs as farm labourers. The first years were generally spent as farm hands, railway employees, bush workers or as urban labourers in the winter time. Such jobs permitted the accumulation of settlement capital, experience with Canadian conditions, an opportunity to learn the language and a chance to assess homesteading possibilities in different western areas. By 1914, single men and families were not only scattered across the West but had established permanent settlements in such places as Edam and Shackleton, Saskatchewan, East Kildonan, Manitoba and Neerlandia and Nobleford, Alberta.

The settlement in the Nobleford area, known as Nieuw Nijverdal, was founded in 1905 by Dutch Americans from Iowa who had been drawn to the newly opened western lands, and who had dry land farming experience. The Americans quickly recruited additional homesteaders from the United States and from the Netherlands. Sharing religion, customs and farming techniques, the community maintained a steady growth until the available land was exhausted and interest turned to other areas in Alberta, such as the Peace River district.

The settlement in Neerlandia, 90 miles (145 km) north of Edmonton, was begun in an attempt to build a community in which Dutch culture, their religion and a sense of ethnic unity could be preserved. Homesteads were staked out in January, 1912, log houses and barns erected, and settlers recruited from Edmonton and the surrounding area. This recruitment and ongoing settlement made possible the construction of roads, the establishment of a post office, school and church, and the formation of a co-operative society. Trading labour among themselves and working co-operatively on community projects, the settlers of Neerlandia attracted other immigrants who feared isolation on the Prairies. By 1913 the community had recruited some sixty Dutch families and promised to become, like Nieuw Nijverdal, a symbol of what could be achieved on the Canadian Prairies by the Dutch.

Although the Netherlands remained neutral, the First World War, with its attendant disruption in European and Canadian societies, brought immigration to a standstill. However, the postwar period once again spurred on immigration to Canada from the Netherlands. Continued population growth in Holland and the scarcity of land impelled agriculturalists to seek opportunities elsewhere. While the established communities in the Canadian West continued to draw immigrants, free or cheap arable land was rapidly diminishing. Winnipeg and the urban centres of the west offered limited opportunities for Dutch labour. Even the truck garden trade, which had developed outside Winnipeg in East Kildonan prior to the Second World War, had but small absorptive capacity.

As the West's drawing power diminished, Ontario came to hold more significance for the Dutch immigrants. Between 1920 and 1929, an estimated 14,909 Dutch immigrants came to Canada, the majority taking up farm labour positions in Ontario. They were encouraged by the Canadian government, Canadian railways, Dutch emigration societies and emigration agents. The mixed farming areas of southern and southwestern Ontario appealed to the Dutch agriculturalists. The postwar move to the urban areas by Canadians provided agricultural jobs which had not previously existed. As in the West, a number of years were spent at these jobs until experience and capital permitted independent settlement. Churches were formed, and as the Dutch community grew, other immigrants were drawn to these areas to benefit from the pioneering work of the earlier immigrants.

The coming of the Depression put an end to this movement. Only close relatives or immigrants with capital could hope to make a beginning in Canada. The number of Dutch immigrants fell from a high of 2,485 in 1929 to a low of 148 in 1934. While there was some increase in the second half of the decade, much of this immigration was designated for settlement in northern British Columbia along the railway line. The majority of pre-Depression immigrants simply sought to survive the devastating effects of the economic decline, although some failed and were either deported or repatriated to the Netherlands. A number of those who faced economic ruin were resettled under federal, provincial and Netherlands government auspices on the Holland Marsh, located some 40 miles (64 km) north of Toronto. Although the first years were extremely difficult, a beginning was made at developing the area for market gardening. The coming of the Second World War was to have a tremendous economic benefit for these settlers, and was to prepare settlement opportunities for postwar immigrants.

The Nazi occupation of the Netherlands in 1940 brought an end to even the limited emigration of the previous decade. A few refugees made their way to Canada; prominent among them was the Crown Princess Juliana with her consort Bernhard. She and her family formed the core of a Dutch-Canadian group which worked actively for the war effort and Netherlands relief. While resident in Canada she gave birth to a daughter, Princess Margriet, and formed deep attachments to the Canadian people. These attachments came to be shared by the Dutch public as a whole when Canadian troops played a prominent role in the liberation of the Netherlands from Nazi occupation.

At the conclusion of the war, the Netherlands was in a state of economic ruin. Opportunity seemed to be stifled, the population continued to grow and land seemed even more scarce. The outbreak of war in Indonesia and fears of an imminent Russian invasion of Western Europe combined to stir a renewed interest in emigration. As the United States was virtually closed because of immigration restrictions, Dutch interest turned to Canada. This interest was heightened by favourable reports from war brides of Canadian servicemen and the interest of prewar Dutch settlers. The Canadian and Dutch governments quickly concluded an immigration agreement for the entry of Dutch farm families and single agriculturalists. The Netherlands Farm Families Movement encouraged the settlement in Canada of agriculturalists who would become independent farmers as soon as possible.

Under these conditions the emigration to Canada grew quickly. Between 1946 and 1950 some 25,966 Dutch citizens arrived in Canada. From 1951 to 1957 the numbers increased rapidly to 103,342 with the peak years being 1952 and 1953 when 20,653 and 20,095 Dutch immigrants entered Canada. Emigration fever had a dramatic effect, particularly in the rural areas of the Netherlands where whole villages emigrated to Canada bringing along their butchers, bakers, ministers and even some prefabricated homes. While the immigrants remained primarily agricultural, by 1953 significant numbers of people with business, professional, technical and other non-agricultural backgrounds were permitted entry. These urban immigrants, like their agricultural counterparts, were placed and aided by the member organizations of the Canadian Netherlands Immigration Council which looked after their welfare until they were independent. The Canadian government supported this work with the result that the settlement process was orderly and successful.

The postwar emigration was, in the main, directed to those areas where there were sufficient economic opportunities. Fortunately, many of these areas had been settled by the prewar immigrants and they and the Dutch churches were prepared to lend a helping hand in the settlement process. As a result southern Ontario, Alberta and British Columbia became centres for immigration settlement.

As the Netherlands experienced a dramatic economic upturn in the mid-1950s the pressure for emigration began to decline. Massive industrialization and growing exports produced a shortage of labour, accompanied by high wages and good job opportunities. Surplus labour from agricultural areas was absorbed into the growing economy and there was little desire for emigration. In recent years this slowdown has been somewhat altered in that many professionals in the Netherlands are now searching for areas of broader opportunity as their society is becoming more and more structured, and the individualistic Canadian

society still seems to offer a better opportunity for professional and personal growth.

According to the 1971 census, nearly half the Canadians of Dutch origin, some 206,940, were living in Ontario. Only 12,590 were resident in Quebec. British Columbia topped the list in western Canada with 70,530, followed by Alberta with 58,565, Manitoba with 35,305 and Saskatchewan with 19,040. In the Atlantic Provinces 14,845 were living in Nova Scotia, 5,360 in New Brunswick, 1,245 in Prince Edward Island and 665 in Newfoundland. Fewer than 500 were living in either the Northwest Territories or the Yukon. Among the cities, Toronto was the leading choice of settlement with 44,430, followed by Vancouver with 31,965.

In comparison with other Canadian ethnic groups, Dutch Canadians do not seem to place great value upon the retention of their native language or culture. In the 1961 census, for example, only 38 per cent of the 430,000 persons of Dutch extraction reported Dutch as their mother tongue, the lowest level of mother tongue retention reported by any of the non-British, non-French ethnic groups. While some observers have noted that the Netherlands is a cosmopolitan culture owing to its foreign trade and therefore its citizens are more likely to integrate in foreign cultures, that appears to be only part of the answer. The majority of immigrants who came to Canada from 1890 to 1960 were rural immigrants with limited educations and with limited exposure to the Dutch intellectual and artistic tradition. A majority of these immigrants found their cultural tradition centered upon the Reformed religion. Furthermore the Dutch government, emigration societies and the Dutch-Canadian churches stressed the necessity of becoming Canadian as quickly as possible. For many then, language and tradition were unimportant as long as the

Dutch Calvinist heritage was retained. Roman Catholic immigrants have by and large joined existing Canadian parishes and through the process of intermarriage have become part of the larger Canadian society.

The two major Dutch Calvinist churches in Canada are the Christian Reformed Church and the Reformed Church. The Christian Reformed Church is the larger denomination. It is to be found both in urban and rural communities and tends to be exclusive in nature, discouraging intermarriage with non-Calvinists and encouraging the view that the church is the cultural and social center. As a result many organizations have grown up to serve the religious and social needs of its adherents. They include boys' and girls' groups, young people's societies, men's and women's societies and choral groups. Involvement in the more secular areas of life has led to the formation of Dutch-Canadian credit unions, immigration societies, burial societies, a Christian labour union, parental school associations and involvement in Christian higher education. The Reformed Church has been less exclusive and more accommodating to Canadian society. Initially upon arrival in Canada many joined the Presbyterian or United Church only to find the religious doctrines to be too "liberal". With the development and expansion of the church in the 1950s, Reformed churches were established in both rural and urban areas, and like the Christian Reformed Churches, societies were organized to provide for the religious and cultural needs of the Reformed church community.

Dutch social clubs which have been formed in many Canadian urban centers tend to pull their main membership from the non-reformed Dutch-Canadian group. As a result many members are native-born Canadians who have married Dutch immigrants. A number of these organizations have organized charter flights to and from the Netherlands and have attracted members who are solely interested in air charter transportation at a reduced rate. These organizations tend to have little impact upon either the Dutch-Canadian or Canadian communities as they are largely social in nature. They occasionally sponsor dances, dinners or involvement in local civic activities. They do not in any sense form a united political or social lobby and seem content to sponsor annual Saint Nicolaas celebrations on December 5 or give expression to Dutch-Canadian amity. Some have also sponsored the foundation of Dutch soccer clubs and keep alive the interest in that sport.

The Dutch-Canadian community is served by a number of publications which carry church news, news of the Dutch-Canadian community and events of importance occurring in the Netherlands. Some of the better known newspapers are the *Calvinist Contact*, a Hamilton weekly which is the organ of the Christian Reformed Church and publishes in Dutch and English, the *Nederlands Courant*, a Toronto weekly published exclusively in Dutch, and the *Windmill Herald*, a New Westminster, British Columbia bi-monthly which is published in both Dutch and English. Some clubs and schools produce monthly publications while radio stations in both Toronto and Vancouver broadcast weekly "Holland hours" featuring news from the Netherlands and Dutch recordings. Programming primarily devoted to the Netherlands has appeared on local cable television in Calgary, Alberta.

Immigrants from the Netherlands have made an impact upon many sectors of the Canadian society. Perhaps their greatest influence has been in the field of agriculture. The arrival of the Dutch agriculturalists after the Second World War helped to counteract the movement of long-established Canadian farmers to urban areas, particularly in southern Ontario, and to supply much needed agricultural labour. They also brought with them a wealth of experience in dairy farming, market gardening, horticulture and in intensive farming methods. In Alberta they helped to introduce stripfarming and used irrigation to make the land more productive, and elsewhere reclaimed swampland and introduced better systems of agriculture. Their experience was put to the test in such places as the Holland and Thedford marshes in Ontario and the Pitt Polder in British Columbia. Dutch Canadians have also been instrumental in the development and expansion of greenhouse techniques for the growing of off-season vegetables and flowers. This industry has shown phenomenal growth particularly in and around the urban centers of Canada.

Individuals of Dutch origin have enriched the political, intellectual, artistic and cultural life of Canada. An early Dutch immigrant, Robert Insinger, served as representative of Yorkton to the territorial legislature before Saskatchewan became a province. At the present time Dutch Canadians serve on municipal and provincial boards, and in various capacities in both the federal and provincial governments, either elected or appointed. Increasingly, Dutch Canadians are attending university and moving into various professions including academic fields. The artistic life of Canada has been enriched by painters, sculptors, designers, weavers, pottery makers and craftsmen working in stained glass, mosaics and jewellery. One of Canada's most famous painters, Cornelius Krieghoff (1815–72) was born in Amsterdam. Dutch musicians have made important contributions as conductors, soloists, teachers and members of Canadian orchestras. Other individuals of

Dutch extraction have brought honour to Canada as dancers, figure skaters and athletes.

The Dutch have tended to integrate completely into the Canadian scene, but in doing so they have made important contributions in many fields. Gifts from the Dutch to Canada, such as the Flentrop organ for the National Arts Centre in Ottawa in Centennial Year, the carillon tower which forms part of the provincial museum complex in Victoria, British Columbia, and the tulips which bloom every spring in Ottawa remind Canadians of the very visible Dutch imprint on the Canadian landscape.

# Ecuadorians

UNTIL 1969, when Ecuador became the second largest producer of oil in South America, most of the country's inhabitants worked the land. The 1950s marked the beginning of large-scale migration from rural areas to large cities, which in turn resulted in the emigration of thousands of Ecuadorians to the United States. In 1963, immigration laws in the United States became more restrictive, and many Ecuadorians had found other countries to which to emigrate. About seven years later, they discovered that Canada was in need of unskilled workers. Soon after, Toronto's College Street and Montreal's Boulevard Saint-Laurent became the areas where an Ecuadorian could find a home away from home. Other communities developed in smaller cities such as Sudbury, Ontario. Ecuadorians migrated in search of better jobs and homes, more education and security.

During the early 1970s Ecuadorians

arrived in Canada by the thousands, an unofficial estimate placing the number at 20,000, most settling in Montreal and Toronto. In the mid-1970s their presence began to be felt in a substantial manner.

Many families came to Canada after 1973, bringing with them a taste of their native country and the security of a home. The community was now ready to create its own cultural atmosphere in Canada. It is not unusual to attend an Ecuadorian dance and find over five hundred couples dancing to a cumbia, bolero or tango. The largest Latin American newspaper was founded in 1973 and continues to be directed by a Canadian of Ecuadorian descent. The first television program in the Spanish language ever seen in Canada was also initiated and directed by a young Ecuadorian immigrant. In the sports field, the Ecuadorian-Canadian Soccer League holds weekly matches in Toronto and Montreal.

Ecuadorian social clubs entirely organized and run by Ecuadorians are actively engaged in sporting competitions and educational projects designed to maintain their language and culture. Unlike more politically-oriented groups, these clubs provide a focus for the entire community.

The influence of the Canadian business system has made a powerful impression on hundreds of Ecuadorians. They can be found in the insurance field, real estate, the communications media and advertising. Others have become small businessmen. Almost without exception they found their first customers among the Ecuadorian community. A number of Ecuadorians have a particular skill in working with gold and thus are employed in the jewellery business. The great majority, however, both men and women, are employed in factories and in service industries.

As of 1977 approximately one-half of Ecuadorian immigrants in Canada were under thirty years of age. Hundreds of this group were either school-age children or younger. Therefore, programs of the Ecuadorian community to strengthen itself will succeed only if they reach the young people. In the mid-1970s, as Ecuadorians move up the economic ladder, many young couples are leaving the traditional immigrant neighbourhood areas of Toronto and Montreal for the suburbs. These moves are bringing with them isolation from the Ecuadorian community, a loss of language among the children and more integration into Canadian society at large.

It is difficult to assess the consequences of this growing residential movement of the Ecuadorian community. But it can be safely assumed that only a deep understanding of their cultural values as Ecuadorians, together with the arrival of new immigrants from Ecuador, will help to maintain the group in Canada. This represents a challenge to both Ecuadorians and to Canadians as a whole.

# Egyptians

EGYPTIANS HAVE TRADITIONALLY been closely tied to their homeland, and have been reluctant to leave it. Starting with the Second World War, however, they began to come into closer contact with other Arab countries which were experiencing economic and social development. Thousands of teachers, technicians and professionals from Egypt travelled to these countries to work. Beginning in 1956 many started to look beyond the limits of the Middle East, and with increasing economic, political and economic problems in the country, the first Egyptian immigrants began to seek wider opportunities. Canada for them was a sanctuary, and a country that could fulfill their personal aspirations.

Egyptian immigration into Canada was miniscule compared to that of other groups prior to 1956. After that date many Egyptians emigrated to Canada and, as word of their initial success spread back to their native land, friends and relatives were attracted. The wave of Egyptian immigrants continued to grow steadily, especially after the implementation of new political measures in Egypt after 1961.

Between 1900 and 1910, only 50 Egyptians were admitted to Canada, and that number fell to 21 immigrants in the period 1911–20, and even lower to 13 between 1921 and 1930. Immigration was so small that no records were kept between 1931 and 1954, but between 1955 and 1960, 126 Egyptians entered Canada. The numbers jumped dramatically between 1961 and 1965, when 6,038 Egyptians came to Canada. Between 1966 and 1970 a further 7,839 arrived, and between 1971 and 1975 arrivals totalled 4,061. According to official statistics, then, fewer than 300 Egyptians were admitted up to 1960, while a total of 17,938 were admitted between 1961 and 1975, with the greatest influx arriving between 1961 and 1970.

Between 1956 and 1975, 18,047 Egyptians were admitted to Canada, the vast majority, 67.6 per cent, going to Quebec, 25.8 per cent giving Ontario as their destination, and only 6.6 per cent reporting that they were going to settle elsewhere in Canada. Therefore, 93.4 per cent of the Egyptian immigrants during this period went to either Quebec or Ontario. In Quebec the heaviest concentration of Egyptian Canadians was in Montreal. It is also interesting to note that in the period 1961–71, of

14,607 Egyptians who entered the country, 6,609, or slightly less than half, were members of the labour force, the remaining 7,998 being dependents or children under the working age. Of these workers, 76.5 per cent were either professional, semi-professional or other white collar, while only 22.5 per cent were blue collar workers, and one per cent did not state an occupation. It is estimated that since then, Egyptian Canadians have remained within the above settlement patterns.

Certain characteristics can be drawn from an analysis of Egyptian immigration to Canada: the size of the Egyptian population in Quebec is increasing, making it one of the largest centralized ethnocultural groups in Montreal. Canadians of Egyptian origin have a high percentage of professionals and white-collar workers among their ranks, and as a consequence Egyptian Canadians tend to be concentrated in urban areas—Toronto, Ottawa, Windsor, and Montreal. There are almost none in the farming sector.

The Egyptian immigrants' high level of education and their knowledge of English and French have aided their rapid integration into Canadian society. Since the British and French presence had been felt in Egypt for two generations, the two official languages of Canada were spoken by many Egyptians before they came to this country. In addition, there was intense pressure on parents of young families to learn either English or French in order to speed the children's integration into Canadian society, and many of them took language classes at night school.

Egyptian immigrants have come to Canada for either political, economic or social reasons. Most Egyptian immigrants come on a permanent basis and with their whole families. Although many frequently visit their homeland, they return to Canada with ties to their adopted land much stronger than when they left, due in large part to the standard of living they have attained in Canada and the opportunities that are available to them.

The Egyptians in Egypt form a homogeneous population, since 90 per cent of them are Sunni Muslims (or Sunnite Moslems). The largest non-Muslim community is the Coptic Christian group, while other non-Muslim groups include Jews and Greeks, Italians, Armenians, Syrians and Lebanese of various religious denominations.

While the Sunni Muslims form a distinct group in Canada as well, there are quite a number of varieties of Christianity among Canadians of Egyptian origin, including Maronites, Melkites, Antiochian Orthodox, Protestants, Syrian Catholics, Armenians, Roman Catholics and others. Each of these groups has its own churches and distinct communities in Canada, with the attendant social and religious organizations.

One of the most important developments in Egyptian religious life in Canada is the emergence in this country of the Coptic Orthodox Church, one of the world's oldest Christian churches. The word "Copt" means "Egyptian", and Coptic Christians represent the descendants of the once great church of Alexandria, founded by St. Mark. Their religious head is the Coptic Patriarch of Alexandria, who lives in Cairo. The rites of worship of the Coptic Church are derived from the original Greek liturgy, and are celebrated in the Coptic tongue with a mixture of the vernacular Arabic.

St. Mark's, a Coptic Orthodox Church, was founded in Toronto in 1963. It is considered the first Coptic church in North America. Another St. Mark's was founded in Montreal in 1967, and there are now two Coptic churches in that city. Pope Shenouda III, the Coptic spiritual leader, visited Canada in 1977, the first visit for any Coptic Orthodox Patriarch to the North American continent. It is estimated that there are approximately 1,100 Coptic families in Montreal, with a similar number in Toronto. A few hundred are scattered across the rest of the provinces. There are also about 6,000 Orthodox and Catholic Copts in Canada.

The Muslims are concentrated to a large degree in Canada's urban areas, and there are mosques in Montreal, Toronto and Ottawa to serve them, as well as in other smaller centres. There are a number of Muslim associations to provide services and social activities for this group, including the MSA Islamic Services of Canada in Toronto, the Islamic Centre of Quebec in Montreal, the Ottawa Muslim Association, the Muslim Society of Waterloo and others.

Egyptians traditionally celebrate a variety of religious and social festivities. The Egyptian Christians celebrate the traditional Christian holidays such as Christmas and Easter. Each church or rite also celebrates its own patron saint day which has become a traditional religious and social event which brings Egyptian Canadians together and gives them an opportunity to exchange their views and talents.

The Muslims celebrate Mawlad el Nabi (The Birth of the Prophet) and Ramadan. Ramadan, the ninth month of the Muslim calendar, is the sacred month in which Mohammed received the first of his revelations from God. Complete abstinence from food, drink and any sexual activity from dawn to dusk during Ramadan is strictly required. The Muslims celebrate the end of Ramadan with Eidul Fitr followed by Eidul Adha, as well as Mawlad el Nabi, and other religious days, in association with other Muslim ethnic groups. Egyptians also celebrate Cham-el-Nessim, when they traditionally enjoy nature by having picnics which include Egyptian foods such as dry fish, falafel, shish kabab and green salads.

The Egyptian community in Canada is served by the newspaper *Arc*, an Arabic-language monthly published since 1973 in Montreal, which also contains articles in English and French. A second newspaper, *Jerusalem Times*, was published in Vancouver from 1973 until 1977.

Egyptians in Canada also read other Arabic papers such as the Lebanese *Canadian Middle East Journal* and the Syrian *Arab World Review*, along with Arabic journals and newsletters published by other Arabic associations and organizations in Canada. These Arabic publications promote Arabic culture and provide services to all members of the Arabic community. The publications repeatedly call for the establishment of a single national Arabic organization to create a stronger voice for the various Arab associations in Canada.

The Egyptians have a weekly radio program on one of Montreal's stations. This program, heard each Sunday, has replaced a Lebanese hour, which was the first Arabic-language program in Canada. An Islamic radio program is heard in Montreal each Saturday on the same station.

Migration to Canada did not fundamentally alter the Egyptian's sense of identity. To many Egyptians, especially those who were able to remain in the same occupation, the change of countries made little difference. They have maintained the same values and loyalties, continuing to consider themselves as Canadians of Egyptian descent, and are keenly aware of events in their homeland.

Egyptians are very interested in passing their cultural heritage on to their children.

They have a reverence for their language, and Arabic-language classes have been formed, such as the Nil Cultural Centre which was established in 1974 to acquaint Canadians with Arabic culture and to encourage the teaching of Arabic. The cultural centre Bois de Boulogne is used for the same purpose.

The Egyptian community has begun to expose its art, literature and music to the Canadian public through different channels. Pharanoic, Coptic and Islamic forms are themes from Egyptian life which, with modern adaptations, lend colour to many Egyptian folkdances that are performed in Canada. Both individuals and groups promote Egyptian cultural exchange by showing films or organizing tours for Egyptian folkloric troups such as the famous Reda Troup and others which have visited Canadian cities from time to time.

Egyptian painting has been shown in Montreal, Toronto and Ottawa, and the Egyptian artist Sami Nasr has had paintings exhibited in the city halls of Montreal and Ottawa and the National Public Library in Quebec City. The Egyptians' love for music is exhibited in numerous bands made up of first and second generation immigrants; bands which blend the Egyptian and the Western at the many Egyptian festivals which are organized.

A number of Egyptian clubs are being formed, especially in Montreal. In 1976, Circle Saint-Marc was formed by a group of graduates from Saint-Marc College in Alexandria, Egypt. Another centre of activity in Montreal is the Circle Heliopolis, recently formed by a group of former students and Boy Scouts from the Maronite Schools in Egypt.

Both clubs promote social and cultural activities. Circle Heliopolis has formed a school for children seven to 10 years of age to teach the Arabic language and the Oriental heritage. It also presents plays and Egyptian dances, and is planning to form a Boy Scout troop. Circle Saint-Marc has organized activities that include a variety of games and sports.

While the Egyptian presence in Canada was not significant before 1966, Canadians of Egyptian descent have made a number of valuable contributions to Canadian cultural and athletic fields. The emergence of new groups and organizations dedicated to helping Canadians better understand Egyptian culture is resulting in an appreciation of the Egyptian presence in Canada by all segments of the larger Canadian society.

# English

IT WAS ENGLISH sponsorship of the voyages of John Cabot, an Italian explorer, that led to British interest, exploration and settlement of what is now Canada. In 1497, five years after Christopher Columbus was the first European to discover the West Indies, Cabot set sail to find the northwest passage to the Orient, but instead brought back tales of seas swarming with fish, leaving little doubt that his North American landfall on June 24, 1497, had been made somewhere between Labrador and Maine, probably on Newfoundland. Cabot's voyage and subsequent expeditions made by his son Sebastian led to the development of the fisheries on the Grand Banks of Newfoundland and laid the basis for English claims to Newfoundland and the Atlantic seaboard.

In the latter part of the sixteenth century, other explorers like Martin Frobisher and John Davis tried to reach the East by way of a northwest passage around North America, but their ships were always stopped by ice floes in dangerous seas between Greenland and Canada. Then in 1610 Henry Hudson pushed his way into the large inland sea that now bears his name. Later in the century other British explorers such as William Baffin and Thomas James helped to reinforce Englands' claim to the area.

This claim was not permanently established, however, until England learned of the region's potential wealth in furs from Pierre-Esprit Radisson, a voyageur from New France. Then Prince Rupert, a cousin of King Charles II, and seventeen associates obtained from the king their incorporation as "The Governor and Company of Adventurers of England trading into Hudson Bay" (1670). The company was granted the exclusive monopoly on trade through Hudson Strait and possession of Rupert's Land, the drainage basin of Hudson Bay. From company posts at the river mouths, British explorers such as Henry Kelsey, Anthony Henday and Samuel Hearne pierced the interior of the continent. Hearne became the first European to reach the Arctic Ocean overland when he explored the Coppermine River in 1771–72. In 1774 he founded the first inland post to be established by the company

As the French and British empires spread in North America, their main lines of expansion began to clash, particularly in the fur trade. This resulted in a mounting struggle and by the middle of the eighteenth century in a conflict for the heartland of the continent.

The fighting in North America became part of a worldwide struggle for trade and empire between two long-standing enemies. From India to North America the British fleet and British arms eventually triumphed. With the capture of the French fortress of Louisbourg in 1758 and Quebec in 1759, France's empire in North America was shattered. By the Treaty of Paris in 1763, New France became another British colony.

The American Revolution of 1775–83 reduced Britain's empire in North America by half, and triggered the first reorganization of British North America. By 1792, the year after the Constitutional Act came into effect, Britain's possessions in North America included Newfoundland, Rupert's Land, the Island of St. John (now Prince Edward Island), Cape Breton Island, Nova Scotia, New Brunswick, Lower Canada (now Quebec) and Upper Canada (now Ontario).

By the late 1770s, English exploration of the western coastline of Canada had begun with the arrival of Captain James Cook at Nootka Sound in 1778. Here he refitted his ships, traded with the Indians and claimed the land for Great Britain. Captain George Vancouver, who accompanied Cook on the voyage into Nootka Sound, later commanded an expedition to the Sound to secure the return of British property that had been seized by the Spanish. While in this area he meticulously charted the northwest coast of British Columbia for the British navy.

The first English colony to be established in what is now Canada was founded in Newfoundland by a small group of fishermen who came to Conception Bay from Devon in 1611. A successful colony was not established until 1637, this time by Sir David Kirke and some associates. Despite imperial mercantile policy which treated Newfoundland as a fishing station and not as a colony, the island's population grew until by 1763 it exceeded 10,000 people.

There was little English settlement in Nova Scotia until 1749, when Great Britain, determined to establish a naval base and settlement to counterbalance the French fortress of Louisbourg, sent out Edward Cornwallis and some 2,000 colonists to found Halifax. Among the settlers, mainly disbanded sailors and soldiers, were many English. They were soon joined by merchants and fishermen from New England who were in turn followed by immigrants from the other seaboard colonies.

Before the end of the Seven Years' War in 1763, however, England's main colonization efforts in the New World were concentrated farther south along the Atlantic seaboard where the thirteen American colonies extended from what is now the state of Maine in the north to the state of Georgia in the south. Even after New France was ceded to Britain, not many English settlers came out or moved across the border from the Thirteen Colonies to Quebec. Most of those who did were merchants who sought to take over the control and direction of the fur trade.

It was the American Revolution that brought thousands of new English settlers to Canada. Between the outbreak of hostilities in 1775 and especially after the Treaty of Paris in 1783, large numbers of political refugees whose loyalties remained with Great Britain journeyed to Nova Scotia and Quebec. Among the approximately 25,000 newcomers to the Maritime Provinces and the 12,000 to 15,000 who flocked to Quebec, many were of English origin. Most were artisans and farmers, only a few being professional men.

The coming of the Loyalists changed the composition of the Canadian people from one that was predominantly French to one that was predominantly British. It also precipitated the creation of two new provinces, New Brunswick and Upper Canada (now Ontario) and the introduction of elected assemblies in both Upper and Lower Canada.

Equally important, the arrival of the

Loyalists continued the colonial tie with Great Britain. As a result, Canadians maintained an interest in the culture and political developments of Great Britain and adopted the British model of political institutions instead of the American one.

Among others, English settlers began to pour into Canada from the United States until the War of 1812. After the war, American immigration fell off drastically, to be superseded by a mass influx of new settlers from England and other parts of the British Isles.

In the decade following the Napoleonic Wars, England along with the rest of Great Britain was gripped by an emigration fever caused by soaring unemployment, depressed wages, burdensome poor rates and agricultural uncertainties. With conditions such as these providing the necessary impetus, many ordinary people, despairing of winning economic and social reforms at home where the landed interests controlled Parliament, decided to emigrate. By 1819 approximately half the British subjects who sailed for British North America were English. From the industrial midlands and the farming areas of England came thousands of emigrants, their numbers peaking in years of depression and severe unemployment in the home country. Between 1815 and 1855, almost one million British emigrants, a large percentage of whom were English, landed in British North American ports.

After Confederation in 1867, immigrant children began to play a significant role in English settlement in Canada. Children from private homes, industrial schools and poor law schools were given free passage, becoming wards of various societies after their arrival in this country. Between Confederation and the outbreak of the First World War in 1914 more than 60,000 British children, most of whom were English, were settled on farms and in towns across the country.

The opening of the Canadian Prairies to settlement attracted another large influx of English settlers. In 1901, fewer than 10,000 English immigrants arrived in Canada, but in 1906, three years after the decision was made to establish an immigration office in central London, more than 65,000 newcomers disembarked at Canadian ports. In 1913 a record number of 113,004 English immigrants arrived from overseas. With the exception of one notable group most of these newcomers came as individuals in search of a better standard of living and freedom from the rigidities of English class structure. Many hoped to do this in the West, where there was still an abundance of free land.

The exception was the Barr Colony, which was founded in Lloydminster, Saskatchewan, in 1903 by the Reverend Isaac Barr, a Canadian-born Anglican clergyman. Anxious to save Canada for the British empire, Barr, aided by a partner, recruited almost 2,000 Englishmen, most of whom came from the cities, for settlement in the northwest. Despite spectacular, almost tragic beginnings, the colony eventually became a thriving venture.

The outbreak of the First World War brought immigration to a standstill, and when the war ended the large numbers of immigrants expected from Europe did not materialize. Immigration from the British Isles did not return to its former level mainly because there was now increased economic opportunity in Great Britain.

Attempts were made to stimulate immigration by means of the Empire Settlement Act, passed by the British government in 1922, which provided for training and financial assistance of emigrants. Under this Act the British government helped 130,000 emigrants from Britain to settle in Canada. Assistance was also given to discharged British soldiers to emigrate, and 26,560 came to Canada. Nevertheless, the number of English emigrants destined for Canada continued to diminish throughout the Depression years of the 1930s and the Second World War, rising significantly only in 1944 and 1945.

With the cessation of hostilities, another large exodus of English emigrants began. Over 7,000 Britons came to Ontario during the late summer and fall of 1947. Many of these who came to Canada were trained industrial workers, artisans and technicians who were profitably absorbed into the Canadian economy. Others who came were investors and executives who helped to initiate this expansion. In addition, there were English brides of Canadian servicemen and English children who had been evacuated to Canada during the war and who had decided to stay in this country permanently. Many of the English servicemen who had participated in training programs in Canada also returned after the war.

The year 1957, which followed the Suez Crisis of the autumn of 1956, saw by far the greatest number of English immigrants, 75,546, arrive in this country since 1913. Another peak year for English immigration was 1967, Centennial Year, when over 43,000 English emigrated to Canada. Since then, however, the numbers have fallen off considerably.

At the time of the 1971 census, Ontario had the largest number of Canadians of English origin, 2,999,375, followed by British Columbia with 806,935, Alberta with 457,235, and Newfoundland with 418,775. Nova Scotia and Quebec were next with 393,435 and 389,790 respectively.

Representative institutions, the traditions of the British and English Common Law are among the most important in the list of Canada's inheritances from Great Britain. Nova Scotia received its first legislature as early as 1758, but the Province of Quebec had to wait until the implementation of the Constitutional Act of 1791, a far-reaching act which determined the general shape that government was to assume in British North America. At this time, Quebec (or rather Lower Canada and Upper Canada, because the former province was divided by order in council) received a governor and a legislature, the latter consisting of an appointed council and an elected assembly. Upper Canada, the home of most of the Loyalists, also received English common law.

Reform movements and rebellions in British North America eventually pointed the way to responsible government, the system whereby the ministry or cabinet which governs a country is responsible, as a body, to Parliament. This practice, which is the extension of the British cabinet system to colonial government, was introduced in Nova Scotia in January, 1848, and two months later in the Province of Canada. The British North America Act of 1867 established a federal government system embodying these principles. Its upper house however, is called the Senate; its lower house, the House of Commons.

In the realm of law, Canadian civil law in nine out of ten provinces is based largely on English common law. (French civil law is maintained in Quebec.) The whole judiciary, or system of courts, is modelled on the English system of justice.

Fishing, lumbering, ship building and farming were the earliest Canadian industries, and in all of these the English played an important role. Indeed, English enterprise, skill and hard work have been at the forefront in the development of Canada from a rural economy into a modern industrial state.

Various well-known institutions that are active throughout the world today, such as the Red Cross, the Boy Scouts and Girl Guides, came to Canada from England. For example, the Canadian Red Cross Society began in 1896 as a branch of the British National Society for Aid to the Sick and Wounded. The Boy Scouts were first organized in Canada in 1908, the same year that the Scout movement was organized in England by Lord Baden-Powell. The Girl Guides, started in England the following year, came to Canada in 1910 when a company was formed in St. Catharines, Ontario.

At the time of Confederation, Canadians of English origin constituted only 20.3 per cent of the total population of the four original provinces. Their proportion rose slowly however, even during the heavy continental immigration that occurred between 1896 and 1914. There were 2,545,358 Canadians of English descent in 1921, and this number increased to 3,630,344 persons in 1951. In total, 708,620 English immigrants came to Canada between 1946 and 1973. England was the leading source country for immigrants in 1951, 1968 and 1973 and was second in 1960 to Italy.

The English have always had a tremendous impact on Canadian society. Today their influence permeates every aspect of Canadian life, from government, law and the professions to industry, commerce and the arts.

# Estonians

THE VAST MAJORITY of Canada's Estonians came with the mass migration which left Esto-nia, a Baltic country, during the Second World War. Before this, however, there were a few Estonian settlers in Canada who lived mostly in the western provinces, to which they were attracted by the promise of free land. The largest groups went to Alberta, where by the first decade of the century the areas around Stettler and Lethbridge contained substantial Estonian communities. Other settlers went to Saskatchewan and British Columbia, and the beginnings of a community organizational structure can be discerned in each settlement during this period.

A notable effort in this early stage of Estonian settlement was made by Admiral Johann Pitka, a hero of the Estonian war for independence of 1918–20. In 1924 he led an expedition into the interior of British Columbia with the express purpose of founding an Estonian settlement. Located near Fort St. James on Stuart Lake, the settlement attempted numerous agricultural ventures as well as lumbering operations as a means of subsistence, but difficulties in communicating with the outside world were insurmountable, and the venture was abandoned. Admiral Pitka returned to Estonia, while other members of the expedition settled elsewhere in Canada. The only remaining traces of the expedition can be found in some of the geographical names of the area, including Pitka Mountain, Pitka Point, and the Linda River, named after the Admiral's daughter.

The most significant wave of Estonian emigration occurred in 1944, when some 72,000 individuals fled the country either to Germany or to Sweden before the Soviet advance. About 40,000 found themselves in Germany at the end of the war, and about 13,500 of them entered Canada between 1946 and 1955. Emigration from Estonia ceased with its incorporation into the Soviet Union, and the Estonian population in Canada has remained fairly unchanged since the early 1950s. The largest Estonian community outside the home country is in Sweden, and because of the great number of intellectuals and professionals who chose to live in Sweden, it remains one of the most important Estonian émigré centres in the world though many Estonians from Sweden have emigrated to Canada and the United States. Sizable Estonian communities can be found in the United States and Canada, with groups of several thousand members also in England, Germany and Australia.

According to the 1971 census of Canada, there were 18,810 Canadians of Estonian origin living in this country. Of this number, 14,520 (77.2 per cent) claimed to have a knowledge of the Estonian language, and this extremely high index of language retention is obviously related to the recency of mass Estonian immigration to Canada after the Second World War.

Another rather interesting feature of Estonian settlement in Canada is the overwhelming concentration of this group in the province of Ontario. In that province, more than 13,700 Canadians of Estonian origin reside. Sizable communities can also be found in British Columbia, with 2,265 Estonian-origin Canadians, or 12.1 per cent of the total Estonian population in Canada; Quebec with 1,440, or 7.6 per cent; and Alberta with 845, or 4.5 per cent. These figures are based on 1971 census statistics.

Because of the high educational and professional qualifications held by most postwar Estonian immigrants to Canada, they were naturally attracted to the urban centres of Ontario rather than to the agricultural, forestry and mining areas of western Canada. Furthermore, since immigration from Estonia

has virtually ceased, these settlement patterns are unlikely to change in the future. When one compares the number of Estonians listed in the 1961 census, 18,550, it can be seen that there was an increase of only 260 persons over the decade before 1971.

The overwhelming majority of Estonians are Lutherans, although there are also Baptists and other religious groups. Estonian congregations have been established in all of the major centres of Estonian population, with several in Toronto, where the Estonian Baptist congregation has also conducted radio broadcasts with an international listening audience.

Because almost all Estonians in Canada are associated with the great migration of 1944, the organizational structure of their communities has assumed certain characteristics. In the first place, the concentration of Estonians in Toronto has made that city the centre of most of the Estonian organizations in the country. The Estonian Federation in Canada was founded in 1950 in order to unite these organizations under one co-ordinating umbrella dedicated to the promotion of Estonian cultural, economic and social interests.

Connected with the events of the Second World War and its aftermath, both the Estonian War Veterans' League in Canada and the Estonian Relief Committee were set up to assist needy compatriots whose lives were shattered in the conflagration. An important function of any ethnic community is education, and in this respect the Estonian communities have attempted to preserve their heritage in the generation born in Canada through a concerted educational program. Where population warrants it, supplementary schools in the Estonian language have been set up. Organizing this activity is the Estonian Teachers' Association, which strengthens its activities by maintaining links with similar educational bodies in the Estonian communities of the United States, Sweden, Germany and England.

Soon after the war numerous Estonian publishing houses were established in Sweden, and some of this activity was transferred to Canada. Two independent Estonian-language newspapers have been established in Toronto; *Meie Elu* (*Our Life*), a weekly, and *Vaba Eestlane* (*Free Estonia*), a semi-weekly.

Among the overall community organizational activities, the existence of a large number of specialized associations should be noted, such as theatre and art clubs, a lawyers' association, and the sports club *Kalev*. An active co-operative movement, the Estonian (Toronto) Credit Union, also exists within the Estonian community. The Estonian Boy Scout and Girl Guide movement and summer camps have been an important factor in promoting language retention and cultural identity. Tartu College in Toronto, residence for students of the University of Toronto, constitutes an important centre for the activities of Estonian university students and academic organizations.

Nearly every Estonian community has its local associations, and those cities with larger Estonian populations are able to support the activities of Estonian choirs and folk-dance ensembles. Notable efforts have been made in the field of drama ever since the Estonian National Theatre was founded in Toronto in 1948, and summer festivals devoted to music, song, dance and sport regularly appear on an annual basis. Since 1956 every four years a major festival is organized jointly by Estonians in Canada and those in the United States. The site of the festival alternates between the two countries.

A more significant event for Canadians of Estonian origin occurred in the summer of 1972, when the community held the first Estonian World Festival, in Toronto. The eight-day event gathered some 12,000 Estonians from around the globe. Besides the political discussions and conferences of various Estonian organizations, the festival presented folk dancing, massed choirs, gymnastics, athletic competitions, theatrical performances and a beauty pageant.

Estonian weavers are active in both Toronto and Montreal, and in 1957 the Saskatchewan Arts Board brought an Estonian weaver to Regina, to instruct on four-harness looms. Estonians in Canada excel also in leathercraft, and artists in Montreal and Edmonton in particular have won recognition for their work. A considerable number of Estonian painters and sculptors have won recognition in Canada.

While the Estonian presence in Canada has been significant only since the Second World War, and while immigration from that country has virtually ceased there is nevertheless a viable Estonian community in Canada which is dedicated to preserving the language and traditions of the homeland. Their contributions in many spheres of Canadian cultural life are evident, especially in proportion to their relatively small numbers, and it can be assumed that the Estonian heritage will continue its presence in this country in the years to come.

# Fijians

THE FIJI GROUP of islands is situated in the western Pacific, some 1,100 miles (1,770 km) north of New Zealand and 1,500 miles (2,414 km) northeast of Australia. This group comprises more than 300 islands, ranging from tiny coral atolls and rugged limestone islands to the two islands of Viti Levu and Vanua Levu, which together comprise 6,148 (15,923 km²) of the group's total area of 7,022 square miles (18,187 km²).

Fijian society is pluralistic, comprising several communities with both physical and cultural differences which form economically and socially identifiable segments. The major Fijian population groups are Fijians, Indo-Fijians, Europeans, Euronesians, Chinese and other Pacific islanders. These groups are segmented, yet are linked in the overall social structure of the country.

Practically all of the Fijian immigrants to Canada are Indo-Fijians, or Fijians of East Indian origin. They are descendants of indentured labourers from India, who came to Fiji to work on the sugar plantations when the large-scale cultivation of sugar cane by modern methods was introduced to the islands during the nineteenth century.

Altogether, it is estimated that 60,000 Indians went to Fiji either as indentured labourers, merchants or traders from 1879 until 1916, when indentured Indian immigration was stopped. Indo-Fijians gradually improved their economic status in Fijian society, rising from poorly paid labourers to become leaseholders or landholders. Today, Indo-Fijians are the largest population group in Fiji, forming 50 per cent of the total. It is said that Indians occupy most of the middle level businesses in Fiji. As they acquire affluence in Fijian society, Indians, particularly the young ones, are given opportunities to receive an education, hence entering various professions and occupying higher positions in the civil service.

Indo-Fijians emigrate to Canada primarily for economic reasons. Dependant largely upon agriculture (sugar cane), Fiji's industries are relatively few and small. There has been much under-employment in the country, especially among the educated youth, simply because there are not enough jobs for this segment of the population. Prevented from migrating to the two neighbouring countries of Australia and New Zealand under the terms of the "White Australia" policy of immigration and its New Zealand version, Indo-Fijians chose to come to Canada.

As an identifiable group, Indo-Fijians are among the newest arrivals in Canada. First Indo-Fijian immigration is said to have begun about 1964, and most of the immigrants have come in the late 1960s and 1970s. Few Fijians have been here as long as ten years. The recency of Indo-Fijian immigration to Canada is documented in Canadian immigration statistics which show that in the 1960s only 843 Indo-Fijians entered Canada. From 1970 to 1975, however, the number of migrants increased significantly, as a total of nearly 7,000 listed Fiji as their country of last permanent residence. The Indo-Fijian community is one of the smallest in Canada, currently consisting of approximately 8,000 persons.

According to the immigration statistics, the choice of residence location for the Indo-Fijian immigrants has usually been British Columbia. Greater Vancouver alone holds some 5,000 Indo-Fijians today. In fact, the community in Vancouver is the biggest Indo-Fijian community outside the Fiji Islands. The Indo-Fijian immigrants are primarily attracted to this area because they can find work in the lumbering industry there rather easily (the industry is one of the areas in which East Indians, primarily from the subcontinent, have been actively involved since the nineteenth century), because that province is closest to their homeland, and because the climate is more moderate than in many other parts of Canada. A handful of Indo-Fijian immigrants have also come to live in Ontario, primarily in Toronto.

A large majority of Indo-Fijian immigrants received their formal academic education and vocational training before entering Canada, for the average Indo-Fijian immigrant who is seeking employment in Canada appears to have received a high school education with some sort of technical training. One-third of the immigrants' intended occupations, upon entry to Canada, are in the area of managerial positions or self-supporting businesses, with the remainder in skilled or semi-skilled jobs. It is estimated that a significant segment of the employed Indo-Fijians in British Columbia are concentrated in the production, processing and distribution of forest products. Others are engaged in furniture making or work as tradesmen in upholstering. Some others are cabinet makers, mechanics and machinists.

Despite the fact that they are recent immigrants, most Fijians have made a satisfactory adjustment to the Canadian way of life. They appear to have positive attitudes towards the Canadian cultural and educational styles. Those who came to Canada reacted against the depressing economic situation in the islands and have found that their knowledge and skills have been more adequately used in this country. Their living standard has also significantly improved.

The Indo-Fijians, from different religious backgrounds (90 per cent of the immigrants are Hindus and the remaining 10 per cent are Muslims), are united by their common English language in Canada and form one community based on their identity as Indo-Fijians. They wish to be known as an Indo-Fijian community, separated from the greater East Indian

community in British Columbia and elsewhere in Canada. Differences in accepted manners and customs have led the Indo-Fijians to maintain a separate identity from immigrants from the Indian subcontinent.

The East Indian community in Fiji is caste-free. Upon their arrival in Fiji, all Indians, being indentured labourers, were forced to work in the fields irrespective of their caste. This act of emigration and the plantation system made people lose caste and the various restrictions derived from the caste system. Thus, some Indo-Fijians in Canada find it difficult to associate freely with their fellow East Indians from the mainland, some of whom are still influenced by the various manners and customs derived from the caste systems of India.

The Indo-Fijians in Vancouver have formed two associations, the Ramayan Mandoli Association and the Fiji-Canada Association. The aims of these associations are to assist Indo-Fijians to meet one another and to help newcomers to adjust to Canadian society. Their activities are largely social and recreational in nature.

Since Indo-Fijians have found a way of life in British Columbia that offers them a chance to take advantage of their education and training, their integration into Canadian society has been, and will continue to be, swift and to a large degree effortless.

# Filipinos

Since 1946 a total of 49,083 Filipino citizens have immigrated to Canada. Of this number, however, about 72 per cent entered Canada during the period 1970 to 1975. The recency of Philippine immigration to Canada is shown by the fact that between 1946 and 1964, only 770 Filipinos were admitted to Canada. Many of the early immigrants were former Filipino residents of the United States.

The number of Filipino residents in Canada has steadily increased since 1966, when entry requirements were eased, with the result that in 1974 Filipinos ranked sixth among all immigrants entering Canada. Even with possible return migration, either to the United States or to the Philippines, the total number of Filipinos in Canada is today estimated to be over 60,000.

Filipinos comprise one of the fastest growing ethnocultural groups in this country. Based on Canadian immigration statistics, the average Filipino immigrant is young and more likely to be female, possesses a college degree, is proficient in the English language, is a Catholic, and probably comes from Luzon, the largest island of the Philippine archipelago. Although economic and political situations in the mother country are important factors for immigration, a nationwide survey on the Filipino immigration pattern from 1962 to 1972 revealed that the background of Filipino immigrants to Canada represented a group that was relatively well off and happy in the Philippines. However, the lure of better opportunities and the excitement of travel and adventure also attracted them to this country.

Filipinos can be found all across Canada. It is estimated that the largest percentage, approximately 40,000 Filipinos, have settled in Ontario, followed in order by Manitoba, British Columbia, Quebec and Alberta. The largest urban centres are the most popular areas for settlement in every province. About 30,000 Filipinos reside in Toronto, and several thousand in Winnipeg, Ottawa, Vancouver and Montreal. There is not, however, any sign of geographic concentration within these urban areas, with the possible exception of a recent influx of Filipino garment-workers to Winnipeg, which may induce the concentration of this group there.

There are a number of clubs or associations prominent among Filipino Canadians, most of which participate actively in festivals and civic celebrations. These include the Filipino-Canada Association, which can be found in most urban centres, the regional associations of which are affiliated with the United Council of Filipino Associations across Canada (UCFAC). To date, there are approximately thirty-five Filipino associations across Canada which are affiliated with the United Council.

Most of the Filipino communities in Canada publish newsletters, among which are *Balita* (*News*), *Ang Tinig* (*The Voice*), *Ang Tanglaw* (*The Light*), *Bayanihan* (*Togetherness*) and *Kayumanggi* (which indicates the typical brown Filipino complexion). Two regularly published newspapers, *Atin Ito* in Toronto and *Silangan* in Winnipeg have replaced two former newspapers, both Toronto-based, which recently ceased publication. The *Filipino Forum* is a new newspaper published in Montreal which describes Canadian and Filipino events. The *Philippine Times*, published in Chicago with a Canadian section, is mailed to Canadian subscribers.

As a consequence of the Philippines' long history of cross-cultural relationships with various eastern and western civilizations, the Filipinos consider themselves inherently multicultural. It is not surprising, therefore, that they are quickly integrating into Canadian society and contributing their unique culture and heritage to the Canadian way of life.

# Finns

THE FINNISH PRESENCE began early during the European colonization of North America. The first Finnish immigrants arrived in North America with the Swedish settlers who established the colony of New Sweden along the banks of the Delaware between 1641 and 1655. Although the colony was small and short-lived, many of the colonists eventually were integrated into the colonial American society.

Nearly two hundred years elapsed before new Finnish settlers immigrated to North America. Between 1835 and 1865, several hundred Finns settled in Alaska, which at that time was part of the Russian Empire. Since the Russian ships visiting Alaska were manned mainly by Finnish crews, many Finns came there as seamen and remained as settlers. Later some of them moved farther down the coast to settle in what is now British Columbia.

There are three major periods of migration in which Finns came to Canada. The first was the lengthy period stretching from 1870 to World War I, a second during the 1920s and the third was the postwar decade of the 1950s. Until 1920, most Finnish immigrants went to the United States. A small minority immigrated directly to Canada and others were to settle in Canada after settlement in the United States proved less satisfactory, especially after Canadian economic conditions improved.

The main factor in Finnish emigration to North America has been economic. Many Finns, especially from rural areas, experienced great difficulties and were obliged to search for new opportunities. Economic problems were reinforced by political and religious tensions in certain regions of Finland. This, along with attractive economic opportunities in North America which included free land, high wages, the hope of religious freedom and democracy, led to substantial overseas migration from these areas of Finland.

A number of other causes resulted in increased immigration. For example, some Finns wished to escape "Russification" policies from 1899 onwards and particularly, compulsory military service in the Imperial Russian Army. In addition, emigration became easier as it became less expensive for emigrants to travel from Finland to North America. New immigrants encouraged relatives and friends to emigrate by providing passage money and favourable information about the new lands.

In the 1920s, the American Congress established quotas on the entry of immigrants to the United States, and Canada became the main destination of Finnish emigrants. Since this decade coincided with the aftermath of the Finnish civil war, the resulting economic dislocation and political difficulties provided the main motives for leaving the homeland.

The Depression ended this era of Finnish migration to North America when in 1931 the Canadian government limited entry to close relatives of Canadian residents. During the 1930s, more Finns left Canada than arrived. During the Spanish Civil War, many Finns fought in the Canadian Mackenzie-Papineau Battalion on the Republican side. They formed approximately 10 per cent of this force. There were 21,494 persons of Finnish origin in Canada in 1921, a figure which increased to 43,885 after the rapid period of immigration in the 1920s, but by the 1941 census this number had declined to 41,683 Finns.

With the expanding Canadian economy of

the 1950s, the Canadian government embarked on a course of receiving large numbers of immigrants into the labour force. Almost 20,000 Finns arrived in Canada during the 1940–60 period, increasing the population of Finnish Canadians from 43,745 in 1951 to 59,436 in 1961. Since emigration after the Second World War was generally from an urban area in Finland, the postwar Finnish immigrant tended to be urban in origin, have a greater number of skills, and was more inclined to settle in the urban areas of Canada.

As the Finnish economy began to expand in the late 1950s, the number of emigrants to depart for Canada decreased at the same time that Canadian immigration laws were tightening. Only a few hundred Finns a year have arrived in Canada since 1960.

The 1971 census lists 59,215 people of Finnish origin living in Canada. Most live in two provinces, about 65 per cent in Ontario and 19.5 per cent in British Columbia, the total population in each province being 38,515 and 11,510 respectively. Few Finns have settled in the Maritime Provinces. There were 1,865 Canadians of Finnish origin living in Quebec in 1971, mostly around Montreal. There have also been active Finnish communities in the mining areas of northwestern Quebec.

The main concentrations of Finns in Ontario can be found in the districts of northern Ontario, notably Algoma, Cochrane, Sudbury, Thunder Bay, and to a lesser extent Timiskaming. The first Finnish migrants to Ontario settled in the Port Arthur-Fort William and Sudbury-Copper Cliff areas around 1885. Many of them had come from Michigan and Minnesota to work on the construction of the CPR. They then turned to mining and lumbering, and later to mixed farming. Often these small Finnish farmers would be seasonally employed in mining and lumbering.

Thunder Bay has the largest concentration of Canadians of Finnish background. The 1971 census lists 11,105 residents of Finnish origin in the district and 8,350 in the metropolitan area. The Port Arthur section has the greatest concentration and this is most evident in the area of Bay Street, where there are a number of Finnish halls, stores and restaurants. A new shopping centre was named "Keskus" (a Finnish word meaning "centre") in recognition of the long Finnish presence in the region. Outlying communities have names such as Lappe and Finland.

A large number of Finns have also gone to the Sudbury area, because of the availability of employment in the nickel-producing operations. Finns are concentrated in the Antwerp Street, Lockerby and Copper Cliff areas of the immediate district as well as Wanup, Long Lake, Waters and Beaver Lake outside the city. Three Finnish-language newspapers, *Vapaus, Liekki* and *Vapaa Sana*, were founded in Sudbury.

Finns were among the first to pioneer the mining communities of Kirkland Lake and Timmins. Overall, northern Ontario has been especially attractive for Finnish immigrants. Besides the similarity of climate to their homeland, immigrants have found the availability of jobs in the mining and lumbering industries to their liking.

There were only 1,450 Finns in Manitoba in 1971, about half of whom lived in the Greater Winnipeg area, while others had settled in the Red River Valley as farmers. Of the 1,730 Finns in Saskatchewan, most live in rural areas.

Finns first appeared in Alberta about 1900. They worked on railway construction and in some of the mining areas. Many saved money and later bought farms of their own. Today, many are farmers in the Sylvan Lake district near Red Deer. There are also active Finnish communities in both Calgary and Edmonton.

Between 1880 and 1900, a large number of Finnish immigrants travelled from the United States to British Columbia to work in the mining and lumbering communities of Nanaimo, Extension, Wellington and Lady-smith. After working as manual labourers for a number of years, many immigrants of Finnish origin all over North America decided to return to the land. In British Columbia, this movement developed into the most famous Finnish settlement in North America, a utopian socialist commune on Malcolm Island in the Queen Charlotte Strait known as Soin-tula (Harmony).

There were 11,510 residents of Finnish origin in British Columbia in 1971. This was an increase from 1961, indicating that many Finns (including those who were Canadian born) had moved to the west coast to seek work. Over half lived in the Greater Vancouver area, with sizable Finnish communities in Nanaimo, Burnaby, Coquitlam, Delta, Kitimat, Maple Ridge, Richmond and Surrey.

As with the Canadian population in general, there has been a steady trend toward urbanization among Finns. In 1931, 54.2 per cent lived in rural areas; in 1951, the figure was still as high as 46 per cent, despite the rapid industrialization of Canada in the previous decade. By 1971, rural residency had declined to 24 per cent, 22 per cent of which was in Ontario. Most of the Finnish immigrants who arrived in the 1950s settled almost immediately in the urban centres of Canada.

Most Finns are Lutherans, the denomination which is the state religion of Finland. The 1931 census reported that 88 per cent of those of Finnish origin in Canada were of the Lutheran faith. For those born in Finland the figure was 93 per cent. In 1971, 60.3 per cent of Finns were Lutheran, a decline of 10 per cent from 1961. The United Church of Canada has the second largest number of adherents among Finnish Canadians. In 1971, 13 per cent of the Finns were of the United Church faith.

Three sects of Lutheranism have developed among Finnish immigrants in North America: the Suomi Synod congregations, which became a part of the Lutheran Church of America in 1961, and which had strong ties with the state church in Finland; the National Lutheran churches, which had lay as well as ordained ministers and remained independent from Finland; and the evangelical Apostolic Lutherans, who followed the fundamentalist teachings of the Finnish evangelist, Lars Laes-tadius.

In Canada, the Suomi Synod congregations became the most firmly established in Finnish communities. There are congregations in Toronto, Montreal, Sault Ste. Marie, Sudbury-Copper Cliff, Kirkland Lake, Timmins-Porcupine, Thunder Bay and Vancouver. There are Apostolic Lutheran congregations in Toronto and Thunder Bay. The Finnish Pentecostal Church is also active, with congregations in Sudbury, Toronto and Thunder Bay.

An indicator of the retention of a cultural heritage is the use of one's mother tongue. In 1931, 89.5 per cent of Finns in Canada listed Finnish as their mother tongue; another 4.8 per cent spoke Swedish. In 1971, 55.9 per cent listed Finnish, a decline from 67.8 per cent in 1961; 39.8 per cent listed English as their mother tongue. The fact that so many of the earlier Finnish immigrants settled in areas outside the industrial centres was a major factor in the retention of the Finnish language and customs by a large proportion of the Canadian-born Finns. Most of their daily activity, with the exception of school work, was conducted in the Finnish language. There was a greater reliance on the services and cultural contacts of the Finnish community, reinforced with the coming of the Depression.

Many of the postwar Finnish immigrants settled in the cities. They had government assistance in finding jobs and learning English and other skills, and therefore relied on their community and association halls only for social activities. The children, who attended schools in urban areas, had even less need for the social activities provided by the supplementary language schools organized by various groups.

There has been a Finnish-language press in Canada for over seventy-five years. Matti Kurikka edited the first Finnish-Canadian periodical, *Aika* (*Time*), in Nanaimo from 1901 to 1902 to promote the organization of the Sointula colony. When the colony was established, *Aika* was published for about a year (1903–4) in Sointula. The three Finnish-language newspapers publishing today are *Canadan Uutiset* (*Canadian News*), a weekly out of Thunder Bay since 1915; *Vikkosanomat* (*Weekly Messenger*), a Toronto weekly since 1975, which was established in 1974 from a merger of *Vapaus* (*Freedom*) founded in Sudbury in 1917 and *Liekki* (*Flame*) founded in Sudbury in 1935; and *Vapaa Sana* (*Free Press*), a twice-weekly, founded in Sudbury in 1931 and published in Toronto since 1934.

The Finns, once they became established in communities in Canada, developed their own institutions to meet the social and cultural needs of their members. In addition to the Lutheran Church, there were many Finnish social clubs which included a number of temperance groups, the first of which, Lannen Rusko (Western Glow), was established in North Wellington, British Columbia. Several local organizations founded the Finnish Socialist Organization of Canada in 1911, which received its charter in 1923. The Finnish-Canadian Amateur Sports Federation, founded as the Worker's Sports Association in 1925, has had close unofficial ties with the Finnish Organization of Canada (FOC).

Since many Finnish Organization leaders and members were active in the Canadian labour movement and left-wing causes, factions developed in the 1920s and 1930s, leading to the establishment of new Finnish clubs in many areas with more emphasis on social activities. In 1931, the Central Organization of the Loyal Finns in Canada was established in an attempt to provide a national structure for co-ordinating these activities.

The events of the Second World War led to new developments in Finnish-Canadian communities. For example, when the Soviet Union attacked Finland in 1939, a number of Finns in Canada formed the Aid for Finland society to assist their old homeland. The first of the Finnish Grand Festivals, representing most non-FOC groups, took place in 1940, sponsored by the Aid for Finland group.

The Finnish-Canadian Cultural Federation was founded in 1971 in Windsor, Ontario, and was chartered as a national organization in 1973. Thirty-two Finnish groups are associated with this Federation, which is a continuation and an expansion of the activities of the Finnish Grand Festival Committee.

One of the most important contributions of Finnish-Canadians was the large number of soldiers of Finnish descent who served in the Canadian Armed Forces during the Second World War. In the field of modern living, the sauna has been a fixture in every region of

Canada where Finns settled. Today, the sauna has become part of the Canadian lifestyle.

Many Finns who were interested in commercial affairs generally became active in the co-operative movements. Co-operatives are a well-established institution in Finland, and Finns in Canada pioneered efforts to establish producers' and consumers' co-operatives, and were prominent in founding and maintaining co-operatives in Thunder Bay, Sudbury, Timmins, Vancouver, Sointula and many other communities. The largest co-operative in Canada, the Consumers' Co-operative Society, Limited, in Timmins, was started by Finns and is still a viable enterprise long after all Finnish halls have closed in the area.

Finns have a long tradition in Canada of organizing amateur sports clubs, and have been particularly active in developing cross-country skiing, placing many members on Canadian national and Olympic teams. They have also been active in track and field and in gymnastics. Today, there are also special clubs among Finns to promote outdoor recreation such as hunting and fishing.

On a cultural level, Finns have actively promoted music and the arts, sometimes as part of their local clubs and on other occasions through distinctive clubs specializing in a given activity. In Toronto, Sudbury, Vancouver and Thunder Bay, there are choirs and bands that promote Finnish music and hold concerts. There are distinctive Finnish arts and crafts clubs in Toronto and Thunder Bay. Some groups specialize in folk dancing and gymnastics. In some communities, there are lodges of the Knights (and also Ladies) of Kalevala which promote a better knowledge of Finnish culture in the community as a whole.

Since 1970, various Finnish communities in Canada have organized Finnish Senior Citizens' clubs, with branches in Toronto,

Sudbury, Vancouver, Timmins, Kirkland Lake, Beaver Lake near Sudbury, Sault Ste. Marie, Thunder Bay and Vancouver. Many of these senior citizens use the halls of local Finnish groups in their areas.

While Finns are often connected with outdoor activities, they are also involved in many aspects of Canadian life which vary from the promotion of the arts to the establishment of clubs for senior citizens. Their contributions have been varied and widespread, and Canada as a whole has been enriched by their presence.

# French

THE FRENCH PRESENCE in Canada dates back to the early years of the seventeenth century, when the French became the first European inhabitants of Canada. Here they settled in Acadia, an area lying within the present boundaries of Nova Scotia, New Brunswick and Maine, and the St. Lawrence River Valley. Later they spread across the continent, carving out an empire known as New France that stretched from the Atlantic to the Rocky mountains and from Hudson Bay to the Gulf of Mexico.

The early pages of Canadian history were written by a Frenchman, Jacques Cartier, who took possession of the newly discovered land in the name of the king of France when he raised a thirty-foot wooden cross on Pointe Penouille at the entrance of Gaspé in 1534.

The establishment of permanent settlements in New France did not begin, however, until 1608 when the city of Quebec was founded by Samuel de Champlain. This centre and later settlements at Trois-Rivières (1634) and Montreal (1642) grew very slowly because the monopolistic trading companies that controlled the colony were reluctant to encourage any development that was incompatible with the fur trade, at that time North America's chief attraction. New France struggled along until 1663, when it came under royal administration and received a new lease on life. One of the first events of the new regime was the arrival of eight companies of the Carignan-Salières Regiment who checked the Iroquois, thereby permitting the colony to develop in peace. The colony flourished, aided by immigration from France and government policies which encouraged early marriage and penalized bachelorhood. In fact, the first twenty years after New France became a royal colony witnessed the greatest growth of the country. These years also saw the emergence of the pattern of large families, a factor which was to play an important role in the phenomenal increase and tenacious survival of the settlement. From 6,000 inhabitants in 1668, the population grew to 25,000 in 1722, 42,000 in 1730, and between 60,000 and 70,000 in 1760. Between 1663 and 1760 only 10,000 persons emigrated from France to New France.

Another principal centre of French colonization in the seventeenth century was Acadia, where Port Royal, which overlooked the Bay of Fundy, was founded. When Acadia was ceded to Great Britain in 1713, there were some 1,600 French-speaking colonists in the area, most of whom had settled in the Annapolis Valley where they had developed an efficient technique for diking the marshlands. In 1755, when hostilities broke out between the French and the English in the Ohio Valley, the governor and council of Nova Scotia expelled some 7,000 to 8,000 Acadians from the province and dispersed them among the English colonies on the Atlantic seaboard. When Louisbourg on Ile Royale (Cape Breton) was retaken by the British in 1758, Acadians from Ile Royale and Ile Saint-Jean (Prince Edward Island) were rounded up and sent to France, the American colonies and England. Some of the Acadians deported to the American colonies settled there permanently, while others went to Louisiana. Still others made their way back to the Saint John River, to Cape Breton and to Nova Scotia, where they were allowed to remain because there was no longer any danger of a French attack. Today they constitute a special branch of the French-Canadian family, with Moncton, New Brunswick, being their cultural centre.

French farmers established Ontario's first agricultural settlement at Windsor in 1749, and are well represented in northeastern Ontario and those counties which lie along the St. Lawrence and Ottawa Rivers from Ottawa to Cornwall. French-language schools and numerous cultural and educational organizations work towards the preservation of French culture and customs in Ontario.

French Canadians made their way to the west as early as 1634, when Jean Nicolet explored as far west as Lake Winnipeg. A century later, between 1731 and 1743, Pierre de la Vérendrye and his sons carried out the last great French-Canadian explorations in North America, pushing towards the Rockies in the traditional search for a route to the Pacific and the continuing effort to tap new fur supplies. The first permanent settlement in western Canada was established in 1818 when a number of French Canadians founded St. Boniface, now part of Greater Winnipeg. Today St. Boniface is the focus of French culture in the west and the site of an annual carnival, *le Festival du Voyageur*, which commemorates the role played by the French in exploring and settling this part of Canada. Other concentrations of French Canadians are found north of Edmonton, Alberta, in southern Manitoba and southern Saskatchewan.

The French-Canadian population continued to grow rapidly after the Conquest, so much so that Governor Guy Carleton predicted in 1767 that the flow of British immigration would never manage to drown the "new subjects" born in Canada. Carleton's prophecy proved justified when one realizes that the birth rate and the mortality rate in the period 1760–70 were 65 per thousand and 34 per thousand respectively, leaving a surplus of births.

In 1814 there were 335,000 people in Lower Canada (Province of Quebec), of whom the great majority were French-speaking. By comparison, there were 150,000 people in the Maritime Provinces, and only 95,000 inhabitants in Upper Canada, now the Province of Ontario. The first census after Confederation recorded a population of 1,082,940 French Canadians in the four original provinces, or almost 32 per cent of the population, and 929,817 in the Province of Quebec.

In 1971 French Canadians constituted almost 29 per cent of the total Canadian population. Of the 6,180,120 recorded in the census, 84 per cent lived in Quebec, 8 per cent in Ontario, 4 per cent in New Brunswick and 2 per cent in Manitoba.

Despite periods of heavy emigration to the United States, the French-Canadian population has grown steadily, accounting for between 27 and 32 per cent of Canada's population. It has done so largely through natural increase, because immigration from France had been insignificant. In fact, organized systematic immigration from France ceased altogether long before the Treaty of Paris was signed in 1763.

There were many reasons for this dearth in French immigration, but the major factor was the climate, which made it difficult for early immigrants to establish themselves in the French-speaking areas of the country. French immigration to Quebec remained insignificant until the years immediately following the Second World War. Then it increased significantly, reaching a peak in 1951, the year that 8,279 French-born immigrants arrived in Canada. Today between 2,000 and 3,000 French-born immigrants arrive in this country each year, the vast majority of whom settle in Quebec. This is relatively a very small number when compared to immigration from other countries.

To encourage immigration from France, the Quebec government has re-opened an immigration office in Paris (an office had been organized in 1869). It is administered by Quebec's Department of Immigration, the first provincial or federal department at any level in postwar Canada to concern itself solely with seeking immigrants, although the portfolio generally combines other responsibilities as well.

Under French rule, the Canadians had dominated the Superior Council, which had legislative as well as judicial functions, and the officer corps of the Marine troops; the last Governor-General of the French regime was a Canadian. During the first years of British rule, the French Canadians played only a marginal role in public life. This changed, however, with the implementation of the Constitutional Act of 1791, a British piece of legislation which provided for an elected House of Assembly and an appointed Legislative Council in Quebec, at that time called Lower Canada.

From the outset *Canadiens* made good use of their new representative institutions to defend their cherished language, religion and traditional agricultural society.

Since Confederation, three French Canadians have occupied the office of Prime Minister of Canada.

The seeds of a growing social revolution were sown during the 1950s, a period of rapid industralization and urbanization in Quebec, and the traditional ideal of a Quebec of large families grouped in and protected by their parish largely disappeared. Taking its place was a new urban concept which stressed mobility, more sophisticated services and amenities and the repeated intervention of the state to achieve desired social and economic change. Equally significant was the view that the state, that is, the Government of Quebec, the most important institution controlled by French Canadians, or the "Quebecois", could be used to give them a larger share of the ownership and direction of their own economy.

For the first few years of the Quiet Revolution everything seemed possible in Quebec as the public school system, public finance, the civil service, labour unions and virtually all of Quebec's institutions were reformed. What changes will occur in the future remains an important question.

Canada is a composite of many different linguistic and ethnocultural communities. This composite includes the Native Peoples, the French and the English, and the other immigrants who have chosen Canada as their new homeland. The long struggle of the French Canadians to maintain their institutions and culture and to survive as a people created an atmosphere conducive to the preservation of the basic linguistic and cultural values of the various ethnocultural communities within Canada. The continued presence of an important French component in Canada ruled out the possibility of imposing a policy of uniformity with homogeneity as its goal. In this atmosphere were created the conditions which made multiculturalism within a bilingual framework an official Canadian government policy in 1971.

# Georgians

GEORGIA IS A SOVIET REPUBLIC situated between the Black and Caspian Seas, bordering on Turkey as well as the Soviet republics of Russia, Armenia and Azerbaijan. The Georgians living in Canada today are a very small group, comprising at most a few dozen families. Precise statistics are impossible to present, since "Georgian" does not appear as a national designation in the Canadian census statistics. One can only estimate the true number of Georgians in the country by reference to the members of the Georgian-Canadian community and their estimates of the total numbers.

Many Georgians emigrated to other parts of Europe and to the United States before 1921, when the Soviets occupied Georgia and effectively sealed off further emigration. The first recorded Georgian in Canada was David Turkia, a tailor who resided in Toronto as early as 1908. Following him was Nestor Metroveli (anglicized to Mike Mitto), born in Georgia in 1895. He emigrated to Canada in 1913 after being discharged from the Russian army, and despite his lack of formal education, he made a successful career for himself as a prospector, helping to discover the Val d'Or mines of Quebec.

Although Georgian immigration to Canada has always been, at best, sporadic, certainly the largest number of Georgians to enter Canada came after the Second World War, largely by way of Europe. Among these were Georgians who for one reason or another found themselves outside of the Soviet Union at the end of the war, but there were also some first-wave Georgian émigrés from Paris. These latter individuals tended to settle in Montreal, while the rest for the most part settled in southern Ontario. At present there are only a few Georgians residing in western Canada, while the largest number can be found in Toronto, Hamilton and St. Catharines.

Because of the small number of Georgians in Canada, the features of a community life that can be found among larger ethnic groups cannot be supported by the scattered population. Churches, schools or organizations are not maintained by this group, but contacts within the community are preserved both on an individual basis and through the much larger Georgian community in the United States where an organizational structure has been established.

Obviously, for such a small group, the problem of assimilation is of prime importance. With few opportunities to transmit the Georgian language to the next generation, with no community structures capable of reinforcing national affiliation, and in the absence of a distinctive religious structure, Canada's Georgian community faces overwhelming difficulties. Attempts are being made to preserve a sense of national identity, reinforced by contacts with other Georgians living abroad, in the United States, or in Europe. It is hoped that the friendships made by the younger members of the community with their peers abroad will help to preserve a sense of common Georgian cultural affiliation and origin in the years to come.

# Germans

THE TERM "GERMAN" is most complex. Few Canadians of German-speaking origin are *Reichdeutsch* (from Germany); most are *Auslandsdeutsch* (from other lands). They come from Estonia in the north to the Black Sea in the south, from Alsace on the west to the Caspian Sea on the east. They may be Roman Catholic, Jewish, Mennonite, Lutheran or some other Protestant denomination. Their native language may or may not be German.

Approximately two thousand German newcomers landed at Halifax from its founding in 1749 until 1752. They were not, however, the first German immigrants to arrive in what is now Canada. A small number of settlers of German origin, some of them demobilized soldiers who had served under the French Crown at Port Royal, Louisbourg and Quebec, are known to have established themselves in New France as early as 1664, the date when Hans Bernard, the first recorded German settler, purchased land near Quebec City. The "foreign Protestants" who arrived in Halifax between 1749 and 1752, however, represented the first organized attempt to settle Germans in this country. As such, they spearheaded a movement that would result in Canadians of German origin becoming the third largest ethnocultural group in Canada, ranking in numerical importance behind the British and the French.

The Germans who made up this initial wave of immigration came from the principalities that were suffering from severe economic problems, religious persecution or the ravages of war. They had been recruited by the British government, which wanted to see Nova Scotia populated by sober, industrious and loyal subjects. The new arrivals were accommodated, supplied with provisions, and put to work in the small, palisaded seaport of Halifax. Then, in 1753, some 1,600 of them were moved to Merligash on the coast, some 60 miles (97 km) southwest of Halifax. In their new home, renamed Lunenburg, they became fishermen and boat builders, specializing in the world-renowned 'bluenose' schooner.

The next group of Germans to arrive in Nova Scotia came from Europe and from Pennsylvania, where most Germans in the Thirteen Colonies were concentrated, between 1760 and 1770. They settled in Annapolis County, Nova Scotia, and in Albert County, Coverdale Parish, Elgin Parish and Hillsborough Township, areas which later became part of New Brunswick.

Among the thousands of United Empire Loyalists who journeyed to British North America during and after the American Revolution were many persons of German origin who had settled earlier in Pennsylvania, New York, and as far south as Georgia. Some of these formed part of the large number of Loyalists who had sailed from New York to Halifax in the late summer and autumn of 1783. Most of the remaining German Loyalists formed part of two other distinct groups, one which moved up the Hudson River valley by Lake Champlain and down the Richelieu River to Sorel, and the other which consisted of persons who made their way over the Niagara frontier. There were ordinary civilians of German origin in the Halifax group, as well as members of militia regiments and German regiments who had fought for the British Crown. Many of these newcomers were

assigned land in Stormont and Dundas Counties, where German names and Lutheran churches are still very much in evidence.

Other Germans who settled in Canada immediately after the Revolution were discharged members of German regiments that had been recruited in various German principalities and sent to this country to defend it against invasion by Americans. An estimated 1,200 soldiers from Brunswick regiments remained in Canada, with several hundred of them settling in Lower Canada and the rest in Upper Canada, Albert County, New Brunswick and in Nova Scotia, where they established the Hessian Line and Waldeck Line settlements.

In 1792, shortly after John Graves Simcoe was appointed Lieutenant-Governor of Upper Canada, a proclamation was issued inviting native Americans who still sided with Great Britain to take up free land in the new province. Among the "late Loyalists" who responded were many settlers of German origin.

Between 1792 and 1837, German settlers arrived from New Jersey and Pennsylvania. Although they were not of Dutch origin, these people became known as "Pennsylvania Dutch." The majority of these settlers were Mennonites who sought not only free land, but also religious freedom and exemption from military service. One group settled in the Niagara district in the present counties of Welland, Lincoln and Haldimand, another group in York County at Whitchurch, and the third group, the most important, on the Grand River. There were also settlers of German Lutheran and Catholic origin who settled in the Grand River area in the 1820s. These settlers contributed to the industrial development of the area. The Grand River settlement became the nucleus of the German-speaking district of Waterloo, the site of the twin cities of Kitchener (called Berlin before 1916) and Waterloo, which together form the capital of Ontario's Mennonite community.

Many German immigrants who arrived from Europe in the nineteenth century settled in Perth, Huron, Bruce and Grey counties. Others, chiefly from Prussia, settled along the Ottawa River in Renfrew County and on the opposite shore in Quebec's Pontiac County. By the middle of the nineteenth century, German settlers could be found throughout Ontario, concentrated in the above-named areas. Most were farmers, whose farms could be distinguished by well-maintained houses and enclosure patterns.

Direct immigration from Germany to Canada continued until the middle of the 1870s, with Ontario being the chief destination. Then the picture changed drastically because of the prosperity of the newly established German Empire. Immigration from the homeland declined, to be superseded by a large immigration of German-speaking Mennonites from Ukraine. These people became one of the pioneering groups of the Prairie Provinces.

In the last quarter of the nineteenth century, a scarcity of free or cheap land in the United States and eastern Canada, and the decision of the Canadian government to grant free homesteads to settlers through the Dominion Land Act of 1872, combined to give settlement on the Prairies a great boost. Still greater encouragement was provided by the construction of the Canadian Pacific Railway (1881–85) and by an aggressive immigration policy which during Clifford Sifton's administration as Minister of the Interior (1896–1905) began to shift Canadian publicity to rural areas in central Europe. As well, correspondence between immigrants and relatives and friends in Europe helped encourage immigration to Canada.

Mennonites from Ukraine were the first settlers to arrive in Manitoba after it became a province in 1870. Between 1874 and 1880, over 7,000 of them settled in one of two regions: the East Reserve, east of Ninerville and west of Steinbach; and the West Reserve, east of Morden and west of Rosenfeld. Within twenty-five years of their coming, most had prospered, confirming the belief that prairie soil was fertile and could support agricultural settlements in areas hitherto considered frozen wastelands.

During the last two decades of the nineteenth century and the first decade of the twentieth, immigrants poured into the area in a great flood. Thousands of these settlers were of German origin, many from eastern and southeastern Europe. By 1914, about 35,000 Germans had settled in Manitoba, representing 7.5 per cent of the total population. Saskatchewan and Alberta both experienced a spectacular growth in German immigration, in Saskatchewan's case from less than 5,000 in 1901 to over 100,000 in 1911.

Most of the German-speaking settlers on the Prairies did not come from the German Empire, but rather from Austria-Hungary, the Russian Empire and the Balkan countries where German colonies had been established during the eighteenth century. These settlements had expanded rapidly and since large families were common, a shortage of land and an increasing class of landless workers had developed. In some areas growing nationalism led to the abrogation of their original rights and privileges, and many of these Germans decided to emigrate to Canada.

Although a small number of German settlers came to British Columbia under the auspices of the Hudson's Bay Company, their settlement there in any number dates only from the Fraser River valley gold rush of 1858. Most of the Germans who took part in this gold rush and a later one in the Cariboo Mountains did not make their fortune, but settled down to make a comfortable living as grocers, farmers, craftsmen, shopkeepers and brewers. The period of prosperity for British Columbia in the first decade of the twentieth century boosted the German population in the province to 11,800 persons by 1911, but the slump which began in 1912 and the outbreak of the First World War effectively curbed German immigration to the province. The First World War proved to be a watershed in the history of all German Canadians, for it marked the end of the first phase of their colonization and the beginning of a period of anti-German sentiment.

With the outbreak of the First World War, the Canadian government restricted direct immigration from Germany. Germany was not admitted to the status of "Favoured Nation" until 1927. One of the many groups to move to Canada on religious grounds was a party of some fifty German-speaking Hutterites who came to Canada shortly after 1918 from Dakota. Nearly all of them settled in Manitoba and Alberta, where their communal way of life sometimes brought them into conflict with government and local people alike.

Between 1919 and 1935, some 97,000 German-speaking immigrants arrived in Canada from Poland, Austria, Czechoslovakia and Germany. The majority were farmers who settled in the vicinity of older German settlements on the Prairies. A number were artisans, labourers and shopkeepers, some of whom settled first in eastern Canada and the Prairie Provinces, and then moved on to British Columbia.

During the Depression years of the 1930s, immigration to Canada fell off sharply, not to reach its former volume until after the Second World War. In the late 1930s, however, there was a small flow of Jewish refugees from Nazi Germany. Another group was composed of approximately 1,000 Sudeten Germans who, because of their Social Democratic political affiliation, emigrated to Canada from Czechoslovakia in 1939 to escape Nazi rule. Although they were skilled industrial workers, many settled on abandoned farms in northern Saskatchewan and on uncleared land in the Tomslake region of northeastern British Columbia.

After Dunkirk, people of German or Austrian origin living in Britain as refugees from Nazi oppression were reclassified as "Friendly Aliens" and either interned in Britain or sent to the Dominions for detention. By September, 1943, however, all of the 6,700 detained in Canada had been released. Over 1,500 of them returned to England, but the remainder, who included a number of scientists, businessmen and professionals, settled in Canada.

Among the large number of displaced persons who came to Canada between 1947 and 1950 were German-speaking refugees from Eastern Europe, many of whom were Volksdeutsche originating in the Danube areas of Roumania, Yugoslavia and the former Austria-Hungary. Although mainly a rural people, they tended to settle in the urban areas of Canada, particularly in Ontario, Quebec and western Canada.

In 1950 a ban on the immigration of German nationals, which had been in force since 1939, was lifted and regulations governing the admissibility of immigrants were broadened considerably. The numbers of Germans entering the country therefore increased dramatically. Between 1951 and

1960, some 250,000 German immigrants arrived, a figure exceeded only by those for Italian and British immigrants. By 1958, new Canadian immigration regulations designed to maintain the immigration flow at a realistic level went into effect. By this time, however, the Federal Republic of Germany had begun to prosper and large-scale emigration of its people had come to an end.

The 1971 census recorded 1,317,200 persons of German descent living in Canada, and since they constituted 6.1 per cent of the total population, they are Canada's third largest ethnic group. In Saskatchewan, Alberta and British Columbia, they are the second largest group after the British. Nearly a third of their number live in Ontario, mainly in the Golden Horseshoe area, the region that encompasses Lake Ontario, the Grand River valley, the Niagara Peninsula and south-western Ontario. At the time of the census there were more than 116,000 living in the Metropolitan Toronto area.

After Ontario, the greatest number of German Canadians live in Alberta, followed by British Columbia, Saskatchewan and Manitoba in that order. In 1971 there were approximately 90,000 living in Vancouver, 62,440 in Edmonton and 62,000 in Winnipeg. In eastern Canada, except for Ontario, their numbers are modest. Approximately three-quarters of the 50,000 German Canadians in the Province of Quebec at the time of the census were living in Montreal. In the Maritimes, there were some 40,000 German Canadians in Nova Scotia and about one-fifth that number in New Brunswick. There were 2,375 living in Newfoundland and 955 in Prince Edward Island.

Most Canadians of German origin belong to the Protestant churches. According to the 1971 census, 24.5 per cent were Lutheran, 15.8 per cent were members of the United Church, and 25.7 per cent were Roman Catholics. Another 9.6 per cent were Mennonites or Hutterites, and a small percentage were Anglicans.

In the early German-Canadian settlements, the life of the community revolved around the church which, in addition to caring for the spiritual welfare of its members, organized language schools for the young, provided care for the needy and supplied recreational facilities. The two oldest continuing German-Canadian clubs are the German Benevolent Society of Montreal, founded in 1835, and the Germania Club in Hamilton, organized in 1864. During the late nineteenth and early part of the twentieth century many other clubs and organizations were formed by German Canadians, but few survived the wars. During the inter-war period a number of local and political clubs were formed, most of which did not continue after the Second World War broke out. After the war, many old clubs were re-established and new ones organized to help thousands of recently arrived German-speaking immigrants adjust to life in their adopted country. Clubs with a purely cultural interest also sprang up, including the Cultural Circle of Vancouver and The Ring of Montreal.

The German musical tradition in Canada is a long-standing one. One of the oldest musical societies in the country, the Quebec Harmonic Society, which was established in 1820, was founded by a German, Henri Glackemeyer (1751-1836). Today many clubs have choir groups. Two of the oldest choirs in Canada, Germania of Hamilton and Concordia of Kitchener, were formed before Confederation. Most choirs belong to one of three regional organizations: the German-Canadian Choirs Association in eastern

Canada, the Prairie Choir Association in the West, and the Pacific Choir Association in British Columbia.

While both the Danube Swabians and the Sudeten Germans have their own active, well-established clubs, the national umbrella organization of Germans in Canada is the Trans-Canada Alliance of German Canadians, which was founded in Kitchener in 1951 to preserve the diverse cultural heritage of German-speaking Canadians. The Alliance, to which most of the clubs belong, operates like a large corporation with many different sections, each with its own head.

Festivals and celebrations of all sorts are popular among Germans, especially the recent immigrants. One of the most popular celebrations is Mardi Gras. This festival is followed by others, including May Day celebrations, Bavarian, Alpine, children's and other special festivals. German Days, which attract many thousands of visitors, are celebrated in the summer picnic season. The Danube Swabians also have their special days, and celebrate *Kirchweihfest*, a folk festival originally religious in character, in the autumn. The largest German festival is *Oktoberfest*, which first made its appearance in the 1960s under the sponsorship of German clubs. The largest Oktoberfest is now held in Kitchener, Ontario, where it has developed into a major tourist attraction and a cultural heritage celebration.

In most German communities, there is a great deal of preparation for the Christmas pageant, with the traditional Christmas scene, carols and performances from the Old World. The custom of a lighted evergreen tree, which originated in Germany during the early years of the sixteenth century, was introduced to Canada in 1776 by Baroness von Riedesel, whose husband commanded the Brunswick troops. The practice spread, and by 1850 Montreal newspapers were reporting that Christmas trees were in common use.

The first German-language publication in Canada, *Halifax Zeitung,* appeared in the 1780s to meet the needs of German- speaking settlers in Nova Scotia and German troops who were stationed there during the American Revolution. In 1835, Ontario's first German-language paper, *Das Kanadische Museum und Allgemeine Zeitung (Canadian Museum and General Newspaper)* published its first edition. It was later replaced by *Der Deutsche Kanadier (The German Canadian).* Numerous German-language newspapers were published in Ontario between 1850 and 1914, but most of them were short-lived enterprises with very small circulation. Two notable exceptions are *Mennonitsche Rundschau,* which still publishes, and *Der Nordwesten (The Northwestern),* which published between 1889 and 1970 until it merged with its rival, *Der Courier (The Courier),* which had been founded in Regina in 1907.

German-language newspapers disappeared from the scene during the First World War because of a government ban against their publication. Some papers continued to publish in English, but the majority ceased, never to appear again. The ban was lifted in 1920, and for a short while the newspapers enjoyed a revival. The Second World War again saw them slip out of sight, and it was not until after the war that the German-language press began to take on a new life, inspired to a great extent by the large-scale immigration of ethnic Germans after 1948 and the influx of German nationals after 1951. There are now two large newspaper chains, the *Courier Nordwesten* and the Reprich chain, as well as religious papers and special interest publications.

German-language broadcasting is found on privately operated radio stations. There is no typical format for these broadcasts, but

German music is very popular in general, and there are some German-language television programs on cable networks.

Canadians of German origin have contributed to all facets of Canadian life. Their most important contributions, however, rest in the field of agriculture, as the Upper Canada Loyalists and the Mennonites converted virgin countryside into productive soil, and German farmers began grape growing in the Niagara Peninsula. German-Canadian craftsmen have established themselves in wood processing and furniture production, tanning, brewing, the production of rubber goods, textiles and buttons.

Science, the arts, politics and the food industry have all felt the impact of the German-Canadian presence. It is therefore valid to say that since the beginnings of European settlement in Canada, German-speaking people have contributed to the growth and development of our country.

# Greeks

THE HISTORY OF GREEKS in what is now Canada is believed to have started about one hundred years after the voyage of Columbus. The first Greek to arrive in Canada is considered to be Juan de Fuca, whose real name was Apostolos Valerianos, who came from the island of Kefelonia. Valerianos was a seaman for forty years and a pilot for the Spanish government. He explored the coast of California and in 1592 sailed through the strait between the Island of Vancouver and the State of Washington.

Immigration to Canada from Greece began early in the nineteenth century. The first immigrants were seamen who settled in Nova Scotia. Between 1870 and 1880 there were about 39 Greeks in Canada. In 1901, the number of Greeks was estimated to be about 300, of whom 15 were in Nova Scotia, 66 in Quebec, 65 in Ontario, 27 in Manitoba and 96 in British Columbia. According to the 1911 census, the Greek population in Canada rose to 3,650 persons, most of whom were located in the cities of Montreal, Toronto, Quebec, Halifax, Edmonton and Winnipeg. The early immigrants tended to establish their own businesses, in particular restaurants, confectionery stores, hotels and bakeries. Although most Greeks settled in larger cities, some immigrants went into farming in Ontario and in the western provinces. A small number from the island of Skopelos became fishermen on the Pacific coast.

Until the period following the Second World War, there was a gradual increase in Greek immigration to Canada. In 1921, there were approximately 6,000 Greeks in Canada, with 10,000 in 1931 and 12,000 in 1941. Immigration was halted during the years 1941–45, but when the war ended immigration resumed in large numbers, and included Greeks emigrating not only from Greece but also from Egypt, Turkey, Cyprus, Roumania and other countries. By 1951, the Greek population in Canada approximated 14,000 persons, but in the 1961 census this figure jumped to 56,000. Today, there are approximately 170,000 Greek Canadians, of whom approximately 70,000 reside in Toronto, 55,000 in Montreal, 10,000 in Vancouver and the remainder in other urban centres such as Windsor, Winnipeg, Ottawa, Saskatoon, Edmonton, Calgary, Hamilton and London, Ontario.

The vast majority of immigrants who have come from Greece were villagers who had an economic motive for emigrating. The pre-migration period in Greece was characterized by poverty, traditional dowry requirements for the marriage of village women and postwar economic instability and insecurity. Social factors were also important. Once Greek immigrants became established in Canada, they sponsored the immigration of relatives from their native towns and villages.

In rather broad and generalized terms, the Greeks in Canada can be roughly assigned into five social groups. The "old-timers" are immigrants, mainly of rural stock, who came to Canada before the Second World War and had little or no formal education. They constitute a rather small part of the total Greek population but include some of the most wealthy members of the Greek communities. They strongly identify with Greek culture and are especially active in the life of the Kinotis (community). The Canadian-born are, as a rule, well-integrated within the general Canadian society, but nevertheless maintain strong connections with their ethnocultural group. Members of this group tend to be successful professionals or entrepreneurs. The immigrant elite is a rather small group including highly educated immigrants of urban middle-class origin. Among them are professionals, scientists, artists, ship-owners, and others. The process of the integration of this immigrant group into the mainstream of Canadian society was relatively smooth and rapid. Immigrant entrepreneurs are those immigrants who have come to Canada from rural areas since the Second World War and have relatively low levels of formal education and occupational training. Nevertheless, they have succeeded in establishing themselves financially and constitute a dynamic element in the communities in which they reside. If they do not meet the success they anticipate in one

venture, they are prepared to launch into another. This group is active in the restaurant business, fur business, fruit and grocery whole-sale and retail firms, laundries, real estate firms and theatres. Often the Greek businesses, particularly the small ones, serve an important social function. They are informal gathering places where men, accustomed to the village *cafenio* (coffeehouse) meet to exchange views and information regarding community affairs. The skilled and unskilled Greek workers who came to Canada after the Second World War probably constitute the majority of the Greek population in Canada. They can be found in restaurant and hotel enterprises working as unskilled labour, and in the maintenance enterprises, garment industry, hospital staffs and in heavy industry . These immigrants work hard in order to attain financial security and to establish enterprises of their own.

Despite the differentiations noted above, these five groups share certain socio-cultural characteristics which bind them together as a distinct minority group. They all speak the same language and adhere to the Greek Orthodox Church; above all they desire to maintain and perpetuate these common characteristics which give them a sense of collective identity.

For many Greeks, the church is the centre of their social as well as religious life. Most Greek communities have built an Orthodox church of their own or are using a building which they have bought or rented.

The most important religious festival for the Greeks is Easter, and this is the occasion when many of the customs dearest to the Greek heart are revived each year. It is customary for women to decorate a replica of Christ's tomb with flowers at noon on Good Friday. In the evening the congregation, carrying lighted candles and singing hymns, joins in the procession as the tomb is carried from the church, around the district and back again on a symbolic journey. The congregation assembles again at midnight on Saturday with unlit candles in their hands. They are awaiting the moment when the priest comes from the sanctuary with a lighted candle and announces "Christ has risen". The priest lights the candles of those nearest to him, and they in turn light others, repeating the priest's words, until the entire church is filled with lighted candles. After the service, it is customary to carry the lighted candle home and to make the sign of the cross over the doorway in smoke. In Toronto, for a number of years the midnight service was held at Varsity Arena with close to 10,000 in attendance.

A festival of a quite different sort occurs on Greek Independence Day, the national holiday of Greece, which is celebrated by Greeks everywhere on March 25. It commemorates the day in 1821 when Greece began its war of independence from more than four hundred years of Turkish rule. The Greek communities nearly always perform in native costumes and there may be a special church service, a parade, speeches, dancing and refreshments.

The Orthodox Greeks in Canada are organized into communities in the larger centres, each incorporated under provincial charter and having an elected council. They are under the spiritual guidance of the Metropolitan Bishop of Canada and, through him, the Greek Orthodox diocese of North and South America with headquarters in New York. The aim of these organizations is the preservation of Greek religion, language and culture. Wherever possible the community supports a church and a school. At the school attached to St. George's Cathedral in Montreal, English, French and Greek as well as other subjects are taught. Affiliated with each community is a women's auxiliary or Philoptochos Society. ("Philoptochos" means "friend of the poor".) These auxiliaries are benevolent societies and are active in raising money to help the needy of the community and providing other assistance.

The American Hellenic Educational and Progressive Association (AHEPA) is an American fraternal organization which was introduced into Canada in 1928. Since then, chapters have been founded in many Greek centres across the country. It seeks to cultivate good citizenship and loyalty to Canada, to disseminate information on Greek culture and to promote high standards of ethics among its members. Affiliated with AHEPA is a woman's auxiliary, Daughters of Penelope, and two youth groups, Maids of Athena and Sons of Pericles.

Not as large as AHEPA but also based in the United States is the Greek Orthodox Youth of America (GOYA). Both young men and women may join this organization whose aims are to promote religious, educational, cultural, social and athletic activities in the spirit of Greek ideals.

In addition to these large organizations which cut across the Greek community, there are many regional societies whose members all come from a certain district or town in Greece. These societies are philanthropic and social bodies aimed at assisting newcomers and also helping the regions from which the newcomers emigrated. Some of these organizations, such as the Pan-Macedonian Union and the Pan-Lakonian Federation, are older groups and the Canadian chapters are affiliated with the American parent body. Other organizations have been formed more recently by newcomers.

Among the other numerous organizations,

the Greek-Canadian Cultural Society, founded in Vancouver around 1960, encourages people of Greek origin to become Canadian citizens and to interpret the traditions, ideas and culture of Greece for the people of Canada. The Canadian Hellenic Cultural Society of Toronto consists of members who are university graduates of Greek descent. About 70 per cent were born in Greece and 30 per cent in Canada. Among its objectives are to advance the cultural level of the Greek community and to encourage and financially assist students of Greek descent to obtain a university education. Finally, there is a Society of Greeks from Egypt which draws together a group of Greeks who have settled almost exclusively in Montreal.

The numerous Greek-Canadian newspapers perform an important function in the process of the integration of newcomers into Canadian life. In Toronto, two main newspapers have been published on a regular basis. *Hellenikon Vema* (*Hellenic Tribune*) is an independent Greek-language newspaper, founded in 1958. The main aim of the newspaper is to help immigrants by giving them information about Canada, its laws and its customs. News from Canada and Greece appears in the pages of the newspaper, as well as a sports page and a women's page.

*Eleftheros Typos* (*The Hellenic Free Press*) is another weekly independent newspaper published in the Greek language. It has been published in Toronto since 1966. In addition to regular political news from around the world, especially from Greece, articles of general interest and accounts of local community activities also appear in the newspaper. Numerous Greek newspapers also appear in Montreal. Among them are *Drasis,* a monthly newspaper written entirely in the Greek language and established in 1971; a monthly

*Parikiaka Nea*; and the *Greek Canadian Tribune.* The Greek community in Vancouver publishes the newspaper *Hellenic Echo* and that in Ottawa, the *Hellenic Canadian News.*

Greek Canadians are found in academic life and the professions and are widely involved in many service industries in Canada, including the restaurant and wholesale food business. They combine their knowledge of Greek customs and methods with a desire to make important contributions to Canada, while at the same time making other Canadians aware of their heritage.

# Guyanese

**ALTHOUGH GUYANA** is geographically in South America, its historical development is more akin to that of the former British West Indies. As in the latter area, the plantation economy of Guyana necessitated the large-scale importation of labour, resulting in a racial variation in the country which still exists. The population now consists of approximately 400,000 persons of East Indian descent, over 350,000 persons of African descent, and about 4,000 Chinese, a few thousand Portugese, and a population of Amerindians, the original inhabitants.

Guyanese of Portugese ancestry were the first group to immigrate from Guyana to Canada. In the absence of official statistics, various sources claim that at least 7,000 Portugese, who made their livelihood mainly in business and commercial firms, became aware of Canada through people who were employed in Canadian banking firms in Guyana, and while most of the immigration flow was headed for England, some Portugese Guyanese chose Canada. Many were also influenced by the Scarborough Fathers, a Roman Catholic order which is established in Guyana. The steady trickle of immigrants during the 1950s increased during periods of racial and political unrest at various times throughout these years.

The Guyanese of African and East Indian descent came to Canada either as prospective university students or as landed immigrants in search of better economic opportunities, along with a change in the political and social environment of their homeland. The majority of them settled in Ontario, while smaller numbers went to Quebec. Between 1946 and 1976 at least 25,807 people immigrated to Canada from Guyana. The peak years of immigration were 1973 and 1976, when approximately 14,082 Guyanese came to this country.

Among the newly arrived Guyanese, associations like the Metro Guyanese Community Association in Toronto fill the needs of members who, although they have left their homeland, are still culturally and spiritually attached to the country of their birth. Projects are sponsored which include fund raising for senior citizens' homes in Guyana, restoration of churches and the like. There is evidence to suggest, however, that as many of the members begin to feel more at home in Canada, Guyanese are beginning to sever their links with Guyana and to redefine their goals and roles. Many of them are becoming more involved with groups that are concerned with the needs of the Black community. There are also a few theatrical groups in which Guyanese are involved, through which it is hoped that West Indian culture will be propagated in Canada.

While the recently arrived Guyanese community in Canada is still trying to adjust to its new home, evidence suggests that Guyanese Canadians are beginning to take an active part in the community and cultural life of this country. Many of them are skilled tradesmen, with over one-third of them being in the professional class. This would support indications that the Guyanese have a valuable role to play in the economic life of Canada.

# Haitians

THE ISLAND OF HISPANIOLA was discovered by Christopher Columbus in 1492. The island became a Spanish colony, but in 1697 Spain ceded the western part of the island to France. The French colony became Haiti, in 1804 the first Black country to gain political independence from European colonial powers. With the exception of Barbados, Haiti has the highest population density of any country in the western hemisphere. Since the beginning of the twentieth century, the undeveloped economic and social situation has contributed to the emigration of considerable numbers of Haitian workers to the Dominican Republic, on the eastern part of the island, and to Cuba. Since the late 1950s, the political and economic situation in Haiti has led to the immigration of substantial numbers of educated Haitians to Canada and to other parts of the world.

As Canada's immigration policy changed during the 1960s to eliminate racial discrimination, many Haitians who had completed their studies abroad began to immigrate to Canada, especially to Quebec. Interest in Quebec began to increase in the early 1960s when Quebec, in the midst of the Quiet Revolution, was introducing educational reform.

Many of the Haitians who arrived after 1967 found teaching positions in the Quebec educational system, and settled in the larger urban areas. Since 1972, 12,000 Haitians have immigrated to Canada, and although many of them were classified as professionals, the majority were skilled tradesmen and service workers. These workers are heavily represented in the textiles and plastics industries, and also as domestic servants.

Most Haitians who immigrated to Canada came from the urban centres, and although the language of the people of Haiti is Creole, French is the official language of the country, and it is spoken by all members of the Haitian professional class. It is natural, then, that Haitians would be attracted to Quebec. Most of the Haitian organizations are located in the Montreal area. During the early years, when a large proportion of the Haitians immigrating to Canada considered themselves under self-imposed political exile, many of their associations tended to be politically oriented. These early Haitian immigrants found that their linguistic and cultural similarities transcended the traditional colour distinction, and acceptance into French-Canadian society was relatively simple. Problems of integration into Canadian society appear to be more pronounced among the post-1972 immigrants than among those who came earlier.

Haitian organizations also work to promote and encourage cultural interests through artistic, drama and folklore groups, and through publications dealing with various questions relating to the arts and social sciences.

Haitians are quietly making a solid contribution to Canadian life, particularly in Quebec. For example, a Quebeçois of Haitian origin was elected to the National Assembly as a member of the Parti Quebeçois in November, 1976. In Montreal, a new medical centre was opened, staffed primarily with Haitian doctors. As a major non-white French-speaking group, they add a further dimension to the whole range of ethnocultural groups which make up Canada.

# Hungarians

AN EXACT STUDY of early Hungarian immigration to Canada is complicated by the fact that immigration statistics for this period do not differentiate between Magyar and non-Magyar Hungarian subjects. Today, the term "Hungarian" is used to describe Magyar-speaking people, but until the First World War, the term was a political designation which might also have included some Slovaks, Croatians, Ruthenians, Roumanians, and various other peoples.

The destination of many early Hungarian immigrants to the new world was the United States. Many of the participants of the unsuccessful revolution of 1848–49 sought refuge there, and they were later joined by others whose motivations for emigration were a combination of political and economic grievances. Canada did not attract substantial Hungarian immigration until the 1880s, when some Hungarian settlers in the United States became disenchanted with opportunities there, and decided to seek a fresh start in Canada.

The first Hungarian colony in Canada was established in Manitoba, through the efforts of Count Paul d'Esterhazy. In 1885, under the tutelage of this immigration agent, a group of Magyar and Slovak families from the United States settled in the lands of the Manitoba and

Northwestern Railway Company near the town of Minnedosa. In the following year another group settled the Qu'Appelle Valley of Saskatchewan. Initially, great difficulties were encountered, but a decade later, a new influx of settlers, this time directly from Hungary, led to the strengthening of the Qu'Appelle Valley Colony and the establishment of several others. Numerous settlements bear witness to the Hungarian origin of their founders: Esterhazy, Kaposvar, Otthon, and Halmok. After the turn of the century, the initial agricultural emphasis of the first settlers shifted, and more Hungarians began to appear in mining towns, lumber camps and in railway construction and in cities. Hungarian settlement, which had been concentrated in the farming lands of western Canada, now gradually spread throughout the country, particularly into the industrial centres of Ontario.

In 1901, the Canadian census recorded 1,549 Canadians of Hungarian origin, although it is impossible to determine how many were actually Magyars, and how many were Hungarian citizens of other ethnocultural origin. By 1911, this number had increased to 11,648, and kept growing until the First World War halted further immigration.

The end of the First World War brought with it new political and economic conditions in Hungary, which was divested of its former territories and impoverished by the war. Furthermore, Magyars who now found themselves under non-Hungarian rule had an additional incentive to emigrate, and the 1920s saw a considerable influx of Hungarians into North America. The United States, which might have been expected to have been the primary destination of most of this migration, introduced a quota system which drastically cut down on immigration. As a result, a correspondingly greater number of Hungarians looked to Canada as a possible destination. So extensive was the pressure for immigration that between 1926 and 1930, some 26,000 Magyars entered Canada, the flow coming to a halt only with the onset of the Depression.

Between 1930 and the end of the Second World War, Hungarian immigration to Canada virtually ceased. The few individuals who did enter the country were permitted to do so in the interest of uniting members of families, or were classified as political refugees. Substantial Hungarian immigration into Canada did not resume until 1948 when a more liberal Canadian immigration policy coincided with the existence of a large number of homeless or displaced persons, fleeing the effects of war and the results of Soviet occupation of their homeland. Postwar Hungarian immigration into Canada had a decided political motivation, and of the 12,000 Hungarians who entered Canada between 1948 and 1956, many were from the middle and upper levels of Hungarian society.

When the effects of Stalinist-style rule stirred the Hungarian people to open rebellion in 1956, some 200,000 Hungarian refugees fled to Western Europe before the advancing Soviet armies crushed all resistance. In this crisis, the Canadian government dispensed with the usual screening procedures, and some 37,000 Hungarians were admitted to Canada. This constituted the last great wave of Hungarian immigration. More recently, the number of Hungarians entering Canada has remained at a fairly steady average of about 500 newcomers annually.

Unfortunately, the normal difficulties which accompany the immigration process were exacerbated in the case of the Hungarian refugees of 1956. Not only did these immigrants have to confront the usual problems of learning a new language, acquiring new skills, obtaining employment and establishing themselves in an unfamiliar environment, but the hurried nature of their departure from Hungary, the emotional impact of the events of 1956, and the large numbers of people involved for whom transportation, accommodation and training had to be organized in a short period of time, all contributed to the difficulties experienced by these immigrants. Many had friends or relatives already in Canada, helping in the process of adjustment. Furthermore, many of the immigrants were educated, highly qualified professionals, which made it easier for them to find jobs. Finally, having lived through the upheavals which Hungary experienced during the Second World War, and then under Soviet occupation, many were experienced in adjusting to new conditions. Thus, despite enormous difficulties, the large majority of Hungarians who came to Canada after 1956 successfully integrated into Canadian life.

According to the 1971 census, there were 131,890 persons of Hungarian origin in Canada, of whom 86,835 (65.8 per cent) claimed some knowledge of the Hungarian language. Of this total, the largest concentration of Hungarian Canadians resided in Ontario, with 65,695, or 49.8 per cent of the Hungarian-Canadian population. Substantial numbers were also found in British Columbia (16,600 or 12.6 per cent), Alberta (16,240 or 12.3 per cent), Saskatchewan (13,825 or 10.5 per cent), Quebec (12,570 or 9.5 per cent) and Manitoba (4,405 or 4.1 per cent). The substantial number of Hungarians, 52,070 or 39.5 per cent, residing in Canada's western provinces is a reminder of the original pattern of Hungarian settlement in this country, with the largest number settling on the open farmlands of the west. As immigration patterns shifted, the industries of Ontario and Quebec proved

more attractive. During the Depression, agriculture became unprofitable, forcing many to abandon their homesteads, and swelling the numbers in urban centres, which further contributed to the shift in the ratio of urban to rural Hungarians in Canada. The political immigrants of the last thirty years have reinforced this trend, since most of these individuals had skills which could best flourish in an urban environment.

The largest single concentration of Hungarian Canadians can be found in Toronto, with 23,350 individuals, or 17.8 per cent of the total Hungarian-Canadian population, and this represents just over one-third of the Hungarian-Canadian population of Ontario. The second largest Hungarian-Canadian centre is Montreal, which has 11,480 individuals. This represents 91.3 per cent of all Hungarians living in the Province of Quebec. Other major urban centres with a substantial Hungarian-Canadian population are Vancouver (8,210), Hamilton (7,755), St. Catharines (6,885), Calgary (5,520), Windsor, Ontario (4,010), Winnipeg (3,860), Edmonton (3,230), Regina (3,135), Ottawa (1,965), Kitchener (1,830) and London (2,215). On the whole, it may be said that well over two-thirds of all Canadians of Hungarian origin live in major urban centres.

According to the 1971 census, some 79,880 Hungarians in Canada are Roman Catholic, constituting 60.6 per cent of the total Hungarian-Canadian population. Some of the Catholics belong to the Greek Catholic Rite. There are also substantial numbers of Hungarian Canadians who are members of the United (13,335 or 10.1 per cent), Presbyterian (12,200 or 9.3 per cent), Lutheran (5,515 or 4.2 per cent) and Anglican (4,700 or 3.6 per cent) churches in Canada. The remainder are dispersed among other Protestant denominations, the Jewish faith and adherents of the Byzantine rite. Only a small group claim no religious affiliation.

The Roman Catholic Church has about sixteen parishes throughout the larger centres of Hungarian population in Canada. Among the larger parishes are those in Toronto, Montreal, Winnipeg, Vancouver, Hamilton, Calgary, Windsor, Edmonton, Regina and London. In addition to their religious functions, these parishes also constitute social and cultural centres, as well as centres for the instruction of the young in religion and on occasion in the Hungarian language. For example, the parish school in Toronto has over three hundred pupils. Affiliated with the Roman Catholic Church is the Greek Catholic (Uniate) Church, which among Hungarian Canadians includes four parishes, one each in Kirkland Lake, Hamilton, Windsor and Welland.

The Hungarian Presbyterian Church of Canada is also highly developed, with sixteen congregations across the country from Montreal to Vancouver. In addition to the major centres of Hungarian-Canadian population previously mentioned, each of which has a Presbyterian church, other centres include Welland, Delhi, Brantford and Oshawa, all in Ontario, as well as several congregations in smaller towns in western Canada. There are also considerable numbers of Hungarians belonging to other Protestant denominations, among them congregations belonging to the United Church in Montreal, Toronto, Niagara Falls and Port Colborne. There is also a Baptist congregation in Toronto.

Many Hungarians in Canada are represented by the Canadian Hungarian Federation, an umbrella organization which brings together some 120 local clubs, societies and churches. The executive of the Federation includes 50 directors from all Canada, as well as a plenary assembly which includes one delegate from each member organization.

Although the Canadian Hungarian Federation is a completely independent body, it does send observers to an annual meeting with the American Hungarian Federation and attempts to co-ordinate its activities with those of the American body. Furthermore, the Federation in Canada co-operates actively with other East European ethnic organizations in their common political protest against Soviet domination.

Associated with the Federation is the United Hungarian Fund, which handles fund raising for the Federation. The Fund has established a day care nursery in Toronto and is at present worth some $150,000. Among the aims of the Fund is the promotion of various Hungarian cultural and educational activities, notably Hungarian language schools, as well as the maintenance of an emergency fund for the assistance of refugees from Hungary.

On the local level, the various Hungarian organizations of Montreal are represented by the Grand Committee of Hungarian Churches and Societies, inasmuch as the president of the Committee has the responsibility of acting as a spokesman for the interests of the Montreal Hungarian community in its dealings with other Hungarian groups in Canada. By this method, the difficulties and expense of Canada's distances are minimized, while the interests of the community are promoted.

Another important central organization is the Hungarian School Board, an arm of the Canadian Hungarian Federation dealing exclusively with the promotion of schooling in the Hungarian language. The Board co-ordinates the activities of numerous Hungarian-language community schools in Hungarian churches and Hungarian community centres across Canada. For example, the Toronto Hungarian community can claim five Hungarian-language schools maintained by the community. Similar schools are operated in Montreal, London, Calgary and Winnipeg. Another important function of the Hungarian Board of Education is the preparation of teaching materials and textbooks for use in these schools. Because such materials should be related to the Canadian environment, the Board is at present preparing a series of primers and Hungarian readers for use in the Hungarian community's schools. Because of these and similar educational efforts by other groups, the Hungarian language is currently being offered as a credit course in two Toronto high schools.

For the younger members of the community, the Hungarian scouting groups provide activities for both Boy Scouts and Girl Guides, with active branches in Toronto, Hamilton, Oshawa, Winnipeg, Calgary and Montreal. The regular scouting program includes such features as summer camps, and is supplemented by activities designed to preserve cultural traditions. Most Hungarian churches also have youth groups.

There are numerous organizations for adults within the community. The Hungarian Engineers' Association is a professional group with its headquarters in Montreal, but with branches in other important centres of Hungarian-Canadian population such as Toronto, Calgary and Vancouver. Uniting some five hundred members, the Association plays an important role in maintaining professional contact among its members, as well as organizing the prestigious Engineers' Ball in Montreal.

In Toronto, an important social and cultural role is played by the Hungarian Helicon Society, a cultural organization with about two hundred members, organized into a youth section, and a section for older members. Although it has no branches outside of Toronto, the Helicon Society does have individual members across Canada. As with the Engineers' Association, the Helicon Society organizes an annual ball in Toronto which is the highlight of the community's social season.

There are two veterans' associations active within the community, one composed of former members of the Hungarian army and the other of former members of the Hungarian gendarmerie. Both have branches across the country, and work towards the improvement of the situation of veterans in Canada. In addition to this, the Rakoczi Association, composed of former officers in the Royal Hungarian Army, attempts to provide a bridge between the activities of veterans and civilians in the community. In addition to these groups, there is also the Freedom Fighters Association, with its headquarters in Toronto, and several branches across the country. This group is made up largely of refugees from the 1956 Hungarian Revolution. It works to promote the interests of political refugees, and actively campaigns against Soviet domination of Hungary.

Another group of mutual benefit societies are the Transylvanian Fraternities, made up of Hungarians from Transylvania. There are branches in Toronto, Tillsonburg, Montreal and Calgary working for the interests of Transylvanian Hungarians. The Szechenyi Society, directed from Calgary, promotes Hungarian culture across Canada, sponsors secondary and post-secondary educational courses, helps authors and provides reference material on Hungary to libraries. One of its accomplishments was the establishment of an endowed chair of Hungarian studies at the University of Toronto.

The Society of Canadian Hungarian Writers has an obvious cultural and literary dimension to its activities. Most important Hungarian community organizations are organized around the various Hungarian Houses which exist in many Canadian cities. For example, the Hungarian Canadian Cultural Centre in Toronto provides a meeting place for all of Toronto's Hungarian groups. The Toronto Hungarian House is the largest Hungarian community centre of this kind outside Hungary. Every year it sponsors the Hungarian community's contribution to Toronto's Caravan, as well as hosting numerous other folk festivals and occasional exhibitions. A similar house exists in Delhi, Ontario, which has a large Hungarian population of approximately 1,500 members engaged in tobacco farming. The Kossuth House, located in the countryside, serves the communities of Kitchener, Guelph and Galt, a Hungarian House exists in London, Ontario, and the Club Hungarica performs a similar function in Fort Erie. In the Montreal community, a church auditorium serves this function.

Of considerable interest is the existence of two Hungarian museums in Canada. The Hungarian Historical Museum of Toronto was founded by the Order of Vitez, with the help of two veterans organizations, and contains exhibits illustrative of various aspects of Hungarian history. The other museum, in Oshawa, is dedicated to the Royal Hungarian Air Force, and contains exhibits illustrative of its activities and history.

The publishing of Hungarian-language newspapers in Canada started well before the First World War. The first two papers were the *Kanadai Magyarság (Canadian Hungarians)* and the *Kanadai Magyar Farmer (Canadian Hungarian Farmer)*. After the war, these were replaced by the *Kanadai Magyar Ujság (Canadian Hungarian News)* a Winnipeg-based weekly, and for some time semi-weekly, which existed until recently. With the growth of the Hungarian community in Ontario, publishing activities gradually shifted there. Newspapers were launched in Hamilton, Toronto and elsewhere, but only a few survived beyond a few years. Today, Toronto is the centre of Hungarian publishing acitvities in Canada. The city's largest independent weeklies are the *Kanadai Magyarság (Canadian Hungarians)* and the *Magyar Élet (Hungarian Life)*. The former was founded in 1950, the latter in 1948 in South America and moved to Toronto in 1956. Both provide general news service, contain many advertisements, and cater to Hungarians in Toronto as well as in other cities of North America. There are also some more specialized papers. The weekly *Sporthiradó (Sport News)* concentrates on news of sporting events. The publication *Menorah-Egyenlóség* is a Hungarian-language weekly newspaper serving Canada's Hungarian-speaking Jews. The *Kanadai Magyar Munkás (Canadian Hungarian Worker)* has been the chief press organ of the Hungarian-Canadian left since 1929. The *Krónika (Chronicle)* is a recently established popular journal published monthly by the Hungarian Canadian Cultural Centre. Other Hungarian-language papers and newsletters are published by various clubs and churches. Toronto also has a small Hungarian-language book-publishing industry centered mainly around the city's two larger weekly newspapers.

Not all of the Hungarian press's products appeared in Hungarian. Some were published in English and aimed in part at second and third generation Hungarians in Canada and the United States. An example was the *Young Magyar American*, a popular monthly which was published in Winnipeg during the second half of the 1930s. At present there is the *Canadian-American Review of Hungarian Studies*, published by the Hungarian Readers Service of Ottawa for Hungarian intellectuals and scholars interested in Hungarian studies.

In recent years, the Hungarian community in Canada has acted as host for two important events which have gathered together Hungarians from all over the world. In 1973, the Primate of Hungary, Cardinal Mindgzenty, visited Toronto, and some 10,000 Hungarians attended the event. Two years later, in 1975, the Toronto Hungarian House was the scene of a Hungarian World Congress, which included representatives of Hungarian organizations from all over the world. Each of these gatherings was amplified by exhibitions, folk dancing and other cultural events; in 1975 one such event was a world jamboree of Hungarian Scouts.

Bringing different skills with them and responding to different conditions in their new homeland, the several waves of Hungarian immigrants have made varied yet equally valuable contributions to Canadian life. In general it may be said that early arrivals had helped to carve prosperous farms, towns and provinces from the Canadian wilderness, while the latter groups have provided some of of the diverse skills and talents required by a modern and complex society.

# Icelandic

THE HISTORY OF ICELAND is one of colonization. In 1974 that nation celebrated the 1,100th anniversary of its colonization by Norsemen. Iceland was first settled in 874 by Norwegian chieftans fleeing King Harhals the Fairhaired of Norway. In 930, the first session of Althing, the Icelandic parliament, oldest in the world, declared the Icelandic Republic. The period of the Republic of Iceland lasted from 930 to 1264 and is known as the Golden Age of Iceland.

The first Icelander to be linked with Canada is Leif Ericsson, whose voyages were part of the great Norse era in Europe. Around the year 1000 he made voyages of discovery via Greenland along the eastern coast of North America, the first time Europeans had travelled to this continent. He named this new land Wineland (Vinland). In 1003, an expedition of Icelanders arrived on the continent to examine the possibilities for settlement. The first child of European descent to be born in North America was Snorri Profinnson, during the winter of 1003–04, and many people in Iceland today can trace their ancestry back to this time. These settlers tried to settle in several locations but hostilities with the native people and other factors forced them to abandon their plans for a permanent settlement. The expedition returned to Greenland in 1006.

Recent archeological finds indicate that early Icelandic settlers attempted to establish a settlement in Newfoundland. They did maintain contacts with Baffin Island and Labrador which were instrumental centuries later in opening the way to the later voyages to North America by the Spanish, French, English and other Europeans.

Prior to mass migration to North America, there were sporadic Icelandic ventures to the United States. For economic reasons Icelanders began leaving their homeland in the late 1850s, and the first Icelandic immigrant to Canada arrived in 1872, twenty-year-old Sigtryggur Jonasson. A party of 22 people had left Iceland that year bound for the United

States, where all of those destined for North America had gone since 1855, but Jonasson was determined to come to Canada. He was familiar with the English language and learned of conditions in Ontario. Later, in 1873, a party of 150 Icelanders arrived in Canada, of which two-thirds settled in Rosseau in the Muskoka region of Ontario, while the remainder went on to the United States. The Rosseau settlement did not prove to be permanent, and many settlers left within the year.

In 1874, a group of 365 Icelanders settled at Kinmount in Victoria County, Ontario. From this group, eighty migrated to Nova Scotia and settled at Markland for several years. As an agent for the Canadian government, Jonasson helped settle the Kinmount group. The Icelanders were not satisfied with either of these settlements and began to look elsewhere. In the spring of 1875, Jonasson set out with a number of other Icelandic spokesmen to investigate the possibilities for settlement in the Red River Valley. They decided on an area on the western shore of Lake Winnipeg, because of its fish, game, land and forests.

The settlers left Kinmount in September, 1875, and arrived at Willow Point on October 21 of that year. This move coincided with the arrival of 1,400 Icelandic immigrants in the country, of whom 1,200 moved to the west, settling in what was known as New Iceland. In 1876, Jonasson brought two parties, numbering some 1,200 immigrants, directly from Iceland. They settled at Icelandic River (now Riverton), Mikley (Hecla Island), Hnausa and Arnes. The colony did not prosper at first, so Jonasson and others organized a logging industry to bolster the colony. In 1896, Jonasson was elected to the Manitoba legislature.

The New Iceland colony was situated just north of the Manitoba boundary when it was founded in 1875. For the first months of its existence, the Icelandic colony was part of the Northwest Territories, but became part of the District of Keewatin when the territorial district was organized in 1876. The Icelandic settlers established their own administration, and a constitution was drafted and adopted in 1878. Gimli was the capital of New Iceland, a colony unique in the history of settlement in Canada.

Icelanders in Canada regard New Iceland as the mother of the Icelandic settlement of North America. It functioned as a temporary home for Icelandic immigrants who later moved elsewhere, founding new colonies in Pembina County of North Dakota, the Argyle settlement northwest of Winnipeg, and other rural settlements in Manitoba at Selkirk, Swan Lake, Shoal Lake, Brandon, Piney, Arborg, and numerous other locations.

The Icelandic population of Winnipeg rose spectacularly in the 1880s. Icelanders destined for Gimli would often remain in Winnipeg in search of employment. Gradually the Icelandic community network developed in Winnipeg to meet the social needs of its members. Also, Winnipeg developed into a leading centre for Icelandic culture and activities in North America. The Icelandic population in Winnipeg eventually grew to more than seven thousand persons.

From the establishment of the earliest permanent settlements, Manitoba has always remained the centre for Icelandic activities in North America. Even as late as the 1931 census, 70 per cent of Icelanders living in Canada resided in Manitoba, the main regions of settlement being the New Iceland area, Winnipeg and Argyle. In 1971, 13,070 Icelandic Canadians, 46.9 per cent of the national total, resided in Manitoba.

Icelanders also settled in substantial numbers in Saskatchewan. Churchbridge was pioneered by Icelanders in 1885, and a large number of Icelandic farmers located in north-central Saskatchewan around Foam Lake, Quill Lake and Fishing Lake between 1891 and 1909. Other districts in Saskatchewan settled by Icelanders are Wynyard, Kandahar, Mozart and Elfros. The number of Icelandic families in Saskatchewan has remained fairly constant. In 1971, 3,095, or 11 per cent, of Icelandic Canadians lived in Saskatchewan, approximately the same number as in 1931.

A large number of early Icelandic settlers went to Markerville, Alberta. Since the end of the Second World War, Icelanders have been attracted to Calgary, Edmonton and Red Deer. In 1971, 2,620 Icelanders lived in Alberta.

The most spectacular increase in Icelandic immigration has been in British Columbia. Whereas only 4 per cent of Canadians of Icelandic origin lived there in 1931, by 1971 there were 5,745 people of Icelandic origin living in British Columbia, which was 20 per cent of all Icelandic Canadians. Their main destination has been Vancouver, and to a lesser extent, Victoria. There are also large numbers of Icelanders in the Peace River Valley and in communities along the coast.

Ontario has attracted an increasingly greater proportion of Icelanders over the years, particularly to Toronto, but this province has not proven as attractive to Icelanders as it has to other ethnocultural groups. Only 2,680 Icelandic Canadians, less than 10 per cent of the national total, lived in Ontario in 1971. Few Icelanders have been attracted to either Quebec or the four Maritime Provinces.

The Lutheran Church is the national church of Iceland and, as with most ethnic groups, the newly arrived immigrants continued their national religion in Canada. There were some differences among the early settlers in North America over what form of Lutheranism to adopt. This division stemmed from two of the leading pioneers among the early Icelandic immigrants, Reverend Pall Thorlaksson, ordained in the United States, who followed the views of the Norwegian Synod then largely dominated by the Missouri Synod (German Lutheran), and Reverend Jon Bjarnason, who found these views too conservative and followed the more liberal doctrine of the Lutheran faith as it had been in Iceland. Their disagreement spread throughout the early Icelandic settlements in North America. It had already become established in the Lake Winnipeg communities by 1877, but died down when Thorlaksson and most of his adherents in that region went to the Dakota territory.

The division was short-lived. By 1885, Icelandic Lutherans in both Canada and the United States established the Icelandic Lutheran Synod at Winnipeg. The Synod provided a central organization to service the religious needs of the scattered Icelandic communities in North America.

As with other Scandinavian groups, there has been a gradual shift towards the United Church of Canada among Icelandic Canadians. In the 1931 census, 77.2 per cent of Icelandic Canadians were Lutherans. The United Church was the second largest denomination, with 8.4 per cent. In the 1971 census, there was no individual breakdown within the four Scandinavian groups as to religious affiliation. For the group as a whole, 33.4 per cent of Scandinavians were Lutherans and 26.9 per cent United.

In 1931, 80.6 per cent of Canadians of Icelandic origin claimed Icelandic as their mother tongue. By 1971, this figure had declined to 29.2 per cent. This does not mean that the 7,860 Canadians who claim Icelandic as their mother tongue could speak it readily; rather it could, for many, reflect a pride in having some knowledge of a language other than the two official languages of this country.

There is a record of a handwritten newspaper that circulated in Gimli during the first winter of settlement, 1875–76. *Framfari (Progress)*, founded in 1877, was the first printed Icelandic paper in North America. It ceased publication in 1880. *Leifur* (named after Leif Ericsson) was established in Winnipeg in 1883, and ceased publication in 1886.

In September, 1886, *Heimskringla (The World)* was founded in Winnipeg. This paper supported the Conservatives; for those Icelanders who preferred the Liberals, *Lögberg (The Tribune)* was founded in January, 1888, in Winnipeg. Since Icelandic-language newspapers did not become established in the United States, the above-mentioned publications have always enjoyed a wide circulation on both sides of the border. The newspapers have served as a connecting link for the various Icelandic communities of North America. In 1959, the two papers merged to form *Lögberg-Heimskringla*, which is published in Winnipeg in both Icelandic and English. There are some 3,000 subscribers to the paper.

*The Icelandic Canadian* was established in 1942 by the Icelandic Canadian Club. It is a quarterly published in the English language and contains articles on Icelandic history, culture and social development in North America.

Other periodicals that have served the Icelandic community over the years include *Sameiningin (Unity),* the official publication of the Icelandic Lutheran Synod from 1885 to 1961; *Timarit,* an annual published by the Icelandic National League; and *Almanak,* an annual founded in Winnipeg in 1895 and discontinued in 1954.

As soon as they became established, Icelanders began to develop various organizations to meet the social and cultural needs of their members. The first Icelandic organization outside the church was the Icelandic Society, founded in Winnipeg in 1877. It was reorganized in 1881 and renamed the Icelandic Progressive Society. In 1882, the first Icelandic hall in North America was built in Winnipeg.

The Icelandic National League was founded in Winnipeg in 1919. The central organization was in Winnipeg and chapters were founded in the principal Icelandic communities in Canada and the United States. The aims of the League are the maintenance of Icelandic cultural heritage, co-operation between Icelandic people in North America and Iceland, and the promotion of Canadian citizenship by Icelandic immigrants in their new homeland. There are eleven chapters active today: six in Manitoba, in Winnipeg, Selkirk, Morden, Lundar, Gimli and Arborg; three in Alberta, in Calgary, Red Deer and Edmonton; one chapter in North Dakota, and an honorary branch in Iceland.

The Icelandic Club was founded in 1938 in Winnipeg. This organization uses English exclusively in its activities. It was founded by Canadian-born members of the Icelandic community. The club emphasizes Icelandic heritage in the service of Canada, and publishes *The Icelandic Canadian*. There are Icelandic Canadian clubs in Winnipeg, Calgary, Coquitlam and Montreal, but there is no formal organization linking them. The club in Winnipeg recently amalgamated with the Icelandic National League chapter in Winnipeg, the clubs being similar in outlook since most of their members are Canadian-born and English-speaking.

For many years, the Icelandic Student Society at the University of Manitoba promoted Icelandic culture among students of the second generation. This Society was founded in 1901 but had ceased activities by 1930.

The Icelandic Festival Committee is located in Winnipeg, and organizes Islendingadagurinn, the annual Icelandic Festival of Manitoba. The first Icelanders' Day was held in Winnipeg on August 2, 1890. Its original purpose was to commemorate the granting of a constitution to Iceland in 1874, but it gradually came to be an occasion for honouring the pioneer settlers. The festival was held in Winnipeg until 1932, when the site was moved to Gimli. Today the festival is primarily a social gathering.

Icelanders have established rest homes which are provincially administered. Two such rest homes are the Bethel Home Foundations in Selkirk and Gimli. Another organization is the Canada-Iceland Foundation in Winnipeg which is supported by all other Icelandic organizations. This foundation receives grants and funds to promote Icelandic culture and literature.

In recent years the Icelandic Canadian Youth Organization has emerged, sponsoring dances, plays, and various social activities for Canadians of Icelandic origin interested in learning of their cultural heritage. The organization is rather informal, operating during the autumn and spring of the school year. Much of its impetus comes from students at the University of Manitoba. However, many of its members include high school students and young Icelandic Canadians interested in maintaining their ancestral culture. The organization was formed in the 1972–73 academic year at the University of Manitoba.

Limited to the Lutheran religion, hampered by their lack of fluency in English, and living in isolated rural communities, the early Icelandic settlers faced severe cultural hardships in adapting to Canadian society. Because of this, Icelandic ethnocultural organizations were generally, even in Winnipeg, completely separate from the rest of society.

Several generations of Canadian-born Icelanders have broken down the barriers of isolation through education in Canadian schools and participation in Canadian society. This adjustment is reflected by changes in Icelandic ethnocultural institutions. Many people of Icelandic origin cannot readily participate in social activities conducted in their ancestral tongue. However, Icelandic clubs have adapted by accepting English as their working language.

One of the most distinctive cultural accomplishments of Icelanders in this country has been the establishment of a Chair of Icelandic Language and Literature at the University of Manitoba. Classes in Icelandic had been taught earlier at Wesley (now United) College from 1901 to 1927, and also at the Jon Bjarnason Academy until 1939. With the closing of the Academy, Icelandic-Canadian leaders began to raise funds for an endowment to present to the Board of Governors of the University of Manitoba for establishing a Chair in the Icelandic language. When, in 1951, the endowment fund was over $150,000, the president of the university announced that a chair would be established for the following academic year.

In 1920, Canada won the gold medal in ice hockey at the Olympic Games in Antwerp, the first year of international competition in that sport. Canada's representatives were the Winnipeg Falcons, a team formed by Icelandic sports clubs in Winnipeg (the falcon is an Icelandic national emblem). The Falcons won the Allan Cup in 1920, the Canadian senior hockey championship.

Canadian citizens of Icelandic origin have been very active participants in politics. For such a small ethnocultural group, a disproportionately high number of Icelanders have been elected to the Canadian Parliament and to various provincial legislatures. The success in politics of so many individuals of Icelandic origin can be partly attributed to the fact that Icelanders arrived in Canada earlier than many other immigrant groups.

Icelanders rate high on many counts. This small, concentrated group has, in Canada, produced literary figures, public men, judges, and professors. They are among our oldest "New Canadians", and as such have aided in the settlement and development of Canada in a manner which parallels the contributions of many larger groups in our country.

# Indians (East Indians or South Asians)

THE TERM "EAST INDIAN" has been used to describe the people of the Indian Subcontinent. However, the term Indian or 'Indo-Canadians' has also been used for people from the modern state of India.

Although Indian immigration to Canada has been relatively recent, throughout most of the twentieth century rising immigration from India has brought the total to an estimated 100,000. From the 1950s to the 1970s, approximately 90,000 Indians joined the approximately 2,000 persons of Indian origin who had been living in Canada in 1951. They are rapidly evolving into a significant component of the larger Canadian society.

The census of 1971 showed that 67,925 people of Indian origin resided in Canada. Only 18,795 of them resided in British Columbia, which is surprising since the main concentration of Indians has historically been in the Province of British Columbia. However, recently arrived immigrants have changed the composition of the Indian community completely.

Until the 1950s over 90 per cent of the Indian immigrants entering Canada were Sikhs from the plains of the Punjab on the Indian subcontinent, and more than 90 per cent of them settled in British Columbia. Many of the Sikhs first became interested in Canada when a detachment of Sikh soldiers returned by way of this country after attending Queen Victoria's Diamond Jubilee in 1897. A few retired soldiers of the British Indian Army who entered Canada during the first decade of the twentieth century also sent back word about the opportunities in Canada.

In Punjabi villages stories were circulated of the boundless chances for improvement in Canada. Many Sikhs were willing to emigrate with a view to improving the lot of their families by returning with a fortune.

The 1914 census lists 258 Indians in British Columbia. It was about this time that the steamship companies began to encourage immigration to Canada, and during the 1905–08 period, about 5,000 Sikhs entered the country, beginning with 45 in 1905 and increasing to 2,623 in 1908. Erroneously called "Hindus", they were almost all adult males of peasant origin. They were basically labourers and found jobs in logging camps, lumber mills, mines and railway camps. These early immigrants did not sail from the Indian subcontinent but from ports such as Hong Kong and Shanghai. Instead of returning home after they had served in British armed forces and police in the Far East, they came to Canada.

At the time that the Sikhs arrived, the European population of British Columbia was feeling threatened by the immigration of large numbers of Chinese and Japanese with their growing competition in the labour market and in the general economy of the province. The influx of Sikhs did little to alleviate the situation, and it was not long before racist sentiments were being directed against the Sikhs, who were more distinctive than other Orientals in their appearance. Various measures were taken to stop the immigration of the so-called Hindus. By application of the "continuous voyage" regulation in 1908 and further legislation in 1910, Indian immigration was virtually stopped. The "continuous voyage" regulation stated directly that Indians could come to Canada only by continuous passage from India.

Partially as an attempt to challenge this legislation, in 1914 a Sikh named Gurdit Singh chartered a Japanese ship, the *Komagata Maru*, and brought a group of 376 Indians to Canada. They were refused admission because they had stopped at eastern Asian ports. After two months on board ship in Vancouver harbour, they were obliged to return to the Orient.

In the years 1909–13 only 29 Indians were admitted to Canada. In 1919 an order-in-council was passed which allowed Indians already in Canada to bring their wives and children into Canada, but many immigrants could not afford to do so at that time. For more than a decade, only a small number of dependants were admitted as an "act of grace."

Immigration remained limited until after the Second World War.

During the 1920s and 1930s the number of Indians in Canada dwindled. Some of them returned to India and some went to the United States. In the 26 years from 1920 to 1945, only 675 Indian immigrants entered Canada, so that by the time of the 1951 census there were only 2,147 persons of Indian origin living in Canada.

Indian immigration aroused numerous legislative responses in addition to the measures taken to limit immigration in British Columbia. In 1907 the legislature of British Columbia amended the Provincial Election Act in order to disenfranchise British citizens of Asian origin in the province. The Indians were British subjects, and theoretically could not be excluded from voting in a British dominion. This and other legal measures taken against them seriously limited economic opportunities open to Indians.

Before the Second World War Indian immigrants worked mainly as labourers in railway construction, in logging operations, and at other similar heavy labour projects. Some later found jobs in agricultural pursuits, particularly on dairy farms in the Fraser Valley and on fruit farms in the Okanagan. The majority, however, entered lumbering. It has been estimated that approximately 75 per cent of Indians in the province were occupied in the production and processing of forest products in the prewar period.

At the end of the Second World War eligible Indians were admitted to the full rights of citizenship for the first time, and in 1947 the House of Commons passed a bill which enfranchised Canadians of Asian origin living anywhere in the country. This was the time when India and Pakistan became independent nations and members of the Commonwealth.

In 1951, special arrangements were concluded between Canada and the governments of India and Pakistan which fixed a quota system allowing 150 Indians and 100 Pakistanis to enter Canada each year. Six years later, a new agreement increased the number of Indians allowed into Canada to 300 per year. Further expansion of immigration due to changes in the immigration laws in 1962 and 1967 has resulted in a steady increase in the numbers arriving from India in the past two decades. In 1967, the year that the latest regulations went into effect, 5,924 persons entering Canada listed India as their country of origin, and thus in 1967 alone the number of Indians who migrated to Canada was equal to 90 per cent of Canada's entire Indian population in 1961.

In contrast to the predominantly adult male, former peasant or ex-soldier migrants of the period prior to the Second World War, much of the current Indian immigration consists of a steadily increasing volume of professionally and technically qualified individuals accompanied by their families. Moreover, many of the present day migrants are not coming directly from the Indian subcontinent, but from such places as Fiji, East Africa, Trinidad and Tobago, South Africa, and many other countries. The steady increase of immigrants from these areas, together with the movement from the subcontinent itself, has seen the total number of Indians arriving in Canada grow from fewer than 1,000 in 1963 to more than 6,500 in 1972 and almost 15,000 in 1974. The large number of immigrants entering, coupled with an augmented natural increase consequent upon the establishment of more normal patterns of family life, has witnessed rapid expansion in the size of the Indian population in Canada, from 2,000 in 1951 to nearly 70,000 in 1971 and to over 100,000 today.

According to the 1971 census, among those 67,930 Canadians of Indian origin, 20 per cent, or 13,555, had been born in Canada. Indians lived in every province and territory of the country, although the largest number, 30,925 were in Ontario, followed by 18,795 in British Columbia and 6,510 in Quebec. Since the 1960s, Ontario has been receiving more Indian immigrants than has British Columbia. Metropolitan Toronto had nearly 15,000 persons of Indian origin in 1971, compared with 10,000 in Greater Vancouver. Indians have generally not established ethnic neighbourhoods or residential districts.

It is estimated that a significant segment of the Indian population is concentrated in the production, processing and distribution of forest products. Many other Canadians of Indian origin are now working in other areas of the Canadian labour force. The earlier immigrants of the postwar period tended to be highly educated middle-class people, but in recent years Indian immigrants come from many walks of life.

The educational attainment for the Indian immigrant is still higher than the national average for Canada, and the proportion of skilled technicians and professionals among the Indian immigrants is significantly high, as compared with other immigrant groups. The majority of the immigrants are making a highly successful adjustment to their new environment.

Reflecting the growing ethnic, linguistic and religious heterogeneity of the present-day Indian communities, the group is rapidly changing from being a largely circumscribed and exclusive Sikh society in British Columbia to being a more widely representative cross-section of the Indian people. The influence of the Sikhs in the community has diminished significantly as their share of the total population has declined.

There are more than forty religious and secular organizations and associations counted among the Indian community in Metropolitan Toronto alone. There are also many in Vancouver, where the community has been more firmly established. The associations and groups are generally formed along linguistic and religious lines, although there are several secular associations representing members of the community. The Punjab speaking (mostly the religious Sikhs and the Muslims) and the Gujarati speaking (Hindus and other religious groups), for instance, are the most numerous groups in Toronto. In addition to these, Indian immigrant groups that originated outside the Indian subcontinent tend to maintain their own identity and to form their own associations in Canada.

Religion as an aspect of the Indian social organization in Canada is not as significant as on the Indian subcontinent, but it nevertheless exerts considerable influence on the daily lives of Indian families. Annual festivals such as *Deepavali (Diwali)*, meaning literally "row of lamps" and symbolizing the triumph of good over evil, and *Baisakhi*, marking both the advent of spring and the founding of *Khalsa*, the militant bond of Sikhism, are observed in the temples as important rituals in the life of the individual.

Sikhs have founded their own *gurdwaras* in Greater Vancouver, and seven in other parts of British Columbia. These and other temples have been built and supported by public subscription and donations from the Sikh community. The *gurdwaras* are much more than just temples to the Sikh community, for they also serve as native language schools and social and recreational centres. The Sikh community centre in Vancouver, completed in 1967, contains a school, library, senior citizens'

housing unit and playground.

There are at least two Indian-language printing presses, one in Toronto and the other in Richmond, British Columbia, and several English-language magazines and newspapers. The three regular journals are the bimonthly newspaper *The Canadian India Times* from Ottawa, the weekly magazine *India Digest* from Toronto, and the quarterly magazine *The Indo-Canadian*, published in Richmond, British Columbia. There are also a number of newsletters published by the various groups as well as radio and cable television programs in British Columbia and Ontario which specialize in Indian music and news.

Home and family life are a sustaining force for Indians in Canada. The family provides the individual with security and economic stability, and prescribes the individual's rights as well as obligations. The spirit of an extended family is important in the minds of many Indians, although their family in Canada is primarily a nuclear unit. Marriages generally take place within their own religious and ethnic groups and many of the prospective partners come from the Indian subcontinent. It must also be noted however, that a number of Indian men and women are now marrying Canadians of non-Indian origin.

Indians in Canada, like most Canadians, live according to the general lifestyle of Canadian society but attempt to retain their traditional cultural and religious beliefs. Many wish to instill in their children a thorough knowledge of their religion and to foster the growth of a moral and spiritual interpretation of life according to their religious beliefs. The Indian immigrants are enriching the multicultural character of Canadian society. Indian yoga, cooking and music, along with the long and rich cultural and philosophical heritage of India, are shared among Indians and their fellow Canadians.

# Indonesians

THE LARGE MAJORITY of immigrants from
Indonesia to Canada (nearly 90 per cent) are
Indonesians of Chinese origin. They are the
descendants of labourers from mainland China
who went to Indonesia to work in colonial
enterprises as wage earners from 1870 to 1930.
Many of those who have arrived in Canada
have come for economic reasons, since highly
educated and trained people have few opportunities in Indonesia for employment amidst
the unstable economic and political conditions
of the home country. In addition, Indonesians
of Chinese origin have come to Canada to seek
wider political freedoms. Many suffered
discrimination of some form in Indonesia, even
though they were legally equal to other Indonesian citizens, and they have therefore come
to Canada to seek complete equality.

As an identifiable group, Indonesians are
among the newest arrivals in Canada, most of
the immigrants having come in the 1970s. The
first Indonesian residents in Canada were
students who obtained permanent residency
when their studies were completed. Non-student immigrants began to arrive after 1966
when immigration laws were eased. Between
1966 and 1975 a total of 1,366 Indonesians
entered Canada, and in 1976 it was estimated
that the total Indonesian-Canadian presence
was 2,000 persons. The Indonesian community
is thus one of the smallest in Canada.

Indonesian immigrants usually settle in the
larger urban centres of English-speaking
Canada, with Toronto and Vancouver being
the most popular cities. They are, however,
widely dispersed throughout these and other
metropolitan areas.

The fact that the majority of Indonesian
immigrants are university-educated or have a
high degree of technical training has enabled
them to integrate successfully into Canadian
life. Despite the recency of immigration and
settlement, Indonesian immigrants have a
positive attitude toward the Canadian educational and cultural lifestyle. Since most have
come to Canada in reaction against political
elements in Indonesia, it is important to them
that their anticipation of freedom, political or
otherwise, and of being treated equally as citizens has become a reality.

The group is now in the process of being
organized. Indonesian immigrants in Toronto,
for instance, formed the Indonesian-Canadian
Association in 1969. Young people have also
formed their own group, the Young Indonesian Association of Toronto. The main aim of
these associations is to assist Indonesian
nationals to meet each other and to help
newcomers adjust to Canadian society. Their
activities are largely recreational and social.
There are approximately two hundred families
who are members of the Indonesian-Canadian
Association of Toronto, and a similar type of
association, the Canadian-Indonesian Society,
has been formed in Vancouver.

Indonesians from different ethnic-religious
backgrounds are united by their language and
national identity. Because of language barriers, many Indonesians of Chinese origin do not
affiliate themselves with the Chinese community at large. The majority of them wish to be
known strictly as an Indonesian community.

# Inuit

FOR OVER TWO CENTURIES, it has been common practice to refer to the Inuit as Eskimos. This is not a word, however, which the Inuit use when referring to themselves. "Eskimo" is an Amerindian word meaning "eaters of raw flesh", while the word "Inuit" means "the People," the singular of which is "Inuk", a person.

There are over 20,000 Inuit living in Canada today. Linguistically and culturally, they are an Arctic people whose sphere of influence extends from Siberia in the west, through Alaska and northern Canada, to Greenland on the east. There are some 100,000 Inuit living in the world as a whole.

Like all Canadians, the Inuit were originally immigrants. Inuit immigration, along with that of other North American natives, was a part of the country's prehistory. Both Indian and Inuit groups were fully established by the time more recent European settlers began to arrive.

Their bond to the land of the far north has always been the most important feature of Inuit life. Traditionally, the Inuit lived off the land from what they could hunt or create from immediately available resources. Later, European traders appeared. The Inuit acquired new skills and took advantage of new opportunities, but the land continued to be the chief means by which they made their livelihood. Today, the vast majority of Canadian Inuit are living in communities which are north of the tree line. They are distributed among the Arctic islands and on the mainland of the Northwest Territories, northern Quebec and the coast of Labrador.

No one is certain when the first Inuit moved from Asia, across the Bering Strait and into North America. It seems, however, that these people were part of the last of a series of successive migrations over this route. Archeological evidence suggests that the Inuit arrived over 5,000 years ago in what is now Alaska. Early Inuit development occurred in three main phases: the Denbigh Flint, which evolved into the pre-Dorset phase; the Dorset phase; and the Thule phase. Each of these cultural phases overlapped considerably and contained regional variations necessitated by the availability of game and other resources. Each phase was, however, a stage of development north of the tree line, and each was nomadic-hunting in nature.

The Denbigh Flint culture was the first to have arrived from Asia. Evidence of this culture was first found at Cape Denbigh, Alaska. The most significant feature of the Denbigh Flint people was their skill in the formation and use of chipped flint tools. The pre-Dorsets were the Denbigh's immediate inheritors. They are known to have hunted with bows and arrows and harpoons, and to have lived in skin tents in summer and small semi-sunken villages in the winter. They began migrating eastward about 2500 BC, and remnants of their culture have been found throughout Arctic Canada as well as Labrador and Greenland.

The Dorset culture is believed to have begun as a response to a warming of climate between 1000 and 800 BC. The earliest Dorsets were probably located in the Foxe Basin region, although the first evidence of their existence was uncovered at Cape Dorset on Baffin Island. The Dorsets made widespread use of soapstone lamps, which were fuelled by animal oil, for heating, lighting and cooking. As well, they used sleighs shod with bone or ivory for travel. They are remembered in legendary Inuit history as the *Toonit*. The Dorsets eventually settled throughout most of pre-Dorset territory, although they did not extend as far westward (Coppermine seems to have been their western limit), but they went even farther south than the pre-Dorsets, down the coast of Labrador and into Newfoundland.

Evidence of the birth of the next cultural development, labelled the Thule, was found in northern Alaska and dates back to about the year 900. Inuit oral history contains stories of how the Thule people invaded and took over the regions of the Dorsets. This cultural replacement process appears to have been completed by about 1300.

The Thule culture was the direct antecedent of what has come to be regarded as the traditional Inuit way of life. The Thule were primarily a whale-hunting people, but also proved capable of adapting themselves to a life based on whatever a particular region had to offer, and are known to have made use of musk-ox, caribou, walrus and most other Arctic game. The Thule were the first Inuit to make use of dogs to haul sleds, and for hunting seal and polar bear. Their culture was an elaborate one and they were skilled artists. The remains of their stone, turf and whalebone houses can still be seen throughout the Arctic.

The approximate date by which the Thule culture had become that of the traditional Inuit was 1700. Traditional Inuit life is portrayed as a single, cohesive entity, integrating small hunting bands, seal hunting, igloos, kayaks, sled dogs and parkas. Such a picture is a considerable oversimplification. The Inuit of the Mackenzie Delta lived in relatively large groups, built their winter houses of logs and depended mainly upon

whale meat for their survival. The Labrador Inuit had a similarly rich environment and also lived in large groups. The Copper Inuit were noted for their skill at sealing through the ice, and for their use of local copper to make tools. Their region was centred on Victoria Island and was considerably less abundant than that of other Inuit. They spent most of their time in small groups of fifteen to twenty persons and, like all small-group Inuit peoples, came together in bands of about one hundred in winter. During the winter season a community meeting place would be erected alongside the smaller family homes.

In addition to the aforementioned groups, there were the Caribou Inuit of the Keewatin District, for whom survival depended on the movement of the caribou herds. As well, the Netsilik Inuit, the Sadliq Inuit, the Igloolik Inuit, the Ungava Inuit and the Inuit of south Baffin Island also composed distinct groups. Each of these groups had its own particular lifestyle which was manifested in such external features as differences in personal ornamentation and style of dress.

In short, regional differences formed an important part of the traditional culture of the Inuit. There were, however, major elements which were common to all these regional ways of life. One such element was the Inuktitut language, which was common even though it contained many dialects. Social customs also possessed an underlying similarity. All groups, for instance, gathered together for songs and drum dances, for contests such as finger pulling, and games of skill such as wrestling. All groups depended on some method of community disapproval for the maintenance of order.

Religious beliefs everywhere centred on a spirit world based in nature, entailing the observance of certain taboos, and accessible through the mediation of shamans. There was, too, the common acceptance of the necessities of northern survival: the necessity of sharing; for the acceptance of death for the weak in times of scarcity; for the enduring of hardships; for concern with the good of the group. Above all, there was a total reliance on northern resources: meat and fish, including caribou, whale, seal and musk-ox, which were caught by men everywhere for food; skins, especially caribou and seal, prepared by the women for clothing and shelter; animal bones and flint for tools and weapons; dogs for travel; the snow itself, in the right conditions, for blocks to build winter homes. Together, these common elements may justly be regarded as forming the basis of a traditional way of life.

Traditional Inuit life lasted in some parts of the Arctic until about 1920. In other regions, the next phase, one of a decline in the traditional way, started much earlier.

The traditional period was a time of fights and quarrels, of natural disasters and of outstanding men. Inuit oral history records many of these events. It is known, for instance, that the Mackenzie Inuit engaged in fairly widespread fighting with the Déné Indians; that in the nineteenth century a journey was taken from Byot Island to Greenland led by a man named Kridlak; that the Ungava Inuit were harrassed by the Naskapi Indians when the latter obtained guns. As yet, the compilation of a completely detailed picture has not been undertaken.

The Inuit's first significant contacts with Europeans occurred with fishermen on the Labrador coast some time during the fifteenth century. This initial exposure became the first step in a long process which eventually made the Inuit of the present Canadian Arctic into Canadians, and created an environment which necessitated a complete restructuring of Inuit life.

Major early factors in this transformation process were the Arctic whaling industry of the nineteenth century, the white fox fur trade of 1900–39, and the activities of various missionary groups. Later developments involved the establishment of RCMP posts, the construction in the 1940s and 1950s of Arctic military bases, and the increasing availability of government programs, services and constraints. Most recently there has been the exploration for, and the exploitation of, Arctic mineral resources such as oil and natural gas.

The Inuit's response to these external excursions was to shift the emphasis of their lives away from the land. Region by region they began to participate in the search not just for food and clothing, but for articles of trade, such as whale meat and bone, seal and fox fur.

Ostensibly, these changes were progressive. Inuit life became easier through access to manufactured goods, including rifles, cloth, matches, snowmobiles, radio and telephones. There were, however, grave disadvantages associated with these shifting lifestyles. For the first time, the Inuit were dependent not only upon themselves and the land, but also on external markets. When these markets collapsed, the people were suddenly cut off from their newly adopted means of support, and periods of very real hardship occurred. For example, the whale oil market collapsed in the eastern Arctic around 1850. In the western Arctic, the demand for whalebone declined about 1900. Famine occurred when the fox fur trade experienced major declines after 1930. In the face of these events, there could be no compensatory return to traditional ways. On the one hand, the old pre-rifle skills had been lost and manufactured goods had become a necessity. On the other, the rifle had caused sufficient depletion of Arctic wildlife so that total dependence on Arctic country food resources was impossible. Population increases also influenced the shift away from the traditional lifestyles.

Ultimately, the necessity for external goods caused the Inuit to switch to a cash economy. Although this change has been relatively successful, results in some areas indicate major problems. The North is not easily suited to the creation of jobs, nor have the Inuit had adequate time to adjust to the educational and social requirements imposed by a wage-earning economy.

The change in Inuit life from land-dependence to trade-dependence to cash-dependence has caused a major change in Inuit residence patterns. It began with the need to have access to trading posts, and then with a tendency to form somewhat more settled communities in the vicinity of these facilities. The trend toward centralized settlements continued as military establishments provided wage-earning opportunities, governments set up central schools and nursing stations, and private industry created employment opportunities. This second phase of development had the most marked effect on Inuit life. It has meant that external agencies have become the controlling factor in the formation of Inuit communities.

Loss of independence and control were both detrimental to Inuit-Canadian life. Especially serious was the deterioration of Inuit standards of health, as the Inuit, early in their contacts with Europeans, found themselves to have little resistance to new diseases. Partly, too, their deteriorating health was associated with their changing lifestyle. Time spent trapping fox for the fur trade could not be spent in hunting caribou for food. There was an increasing reliance on external goods for food and clothing. Diet became less nourishing,

clothing less suited to Arctic conditions. The situation worsened as Arctic goods found fewer ready markets and wildlife numbers decreased. Recent government medical programs and payments have allowed for some improvements, but problems remain owing to the low income levels frequently experienced.

Change in status, situation and physical well-being have meant that the Inuit experienced a severe degree of what is currently known as "culture shock." One other factor that should also be recorded is the lack of respect by outsiders for Inuit ways and beliefs, and the systematic attempts by various groups, particularly missionaries and educators, from early days up to the 1960s to undermine the Inuit confidence in their traditions. It is a factor which has had grave consequences in terms of Inuit disorientation. This, in turn, has increased Inuit susceptibility to the notion that they must remain in poverty, and to standard social problems related to hopelessness of life, such as alcohol abuse.

By 1950, Inuit life in Canada had deteriorated to a very serious extent. Up to this time, little interest had been shown by the various levels of Canadian government. The RCMP had administered justice and, in conjunction with traders and missionaries, welfare and medical aid. Education had largely been in the hands of the churches. From 1950 on, however, government involvement has increased. An extensive program to cure TB was carried out in the 1950s. Hospitals, nursing stations and schools have all been established on a regular basis; a housing program has been undertaken; communications have been improved. In short, the Inuit have gradually come into touch with those services common throughout the rest of Canada. Yet even these improvements have caused larger problems, since in many cases government involvement in Inuit life has come to represent the final loss of Inuit control over Inuit events.

The Inuit of the 1970s have at least superficial access to the full range of modern technological advantages and to the rights, freedoms and privileges accorded to other Canadians through the Territorial Council of the Northwest Territories, the provincial governments of Quebec and Newfoundland, and the Government of Canada. They are also acknowledged as being among Canada's most disadvantaged citizens.

They are not happy with this situation. Nor are they prepared to accept the idea that outsiders know best. Important initiatives are being taken, just a few of which can be described below. Most of these initiatives have been taken with outside help, frequently in the form of government advice or financing. They are, however, essentially Inuit developments.

In 1958, the first Inuit Community Council was formed at Baker Lake in the Northwest Territories. This form of local government has now spread to all Inuit communities. In 1971 the Inuit national organization, Inuit Tapirisat of Canada, was founded. Its aim is to give the Inuit a voice in negotiations with government, a chance to participate fully in Canadian society, and an opportunity to maintain and develop their culture. Inuit Tapirisat now has its headquarters in Ottawa and operates through six regional affiliates: the Northern Quebec Inuit Association, COPE (The Committee for the Original Peoples Entitlement), the Labrador Inuit Association, the Baffin Region Inuit Association, the Keewatin Inuit Association, and the Kitikemot Inuit Association.

The Inuit are not a conquered people. Prior to the present decade, however, they had not been the subject of any attempt by any government to enter into formal agreements regarding the land on which they live. This issue has become a matter of increasing significance, as external excursions have become more pressing, and especially as external interest in the exploitation of Arctic natural resources has grown. To date, the Northern Quebec Inuit Association is the only group to have participated in the drawing up of a final agreement, settlement of which, subject to community ratifications, was announced in November, 1975.

Inuit Tapirisat has caused major studies of land use and occupancy by Inuit in the Northwest Territories to be undertaken, as well as studies of renewable and non-renewable resources. A proposal for the settlement of land claims, based on these studies, was put forward in February, 1976. The proposal was withdrawn. However, a new proposal was approved at a general assembly of Inuit at Frobisher Bay on October 17–22, 1977. Issued in the form of a proposed agreement in principle, the two-page statement emphasizes that Inuit of the Northwest Territories are seeking the right of political self-determination within Canadian Confederation; protection of their lands, waters and wildlife; preservation of their language and culture; and the right of compensation for past, present and future use of Inuit lands.

The proposal calls for the establishment of a new territory called Nunavut ("Our Land") with its own government. The territory would cover approximately 1.5 million square miles, generally everything north of the tree line.

The Labrador Inuit Association has also begun a land claims project. Ultimately, this association will present its own proposal. The Inuit everywhere have asked that their claims be settled before any further major development of the North is allowed to take place.

COPE has been involved in presentations

to the Mackenzie Valley Pipeline Inquiry in pressing for the retention of a moratorium on development at Cape Bathurst and of a land freeze at Tuktoyatuk, and in efforts to prevent offshore drilling in the Beaufort Sea. Activities have also been undertaken by various groups for the alleviation of social problems. An Inuit non-profit housing corporation has been set up, work has begun in several centres on problems related to alcohol abuse, a project— Maliiganik Tukisiiniakvik— for the improvement of legal services and facilities has been established at Frobisher Bay, and discussions have been entered into by all major associations for the improvement of government programs.

The Inuit have not yet discovered a satisfactory means of ensuring appropriate standards of living for the majority of their people. A development which has, however, resulted in an improvement in almost all Inuit communities is the community co-operative. The first co-ops were begun in 1959. They are well adapted to Inuit society in that they are based on the principles of group sharing and group welfare. In 1966, federations of regional co-ops began to take place for the provision of additional economic stability and marketing power. The Quebec Federation, formed in 1967, now has its own marketing service in the south; the Northwest Territories Federation took over Canadian Arctic Producers Ltd., a government-sponsored non-profit company based in Ottawa, in 1973. Co-ops are involved in a wide range of enterprises including air service at Pelly Bay, school building at Povungnituk, and retail stores in a number of centres. The most famous aspect of co-op endeavour is the distribution and marketing of Inuit works and handicrafts. The soapstone carvings, prints, batiks, articles of clothing and works of embroidery of Inuit artists and

craftsmen everywhere are now widely available throughout Canada and in various parts of the world. A most recent Inuit enterprise has been the establishment, by Inuit Tapirisat, of the Inuit Development Corporation, which is intended to serve as the business arm of the Inuit of the Northwest Territories.

Considerable effort is being made by all Inuit associations to ensure not only the preservation of Inuit culture, but also its increased vitality and growth. The Inuit Cultural Institute, formed at Eskimo Point, and the Inuit Cultural Association, founded at Igloolik, provide two examples of work in this area. The Northern Games, which first took place in 1970, have been established as biennial celebrations of northern people's physical skills and pastimes. At present, the most obviously flourishing aspect of Inuit culture lies in the area of visual and plastic arts. Breakthroughs into new media have been achieved: into soapstone rather than ivory carving at Port Harrison in 1950; into print making beginning at Cape Dorset in 1957; still later into work with duffle and other cloths. New cultural developments lie in the production of books by Inuit authors and films by the Inuit film company Nunatsiakmiut.

Government authorities have, by and large, come to accept the necessity for increased openness to Inuit life and customs in the school system. Although Inuit children are still being sent to high schools in the south, more local schools are being built. Also, curricula are being developed to relate better to the facts of Inuit life, and to provide for the teaching of Inuit history and other subjects. Inuit classroom assistants are being hired to facilitate the use and strengthening of Inuktitut in the primary grades. The Inuit are endeavouring to see that these developments are continued, broadened, and made still more meaningful. Adult education programs and on-the-job-training are also considered highly relevant. For example, Inuit Tapirisat is currently involved in the promotion of a management training program.

In 1974, the Northern Quebec Inuit Association prepared and presented a brief expressing its members' concern in the field of communications. The underlying message was relevant to Inuit everywhere in Canada: programming and systems dominated by southern requirements and lifestyles could not fully serve the Inuit or provide them with a proper means of self-expression. Since that time, NQIA has been instrumental in the establishment of its own communications society, Taqramiut Nipingit, Inc. This society, in turn, is setting up high-frequency radio stations in various Quebec Inuit communities. A similar radio operation is provided by Western Arctic Communications to such centres as Paulatuk, Northstar Harbour, Holman Island and Tuktoyatuk. Several Inuit newspapers and magazines are also in operation, including *Inuit Today*, published by Inuit Tapirisat; *Inuvaluit*, the organ of COPE; *Inukshuk* appearing in Frobisher Bay, the *Messenger* at Eskimo Point; and *Tuturuat* at Povungnituk. Radio programming for production over CBC Radio is also being carried out, sponsored by Inuit Tapirisat and its affiliates.

These are some of the responses currently being made by Canada's Inuit to the facts of their lives as Canadians, a life which has, at times, been unsatisfactory but which the Inuit desire strongly both to change and to keep the same. The Inuit want change in that they desire better lives for themselves through science and technology, but they want to retain their culture and traditions, their lands and their customs that have been theirs for centuries, and which originally formed the basis for civilization in Canada.

# Iranians

THE PEOPLE OF IRAN, formerly and more popularly known as the Persians, come from one of the Islamic countries of the Middle East, where flourished one of the earliest civilizations in recorded history. In the twentieth century Iran has become a very important country because of its vast petroleum resources.

As an identifiable group, Iranians are among the newest arrivals to Canada, most of the immigrants having come in the 1970s. Few immigrants have been here as long as 10 years. Between 1946 and 1965, only 283 people entered Canada from Iran. The early Iranian residents were students who obtained permanent residency when their studies were completed. Non-student immigrants began to arrive after 1966 when new immigration laws came into effect and entry requirements were eased. From 1966 to 1975, the number of immigrants had increased relatively, with 1,730 immigrants being recorded from Iran. Other Iranians came from countries such as West Germany, France and England. Therefore, according to immigration statistics, between 1946 and 1975 a total of 2,438 Iranian citizens immigrated to Canada. The Iranian community is one of the smallest in Canada, consisting of perhaps a few more than 3,000 persons.

Immigration statistics show that the choice of place of residence for the Iranian immigrants has almost always been the largest urban centres in Canada, in particular

Toronto, Montreal and Vancouver. They are, however, widely dispersed throughout the cities and surrounding suburbs.

Due to the recency of settlement and limited size of the population, the Iranians in Canada are not yet formally organized. The Iranian culture is predominantly Islamic; approximately 98 per cent of Iranians profess Islam, the official religion of that country, and Iranian immigrants belong to the Islamic community at large in Canada.

Since the Iranian community is very small and scattered, activities are centered around family, kin and friends, and interpersonal ties formed by the family and friendship group are more important than ties afforded by a formally organized association.

The Iranian community may take its own definite shape by the time that sufficient numbers of the immigrants have gathered to form a "community" and when the majority of those immigrants become firmly established within Canadian society.

# Irish

IRELAND IS A PREDOMINANTLY Roman Catholic country where Gaelic was once the universal language. During the Middle Ages, the influence of the church in Ireland made the country the centre of ecclesiastical learning in Western Europe and the first country north of Italy to produce a written literature in its native language. This golden age came to an end, however, with the Norse invasions of the ninth and tenth centuries. With the subsequent invasion of the Normans under King Henry II in 1171, the country entered a centu-ries-long period of domination by England, and the Irish fared badly under English rule. In fact, before Southern Ireland gained Dominion status and Northern Ireland acquired its own Parliament (1921), conflict, repression and rebellion were commonplace.

Annual emigration was slight before 1783, averaging perhaps a few thousand a year, the majority of whom were Scottish Irish from largely Protestant Ulster. During the long French Revolutionary and Napoleonic Wars, substantial emigration occurred only during the temporary peace of 1801–02. But with the advent of a permanent peace of 1815, emigration gained a considerable momentum. Several factors combined to swell it, the most important by far being overpopulation.

Ireland's climate, the fertility of its soil, the character of its agricultural system and the ease with which a bare subsistence could be obtained by growing potatoes had all combined to encourage population growth in the early years of the nineteenth century. By the 1840s, when the largest Irish exodus to North America took place, Ireland was the most densely populated country in Europe with a population of 8.25-million people surviving on about 13.5 million acres of arable land. Over 60 per cent of these people were engaged in agriculture, and of these, over 80 per cent were said to be living in the midst of squalid surroundings, destitution and disease. To further complicate matters, there was a high birth rate but no corresponding growth in industry and agricultural improvements. When agricultural improvements were introduced, the small farmers and the labourers or cottiers were often adversely affected.

It was nevertheless the failure of the potato crop, the only source of food for thousands, that provided the greatest impetus for emigration. Between 1828 and 1845 there had been thirteen years of partial crop failures. In 1846–47, however, the blight was more widespread and devastating than it had ever been before and with typhus following upon famine, huge numbers died. For those that lived, emigration offered the only hope for the future.

To agrarian distress was added urban discontent, caused by unemployment in the handweaving industry. In 1830 it became particularly severe after customs duties were removed and Ireland was flooded with factory-made products from England. As a result of developments such as these, many artisans and craftsmen were displaced.

Ireland, like Great Britain, was also hard hit by depressions such as the Great Depression of the 1880s. During this period it was estimated that a half-million Irish were short of life's necessities. Once again, emigration became very attractive.

Irish historians cite evidence showing that their ancestors landed in Canada centuries before the Norsemen and French. In addition Irish documents reveal that as early as 1594, fishermen, some of whom may have become settlers, were sailing between Ireland and Newfoundland. In neither case, however, was a permanent imprint made upon what is now Canada.

It has never been disputed, though, that substantial numbers of Irish settled in New France during the French regime. Of the 2,500 families that comprised the population of New France in 1700, a hundred were shown by parish registers to have originated in Ireland. In thirty other cases either the husband or wife was of Irish origin.

This Franco-Irish element was augmented by the addition of soldiers who had served in the "Irish Brigade" on the Canadian frontier between 1755 and 1757. This brigade had been brought from the West Indies, and many of them settled in the New World upon leaving the service. Meanwhile, at the eastern end of the continent Irish were filtering into Nova Scotia after the founding of Halifax in 1749. Some of these new arrivals were disbanded soldiers and sailors who had come to the colony with Edward Cornwallis, Halifax's founder. Others were indentured servants from Newfoundland or Virginia seeking an escape from the hard obligations which were their lot. Although theirs is a story of individual rather than group migration, the Irish nevertheless formed about one-third of Halifax's population by 1760.

During this period the Irish were also establishing themselves in Newfoundland. Although Catholics in the colony were subjected to all the disabilities of those in Ireland and were also required to pay special taxes, the Irish nevertheless constituted a significant part of Newfoundland's population by 1753. Newfoundland became still more attractive to Irish emigrants after 1784, the year Reverend James O'Donnell, the real founder of the Roman Catholic Church on the island, arrived from Ireland as Prefect Apostolic.

The first large migration of Irish to the Atlantic Provinces, in fact to any part of the country now known as Canada, occurred in the 1760s when Alexander MacNutt, an Ulsterman, brought a total of 470 Ulster Irish to Halifax in 1761 and 1762. MacNutt had grandiose plans for the peopling of Nova Scotia by Irishmen, but insufficient resources for implementing his schemes. When the British government realized that he could not fulfil the conditions of his huge land grant and that his ambitious projects were accelerating the depopulation of Ulster, it halted his colonization activities.

Nova Scotia also received hundreds of

Ulster Irish from Londonderry, New Hampshire, in these years. They settled around Truro and Onslow. Later in the century the province's Irish population was reinforced by the arrival of the United Empire Loyalists of Irish origin.

Large-scale Irish settlement in Upper Canada (Ontario) did not begin until after the Irish rebellion in 1798. It received additional stimulus in 1823 and 1825 when a failure of the potato crop, misery and disorders in Ireland inspired a government attempt to solve problems at home and populate the colonies by providing assistance to Irish emigrants going to Upper Canada.

The task of superintending the settlement of such immigrants fell to Peter Robinson, who received his commission while in London with his brother, John Beverley Robinson, then Attorney General of the province. Robinson hastened to Southern Ireland, where he collected the names of all those who wished to emigrate. Eventually almost six hundred were selected and sent to Upper Canada, where they settled between the Perth settlement and the Ottawa River. Two years later Robinson, who was made Commissioner of Crown Lands in 1827, brought out another contingent of Irish settlers, some two thousand in all. Most of these settlers were located north of Rice Lake where, around the new village of Peterborough which was named after Robinson, a flourishing community soon sprang to life. Nearly all the new arrivals were young farmers and their families who, with the aid of some government assistance, quickly adapted to life in the backwoods of Upper Canada.

From the points of view of both the emigrants themselves and of Upper Canada, the two Irish settlements were highly successful. Nevertheless, the government decided not to repeat the experiment because of the cost involved. In any event, the favourable publicity surrounding the settlements was enough to induce thousands of other Irish emigrants to journey to the New World without government help.

Peter Robinson also selected hundreds of Irish for settlement on free lands in the Townships of Goulbourn and Huntley in Carleton County and Ramsey Township in Lanark County. These immigrants, who arrived after 1828, provided much of the manpower that went into the building of the Rideau Canal.

Another individual who helped a large number of Irish immigrants to settle in Upper Canada during these early years was Colonel Thomas Talbot, the most remarkable promoter of settlement in the province's history. A former army officer who was descended from one of the most famous families of the Anglo-Irish aristocracy, Talbot founded the Talbot Settlement on 5,000 acres of land fronting Lake Erie. St. Thomas, Ontario, named after Talbot, was the capital of the domain. Between 1804 and 1837, when he was forced to hand over his colonizing agency to the provincial government, he succeeded in settling thousands of colonists, many of whom were Irish, in twenty-seven townships.

Irish emigration to Canada peaked during the "Hungry Forties", when countless thousands of destitute Irish, most of them peasants, were driven from their homeland by famine. In 1847 alone an estimated 80,000 Irish embarked from Liverpool and from 18 Irish ports for the Province of Canada. More often than not, these emigrants were jammed together in narrow, unventilated quarters and forced to endure a voyage which became a brutal test of mere survival. If they were not ill when they began the trip, the chances were high that they would become the victims of typhus, cholera, or measles before the voyage had ended. In August of 1847, for example, the editor of the *Montreal Witness* calculated that of the 60,000 Irish immigrants who had arrived in the St. Lawrence that season, one-third of the males from 16 to 60 years of age were either dead or sick. Today a huge, rugged boulder, which stands on a grassy island on Bridge Street near the entrance to Montreal's Victoria Bridge, guards the bones of thousands of Irish immigrants buried there and nearby.

As a result of the large numbers of Irish who poured into Canada during the 1840s and 1850s, the Irish constituted the largest group in the "British" category at the time of Confederation. When the first census was taken in 1871 they numbered 846,414 in Canada's four original provinces, the English 706,369 and the Scots 549,946. The Irish were second only to the French in number. After Confederation, Irish immigration was overtaken by immigration from England and Scotland, Ireland's population having been drastically reduced by disease, famine and emigration between 1845 and 1851. When the 1971 Canadian census was conducted there were an estimated 1,581,730 Canadians of Irish origin, of whom by far the largest number, 772,875, were living in Ontario. The next largest Irish populations were to be found in British Columbia (176,980) and Quebec (139,100).

In almost all of the larger centres in early British North America there were chapters of the National Society of St. Patrick, which kept alive memories of the homeland and assisted Irish compatriots. In Montreal, the St. Patrick's Society was the earliest of the city's national societies, its constitution having been drafted in 1834.

The first Irish historical society in what is now Canada was founded in Halifax in 1786. Its constitution stipulated that members should celebrate the feast of St. Patrick, Ireland's patron saint, annually and provide relief to their kindred in need. The celebration of St. Patrick's Day on March 17 is now a custom enjoyed by both Irish and non-Irish Canadians alike.

With increased Irish immigration, Irish societies proliferated, becoming important instruments along with the Roman Catholic Church in preserving the identity of the Roman Catholic Irish community. For Irish Protestants, there was the Orange Association of British North America, organized shortly after immigrants from the north of Ireland began to land in this country. Today there are more than thirty-five Irish organizations in this country, the majority of which are located in Ontario, Quebec and the Atlantic Provinces. In Montreal alone there are at least nine different Irish organizations, including such diverse groups as the Ancient Order of Hiberians, the Irish Protestant Benevolent Society and the Jewish Sons of Erin.

Irish societies have been established in most cities from Corner Brook to Vancouver. Some groups, such as the Toronto Irish Immigrant Aid Society and the Irish Choral Society of Scarborough serve special interests in their communities. There are also many Irish clubs and associations which cater to social and sports activities. These include such groups as the Gaelic Athletic Association of Lasalle, Quebec, the Sudbury Shamrock Club and the Irish Sports and Social Society of Edmonton.

Personalities of Irish descent who have made an impact on Canada's development are legion. In the eighteenth century, for instance, Sir Guy Carleton, later Lord Dorchester, the first Governor-in-Chief of British North America, supplied many of the ideas that were incorporated into the Quebec Act of 1774, the act which helped to ensure the survival of

French Canada as a distinct community by guaranteeing it freedom of Roman Catholic worship, the maintenance of French civil law and the continuation of the seigneurial system. Sir Guy also directed the evacuation of troops and Loyalists from the port of New York in 1783. His brother, Thomas Carleton, was the first Governor of New Brunswick.

No less important is the role played by thousands of Canadians of Irish origin who literally built Canada. In the nineteenth century Irish Canadians supplied much of the brawn and labour that went into the construction of the country's canals and railways. As a matter of fact, before the great wave of Irish immigration subsided in the closing years of the century, Irish-Catholic workers from Southern Ireland (now known as the Irish Republic) were synonymous with railway construction. To these Irish-Canadian labourers, Canada owes a great deal of her early development.

# Israelis

*See also Jews*

THE ISRAELIS ARE one of the most recent additions to the Canadian ethnocultural mosaic. It is estimated that there are approximately 25,000 emigrants from Israel in Canada today. They first started arriving during the 1946–50 period, when 435 persons who gave their last permanent residence as Israel immigrated to Canada. The figure jumped substantially for the 1951–57 period, with 6,842 Israelis immigrating. The total for the period 1946–73 was 23,636 persons from Israel who immigrated to Canada.

The Israelis in Canada constitute three main groups. One group includes Jews of European origin who immigrated to Canada after living in Israel for some time. Their mother tongue is either Yiddish or that of the country of their origin, mainly Eastern European. Another group consists of Jews who had immigrated to Israel from one of the Arabic countries, and whose mother tongue is either Arabic or French. The third sector of the community comprises the Sabras, the native-born Israelis, whose mother tongue is Hebrew and whose lifestyle, values and aspirations do not derive from life in the Diaspora but rather from Israeli environment and culture, which includes their particular family background.

The establishment of the state of Israel in 1948 was a milestone in the realization of the Jewish Zionist ideology which called for the creation of a fully autonomous Jewish nation. From its very beginning, Israel had to cope with grave problems of how to absorb hundreds of thousands of newcomers, refugees and displaced persons, many of whom found a haven in Israel. As a consequence, the complex process of nation-building conducted under difficult conditions such as this and others has been accompanied by a reverse emigration from Israel. Canada has been one of the most attractive destinations.

Israelis have emigrated to Canada for a variety of reasons. Those who came from 1948 to the mid-1960s were mainly European Jews who had immigrated to Israel in the mid-1950s. They left Israel because they were dissatisfied with their economic prospects there. The Jews from the Arab countries were often unable to identify with the Israeli social and cultural milieu, and the Sabras came to Canada to take advantage of educational and technical training and decided to stay, or they left because of an economic recession in Israel that followed the 1973 war. They also came from any of the three groups to join their relatives or because they married Canadians.

The Israeli community in Canada is heterogeneous in many respects such as education and occupational skills and, as in the case of many immigrant groups, is not free from ambivalent feelings about the decision to settle permanently in Canada. In many ways, the life of the Israeli community in this country can be described as a minority within a minority. The Israelis, particularly the native born, tend to reside in a predominantly "Israeli" neighbourhood. They patronize Israeli neighbourhoods, regularly follow the Israeli press, and are closely attached to events in Israel. No formal Israeli groups have been established in Canada, and the Israeli community does not publish a newspaper of its own.

The lack of official organizations representing the Israeli community may be explained in part by the fact that the Israelis constitute a part of the broader Canadian Jewish community. Although this process of interaction between these two communities has not always been harmonious, the Israelis participate along with Canadian Jewry in Jewish religious life and in the activities of the Jewish community organizations. In particular, they are involved in organizations that centre around the language and culture of Israel, thus enriching the cultural life of Canadian Jews with elements of the authentic Israeli culture.

# Italians

ALTHOUGH ITALIAN EMIGRATION to this country did not assume major proportions until the closing years of the nineteenth century, Italy's close association with Canada is a long-standing one, dating back as far as the fifteenth century. At the end of that century, when European powers were seeking a shorter trade route to the Orient, Italian navigators became the first to discover and explore the eastern coast of what is now Canada. The most famous of these was Giovanni Caboto (John Cabot) who in 1497 sailed from England to Canada's Atlantic coast. A citizen of Venice, Caboto was sponsored by Henry VII of England in whose name he claimed the territory, believed to have been either Newfoundland or Cape Breton Island, where he landed.

In 1524, Giovanni da Verrazano made a similar voyage of exploration for Francis I of France. Landing on the shores of what is now North Carolina, he explored the coast for a considerable distance northward, possibly as far as Cape Breton Island.

In the seventeenth century, Italian soldiers from the Carignan-Salières regiment, which had been sent to New France to quell the Iroquois, gave up military careers to settle along the Richelieu River and close to Montreal. Their example was later followed by Italian soldiers who had served with the de Meuron and de Watteville Swiss mercenary regiments in the British army during the War of 1812. When these regiments were disbanded in 1816, many of the Italian soldiers decided to remain in Canada, where they settled around Drummondville, Quebec, and in southern Ontario. The names "Martin" or French "Martin" or "Martineau", generally considered to be Scottish or Irish or French today, may very well have once been "Martini" or "Martino". Similarly, the names "Desliettes" and "Desilets", "Duluth" and "Delude", may have come from the Italian name "De Lietto".

It was not until the late nineteenth century that Italians began to emigrate to Canada in significant numbers. By then, Italy had become a unified state. Instead of improving the lot of the peasants, however, unification had served only to pass the reins of power to the middle class, which appeared unwilling to aid the poor. With the social promises of the "Risorgimento" unfulfilled, and another period of deprivation and frustration setting in, millions of peasants, particularly from the overpopulated south, opted for a new life in South America, the United States and Canada.

Steamship agents and recruiters promoted the crossing to North America, where intensive labour was needed and seasonal work was available on the transcontinental railways, in mining and in industry. During this period Raffaele Veltri formed the Welch Railway Construction Company, which is still in existence. Mr. Veltri died in Thunder Bay in 1975, but his private diary tells of the building of the CPR as early as the 1880s. After this time thousands of Italians came to work on the CPR, the Grand Trunk Pacific and the National Transcontinental. It is estimated that in 1904 there were between 6,000 and 8,000 labourers in Montreal alone.

From the turn of the century until the First World War, migrant Italian workers, often bachelors, came to Canada from Italy and from the "Little Italys" of the American east coast. Many returned after the summer's work to contribute income earned in Canada to the upkeep of southern Italian villages and for the provision of dowries for sisters and daughters. Those who did not return to Italy wintered in the railhead cities, especially in Montreal.

As railway work gave way to interurban and street railway development, more Italians stayed in the cities. Thus by the First World War, the migratory nature of Italian immigration to Canada began to change. The migrants were becoming immigrants. Instead of returning to Italy, young men sent for wives or relatives and so the "chain migration" process of close-knit families replaced recruitment as a reason for immigration. Italian business districts grew up in the major cities; the *ambiente* of Little Italy emerged. The *padrone* who had recruited labourers for the railway companies was joined by a more settled middle class of importers, shopkeepers, priests, caterers, and undertakers. By 1914, half the fruit merchants in Toronto were of Italian descent.

The extension of settlement caused by railway work, the initiative of skilled tradesmen, the lure of a potentially rich country, and the development of mining industries meant that most Canadian towns had an Italian population before the Second World War. There were, for instance, 112,625 Canadians of Italian origin in 1941, compared to 98,173 in 1931. This figure represented 1.0 per cent of the total Canadian population in 1941. Around Sault Ste. Marie, the Lakehead and Hamilton, for instance, substantial numbers of Italian Canadians worked in industry. In British Columbia, Italians who were former railway workers became truck farmers or orchard and vineyard operators.

The years of Fascism and the Second World War were difficult for many Italian Canadians, although the vast majority maintained the best cultural values of the old country along with loyalty to Canada. After the war, Canada's need for workers soon overcame the residual hostility to former enemies. Official government encouragement combined with the tightening of immigration laws in other countries and overpopulation in Italy produced a second great wave of Italian immigration to this country. Family chains, long interrupted, were renewed and sponsorship of friends and relatives grew rapidly. In 1951, there were 152,245 Canadians of Italian origin, this figure climbing to 450,351 in 1961 and 730,820 in 1971. Italian Canadians were 1.1 per cent of the total Canadian population in 1951 and 2.5 per cent in 1961.

As a result of the large postwar influx, Toronto became the largest "Italian" city in Canada with a population of 271,755 Italian Canadians in 1971. It outstripped Montreal, where the largest number of Italians and Italian enterprises were located before 1945. In addition to those who have settled in the Metropolitan Toronto area there are about 150,000 Italian Canadians living in other parts of Ontario, the province which has over 60 per cent of Canada's Italian population, which stood at 730,820 persons in 1971, or 3.4 per cent of the total Canadian population. Other cities with large Italian-Canadian populations in 1971 included Montreal (160,000), Vancouver (30,000), Niagara/St. Catharines (29,705), Hamilton (25,000), Windsor (20,000), Sudbury (10,340) and Winnipeg (9,400).

A more recent phenomenon is the development of Italian-Canadian suburbs and ex-urban areas to the north and west of Toronto. These areas represent not a sense of distance from fellow Canadians, but rather the natural expansion into preferred housing and settings by the more successful new immigrants. The Italian attachment to the land and the building skills of many Italian Canadian facilitate this move to the country.

In Quebec, most Italians live in Montreal and suburbs like St. Leonard. There are smaller Italian-Canadian settlements in Quebec City, Sherbrooke and Sept Iles. In Quebec many Italians have tended to learn French instead of English because they have close contact with French-speaking workers. Shared religion and contact, particularly in the artisan skills, has led to a striking amount of intermarriage between Italian Canadians and French Canadians in Quebec.

Many Italian newcomers have been attracted to the West Coast. After Ontario, with 463,095 Italian Canadians in 1971, and Quebec (169,655), the largest group was in British Columbia (53,795). Of this number, 29,530 were living in Vancouver, with Trail also having a relatively large Italian-Canadian population. Among the Prairie Provinces, 24,805 Italians were living in Alberta in 1971, 10,445 in Manitoba and 2,865 in Saskatchewan. Most were living in urban centres such as Calgary, Edmonton, Lethbridge, Winnipeg and Regina. Of the Italian population in the four Atlantic Provinces (5,750 in 1971), 3,770 were in Nova Scotia, the majority on Cape Breton Island or in the Halifax area.

In 1964, the centenary of organized Italian settlement in Canada was observed. Celebrations in the form of lectures, banquets, dances, parades and church services started in most Italian-Canadian communities on October 12, Columbus Day, and continued until the end of the month, climaxed by a grand ball. On October 30, 1964, a specially designed mosaic plaque, fixed to one of the inner walls of the Ontario Legislative Building in Toronto, was unveiled. Where once there was a tendency for celebrating the local saint days and other religious feasts of Italian-Canadians, Columbus Day is slowly replacing these events as an Italian-Canadian holiday. Week-long festivals or Italian Weeks are held in Thunder Bay, Hamilton (Festitalia) and Ottawa. Throughout the year, the Italian-Canadian communities have their own activities where their own folklore groups (for example, Sicilia Bedda, Club Abruzzi), drama groups (such as Compagnia dei Giovani) and other organizations participate. The Italian-Canadian communities are developing a mixed culture which is neither totally Italian nor English Canadian.

Most of the early Italian immigrant organizations in Canada were mutual aid societies that provided members with financial help and funeral costs. These clubs and organizations nearly always drew their members from the *paese* (home area) of the newcomers and excluded other Italians. With the passage of time, however, more inclusive clubs were formed. Two of the most important of these institutions, which are still active, are the Order of the Sons of Italy and the Order of Italo-Canadians.

The Italian Canadian Workmen's Association, whose main strength is in Montreal, is made up almost entirely of immigrants who arrived in Canada after 1952. Its chief purpose is to help solve the problems of Italian immigrant workers. In recent years, however, there has been a growing effort within the Italian-Canadian community to bring their various organizations together into one or more large federations. A co-ordinating committee in Montreal and an Italo-Canadian Brotherhood Society in Vancouver were established. Finally, in 1970, the Federation of Italian Canadian Associations and Clubs was created in Toronto, bringing together over sixty different clubs and organizations. Along with the Italian Department at the University of Toronto, it has worked to further education in both the Canadian and Italian cultures. It has also shown an interest in everything from Italian-Canadian sports to immigrant problems and the use of cable television. Its member clubs include such diverse organizations as the *Famee Furlane*, which serves the needs of a regional group, the Italian Immigrant Aid Society, the York Italian Band, the Italian Pastoral Commission and the Italian Philatelic Club.

The Order of the Sons of Italy has an association with a similar organization in the United States. The first lodges in Canada were established in Vancouver in 1905, Sault Ste. Marie in 1915, and in Montreal in 1919. In 1924, several branches broke away to form the Order of Italo-Canadians. The lodges of both orders are often divided according to members' political affiliations.

All of the Italian organizations, particularly the two latter ones, played an important role in the lives of the early immigrants. They provided material and spiritual support in times of illness, accident and death, and served as social and recreational centres. In recent years, however, membership has fallen off because many Italian Canadians no longer feel the need for this kind of help, and many postwar immigrants appear to have found sufficient support and companionship in their families, in the wider circle of relatives and in the local parish. Some have not joined any organizations at all, while others have founded new organizations.

Italian Canadians have been instrumental in organizing unions in the construction industry, and they are the presidents of many locals of the affiliates of the Labourers International Union. There is the Italian Canadian Workmen's Association in Montreal, and the Union of Injured Workers (APIO) exists in Toronto and in some other cities in Ontario, notably Ottawa.

Cultural organizations such as the Dante Alighieri Society promote the spread of Italian language and learning. The Club Venezia, composed largely of Italian Canadians from Venezia, and the Giovanni Caboto Club promote cultural and sports activities. In Toronto, Italian is now part of the secondary school curriculum of about 5,000 Italian-Canadian children. It is expected that this recognition of the Italian language will expand throughout the province shortly.

Unlike the mutual aid societies and those cultural groups that transcend localism, more recent organizations tend to represent specific economic and social groups within the Italian-Canadian community. The Canadian-Italian Business and Professional Men's Association, for example, was founded in 1952 and now has branches in several Canadian cities. The association promotes business among Italian Canadians, the employment of Italian-Canadian labour, and assistance to newcomers in the Canadian community. Toronto and Montreal have Italian Chambers of Commerce.

COSTI (Centro Organizzativo Scuole Techniche Italiane), an Italian community centre founded in 1961 with branches in Toronto and Hamilton, is a private institution which helps newcomers become an integral part of the social and economic life of the country. It publishes a monthly bulletin, *Il Ponte (The Bridge)*, in Toronto. Another Toronto-based organization is Centro Organizzazione Italiano. Under its auspices Italian-Canadian law students and university graduates provide free legal aid and counselling to their fellow countrymen. Organizations serving the Italian-Canadian community do not exist only in Toronto; there are over four hundred associations, clubs and cultural organizations coast to coast.

In January, 1974, the National Congress of Italian-Canadians was formed, uniting Italian-Canadian associations across Canada and serving the needs of over 800,000 members of the Italian community. The organization's role is to act as a link between Italian-Canadian organizations and to provide a means of consultation between the Italian-Canadian groups, the federal government and related organizations. The organization also encourages Italian Canadians to become involved in public affairs and fosters the retention and interpretation of Italian culture in Canada.

The Italian-language press in Canada shows both variety and vitality, including as it does a daily newspaper, *Il Corriere Canadese* which is distributed throughout Toronto, weeklies which are published in Montreal, Toronto, Vancouver and Windsor, and semi-monthly and monthly publications. The Italian-Canadian media are perhaps the best developed of the third-language media with over twenty-five newspapers published on a weekly or bi-weekly basis.

Many radio stations in the metropolitan areas have daily transmissions in Italian, while TV stations carry weekend variety and news shows in the Italian language. There are few other ethnocultural groups in Canada as well organized in the area of television broadcasting. The Italian television programs in Montreal, Toronto, Hamilton and Windsor have very large viewing audiences.

The contributions made by Italian Canadians to the development of Canada range over a wide variety of fields, reflecting the vitality and energy of the Italians, their capacity for hard work and their appreciation of the arts. In the early years of this century, when Canada was being transformed from a wilderness nation to a modern industrial state, Italian Canadians provided much of the manual labour that went into building railways, roads, canals, harbour installations and other construction projects. Some of the Italian labourers involved in these projects later went on to found their own successful construction companies.

Italians continue to contribute their skills to Canada's construction industry. They are at work on subways, industrial plants, new towns in the north, housing developments, office and apartment buildings, shopping centres and other projects. In Ontario alone, Italian labour is estimated to make up 70 per cent of the working force in the construction industry. As a result, new Italian-Canadian construction companies have mushroomed since 1946. Because of their special knowledge of mosaic and stucco work, both of which have been developed to a high degree in Italy, Italian artisans have been responsible for most of the work of this type on Canadian buildings. The sons of such men are beginning to contribute to Canada as architects and engineers.

Italians, with their strong sense of form and design, have also played a major role in the clothing industry. In Montreal and Toronto, many clothing manufacturers and dress-making firms employ Italians as shop foremen, cutters and designers. In the manufacture of food products, a number of Italians have gained prominence. This is true also of the wine-making industry and fruit and vegetable marketing industries as well. An early immigrant, Charles Honore Catelli, established a successful pasta manufacturing plant in Montreal. Pasquale Gattuso, born in Canada of Italian parents, founded a Montreal firm which processes oil and Italian foods. With the new migration of the post-1950s, a large number of food processors and importers have

emerged to serve the needs of both the Italian community and Canadians as a whole. Italian Canadians have also done a great deal to liven up the Canadian restaurant scene.

In the musical life of Canada, Italians have established a fine tradition as teachers of vocal music, composers, classical and jazz musicians, conductors and arrangers. The Italian love of opera has aided the growth of young opera companies in Canada.

Before the First World War most Italians who emigrated to Canada were migrant workers who returned to Italy after a summer's work on Canadian railways and other construction projects. Since then, however, the migrants have become immigrants and citizens, playing a major role in many phases of the development of this country.

# Jamaicans

JAMAICANS ARE PREDOMINANTLY of West African descent, with a small percentage of European, Chinese, East Indians, Lebanese and racial mixtures of all these groups. These people have lived in Jamaica, sharing common political, educational, economic and, to some extent, social institutions based on the British model. Over a period of more than three centuries, this interaction has produced unique cultural attributes. Jamaicans of diverse racial origins have more in common with each other than they do with the inhabitants of the countries from which their ancestors came.

With the exception of a group of 556 Maroons who arrived in 1796 after successfully defying British attempts to enslave them in Jamaica, Jamaican immigration to Canada is a relatively recent development. Although they have settled in Canada since the eighteenth century, it is only since 1968 that the Jamaican population in Canada has assumed a significant dimension, with more than half the population having arrived since 1971. Jamaicans form the largest group of West Indians now living in Canada. The exact number of people of Jamaican origin is unknown, but official Canadian government statistics in 1976 estimated a total of 58,832 people living in Canada whose birthplace was Jamaica.

Prior to 1962, there was a very heavy wave of emigration from Jamaica, but the object of this exodus was Great Britain, where there was still an "open door" immigration policy. At that time, Canada's official immigration policy favoured applicants from European countries, but an immigration scheme was introduced in 1955 which allowed single, childless, female immigrants between the ages of 25 and 30 to enter Canada and work as domestics in a Canadian home for a minimum of one year, after which they could become eligible for landed immigrant status. Only 2,690 women arrived from the West Indies, including Jamaica, under this scheme during the ten-year period 1955–65.

A new immigration policy in 1967 introduced a point system which took into account an applicant's age, occupation, skills, education and training, and employment possibilities in Canada. Another category of eligibility was added, that of nominated relatives, "midway between sponsored dependants and independent applicants", enabling immediate relatives resident in Canada to sponsor or nominate family members in Jamaica. This development accounted for the marked increase of sponsored or nominated immigrants arriving during the 1970s.

The majority of Jamaicans emigrating to Canada seek to achieve a higher standard of living and opportunities for personal advancement. A few, however, have left because they wanted to work and travel in other countries with a less crowded atmosphere than the small island of their birth. Some also came as university students and later applied for landed immigrant status. Since 1973, many Jamaicans of the managerial and professional group have come to Canada because they were unable or unwilling to come to terms with changes which are currently taking place in Jamaican society, most notably the movement away from the traditional social order. Others felt that Canada offered an opportunity to discard traditional class-conscious attitudes.

The data regarding Jamaican settlement go back only as far as 1973, but the current trend is similar to earlier periods. The majority have settled in Ontario, followed by Quebec and British Columbia. The following breakdown for 1973 and 1974, the two years of heaviest immigration, typifies the general trend of settlement. Ontario received 19,194, while 1,500 went to Quebec and 371 to British Columbia. The majority have settled in Toronto and Montreal. At least 54 per cent of the West Indian population in Toronto is of Jamaican origin, and the majority have arrived within the last decade. As many live in the suburbs as in the downtown areas in both Toronto and Montreal, although there are small concentrations downtown.

In the occupational area, the only information available on Jamaicans concerns their intended occupations in the new country. A relatively high percentage of managerial and professional people came to Canada from 1972 to 1974. These people, like all Jamaicans, speak English, the official language of Jamaica, and all of the immigrants speak "patois", a dialect which has its roots in both Africa and England.

Music, dancing and religious services provide community activities shared by Jamaicans and other Canadians. Recent Jamaican immigrants have come from an environment in which church attendance is regular, and many continue to attend church in Canada. In the case of the Pentecostal church, whole congregations have been rejuvenated by the influx of Jamaicans whose major social activity is the weekly session in church.

In each city where there is a sizable Jamaican population, there are Jamaican-Canadian associations, the functions of which vary with the size and involvement of the membership. For the most part, they are concerned with helping newly arrived immigrants adjust to life in Canada, and with working in conjunction with the Jamaican High Commission on problems of a consular nature. Unfortunately, these organizations tend to lose many of their members as soon as the immigrants have managed to find their places in society at large.

*Contrast*, which was recently combined with *The Islander*, has for several years been the "voice" of Toronto's Jamaican community. The Jamaican Canadian Association is one of the oldest Black organizations in Toronto, working in the interests of both new immigrants and established Canadians of Jamaican origin. To foster cultural exchanges between Jamaica and the community in Canada, several Jamaican artists and a major playwright staged productions in Toronto in 1976. There are a number of Alumni Associations. The Kingston College Boys' Association, for example, supports its old school financially and in other ways, and provides recreational and cultural activities for its members.

# Japanese

JAPAN'S EARLY HISTORY is lost in legend, and reliable records date back to only AD 400. The country was originally inhabited by numerous clans and tribal kingdoms, and turned into a state of warriors under the Shogun after the twelfth century. The first European contact with Japan was made by Portuguese sailors in 1542, but the Japanese were almost completely successful in keeping out Westerners and Christianity until, in 1853, the American Matthew Perry obliged the country to open trade relations with the West.

Canada's first contacts with the Japanese were accidental. Three lost survivors from Owari (Nagoya) drifting helplessly in their storm-wrecked fishing boat were washed ashore on the Queen Charlotte Islands in 1833. They were rescued and eventually returned to Japan. This was the earliest recorded landing of Japanese on Canada's Pacific coast, then a virgin frontier called New Caledonia. More likely than not, other castaways, enduring similar ordeals, were carried by the Japan Current or Kuroshiwo, to reach these shores.

The story of the Japanese in Canada begins in 1877, nine years after Japan rescinded the rule promulgated by the Tokugawa shogunate rule which forbade its subjects to have contact with foreigners. It was the time of Japan's westernization. Her social, educational, political and economic systems were being restructured. Overnight, Japan was undergoing a frantic transformation from a feudal state to a modern nation. Bright young men were encouraged to go abroad and learn from Europe and America.

Manzo Nagano was such a restless young man. He was born in Nagasaki in 1853, the year that Commodore Matthew Perry anchored his American fleet in Tokyo's Bay to "persuade" Japan's rulers to end the country's trade isolation from the West. Engulfed in the fervour of the period, this adventurous young carpenter stowed himself aboard a British ship, heedless of its destination, to begin his epic voyage.

When Manzo Nagano disembarked and touched land, presumably in May, 1877, at New Westminster, British Columbia, he stepped into history. Although unaware of where he was, he became the first known Japanese to settle in Canada. It was through chance, not design, that Nagano led the pioneer generation of Japanese, the Issei, into this country. However, as a rugged and resolute individual, he is symbolic of the patient, hardy and industrious spirit of the Issei who were to contribute immensely to the early development of western Canada.

Among those who followed was Gihei Kuno who, when he saw the teeming red salmon fighting up the Fraser River in 1877, urged his fellow villagers from Mio in the Wakayama prefecture to come to Canada. They came in such numbers that they became the core of Steveston (now part of Richmond, British Columbia) and even today their descendants comprise a strong segment of the Japanese-Canadian fishermen. Much of the techniques and gear used in the West coast fishing industry were those introduced and developed by the early immigrants.

Yasukichi Yoshizawa was another early immigrant who with three companions rowed steadily from Vancouver for six weeks, braving miles of unknown coastal waters to be the first Japanese to reach the rich fishing grounds of northern British Columbia. Possibly the most daring Issei was Jinzaburo Oikawa who, in 1906, with a company of men and at least two young women, purchased and sailed a retired vessel to reach Canada. Although this was an illegal act, the authorities, after negotiation with the Japanese consul and in admiration of the group's exploit, permitted them to remain.

By 1889, when a Japanese consulate office was opened in Vancouver, Japanese merchants and shopkeepers were operating there as well as in Victoria. The most successful of these early businessmen was Shinkichi Tamura who participated in many ventures, among them organizing a trust company bearing his name. He retired to Japan where he was elevated to the House of Peers.

Most of the early immigrants were of peasant stock. After labouring in the mines or on the railway, or in logging camps or sawmills, many used their savings to purchase uncleared land in the fertile Fraser and Okanagan Valleys. This movement was led by men such as Jiro Inouye and Yasutaro Yamaga, who counselled other farmers and organized a co-operative in the Lower Fraser. Using Japanese techniques, the hard-working pioneers soon dominated the fruit industry and market gardening in the Fraser Valley, becoming the targets of racial hostility based on envy and fear of economic competition. The increase in immigration caused by American regulations closing the continental United States to Japanese led the Canadian government to adopt a policy which limited immigration through agreements with the Japanese government.

Immigration from Japan began slowly. In 1896 there were no more than 1,000 Japanese in Canada, but this number had increased to

4,738 by 1901 and 9,057 by 1911. Consequently, the immigration of single men was sharply reduced and was replaced with a movement of family members, especially of brides of Japanese already settled in Canada.

Japanese immigrants settled predominantly in British Columbia, since the province was closest to their homeland and could be reached with the least expense. It had a favourable climate and provided employment opportunities in the expanding fishing, lumbering, mining and railroad industries. In the early years, Japanese Canadians were employed in those major industries mainly as manual labourers, but as they gained skill and knowledge they were able to move into farming, self-supporting fishing and occupations of a commercial nature.

The contributions of the pioneer Issei to the early development of western Canada were vital and considerable, but were not without a heavy price. The cemetery in Cumberland on Vancouver Island where they worked in the coal mines as early as 1890 is filled with shattered victims of colliery explosions and logging accidents. A rail disaster in 1904 near New Westminster snuffed out twenty-three young Issei lives while a snowslide on the CPR line in 1910 claimed thirty more.

When the First World War erupted in Europe, many offered their services to their adopted land. Nearly two hundred proceeded overseas, to win battlefield awards and citations. Fifty-four Issei failed to return.

From the beginning some Canadians were hostile towards Asians in British Columbia. That hostility was based on a fear of the "yellow peril", fostered by the idea that British Columbia would be overrun by a population which differed greatly, racially and culturally, from the Anglo-Canadian charter group. The Japanese were seen as a threat to "white" standards of living and as not able to be assimilated into Anglo-Canadian culture.

Anti-Oriental sentiment was sometimes violent, as in the 1907 Vancouver riot. On September 7, 1907, a mass meeting and a parade for anti-Oriental agitation was held by the Asiatic Expulsion League in Vancouver. The crowd turned into a mob of one thousand who marched on Chinatown and little Tokyo. The riot contributed to the first concrete restriction of Japanese immigration to Canada, in which Japan agreed voluntarily to restrict the number of emigrants.

From 1895 to 1902 the Legislature of British Columbia had passed a series of measures disenfranchising British citizens of Asian origin in the province. Disenfranchisement meant exclusion from a whole series of activities in the political and economic life of British Columbia. Exclusion from the voters' list made Asians ineligible for certain trades and professions and for employment in certain occupations. In addition, federal and provincial regulations cut back the number of licenses issued to Asians in the fishing and lumbering industries, reducing employment opportunities in these traditional fields. Discrimination practised by the larger society either by law or custom limited job opportunities, restricting Asian participation in the mainstream of Canadian society.

Discriminatory regulations applied to both immigrants and Canadian-born Japanese Canadians, who by 1941 comprised 70 per cent of Canada's 23,450 Japanese. While pressure from British Columbia citizens and politicians had led to restrictions on Japanese immigration in 1908, female Japanese entering as wives were not restricted. By 1928, tighter controls had greatly reduced female immigration but a population ratio of 7 females to every 10 males in British Columbia had been reached. The Canadian-born or Nisei generation began to appear in about 1910, with the birthrate peaking in the early 1930s. Immigration figures of the time show that whereas in 1908, 7,985 Japanese immigrated to Canada, this fell off to 508 persons in 1909. Only in 1919, when 1,181 Japanese came to Canada, did figures reach over 1,000 immigrants per year until after the Second World War. In 1921, there were 15,868 Japanese Canadians. This figure reached 23,342 in 1931, and did not rise much above 23,000 until 1961.

The Nisei began to come of age in the mid-1930s, during the most difficult of times. Canada and the world were still in the grip of the Depression. Discriminatory hiring practices against Asians by both business and government in British Columbia harshly restricted employment opportunities. Japanese-Canadian fishermen were being forced from their livelihood by the reduction of licenses issued to them. Added to these and other difficulties were those caused by the Japanese invasions of Manchuria and China. Politicians and agitators exploited this Asian situation to harrass Japanese Canadians by questioning their loyalty and making unfounded charges.

The maturing Nisei saw the basic problem in the denial of the franchise to all of Asian background, both naturalized and native-born. In 1936 they formed the Japanese Canadian Citizens' League, whose first act was to send a delegation to Ottawa to plead for the right to vote.

When Canada declared war on Germany in 1939, Japanese Canadians responded with acts and expressions of loyalty, and pressure against them seemed somewhat eased. In 1941 there were 23,450 persons of Japanese ancestry in Canada with 22,096, or 96 per cent, in British Columbia. In Vancouver alone there were 8,448 Japanese, while others were scattered in Victoria, on farms along the lower Fraser River and in the Okanagan Valley, and in a number of coastal fishing villages and lumbering areas.

The apogee in the history of discrimination against the Japanese Canadian came when war was declared on Japan in 1941. The removal from the so-called defence zone in British Columbia of all Japanese Canadians, whether Canadian citizens or not, became the wartime policy of the Canadian government. The government uprooted the Japanese community, breaking up families and selling all the real and personal property of the evacuees.

The Japanese were moved either to road work, farming or industrial projects set up by the government, or to the relocation and internment camps. Thus, as a result of the evacuation, 2,500 were in the sugar beet fields of Alberta, 1,000 were farming in Manitoba and 3,000 were either in self-supporting projects in British Columbia or in road projects or industry in eastern Canada. The remaining 12,000 were relocated in the British Columbia interior. Because of the opposition from already settled areas, scantily inhabited and isolated ghost towns were selected. Approximately 4,800 were sent to Slocan, 1,500 to New Denver, 930 to Sandon, 970 to Kaslo and 1,200 to Greenwood. Two completely new settlements were created at Tashme and Lemon Creek, which accommodated 2,600 and 1,800 respectively.

In 1945, all Japanese Canadians were given the choice of agreeing to go to Japan or of moving east of the Rocky Mountains. The "repatriation" scheme was made attractive by offers of free transportation to Japanese Canadians, a cash stake, and the transfer of funds realized from a sale of property, and resulted in the eventual departure of 4,000 Japanese Canadians to Japan. Government policy was to disperse the remainder across Canada. From relocation centres in the centre of British Columbia, a further 3,000 Japanese Canadians were moved eastward and settled in various parts of the country.

In 1949 remaining wartime restrictions were lifted from the Japanese Canadians and they were granted full voting rights. The social and economic climate was also slowly improving so that nearly a hundred years after they first arrived in this country the Japanese Canadians were accepted into the mainstream of Canadian society.

The 1971 census recorded a total of 37,260 Japanese Canadians, with more of them living in Ontario (15,600) than in British Columbia (13,585). A large proportion, about 70 per cent, were born and raised in Canada. Today there are an estimated 15,000 Japanese Canadians in Metropolitan Toronto alone. The number of postwar Japanese immigrants has been increasing gradually since the 1967 change in the immigration act, but it has only once exceeded 100 persons per year. According to the immigration statistics, a total of 9,286 Japanese entered Canada between 1946 and 1975, but many returned to Japan within a few years. The most recent immigrants are highly educated technical or professional people.

Prior to the Second World War Japanese communities on the West Coast sustained many organizations of both a religious and secular nature. By 1934 there were 230 Japanese-Canadian organizations of which 84 were to be found in Vancouver alone. There were trade associations, prefectural associations and friendship groups, and these organizations provided the cohesion to keep both formal and informal social networks intact in the Japanese Canadian community.

With dispersal, fundamental change has occurred in the structure of the community. Without the geographic concentration and prewar discrimination, the sense of community defined by such elements as common needs, shared institutions and a feeling of group consciousness has become more diffuse.

At present the main national organization of Japanese Canadians is the Japanese Canadian Citizens' Association, which was re-founded in 1947. It took an active part in the struggle to achieve legal equality and to promote the social welfare of the Japanese after relocation and resettlement. After generally achieving its goals, the JCCA now functions actively at the local community level.

The major Japanese-Canadian publications now come from Toronto, although many were first established in Vancouver. Two semi-weeklies are *The Continental Times* and *The New Canadian*, both of which play instrumental roles in promoting good citizenship and community spirit. *The New Canadian* continued to publish during the war and was the only means of communication for the Japanese, connecting the evacuated communities, scattered individuals and families.

Besides these nation-wide newspapers there are many community-wide organizations and institutions among the Japanese Canadians, including *Ken-jin-kai* (social groups composed of people from the same prefecture in Japan), language schools, and credit unions in addition to various social-cultural clubs. There are over fifty groups in the Japanese community in Canada alone. Throughout the country the Issei are the main, active participants in the organizations, and the Nisei and Sansei (third generation) are also actively involved in community-wide institutions rather than solely Japanese organizations.

A decade after the resettlement of Canada's Japanese minority, erection of a Japanese-Canadian community centre was proposed in Toronto. The Japanese Canadian Cultural Centre, completed in 1964, is no longer exclusively a Japanese-Canadian community centre. The purpose of the centre is to provide a meeting place between the older Japanese Canadians and the younger generations, and between Japanese Canadians and other Canadians in the metropolitan community. Through its various activities the centre serves the larger community by introducing many facets of Japanese culture into the Canadian mosaic. At the same time, interest in such activities as ikebana, bonsai and sumie, judo, karate and other martial arts is growing among both Japanese and non-Japanese.

In 1977, Japanese Canadians marked the 100th anniversary of the arrival of Manzo Nagano with a series of Centennial celebrations on both the national and local levels. Under the direction of the Japanese Canadian Centennial Society, with national headquarters in Toronto, Japanese Canadians sought to preserve and promote a sense of community among the 40,000 Japanese residents of Canada. Throughout the celebration it was hoped that the project would also provide the younger generation with an opportunity to learn the background of their parents and grandparents in Canada.

Some concern exists among Japanese Canadians that with intermarriage they will disappear as an ethnocultural group before the end of their second century. Whatever the future, the first hundred years of Japanese-Canadian history are a unique, unprecedented segment of Canadian history.

# Jews

*See also Israelis*

THE HISTORICAL CONNECTION between the Jewish people and Canada dates back to the eighteenth century when what is now the Province of Quebec was New France. In 1748, Abraham Gradis, a Jewish merchant of Bordeaux who owned and operated many of the merchant ships sailing between France and New France, helped to found the Society of Canada to encourage trade with and material support for the colony. When the British attacked New France he recruited troops at his own expense. However, despite the Gradis family's support of the colony for more than a decade, Jews were prevented from settling in New France under a royal decree of 1685 which barred non-Catholic settlers from its colonies.

The first Jews who settled in Canada came from England to Rhode Island and moved to Halifax in 1751. They were merchants, born in England of parents who had come originally from Germany, and were engaged in the export of timber, dried fish and potash to England and the West Indies. Jewish settlement began when Canada became a British colony. Some Jews served as supply officers with the British army. One of these was Aaron Philip Hart, who came to Montreal as a commissary officer in 1760 and later settled in Trois Rivières where he is credited with founding the first Canadian Jewish family.

Many of these first Jews in Canada were of Spanish and Portuguese origin and emigrated from England or came north from the American colonies. Those with commercial relations already established in England and America continued their enterprises here with great success. The majority settled in Montreal, where their number, although small, enabled them to maintain the traditions of Jewish life. One of the first Jewish congregations, Shearith Israel, established in Montreal in 1768, followed the Sephardic ritual. The first Jew elected to a legislative body in Canada was Samuel Hart, a Halifax merchant. He was elected to the Legislative Assembly of Nova Scotia in 1793 and held his seat for six years.

In 1807, Ezekiel Hart, born in Trois Rivières in 1770, was elected to the Legislative Assembly of Lower Canada. Unfortunately, this happened at a time when the governor of the province, Sir James Craig, was at loggerheads with the representatives of the French-Canadian population. Ezekiel Hart was deemed to be a friend of the governor. When the Assembly met at Quebec in January, 1808, Hart proceeded to assume his seat and took the oath using the Old Testament. The assertion was then made that he had no right to sit in the Assembly, not being a Christian. Although there may have been some racial prejudice involved, it is clear that this was a blow at Craig. The governor dismissed the Assembly, new elections were called, and again the people of Trois Rivières gave Hart a majority of their votes.

When the Assembly was convened in 1809, the opposition was repeated, and Hart was obliged to withdraw. It was not until 1831 that the Quebec Legislative Assembly passed a bill recognizing equal civil rights for the Jewish population. The bill was supported by Louis Joseph Papineau, a prominent leader of French Canada, and was given royal assent in June, 1832.

For almost a century, from 1760 until 1850, the Canadian Jewish community remained small and immigration was minimal. A small number of Jews began to settle in Ontario towards the end of the eighteenth century, but the majority still lived in Quebec. According to the census of 1851, there were 451 Jews in Canada, of whom 348 were in Quebec and 103 in Ontario. The expansion to other parts of Canada began in the 1850s with the first influx of Jewish immigrants from Europe, almost all of whom were from the German states where revolution, war and economic depression drove many Germans, including some 50,000 Jews, from the country between 1850 and 1870. How many immigrated to Canada is not known, but they undoubtedly accounted for much of the increase in Canada's Jewish population, which almost tripled to 1,333 by the time of the 1871 census.

While many of the German-Jewish immigrants were drawn to the older Jewish communities in Quebec, many more pressed farther west into Ontario where they settled in Toronto, Dundas, Lancaster, Hamilton and Ottawa. Towards the end of the 1830s Jewish communities were also being established in the Maritimes and in British Columbia, where Jewish settlers were among the founders of the City of Victoria.

Many of the settlers were of urban background and upon arrival were absorbed by the Jewish communities in metropolitan centres. Their immediate need for social and financial assistance gave rise to the beginnings of organized relief efforts within the Jewish community. The main burden fell upon the Montreal community, since it was the principal port of entry for immigrants from overseas. The first Jewish charitable organization, the Hebrew Philanthropic Society, was founded in Montreal in 1847 to provide assistance for needy and especially destitute immigrants. In 1863 the Society was reorganized as the Young Men's Hebrew Benevolent Society. Similar organizations were founded in Toronto in 1875 and Hamilton in 1878 as immigrants who had first landed in the United States came to Canada after finding conditions unsuitable in the south.

The opening of the Canadian West in the 1870s roughly coincided with the East European phase of Jewish immigration which began in earnest in 1881 and continued until 1929. Thousands of Jews fled from Russia, Roumania, Poland and other East European countries where intensified persecution was manifested in violent pogroms. Between the early 1880s and the turn of the century, Canada's Jewish population increased more than ten-fold to 16,717. Between 1900 and 1920, 138,467 Jewish immigrants were admitted to Canada.

The increasing number of refugees had soon overwhelmed facilities of the Jewish relief agencies in Montreal and Toronto. When a wave of pogroms swept through the Russian Empire in 1881, the burden of receiving refugees fell to the tiny colony of Jews in Manitoba where they had established themselves in the 1870s. Their total population by 1881 numbered only thirty-three, and of these, twenty-one persons comprising eight families lived in Winnipeg.

The settlement of Jewish refugees in the west was finally realized through a combination of events. Anxious to increase Canada's population, the Canadian government instituted a new, free land policy in the west and assigned the Canadian High Commissioner in London the task of attracting as many settlers as possible. World sympathy with the plight of Jews in Russia led to the formation of relief committees in London, Paris, Berlin and New York to assist the emigration of Jewish refugees to North America. In Canada, where Jewish relief agencies could no longer handle the entire burden of immigrant assistance, a movement began in the 1880s towards a Jewish colonization effort to settle the immigrants on the land.

In 1884, two years after their arrival in Winnipeg, the Jewish immigrants were assigned a tract of farmland near Moosomin, Saskatchewan. The first settlement became known as New Jerusalem, but crop failures over the following three years contributed to its demise in 1888. That same year a more successful Jewish farm settlement was founded at Wapella, 20 miles (32 km) from Moosomin, and it endured for fifty years.

In Montreal the Young Men's Hebrew Benevolent Society had become incorporated with the Baron de Hirsch Institute and Hebrew Benevolent Society, named after the Jewish philanthropist who gave considerable financial support to the society's immigrant relief efforts. When Baron de Hirsch established the Jewish Colonization Association in 1891, a colonization committee was formed by the Society in Montreal.

As the largest centre of Jewish population in the west and the third largest in Canada, Winnipeg served as the main cultural and communal base for the western Jewish community. By the end of 1882, Winnipeg's handful of Jews had grown large enough to found their first congregation, the B'nai Israel. A second congregation, the Chevrah Beth El, was formed in 1884. In 1889 the two united and built the city's first synagogue, Shaarey Zedek. Winnipeg also continued to be a principal settlement for immigrant aid. The Jewish Immigration Society, founded in 1912, became the backbone of Jewish war relief work in the west with fifteen branches in operation from

Manitoba to British Columbia by 1916.

Immigration restrictions at the end of the First World War inhibited the continued admission of Jewish immigrants to Canada at a time when events in Europe had rendered their need to emigrate more desperate than ever. Since the majority of Jews were from Poland, Austria, Hungary, Roumania, Ukraine and the Baltic states, they fell within the non-preferred category immediately after the war, and it was not until the early 1920s that Jewish immigration again picked up.

Immigrant aid ceased to be a matter of settlement and relief financing alone. The need for rescue and rehabilitation required the intervention of an agency knowledgeable in governmental regulations and laws. The Canadian Jewish community responded in 1919 by founding the Jewish Immigrant Aid Society of Canada, a national body exclusively devoted to problems of Jewish immigration and immigrant aid. Between 1920 and 1930, more than 48,000 Jewish immigrants were admitted to Canada, almost all of them through the assistance of JIAS. The task of receiving immigrants during this time was shared by some fifty Jewish communities in Canada. About 30 per cent of the immigrants went to the western provinces, about 30 per cent to Ontario, and about 40 per cent remained in Quebec and the Maritimes.

The next phase of Jewish immigration began with the Depression of the 1930s and Nazi rule in Germany; the exodus from Germany beginning in 1933 and rapidly gaining momentum as Nazi anti-Semitism intensified. By the end of 1937, some 140,000 Jews had fled Germany, and they were joined by Jews from Austria, Czechoslovakia, Latvia, Lithuania, Poland, Roumania and Hungary about this time. Of these people, between 1930 and 1940, about 11,000 Jewish immigrants

were admitted to Canada. At the onset of the Second World War immigration from Europe was almost completely stopped, and between 1940 and 1945, only 1,852 Jews were admitted to Canada, most of whom were from the United States. A small number of them were refugees in transit to other countries, and did not settle in Canada.

The Jews who survived the war to emigrate to Canada and other countries were, for the most part, displaced persons. Of the one million persons in this category who could not be repatriated to their homelands, approximately 250,000 were Jews. Canada's postwar immigration policy broadened the categories of admissible immigrants and made special provision for refugees from various camps in Europe, allowing more than 11,000 Jewish displaced persons to be admitted to Canada between 1947 and 1952. Another special group, more than 1,110 Jewish war orphans, were admitted to Canada and placed across the country under the War Orphans Project, part of the government's Group Movement Plan sponsored through the Canadian Jewish Congress.

Postwar Jewish immigration dropped off sharply after 1954. By then, 42,203 Jews had entered Canada since the end of the Second World War. Until the mid-1950s, Jewish immigration to Canada had originated primarily from Europe, and the last influx from this source came in 1956–57 following the revolution in Hungary, when of the 37,000 Hungarian refugees admitted to Canada, 4,500 were Jews.

The Suez crisis in Egypt in 1956 led to the expulsion of 25,000 Jews from Egypt. Some of them settled in Canada, and political developments in North Africa between 1956 and 1969 and the Arab-Israeli war of 1967 brought thousands of French-speaking Jews to Canada from Morocco, Tunisia and Algeria. Of the estimated 25,000 Jews that came at this time, 18,000 of them are now in Montreal and the rest are in Toronto and other urban centres.

At present, it is estimated that there are over 300,000 Canadian Jews. The majority of Canadian Jews reside in the provinces of Ontario (45.5 per cent), Quebec (39.1 per cent) and Manitoba (6.7 per cent), mainly in the cities of Montreal (38.5 per cent), Toronto (37.0 per cent) and Winnipeg (6.5 per cent). English is the major language in the Jewish home (83.9 per cent), while Yiddish (8.5 per cent) and French (3.4 per cent) follow. A large part of the Jewish group (23 per cent) is bilingual in the two official languages.

The Jewish community has established a comprehensive network of institutions, organizations, associations, agencies and foundations to provide for the social, economic and educational needs of Jewish communities throughout Canada, to assist Jewish immigrants in the integration process and to help needy Jews all over the world. The system of Jewish education is highly developed, with different types of schools at all levels.

The Canadian Jewish Congress, founded in 1919 and reconstituted in 1934, is the representative body of Canadian Jewry. Its objects are to safeguard the status, rights and welfare of Jews in Canada; to combat anti-Semitism and promote understanding and goodwill among all ethnic and religious groups; to co-operate with other agencies in efforts for the improvement of social, economic and cultural conditions of Jews all over the world; to assist in rehabilitating Jewish refugees and immigrants; and to assist Jewish communities in Canada to establish community organizations to provide for their social, philanthropic and educational needs.

The Jewish Immigrant Aid Services of Canada, founded in 1919, serves as a national Jewish agency for immigrants and immigrant welfare. The Jewish Colonization Association of Canada, founded in 1907, continues its original function of providing financial aid to Jewish farmers and assisting the migration of experienced Jewish farmers from Europe who wish to settle on farms in Canada. The United Jewish Relief Agencies of Canada, founded in 1939, extends relief to Jewish refugees and other war victims.

The National Council of Jewish Women, B'Nai Brith (founded in 1843 in New York, 1875 in Toronto), The Canadian Union of Jewish Students (1971) and The Federalist Zionist Organization of Canada (1967) are examples of other Jewish organizations in this country which offer their services to the Jewish community. In addition, Jews co-operate with Protestants and Catholics on the inter-religious level through the Canadian Council of Christians and Jews.

The first Jewish newspaper in Canada was an English bi-weekly, the *Jewish Times*, established in Montreal in 1897. In 1908 another publication, the *Canadian Jewish Tribune*, began in Montreal, but soon amalgamated with the *Jewish Times* under the name *Canadian Jewish Chronicle*, now discontinued.

For many years the only daily newspapers published in Canada in a language other than English or French were two Yiddish dailies, the *Jewish Daily Eagle* of Montreal and the *Jewish Journal* of Toronto, both in continuous publication for more than fifty years. With an increase in the number of Canadian Jews whose mother tongue is English, these Yiddish newspapers are now weeklies, as is the *Yiddish Press* out of Winnipeg.

Other weekly publications include the *Canadian Jewish News* of Toronto, the *Jewish Post* and *Western Jewish News* (Winnipeg), and the *Jewish Western Bulletin* (Vancouver). The *Canadian Jewish Weekly* and *Toronto Jewish Press* are published bi-weekly in Toronto. The Canadian Jewish Congress publishes the *Congress Bulletin* and the *Bulletin du Cercle juif* monthly. The Zionist Organization of Canada publishes the *Canadian Zionist*, and the Canadian Hadassah Organization the monthly magazine *ORAH*.

Jews make up less than 1.5 per cent of Canada's population, yet their contributions to the economic and cultural life of this country have far exceeded their proportionate numerical strength. A significant factor in this contribution is the extent to which individual initiative has prevailed in the Jews' efforts to establish themselves and participate fully in the affairs of their community. Many chose to be self-employed and provided the community with important new commercial outlets and services. They also served the professional needs of the community as doctors, lawyers and civic officials.

Their contribution to industrial development is evident in the number of Canadian industries that found their beginnings in Jewish enterprises. Initially Jews were especially active in the founding of the Canadian merchant marine and in the field of railway construction all across the country, in the production of hydro electricity and telephone service. In Toronto and Montreal during the 1920s, Jews first became involved in the clothing industry, and they figured significantly in the development of the industry's labour movements and the establishment of the International Ladies' Garment Workers Union and the Amalgamated Clothing Workers Union.

During the 1880s, when the western prairie territories were opening to settlement, Jews were active in the areas of clothing manufac-turing, wholesaling and retailing, and were among the first settlers to establish farming communities in the west. They have also contributed to Canadian military history, and Jewish immigrant aid organizations made numerous presentations to the Canadian government following both world wars to modify immigration policy, which helped all immigrants, not just those of Jewish origin.

The intellectual tradition, which for centuries has been a major cohesive force in Jewish life, is demonstrated in the number of Jews who have distinguished themselves in science, medicine, law, education, literature and the fine and performing arts. Jews have also given substantial philanthropic support to Canadian participation in arts and culture.

In Canada, the Jewish people, maintaining their ancient prophetic ideals and their steadfast belief in human dignity and human welfare, have contributed a great deal to the country's development and growth.

# Koreans

IN THE PAST, Korea was a cultural bridge from China to Japan. From the end of the sixteenth century until the middle of the twentieth, the country became progressively more isolated from the rest of the world as a reaction against Japanese invasions. Even when China and Japan were finally opened to Western influence in the nineteenth century, Korea was not well known in the West. In 1910 Korea was annexed to the Japanese empire. It was liberated in 1945 at the end of the Second World War but remained relatively isolated until the outbreak of the Korean War, in June,

1950, creating a situation where the country was divided into two sections—a Soviet and Chinese sphere of influence in the northern zone and an American sphere in the south. Almost all immigration to Canada has been from the southern zone.

Since 1967, Toronto has been the most attractive place for Koreans to settle due to job opportunities there. In 1973, Canada stood in third place among countries in which Koreans settled, after Japan and the United States. There were an estimated 3,000 persons of Korean origin living in Toronto in 1972, about 500 in Vancouver and 350 in Montreal, along with a few hundred in other major centres such as Winnipeg, Edmonton and Calgary. With 1,280 new arrivals in 1972, the Korean population reached just under 7,000 in that year. In 1977, the total number of Korean immigrants in Canada was estimated at 25,000. Immigrants came directly from South Korea as well as indirectly from Europe, particularly from West Germany, and from Viet Nam, South America and the United States.

Most Canadians of Korean origin are highly skilled workers or professionals. Several hundred are working as nurses in hospitals across Canada and a dozen or more as doctors. A few are factory workers in Toronto and Brampton. Other professions in which Koreans are found include employment as bank clerks, dentists, accountants, engineers and miners. Korean ministers and social workers have also been located in some of the larger cities, and there are a number of Korean university professors.

Many Koreans have established small . businesses, including food stores, restaurants, and boutiques. Trading companies import ingredients for Korean dishes and materials for arts and crafts. Koreans have also ventured into such varied undertakings as income-tax services, printing shops, auto repair shops, taekwon-do clubs, insurance agencies, travel agencies and real estate agencies.

One of the key organizations in the life of Koreans is the church. The first Korean United Church was established in Vancouver. Within the church body there are youth, senior citizen and women's groups active in recreational, educational and cultural programs. The church also provides a place for new immigrants to meet. Nine United Church congregations serve most of the Korean population of that denomination in Vancouver, Winnipeg, Edmonton, Toronto, Hamilton, Windsor and Montreal. The Korean Presbyterian and Korean Catholic churches in Toronto and London serve those religious denominations.

Club Coreana was organized in 1970 as a social meeting place for Korean students at the University of Toronto. The club has participated in various international activities and campus festivals.

The aim of the Cultural Centre for Korean Canadians in Toronto is to introduce Korean culture to the Canadian public. The Association of Korean Scholars, located in Ottawa, was founded in Toronto in November 1972, and serves the Korean professional community. There is a Korean Canadian Association in most cities where Koreans have settled. The best known are the Korean-Canadian Association of Metro Toronto, the Korean Community of Greater Montreal, the Korean Society of Vancouver, the Korean Association of Manitoba, the Korean Canadian Association of Ottawa, and the Alberta Korean Association, all established between 1964 and 1967. These associations run a variety of cultural, educational, religious and social programs. The association in Toronto publishes a directory and has seasonal outdoor and indoor recreational meetings. It also sponsored a national festival in 1972. The organization has started a Korean-language school for second generation Koreans who wish to preserve their national language.

Similar cultural needs are expressed by the Korean Catholic Community Centre in Toronto, the Korean Church of Toronto, which is interdenominational, and the Montreal Korean Cultural Foundation.

An organization of a different nature is the Ad Hoc Committee for the Orientation of Korean Immigrants in Greater Vancouver, founded in 1972. This organization serves as a bridge between new immigrants and the larger society. The Korean Human Rights Council in Ontario was organized as a social services association in 1974 in Toronto to aid the community and new immigrants.

The *Korean Canada Times*, which started publication in 1971, was the first Korean-language weekly newspaper in Canada. Owing to financial difficulties, the newspaper ceased publication a year later. *Canada News* and *New Korea Times* are weekly publications. Another weekly, the *Korean Journal*, began publication in late 1972. It contains news from Korea as well as news about the Korean community in Canada. Another publication of the Korean community is a quarterly magazine, *The Pioneer*, published by the Toronto Korean United Church, which began in 1970. *Sangjo* is the quarterly of the Korean Vancouver Society. It is published in both Korean and English, and has been put out since 1971.

During 1973, the Toronto Korean United Church sponsored a half-hour radio program every Saturday which contained music, stories, interviews and news about Koreans.

Koreans are known for their proficiency in music and dance. Many love singing, and an important feature of their church organization in Canada is the choir. In 1972, the Toronto Korean United Church choir was invited to perform at the Canadian National Exhibition and at a Korean Festival organized in November, 1972.

National celebrations among Koreans are observed in a quiet way. They include National Independence Day celebrations on March 1, and are related to the movement for independence in 1919 rather than Liberation Day celebrations which are held on August 15.

Korean Canadians enjoy material benefits in life which they would have been unable to achieve in their homeland, but still feel a strong attachment to their native country. Several Korean organizations, notably church groups, in their continuing concern for and desire to help people in Korea, have raised funds to send to Korea for general assistance in their home churches and needy communities. They eagerly seek to educate their children. Their problems, identical to those of other ethnic groups entering a new and different society, are gradually being eliminated as the Korean group continues a successful integration into Canadian life.

# Latvians

LATVIA IS A COUNTRY of some 25,000 square miles, (64,750 km²), situated on the eastern shore of the Baltic Sea and bounded on the north by Estonia, on the south by Lithuania, and on the east by Byelorussia and Russia.

Latvia as an independent state was to last only until June, 1940, when the Soviet army occupied the country and incorporated Latvia into the Soviet Union as a constituent republic. The country was occupied by the Nazis from 1941 until 1944, when the Red Army re-occupied it, with the result that 110,000 Latvians found themselves in Western Europe at the end of the Second World War as displaced persons. Of this number, some 60,000 made their way to the United States, while 12,892 emigrated to Canada.

There was little Latvian immigration to Canada before the Second World War, although some settlement did take place at the beginning of the twentieth century. The Province of Manitoba was one of the few areas where there was any significant prewar Latvian settlement. The Sifton area of the province, near Dauphin, witnessed the settlement of a few Latvian farmers as early as the 1890s, and some others settled around Lac-du-Bonnet on the Bird River, where place names such as Lettonia and Libau testify to the Latvian presence in the area. Latvian political refugees, seeking escape from Tsarist oppression, founded the town of Lettonia in 1906, and quickly established a school there. A Latvian community hall was built in the Lee River district in 1913.

By the time of the First World War, there were several hundred settlers of Latvian origin in the area, although the subsequent difficulties of the Depression drove many to seek work in eastern Canada. Because of the small numbers of people involved, and because of both economic and social pressure, the tendency to integrate was very strong, and only a few individuals were able to retain their Latvian language and national consciousness. The Canadian census of 1941 showed only 975 Canadians of Latvian origin.

Apart from these few hundred early settlers, the bulk of the Latvian population in Canada owes its presence to the effects of the Second World War. The majority of Canadian Latvians found themselves in displaced persons' camps in Germany after the war, and they made their way to Canada after 1946. Between this year and 1956, a total of 12,892 persons of Latvian origin entered this country.

In the 1971 census of Canada, a total of 18,180 persons claimed Latvian ancestry, and of this number, 14,140 (77.8 per cent) claimed some knowledge of the Latvian language. This extremely high percentage of persons retaining all or part of the language testifies to the relatively recent arrival of most Canadian Latvians, as the forces of integration have not yet made themselves fully felt.

A geographical breakdown of Latvian settlement in Canada shows that the overwhelming majority, 13,045 (71.8 per cent), reside in Ontario. Other provinces with a substantial Latvian settlement include Quebec (1,345 or 7.8 per cent), British Columbia (1,145 or 7.4 per cent) and Alberta (1,010 or 5.6 per cent). The largest single Latvian concentration is to be found in Toronto, where over 8,000 Latvians reside, and other large centres for Latvian settlement include Montreal and Hamilton, each of which has over 1,000 Latvian Canadians.

Because of a virtual halt in immigration to Canada from Latvia as a result of Soviet occupation, whatever growth has taken place can be attributed to natural increase. Statistics show that in the years 1958–62, fifty Latvians immigrated to Canada, but that only ten arrived in the years 1963–67 and another fourteen between 1968 and 1973.

Most Latvians are members of the Lutheran Church, although a small Roman Catholic minority also exists. As is to be expected, the Toronto area has the most highly developed Latvian religious life, with three Latvian Lutheran churches: St. John's, St.

Andrew's and the Eastern congregation. Smaller congregations have been able to establish their own churches, including for example St. Peter's Latvian Lutheran Church in Ottawa, with a congregation of several hundred, and Christ Latvian Lutheran Church in Hamilton. These churches also provide programs of social and cultural activities.

Latvian Catholics are organized around the Federation of Canadian Latvian Catholics, which also, in addition to its religious activities, carries on social and cultural activities. In Toronto there is also a small congregation of Latvian Baptists.

The earliest Latvians in Canada were mostly farmers, with only a sprinkling of professionals. Those who came in the postwar period, in contrast, included proportionately more professionally trained and educated people, and for this reason, after initial settlement adjustments, they have been able to enter Canadian society with considerable success. Only a small part of the postwar immigration has entered the agricultural field, with a significant part of this number settling in the Orangeville and Dundalk regions of western Ontario, where they specialize in dairy and poultry farming. Many others have made careers for themselves as engineers, doctors, lawyers, contractors and businessmen, reflecting their educational backgrounds in Latvia.

The Latvian community in Canada is served by several organizations, all of which are linked together in the umbrella organization the Latvian National Federation in Canada (LNAK). This is a highly structured body, founded in 1949 to act as a unified voice in the community's dealings with the Canadian government and with other ethnocultural groups, and to acquaint other Canadians with Latvian people and culture. Possessing specialized departments to deal with matters such as politics, culture, information, education and welfare, LNAK encompasses all of the fundamental aspects of Latvian-Canadian community life. It acts in a political role by promoting its long-range goal of independence for Latvia, and in so doing, collaborates with the umbrella organizations of the other two Baltic nationalities in Canada, the Estonians and Lithuanians. Furthermore, it supports cultural activities, supervises ten Latvian-language Saturday schools, and prepares textbooks and trains teachers as part of its program to preserve the Latvian heritage in Canada. At present its headquarters is located in Toronto.

The central organization of Latvian youth is the Latvian National Youth Federation in Canada (LNJAK). Its basic aim is to promote the preservation of Latvian cultural heritage and to foster friendship. To this end, it is a co-founder with a similar organization in the U.S. of the Latvian Youth Literary Society, Celinieks (The Wayfarer), which among other ventures publishes *Mazputnins (Little Bird)*, a magazine for children.

There are many local Latvian youth organizations which promote numerous activities ranging from modern and folk dancing to drama and various sports. Similar programs are encouraged by Latvian troops of the Boy Scouts and Girl Guides, which retain characteristic Latvian traditions along with their affiliation with the international scouting and guide movements.

A large international Latvian organization is the Daugavas Vanagi, which takes its name from the largest river in Latvia, the Daugava. It was founded as a relief organization at the end of the Second World War, but now has branches in many countries with sizable Latvian communities, and it has broadened its activities to include political work aimed at promoting the cause of Latvian independence and the preservation of Latvian culture. To this end, it publishes an international monthly magazine in Toronto, *Daugavas Vanagu Ménesraksts*, containing a broad range of information of interest to Latvians in general and to organization members in particular.

In Canada, the Daugavas Vanagi has nineteen branches. Together, they unite some 1,500 Canadians of Latvian descent, and promote numerous cultural activities such as publishing, recording music, choirs, educational work and sports. The organization continues its welfare work through various fund-raising events, and maintains links with its sister organizations around the world.

Essential to the Latvian cultural and social activities in Canada is the Latvian-language newspaper *Latvija Amerika (Latvia in America)*. This newspaper emerged out of the union of several earlier Latvian-language newspapers which were founded in response to Latvian immigration following 1946. Three Latvian-Canadian newspapers merged in 1950 to form the *Briva Balss (Free Voice)*, which in turn merged with another Latvian newspaper appearing in Germany, but rising costs ultimately caused the newspaper to be taken over and managed by the Daugavas Vanagi of Canada and the United States, at which point the name *Latvija Amerika* was adopted. At present, the paper is published in Toronto. It is a weekly with both news of the world and items of local interest to Latvians in Canada and the United States.

There are numerous other Latvian organizations functioning in Canada. The Association of Latvian Engineers and Technicians, for example, is a body with obvious professional interests which are to some extent expressed in its support of a scholarship fund to assist Latvian engineering students. Similar professional interests are promoted by the Association of Latvian Business and Professional Men. Those involved in creative enterprises have the Latvian Handicraft Guild, the Latvian Artists Association, the Latvian Press Club, and numerous local drama clubs. Similarly, several sports clubs exist across the country, as well as a hunters' and anglers' club with several branches. The functions of the above organizations are oriented toward culture and service, but the wide range of their functions testifies to the complex structure of interests and activities which the Latvian community has created for itself.

There are many contributions made by Latvian Canadians to the cultural life of this country, particularly in the visual arts, ballet, music and science. One of the most characteristic Latvian cultural activities is the song festival, a time-honoured form of traditional cultural expression dating back to the nineteenth century. The first Latvian song festival took place in Latvia in 1873, with choirs from all parts of the country coming together to perform modern and traditional songs. The first festival was a great unifying force, strengthening an awareness of cultural and national unity. These song festivals were subsequently held at regular intervals, and with the end of the Second World War, the idea of the Latvian song festival, like so many other national traditions, was transplanted to Canada.

It was not until September 1952 that the idea became reality, and some 2,000 Latvians came together in Toronto's Massey Hall to attend this unique cultural celebration. The second festival took place in Toronto in 1957, with some 600 singers performing traditional songs as well as works by contemporary Latvian composers who had settled in Canada.

In addition to the concert of massed choirs, the one-week long program includes symphony concerts, recitals, exhibits of fine arts and handicrafts, theatre performances, folk dancing and many other cultural events. This unique celebration is repeated in Canada every five or six years, alternating with similar events in the United States. The Latvian song festivals are the most spectacular demonstration of the Latvian culture and cultural heritage in Canada.

Even though the Latvian presence in Canada is a relatively recent one, and their numbers are relatively small, their presence is felt everywhere, especially in the musical sphere. They are vitally interested in maintaining their cultural heritage in their new homeland and passing it on to both the younger generation and to other Canadians.

# Lebanese

THE FIRST TWO Lebanese arrivals in Canada came to Montreal in 1882, and in 1885 a small colony grew in Montreal when a few others followed the first immigrants. Life was difficult for these early arrivals, for they had to make a living as door-to-door merchants.

It was not until after 1890 that Lebanese began arriving in Canada in any significant numbers. Most of them came from the Tyre Valley in Lebanon and formed the nucleus of the Lebanese community in Montreal. Some of these people later moved on to Ottawa to form the first Lebanese community in that city. Other groups were soon to follow, each group coming from a particular area or town in Lebanon and settling together in Canada.

The Montreal community were the forerunners of the Lebanese wholesale businesses that later flourished in Montreal, and the Ottawa community, which first centred around Carleton Place, again formed the nucleus of a thriving merchandising trade in that city.

The first Lebanese in Toronto likely arrived in 1888, and was soon followed by others who settled in that city. The Lebanese extended their settlement horizons to include New Liskeard, Ontario, in 1899 and to the Maritimes, Manitoba and British Columbia shortly thereafter, where various small manufacturing industries soon sprang up. The Notre Dame St. East section of Montreal and the Wellington (York) Street area of Toronto quickly became the eastern Canadian centres of wholesale merchandisers of Lebanese and Syrian descent. Many of the businesses in these areas suffered in the Depression, and a vast majority of them went bankrupt, their proprietors moving to other parts of Canada.

The Lebanese who came to Canada during the latter part of the nineteenth and early twentieth centuries were officially classified as Syrians, and the 1901 census classified Syrians (including Lebanese) with the Turks, since Syria was under Turkish control at that time. It was not until 1955 that Lebanese were classified separately in immigration department figures. There were 3,712 Syrians immigrating to Canada between 1901–05, a number which fell to 2,246 for the period 1906–15, 1,272 for 1916–25, 612 for 1926–35 and 89 for the period 1936–45. It is impossible to determine what proportion of these immigrants were Lebanese. It might be assumed that Lebanese formed roughly one-fifth of the Syrian total if it can be assumed that the proportion of 206 Lebanese who immigrated to Canada in 1955 was constant to the 1,160 Syrians who also came at this time. Other statistics, based on the fact that Lebanese immigration (16,618 persons) between 1955 and 1975 exceeded Syrian (3,000), suggest that figures might be approached somewhat differently.

Between 1956 and 1975, 16,618 Lebanese immigrants settled in Canada. Of these, 45 per cent reported Ontario as their destination, and 35 per cent reported Quebec. Therefore, during this time span, Ontario and Quebec accounted for 80 per cent of the total number of Lebanese immigrants, while Alberta attracted another 11 per cent. The Ontario group is dispersed in centres such as Toronto, Ottawa and vicinity, London and Windsor; in Quebec most Lebanese Canadians reside in Montreal, with a few in Joliette, Trois Rivieres, St. Jerome, Sherbrooke and Quebec City.

There are several hundred Lebanese in the Maritimes, most notably in the Sydney/Glace Bay, Nova Scotia region, in Halifax, and in Saint John, New Brunswick. Small Lebanese communities are also found in Vancouver and Winnipeg, but the largest concentrations of Lebanese in the west are centred in the Calgary and Edmonton areas.

Most Lebanese expected their stay to be of short duration when they originally came to Canada, but the success of their commercial ventures encouraged them to stay. They found they quickly integrated into Canadian society, and that any adjustments were of a minor nature. Their organizations helped in this integration process, while at the same time endeavouring to maintain their cultural heritage.

There are non-sectarian associations of a social, charitable or cultural character established by the Lebanese in many Canadian communities. Among these associations are the Canadian Lebanese Syrian Association (CLSA), L'Association des Amitiés Québec Proche-Orient (Quebec Middle East Friendship Asso-

ciation), and the St. Sauveur Immigrant Aid Society. Each of these organizations hopes to promote understanding between Lebanese and other Canadians, and strives to maintain the unique Lebanese culture and traditions in Canada. Because of the growing number of Lebanese in Canada, the international Lebanese Cultural Union established a Canadian association in 1963 with the objective of developing a stronger rapport between Canadians of Lebanese descent and Lebanon.

At present, the Lebanese group exhibits a distinctive variety of religions, sects and rites among its members. Within the community are Maronites, Melchites, Antiochian Orthodox, Syrian Orthodox, Protestants, Druze, Shi'l and Sunni Moslems. Many centres and local associations are provided by each religious group in Canada.

The early Syrians published an Arabic-language newspaper *Al-Shehab*, which appeared bi-weekly in Montreal. It lasted only two years, and attempts to start another paper, *Al Aalamein (Two Worlds)*, suffered a similar fate. The Lebanese community is now served by the semi-monthly *Canadian Middle East Journal* and the monthly *Arab World Review*. The community is also served by the magazine *Trait d'Union*, published since 1963 in Montreal.

The Lebanese presence was initially based around the manufacturing industry, but it has expanded to include many facets of Canadian life. They have brought new foods with them in which Canadians are becoming interested. The Lebanese wish to maintain their cultural heritage, but find it easy to slip into the Canadian mainstream. The construction of community halls is an effort to establish solidarity within the still comparatively small group. With the recent civil war in Lebanon, immigration from that country stepped up again to over 1,500 immigrants in each of 1974 and 1976. It is expected that these newcomers, with the assistance of those Lebanese already in Canada, will quickly assume a contributing role in Canadian society, as Lebanese before them have done.

# Lithuanians

LITHUANIA IS A SMALL COUNTRY located on the southeastern coast of the Baltic Sea. The first recorded Lithuanian immigrants to Canada arrived at the beginning of the nineteenth century as soldiers in the British army. Approximately 150 Lithuanian soldiers in Napoleon's armies had been taken prisoner by the British, and as a means of obtaining their freedom they agreed to enlist with the British forces and serve in Canada during the War of 1812. Enrolled in the regiments of Colonels de Watteville and de Meuron, these Lithuanians assisted in the defence of Canada in battles at Chateauguay and Fort Erie, and with the close of the war settled in Canada and generally integrated into colonial society.

More substantial Lithuanian immigration to Canada began at the close of the nineteenth century, when increasing numbers of Lithuanian agricultural workers left their homeland to escape conscription into the Russian army, or to improve their livelihood. Others had participated in anti-Russian uprisings and were sought by the Tsarist police. Interestingly enough, many of these early immigrants had first travelled to Scotland and England, where they worked in the coal mines. After a time, they decided to seek a fresh start and come to Canada. As a result, a small Lithuanian

colony arose in Sydney Mines, Nova Scotia, during the first two decades of the twentieth century.

Other groups of Lithuanians moved to western Canada, while some grew tobacco in southern Ontario. A substantial number, however, were attracted by the industrial opportunities to be found in Canada's urban centres, and small colonies of about 500 and 300 people settled in Toronto and Montreal respectively. Other centres such as Winnipeg, Calgary and Vancouver contained smaller numbers of Lithuanian Canadians.

By the time that Lithuania had regained her independence, there was a sizable Lithuanian community in Canada. According to the 1921 census, there were 1,970 people of Lithuanian origin in this country. During the next decade, Lithuanian immigration to Canada continued with an additional 3,000 individuals entering the country. The Great Depression of the 1930s had only a marginal effect on Lithuanian immigration, since another 2,000 Lithuanians were added to the Canadian total.

The largest wave of Lithuanian immigration, however, occurred after the Second World War and the Soviet occupation of Lithuania. When Soviet armies entered the country in the summer of 1944, many Lithuanians fled westward, either to Sweden or to Germany. When the war ended, they found themselves in displaced persons' camps, and from there almost 20,000 Lithuanians eventually made their way to Canada.

According to the 1971 census of Canada, there were 24,535 persons who claimed Lithuanian ancestry residing in this country. Of this total, 14,725 (60 per cent) claimed to be able to speak the Lithuanian language. By far the greatest number of Lithuanians were to be found in Ontario, with that province alone containing 15,365 (62.6 per cent). Other provinces with a substantial Lithuanian population include Quebec (3,990 or 18.3 per cent), Alberta (1,845 or 7.5 per cent) and British Columbia (1,630 or 6.6 per cent). Most of the Lithuanians living in Quebec reside in Montreal, but by far the largest single centre of Lithuanian population is Toronto, with a Lithuanian population in excess of 8,000. A third centre of Lithuanian population is Hamilton, with just over 2,000 Lithuanian Canadians, while Vancouver, Winnipeg, Edmonton, London, Ottawa, Windsor and Calgary have Lithuanian communities of several hundred individuals.

The Lithuanians who came to Canada before the war were, for the most part, unskilled workers who sought employment either in farming or, more likely, in industry. Those who came after the war, however, were in large part professional people, as well as skilled specialists who had completed their education and training either in prewar, independent Lithuania or in Western Europe. Although most were able to resume their former occupations, those whose qualifications were specifically tied to the Lithuanian situation, such as lawyers, civil servants, career military officers, teachers and writers, found it more difficult to obtain employment in Canada, and many had to requalify themselves.

As a result of the restrictive measures in force in the Soviet Union, Lithuanian immigration to Canada in recent years has virtually ceased. This may, in some part, account for the decline observed in the number of Lithuanians recorded in the Canadian census of 1961 (27,629) and that of a decade later. Apart from the integration processes which may have caused this decline, there is a likelihood of some emigration to the United States.

Religion plays an important part in the life of the Lithuanian community. Most Lithuanians are Roman Catholics, although there is a small Protestant minority. This balance is reflected in the fact that there are nine Lithuanian Catholic parishes in Canada, and only one Protestant congregation, the latter in Toronto.

The first Lithuanian parish was that of St. Casimir, founded in Montreal in 1916. This was followed twelve years later by the parish of St. John the Baptist in Toronto. All subsequent church foundations took place after the Second World War, as a result of the large influx of Lithuanian immigrants. At present Toronto has three Lithuanian parishes, two Catholic and one Protestant, and Montreal has two parishes. Lithuanian parishes are also to be found in Hamilton, Winnipeg, Delhi, Windsor and London. In addition, there are small Lithuanian-language missions in the cities of Ottawa, St. Catharines-Welland, Sudbury, Edmonton and Vancouver. The Franciscan order maintains two establishments for its Lithuanian brothers in Toronto and St. Catharines, while the Jesuit order maintains a rectory in the Montreal parish of Our Lady of the Gate of Dawn. The Sisters of the Immaculate Conception have established two convents, one each in Toronto and Montreal, and have operated kindergartens within their areas.

The earliest secular Lithuanian organizations date back to 1904, when a mutual aid society was founded in Montreal. A similar society was established in Toronto the following year, and in Winnipeg in 1912. By the beginning of the 1930s, there were some fifteen branches of these societies across the country, but the attraction of more broadly-based Canadian insurance companies in time diminished their appeal.

All Lithuanian-Canadians are considered

members of the Lithuanian-Canadian Community, founded in 1952, with some twenty chapters across the country. Its highest body, the National Council, is located in Toronto. The National Council integrates and coordinates Lithuanian cultural activities in Canada, maintains links with Lithuanian organizations in other countries, particularly with the Lithuanian World Federation, and provides a relief fund for needy compatriots. It also co-ordinates Canada-Lithuania Days, drama and dance groups, choirs and Saturday morning schools where children are taught the Lithuanian language. In the political sphere, the Community is committed to the ideal of an independent Lithuania free from Soviet domination.

Toronto, with the largest Lithuanian community in Canada, also has the largest Lithuanian community centre. In 1973, the Lithuanian House was opened to the public, with banquet halls, a permanent museum and a library. The building has since become a focal point for numerous community cultural and social activities.

Among the most important of the functions of the Canadian Lithuanian Community is the transmission of the Lithuanian cultural heritage to the young. As a result, the Lithuanian-language Saturday school has an important role to play in providing instruction in Lithuanian language, history, religion and folklore. Classes are held between September and May, usually on Saturday mornings. Well over one thousand Lithuanian children attend such schools, of which there are sixteen across Canada.

Lithuanian youth have their own Boy Scouts and Girl Guides organizations, affiliated with the international scouting movement. Furthermore, the Catholic Youth Association, Ateitininkai, also organizes youth activities, concerts, library evenings and summer camps. Those of university age have the Lithuanian Canadian University Students' Association to co-ordinate their activities, organize lectures, exhibitions and concerts, and represent the Lithuanian student community both in its dealings with other Canadian groups and in maintaining links with other Lithuanian student groups abroad. It is affiliated with the North American Lithuanian Students' Federation and works closely with the latter in organizing workshops, study sessions and conventions mainly in the United States.

The Lithuanian community is also involved in sports activities, with some ten sports clubs across Canada. The most prominent are the clubs Vytis and Ausra in Toronto, Kovas in Hamilton and Tauras in Montreal. Lithuanian folklore is preserved by numerous choral and dance groups, of which the largest are Gyvataras of Hamilton, and Varpas and Gintaras of Toronto.

Remaining Lithuanian organizations include the Lithuanian Canadian Catholic Women's Society. This group, founded in 1949, was based on a similar organization established in Lithuania in 1907. Among its concerns are Lithuanian education and cultural preservation. The Siauliai was an organization committed to cultural enrichment. Also, there were several Lithuanian organizations which were founded by the earliest waves of immigrants and which continued their functions until recently. There are also several branches of the Lithuanian American Alliance, an organization based in the United States.

At present there are four Lithuanian-language newspapers published in Canada. The largest is *Teviskes Ziburiai (The Lights of the Homeland)*, a weekly published in Toronto by the Lithuanian-Canadian Roman Catholic Cultural Society. The paper was founded in 1949 and is currently a member of the Ethnic Press Association of Ontario. A newspaper with a somewhat smaller circulation is the Montreal-based *Nepriklausoma Lietuva (Independent Lithuanian)*. Another Lithuanian newspaper published in Toronto until 1976 was the left-wing *Liaudies Balsas (People's Voice)*. A more specialized Lithuanian publication is *Moteris (Woman)*, intended specifically for Lithuanian women. The magazine was originally founded in Lithuania in 1923 and was revived in Canada after the Second World War. It is currently published in Toronto by the Lithuanian Catholic Women's Society.

Lithuanian art, whatever its medium, draws heavily on folklore in both its popular and traditional forms of expression. The most obvious example of this can be found in the numerous Lithuanian dance groups and choral societies active in all the larger centres of Lithuanian population. There is also a strong influence of traditional Lithuanian handicrafts such as weaving on the designs of contemporary Canadian artists of Lithuanian ancestry.

When one looks at the Lithuanian community today, one finds that its members have achieved considerable economic, educational, cultural and social integration into the Canadian system. At the same time they have maintained a distinct ethnocultural community that has recognizable social and cultural objectives of its own.

# Macedonians

THE MACEDONIAN PEOPLE include the original Slavic and Slavicized population inhabiting the area that roughly comprised the lands of the Macedonia of antiquity. Unlike other Slavic nations, the Macedonians have not had the opportunity to enjoy political independence in the modern era.

The Macedonians are not classified separately in the Canadian census and an attempt to estimate their numbers currently living in Canada is difficult. Migration from Greek Macedonia has always been heavy, and many of the Greeks entering Canada are in fact of Macedonian ancestry. Many of them prefer to speak Macedonian, attend a Macedonian church and to subscribe to Pan-Slavic sentiments. As well, in the case of Macedonians emigrating to Canada from Serbia (later Yugoslavia) and Bulgaria, it is virtually impossible, due to lack of adequate statistical classification, to isolate them from their southern Slavic neighbours.

As early as 1896, a few young Bulgaro-Macedonian peasants left the regions of Kastoria and Flovina in south Macedonia and migrated to Canada. They were followed during the next decade by only a few scattered individuals attempting to escape poverty and Turkish oppression. Then in the aftermath of the revolt of 1903, large-scale emigration to Canada, and in particular to Ontario, began. They did not intend to settle permanently, but wished to save money and return home to buy land. Some came to Canada several times for this purpose. About 1910, women began arriving to join their working husbands, an indication that these Macedonians intended to stay. In 1910, there were about 500 Macedonians from the district of Kostur in Toronto. It is estimated that there were about 6,000 Macedonians in Canada prior to the First World War.

Many of these early Macedonian settlers worked as unskilled labourers, and they were quick to form mutual aid societies. Macedonians from the same village banded together to help one another, forming organizations, one such being the Oshchima Benefit Society "St. Nicholas", formed by Macedonian immigrants from the village of Oshchima in 1907.

During the wars, Macedonians came to Canada intent on becoming permanent settlers and bringing their families when adequate funds were available. Many opened small restaurants, variety stores and other small businesses, concentrated in the southern districts of Toronto. Macedonian immigration progressed steadily until the Depression, and then more slowly until the outbreak of the Second World War. Following the Depression, special business associations were formed in which family restaurant owners and other small businessmen pooled their resources and invested them in more prosperous enterprises. It was during this period that the real economic basis of the Toronto Macedonian community was laid.

After the Second World War, Macedonian immigration increased, particularly after 1948 when the civil war ended in Greece. This period also marked the time when Macedonian Canadians began to leave their group concentrations and began to establish themselves in various areas of Canadian cities, especially in Toronto. They still showed a preference for new opportunities and businesses.

The composition of the Macedonian immigrant community underwent considerable change in the mid-1960s. Macedonians coming from Greece were now more integrated into the Greek culture than previously was the case, and many lacked any special Macedonian consciousness. Immigration from Yugoslavian Macedonia also increased in the mid-1960s. Many of these immigrants came from urban centres and possessed professional skills, easily practised in Canada.

Macedonians have integrated easily into Canadian society, with many establishing themselves in professional fields. They do, however, preserve their traditional heritage by maintaining their folk music, dances and celebrations.

The first Macedono-Bulgarian Church in Toronto, Sts. Cyril and Methodius, was established in 1910. St. George's Macedono-Bulgarian Orthodox Church was constructed in Toronto in 1941. The Macedonian Orthodox Church of St. Clement of Ochrid was established in 1962, and Holy Trinity, a small church in Toronto, was built in 1973. There is a Macedonian Orthodox Church in Hamilton dedicated to St. Naum.

The largest Macedonian association is the Macedonian Patriotic Organization, with headquarters in the United States. This association has been organized since 1925 with the aims of working for the establishment of Macedonia as an independent democratic republic within her traditional geographic boundaries, and to promote cultural life among Macedonians in Canada and the United States. The strength of the MPO may be indicated by the thousands who attended its annual convention. There are four MPO branches in Toronto.

The weekly *Macedonian Tribune*, founded in 1927 and published in the United States, is the official publication of the MPO. It has had an English page since 1938 and a special section for young Macedonians.

Today, Macedonians of the first generation are often very involved in the restaurant business, while many of the second generation are established in the professions. They tend to preserve their traditions, although the Macedonian identity may be different among other than first generation Macedonians. Regardless of which country he has emigrated from, the Macedonian in Canada is proud of his background, and attempts to retain it while contributing the best of his culture to the larger Canadian scene.

# Malaysians

THE PEOPLE OF MALAYSIA in Canada come from the Malay peninsula located in the heart of southeast Asia. Ethnically, most Malaysians in Canada are of Southeast Asian origin, establishing in Canada what is known as the Malaysia-Singapore community, which maintains a separate identity from other Chinese or East Indian immigrants.

As an identifiable group, Malaysians are among the newest arrivals in Canada, most of the immigrants having come in the 1970s. Few of them have been here longer than 10 years. Prior to 1969 there were no more than a handful of Malaysians and Singaporeans in Canada, their numbers being so small that they were not listed in Canadian immigration statistics. In 1972, 368 Malaysians and 166 Singaporeans entered the country. In 1973, 647 persons entered Canada from Malaysia and 233 from Singapore, increased by a further 605 from Malaysia and 405 from Singapore in 1974. In 1975, 461 persons

entered Canada from Malaysia and 442 from Singapore, giving an estimated total of persons in the Malaysia-Singapore community in Canada in 1976 of about 3,000 persons, one of the smallest groups in Canada.

Most of this group has come to Canada for political and economic reasons, and their choice of destination is usually either Toronto or Vancouver. Most are well-educated, and because of this they integrate well into Canadian life. A few immigrants are students who return home after completing their studies.

The Toronto community has its own association known as the Malaysia-Singapore Association of Canada, founded in 1973. Student groups have also formed associations in Toronto, Alberta and Winnipeg. The main aim of these associations is to assist Malaysian and Singapore nationals to meet one another and to help newcomers adjust to Canadian society. The Malaysia-Singapore Association of Toronto works closely with the Asian community council and the International Centre.

There are no exclusively Malaysian or Singaporean churches in Canada, but the community's Christian, Moslem, Hindu and Buddhist followers have become adherents of existing institutions.

Malaysia National Day is observed on August 31.

The Malaysian-Singaporean immigrants have made a successful adjustment to Canadian life, and they have a positive attitude towards the Canadian cultural and educational lifestyle. Most of them have come from an environment of political upheaval, and the freedom found in Canada is a welcome reality.

# Maltese

THE ANCESTRAL HOME of the Maltese has long been coveted by other nations because of its strategic position midway between Africa and continental Europe. The Apostle Paul is credited with converting the Maltese to Christianity, and the country has remained staunchly Roman Catholic ever since, despite coming under the domination first of the Byzantines and then the Arabs. The island passed under the protection of the British in 1814 with the establishment of a large naval base there.

In the First World War, Malta assumed the nursing role it had discharged under the Knights of Malta, furnishing thousands of beds for the sick and wounded. During the Second World War it resisted fierce enemy aerial attacks so valiantly that the people were awarded the George Cross as a group. In 1964 the island was granted full independence within the Commonwealth and in 1974 it became a republic.

If there is one single overriding factor which has governed Maltese emigration over the years it is overpopulation, for Malta, although rich in history, sunshine and charm, lacks the natural resources to support a rapidly growing population, estimated to be 322,173 at the end of 1973. Only recently, with the attraction of new industry to the three islands of Malta, Gozo and Comino, an increase in the tourist trade and the opening of new docks has the economic situation begun to look more promising.

The Maltese have looked to emigration to help alleviate the overpopulation problem ever since the middle years of the nineteenth century. In the 1800s, however, emigration took the form of an unplanned, spontaneous movement, usually to the coast of northern Africa and the eastern Mediterranean where there were employment opportunities in trading, general labour and craft work. Not until unemployment became widespread on Malta in 1907 did a significant emigration movement get underway to Australia, Canada and the United States. When thousands were laid off in the naval dockyards after the Armistice in 1918, the Maltese government created an emigration department to promote and control emigration.

Between 1918 and 1920 over 10,000 Maltese left for the United States, Australia and Canada. Emigration then slid to very low levels in the 1920s and 1930s as the principal receiving countries restricted the entry of immigrants because of reduced employment opportunities. Only after the Second World War did the exodus again begin in earnest, this time encouraged by dwindling employment opportunities in the naval establishments and the closing down of British military facilities. Now, however, instead of going to the United States, many emigrants came to Canada.

The first Maltese known to have settled in Canada was Lewis Schikluna who came to St. Catharines, Upper Canada, in 1836 and established a shipyard on the Welland Canal at a spot below where the Burgoyne Bridge now spans the ravine. In 1840 a group of Maltese pioneers arrived in this country, and since then the number of Maltese has continued to grow. The number of Maltese emigrating to Canada remained insignificant until after the Second World War when special provision was made for their admission to this country. The joint program which was worked out by the Canadian and Maltese governments was implemented in 1947 "in recognition of the outstanding service rendered by the people of Malta during the war and to assist them in dealing with their reconstruction problem." The first group of 500 selected workers arrived in 1948 and since then immigrants from Malta have continued to arrive annually, averaging about 300 to 400 each year. Between 1946 and 1950, 1847 persons from Malta immigrated to Canada.

In 1949 a study made by the editor of the *Maltese Journal* of New York revealed that 1,600 Maltese resided in Ontario, of whom 8 per cent were office workers, 2.5 per cent mechanics and 80 per cent unskilled workers. Eight per cent were employed in the meat industry and 1.5 per cent in business. There were 400 Maltese settled in the other provinces.

Since the end of the Second World War, 15,591 Maltese have left the small islands of their homeland for Canada. Although the majority of those Maltese immigrating to Canada stayed here, a small number did journey on to the United States. At the last census count in 1971, there were 9,230 Maltese-born Canadians and approximately 40,000 Canadians of Maltese origin living in Canada.

The Maltese who have come to Canada since the war have by and large settled in industrial centres where it is easiest to find employment, Toronto being the biggest magnet. Today there are an estimated 25,000 Toronto residents of Maltese origin, over 8,000 of whom are concentrated around Dundas Street West where the Maltese Franciscan Fathers have built a church and a parish hall dedicated to St. Paul. Maltese clubs and societies as well as a variety of businesses run by Maltese are also located in this area.

Maltese communities are also found in Hamilton, Oshawa, Whitby, Guelph, London, St. Thomas and Windsor. In addition, several families have settled in other Ontario centres such as Ottawa, Belleville and Peterborough. Outside of Ontario, Maltese can be found in Vancouver, Winnipeg and Montreal.

The Maltese celebrate various holy days and national feasts, including the feast of the conversion of St. Paul on January 25, the shipwreck of the Apostle on February 10, and the usual Canadian holidays. Malta's National Day on December 13 commemorates the anniversary of the declaration of the Republic of Malta in 1974.

Since most Maltese speak English and tend to integrate rather quickly and easily into Canadian society, they have not formed many organizations of their own. Some non-church-affiliated organizations, however, have played an invaluable role in the Maltese community. One of these is the Maltese Canadian Society of Toronto which since 1930 has done a great deal to help Maltese settle into their new way of life. Originally formed by a group of people interested in the social and economic welfare of the Maltese community, it was then primarily a benefit society.

As the community grew, so did the number of societies and clubs. Activities sponsored and organized by these Maltese organizations included social get-togethers, bands, national festivities such as Carnival, Imnarja and Malta Day, a Maltese radio program and Maltese television community programs, and services to help newcomers get settled in the community.

Similar festivities have been taking place in other communities such as Windsor, St. Thomas, Whitby and Guelph. Many other social activities and religious festivities are organized by the parish groups of St. Paul the

Apostle Church and the Franciscan Fathers.

Since soccer is Malta's national sport, the soccer club plays a role in the lives of many Maltese Canadians. Two of the better known clubs are the Toronto Hibernians Soccer Club and the Malta Soccer Club of Canada.

The Maltese arrived rather late on the Canadian scene, but are making an impact on many aspects of Canadian cultural and sporting life. They are dedicated to helping each other, but are also adding the unique Maltese character to the larger Canadian society.

# Métis

THE WORD *métis* is a French derivative of the Spanish word *mestizo*, meaning "to mix." Theoretically, the term Métis refers to those Canadians of mixed Indian and European ancestry, but the matter is complicated by both sociological and legal factors. On the one hand, large numbers of people of Métis descent are thought to have achieved so complete an assimilation into the larger Canadian society over the years that their original ancestry has long been forgotten. Provisions of the Indian Act allow for the registering as Indian of certain non-Indian women and their children and the deregistration, for various reasons, of pure Indians of either sex. Therefore, there are status Indians who are in fact of mixed descent, along with a substantial body of people who regard themselves as non-status Indians.

In a sociological and legal sense, then, the question of who is or is not a Métis is a difficult one. It is possible that in the near future the revision of the Indian Act now being studied will effect changes in the situation. Since a major concern of all native groups at present is the settlement of outstanding aboriginal claims, a legal definition acceptable to all sides will have to be achieved. It would appear sufficient to acknowledge the right of those who currently lay claim to Métis heritage to be so considered.

At present, it is not known exactly how many people would fall into this category, although one source notes that there are at least 750,000 Métis and non-status Indians in Canada. It is clear that in recent years they have become more closely allied and that during this period the overall term "Native" has come increasingly to be used, both in respect to Métis and non-status Indians, as well as status Indians. The Native Council of Canada, the national association of Métis and non-status Indians, currently considers itself as representing this group in all provinces, the Northwest Territories and the Yukon Territory.

There is no official record of the birth of the first Métis Canadian. One can assume, however, that the event dates back to a time shortly after the first Europeans arrived in Canada. What is known is that the rise and influence of the Métis as a group was closely allied with the development of the fur trade, and that Métis communities tended to grow up in the Maritimes, Quebec and Ontario along the waterways that in the seventeenth and eighteenth centuries provided the major method of movement around the country. The Métis played an important part in the fur trade as a whole, acting as interpreters between the traders and various Indian tribes involved; served as guides, entrepreneurs and businessmen; and played an essential role in both communications and transportation.

The first Métis on the Prairies was probably born during the first quarter of the seventeenth century, when explorers began to winter on the west coast of Hudson Bay. By the mid-eighteenth century, when the fur trade had become firmly established in the region, the Métis were present in sufficient numbers to begin to be referred to as a separate group, although their numbers were not the only criteria. Ultimately they became the largest single factor in the population of what is now Manitoba, and remained so until shortly after the establishment of that province in 1870.

The original relationships between the Europeans and the Indians were almost exclusively between the French and the Indians, because of the more aggressive trading policies of the largely French-manned Northwest Company and a fairly liberal attitude on the part of the company towards marriage by its employees. Later, as the rival Hudson's Bay Company increased its hold on the fur trade and Scottish farmers moved into the Red River settlement after 1812, a substantial English-speaking "halfbreed" presence began to be felt. The first Manitoba census, carried out in 1870, recorded a population of 5,757 French-speaking Métis and 4,085 English-speaking "halfbreeds." The complete mixed-blood group represented 82 per cent of the total population, with Europeans only 13 per cent and Indians 5 per cent.

In the Northwest Territories, two fairly separate communities grew up in the Mackenzie valley area; that to the north consisting of the largely English-speaking descendants of the nineteenth century whalers, traders and Athapaskan Indians, and that to the south being closer to the French-speaking Métis of the Prairies.

Historically, the concept of the Métis as a group achieved its most important manifestation on the Prairies. The beginnings came in the Red River area in what was once Assiniboia and is now Manitoba, where both half-breed and Métis communities emerged. The two led fairly distinct lives, separated not only by language and paternal descent (material origins for both were usually Cree or Salteaux), but also by religion and lifestyle. The halfbreeds were usually Protestants and farmers, while the Métis were Catholic and it was they who envisioned and hoped to realize the Métis nationhood.

The Métis had their own language, mainly French but with a strong Cree element. They had distinctive features of dress, such as the Assomption sash. And they had a culture which embraced not only some of the folk music of Europe but also the closeness to the natural environment of all North American peoples. What is more, the Métis of the Prairies, and particularly of the Red River, developed a unique and flourishing economy. Some farming was involved, as were traditional Métis pursuits of trapping and acting as interpreters between Indians and whites. To these were added a highly successful freighting trade and the large-scale hunting of buffalo.

Freighting took place mainly in the spring along clearly defined trails. For many years it provided one of the main means of moving goods in and out of the area through the border town of Pembina to the U.S. commercial centre of St. Paul. With the development of a distinct way of life among the Métis came a growth in political awareness, a sense of independence. The first evidence of this came in response to Lord Selkirk's Red River Colony, first founded at Fort Garry in 1812. Antagonism was aroused partly as a result of rivalry between the Northwest and Hudson's Bay companies and partly through a feeling that farming would prove harmful to the fur trade. When in 1814 the Governor of Assiniboia, Miles Macdonnell, sought to impose restrictions on the sale of pemmican and the running of buffalo, tension began to mount. The Nor'westers were instrumental in convincing the Métis that action should be taken. In 1814–15 harassment of the settlers and the eventual surrender of the governor took place. When the new governor, Sir Robert Semple, arrived in 1816 he and about twenty of his men were killed in what has come to be known as The Massacre of Seven Oaks.

Reconciliation between new settlers and Métis subsequently took place, facilitated by the merging of the Northwest Company with the Hudson's Bay Company in 1821. In 1835 the Hudson's Bay Company took steps to enforce more stringently its monopoly on the fur trade. Various incidents resulted, concluding with the arrest of four Métis in 1849 for illegal trading. Five hundred armed Métis surrounded the courthouse with the result that, although a verdict of guilty was passed down, no sentence was imposed. The trade monopoly of the Hudson's Bay Company was effectively broken. The Métis were able to insist on the later replacement of the judge by a man who could communicate in both English and French.

The culmination of Métis efforts to establish their position as a political entity in Assiniboia came with the negotiations over the sale of Rupert's Land (the entire area between the Red River and the Rockies) by the Hudson's Bay Company to the Canadian government in 1869. This was undertaken without consultation with the region's inhabitants or any arrangements for the retention by those inhabitants of the land on which they made their homes. In August 1869, Canadian government surveyors began to work in Assiniboia in disregard of the Métis settlement patterns. The surveyors were removed from Métis land by a group of some sixteen unarmed men led by Louis Riel.

In that same year, the Canadian government appointed William McDougall as Governor of Assiniboia, and directed him to proceed there and establish and maintain authority. The move was premature, since it required royal proclamation and none had, as yet, been given. Under the leadership of Louis Riel, the Métis formed a national committee. McDougall was turned back across the American border. Then, a provisional government in which all inhabitants were free to participate was established along democratic lines with Louis Riel as president. A bill of rights was declared, designed specifically to ensure fair treatment and full representation for all.

Riel's provisional government was the body which negotiated the terms of Manitoba's entry into Confederation. Riel was, however, deprived of his assured amnesty and a military force was sent from Canada.

After the founding of Manitoba in 1870, a large number of Métis moved into what was to become Saskatchewan. They joined other Métis and halfbreeds along or near the South Saskatchewan River in the Batoche area. The Canadian government was at this time making active efforts to further settlement of the West. Once again, those already there began to feel that tenure of their land was in jeopardy. In 1884, farmers from around Prince Albert joined the Métis and halfbreeds in asking Riel to come from Montana to their aid.

Riel had a concept of the northwest as a land in which Native peoples should be able to develop fully and freely. He drew up a petition, and when the response was unsatisfactory, declared a second provisional government. By this time, the support of white settlers had been reversed and the halfbreeds had decided to adopt a position of neutrality. Indian commitment to what had become an exclusively Métis cause was very limited. A troop of Northwest Mounted Police was defeated at Duck Lake in March 1885 by the Métis, and the government sent in a militia force. The Métis were heavily outnumbered but withstood four days of battle at Batoche. Riel surrendered and was tried in court, sentenced, and hanged.

The founding of Manitoba as a province resulted in the migration of a substantial number of Métis, due in part to the sheer volume of settlers who began to move into the area. The Métis were outnumbered and their political power was lost. In part, the causes for the migration were economic. Steamboats and railways were replacing the freight trails, the fur trade was dwindling, pemmican was no longer in demand, and the buffalo were declining and would eventually disappear. The Métis were to find, as they had found in Quebec and Ontario, that their skills and services were no longer of prime importance. Moves (often repeated several times) to Saskatchewan, Alberta, "frontier" areas of Manitoba, North Dakota and Montana ultimately proved to be only a means of postponing change. The old way of life was passing and the farmer was taking over.

Some Métis kept on moving north and started remote communities in northern Alberta, Saskatchewan, Manitoba and even the Northwest Territories where a life of hunting and trapping could provide a means of support, at least for a time. Others settled into southern communities or took up residence in groups, usually on the edges of predominantly white communities or of Indian reserves. Those who retained an identity as Métis usually did so at the price of being to some extent outcasts. The pattern was much the same in other parts of Canada and has been clearly observed as having an effect in recent years among the Mackenzie valley Métis of the Northwest Territories. One of the chief concerns of Métis leaders in this area at present is to ensure that exploration for and exploitation of natural resources does not prove entirely disruptive of Métis life.

Perhaps the most important development of the second half of the twentieth century has been the increasing movement of Métis to major Canadian urban centres. This migration has occurred generally as a quest for increased opportunity and improved standards of living. It means that Métis are now to be found in significant numbers in a large percentage of Canadian towns and cities.

Since the events following the Riel Rebellion of 1884, the Métis have at various times sought to work together for the betterment of their situation. There was, for instance, the movement in Saskatchewan in 1937 surrounding the original founding of the Saskatchewan Métis Society. The 1960s and 1970s have witnessed a renewed and determined effort in this regard. Canadian Métis and non-status Indians are now more vociferous in seeking to protect their rights, more active in the fields of political and social welfare, more visibly a force in Canadian society, more confident in their assertion that only they can decide the ways and means by which they must live than at any previous time in the twentieth century. Currently, much of their work is being undertaken on the basis of funding by various levels of government, which is a factor to be remembered and taken into account. Nevertheless, it does not alter the fact that the initiatives described in the following pages are essentially Native developments.

In 1961, the Métis Association of Alberta

was founded. It proved to be the first of a new wave of provincial associations working through locals and intent on uniting Métis and non-status peoples so that they might achieve both a political voice and the mechanisms for social and cultural growth. There are now Métis and non-status organizations in the Northwest Territories and in all of the provinces with the exception of British Columbia, where the United Native Nation is open to membership by all of those of Native ancestry. The Native Council of Canada, previously noted as the national association, was founded in 1971 and has its headquarters in Ottawa. Although both national and provincial groups are heavily involved in the planning and implementation of a wide range of programming, their single most important function lies in their ability to make representations to the various governing bodies on relevant issues in a manner which will be assured of a careful hearing.

At the Fifth Annual Assembly of the Native Council of Canada in June 1976, it was agreed that the reaffirmation of aboriginal rights and settlement of claims resulting from that reaffirmation should be accepted as the primary objective of all forthcoming effort. The issue revolves around the special position that the Métis and non-status peoples believe themselves to have regarding authority over Canadian land as a result of their initial residency and settlement on that land. It was the issue which was very much at stake at the founding of Manitoba and which the Métis believe not to have been settled at that time. It was at stake in Saskatchewan in 1885 and has come frequently into the news in recent years, particularly as such new areas as James Bay and the Mackenzie valley become the subject of natural resource development. The Native peoples feel that a favourable decision on their claims will result.

A preliminary study on the aboriginal claims of Manitoba Métis was published by the Manitoba Métis Federation in 1973. Further research is now underway or planned by all provincial associations and the Native Council of Canada. Claims are under negotiation in British Columbia and the Yukon, where treaties were never made. A settlement which may involve Métis and non-status Indians has been agreed to in that part of Quebec affected by the James Bay Hydro Project. The Métis Association of the Northwest Territories, originally included with the Indian Brotherhood of the NWT in the Déné declaration of nationhood, is now committed to the presentation in the near future of its own individual proposal for a Mackenzie valley settlement.

Although aboriginal rights are a priority, the process of development and of resolving difficulties in all areas is regarded as being of the utmost importance. To this end, the Native Council has established a commission for the study of crime and punishment, is working with the Central Mortgage and Housing Corporation for the creation, implementation and extension of housing programs, and has set up a national program on alcohol abuse. Provincial associations have shown themselves active in these and other aspects of social welfare. At the same time, all Native peoples—status, non-status and Métis—have joined together for the formation of groups founded to answer particular needs. Of interest in this field are the local, national and provincial women's groups, and the network of Friendship Centres now operating in urban areas to provide counselling, recreational facilities and cultural meeting places to assist in the adjustment to urban living. In education, one of the most important tasks has been the "education of the educators," the convincing of educators of the necessity for including material relevant to Native children in the curricula, and demonstration to educators of the extent to which Canadian textbooks contain inaccuracies and derogatory information on Native history and Native life. Some success has been achieved, and departments of education in such provinces as Ontario are both upgrading the quality of information on Native topics and gradually withdrawing texts that Native groups regard as unacceptable.

The retention, strengthening and development of cultural heritage is of vital concern to all Métis and non-status groups. From British Columbia to Newfoundland, efforts are being made to ensure the continuation of such traditional skills as beadwork, basket weaving, and wood carving; to record on film such activities as the making of bannock and the preparation of hides; to offer language classes; and to provide facilities for Native music and dancing. Notable in this regard are the annual "Back to Batoche" days of the Association of Métis and Non-Status Indians of Saskatchewan, and the newly formed Native Folk Festival Corporation of Thunder Bay. Also of importance is a program entitled "Native Country", established by the Native Council for the promotion of Native entertainers. Traditionally, Native culture was inseparable from Native spiritual values and perceptions. For a long time, however, every effort was made by those working with Native peoples to ridicule and destroy Native religious beliefs. Revival and growth are now taking place in this aspect of life and also a Native Ecumenical Conference is held every year at Morley, Alberta.

Like many other ethnocultural groups, Native people have found the regular media channels inadequate in the coverage of their events. To fill this need, Native newspapers and communications societies have been formed. At present the Native Council publishes *The Forgotten People* monthly, and each provincial association has its own publication. *Dimensions* is the publication of the Ontario Métis and Non-Status Indian Association. Other groups such as Friendship Centres produce periodicals and newsletters, and the National Association of Friendship Centres has a monthly periodical, *The Native Perspective*. Communications societies are active not only in print, but also in broadcasting, radio and television work. The Alberta Native Communications Society puts out a weekly paper *The Native People*, produces 16 millimetre films, does television work, and provides radio programming to about ten radio stations. The CBC radio program "Our Native Land" is heard throughout Canada and features Native news, broadcasters and performers.

It is generally accepted that Native leadership and Native people as a whole have responded with responsibility and patience to what are almost universally regarded as injustices against the Native people. Their contributions to the early development of our country and the role they played in the political formation of the Prairies places upon Canadians a debt which must be paid through an early and successful conclusion of aboriginal claims and other matters which affect Métis and Native peoples alike.

# New Zealanders

ALTHOUGH A NUMBER of New Zealanders come to Canada each year, very little is known about them as members of a distinct New Zealand national group. There is no information on them in the Canadian census. For this reason, even the most basic information on the size and composition of their population in Canada is unavailable.

New Zealanders share an ethnocultural background with many Canadians of British origin, and their lifestyle is similar to that of other English-speaking Canadians, so they are not a distinctly visible group in this country. As for those New Zealanders with non-British backgrounds, they may choose to become members of their original ethnocultural communities in Canada.

Immigration from New Zealand has risen steadily in the postwar decades. No figures have been kept, however, for the prewar period. Between 1946 and 1965, 4,632 people from New Zealand were admitted to Canada, although they were not all citizens of New Zealand. From 1966 to 1975 another 8,200 people came to this country from New Zealand, some of whom originally came from other countries such as England and the United States.

The personal backgrounds of New Zealanders entering Canada during the past 10 years are identical in most respects to those of other recently arrived immigrants from Asia. Of the 4,950 immigrants who entered Canada between 1966 and 1975 and who were seeking employment, 2,342 (47.3 per cent) reported that they intended to enter the professional or managerial fields, 20 per cent were white collar workers, and 30 per cent were in some sort of manual or service job category. As with many highly qualified immigrants from other countries, New Zealanders have emigrated in search of better economic opportunity.

It is estimated that the largest number settle in British Columbia, followed by Ontario and Alberta. They gravitate to urban centres, in particular Toronto and Vancouver, and have very little trouble integrating into Canadian society. New Zealanders in Canada do not therefore form groups which can be recognized as an ethnocultural community.

There are three clubs of a social nature formed by New Zealanders together with the Australians in Canada, two in Vancouver and one in Toronto. The Australia-New Zealand Association in Vancouver was formed in 1935. TRANZAC in Toronto and the Southern Cross International Association in Vancouver are two other similar associations of a non-profit, non-political and non-sectarian nature with membership open to all nationals.

While New Zealanders are not a visible ethnocultural group in Canada, they continue to contribute to the larger Canadian society through their organizations and their professional skills, are proud of their background and history, and are ready to become active and vital members of Canadian society.

# Nigerians

NIGERIA BECAME A BRITISH COLONY in 1861. The British administered the country as two different regions up to 1914, when the Northern and Southern Protectorates were united into one colony. The north is predominantly Muslim and the south is Christian. Nigeria became independent on October 1, 1960.

Nigerian emigration to Canada is a very recent phenomenon, although a small number of Nigerian students studied in Canada in the late 1930s and early 1940s. As a young state

Nigeria is still in the process of developing the economic and technological possibilities required to industrialize the nation. Many Nigerians therefore seek their university education abroad, and Canada is one of the numerous countries where Nigerians go in search of higher education. Nigerians began to enter Canada in greater numbers in the 1960s, but the influx of Nigerians has dropped since the early 1970s. There was no recorded Nigerian immigration prior to 1963, and between 1963 and 1967, 175 Nigerians emigrated to Canada, the figure rising to 857 persons for the period 1968–73, before immigration dropped off.

In 1975 there were approximately 2,000 Nigerians in Canada. It is further estimated that as of 1974 about 173 had taken out Canadian citizenship. About four-fifths of the total number of Nigerians in Canada are registered students in Canadian colleges and universities. More than 50 per cent of the entire Nigerian student population is sponsored by either the federal government of Nigeria or the various state governments. A few of the students are sponsored by the Canadian International Development Agency (CIDA).

There are close to 1,500 Nigerians in Ontario, with about 500 residing in Toronto and environs, while about 200 are in the Province of Quebec. Nigerians are found in other Canadian cities, including Vancouver, Edmonton, Calgary, Winnipeg and Halifax. An overwhelming majority of Nigerians in Canada belong to either the Ibo or the Yoruba ethnic groups.

There is no national organization of Nigerians in Canada. The only semblance of a national organization that existed in Canada was motivated by the Nigerian civil war (1967–71) when the Ibos organized a national union of Biafrans, primarily to propagate the

cause of Biafra in Canada during the civil war. Various Canadian groups and organizations organized relief funds for the civil war's victims. This Biafran national union withered away soon after the civil war ended in Nigeria.

Nigerians in various Canadian colleges and universities have student unions. These unions are social organizations whose major preoccupation is to organize dances commemorating Nigeria's Independence Day on October 1.

Nigeria was host to the Second World Black and African Art and Cultural Festival in January–February, 1977. Canadian Blacks, with substantial support from the Canadian government, participated in the festival. It marked the first time that Canada has participated in an international Black festival, indicating that the African presence in Canada is beginning to be felt.

# Norwegians

THROUGH THE VOYAGES of Norsemen from their colonies in Iceland and Greenland late in the tenth century, Norwegians can be considered the first Europeans to explore the North American continent. In the year 1000 Lief the Lucky landed at a place called Vinland, thought to be Newfoundland. The Norsemen made at least one major attempt to establish a settlement in the newly discovered land, but the natives drove them off.

The beginnings of the Norwegian movement to North America can be traced to 1825, when the first shipload of Norwegians arrived in the United States. It was not until the 1890s, however, that these people began looking to the Canadian Prairies as land became scarce and expensive in the United States. Until that time, Canada had been little more than a corridor for the vast influx of Norwegian immigrants to this continent. Most Norwegians entered the United States by way of Quebec, since it was the port with the cheapest entry fares. Over a half-million Norwegians stepped ashore at Quebec; few remained in Canada.

In June, 1854, a small Norwegian settlement was founded on the Gaspé Peninsula in eastern Quebec. However, severe weather and land settlement difficulties caused much disillusionment to set in by 1859. By 1862, all but ten of the Norwegian settlers in the Gaspé had left for the United States.

Until 1890, Canadian policies designed to retain at least a sizable portion of the large numbers of Norwegian immigrants streaming through Quebec were a failure. In 1857 the Department of Agriculture had appointed Christopher Closter, a Norwegian, as a Canadian immigration agent at Quebec. From 1873, Canada was advertised in most Scandinavian countries as a home for potential immigrants. Canadian immigration agents travelled to Norway to promote land opportunities in Canada, but potential Norwegian emigrants were indifferent.

The land policies in eastern Canada prior to the construction of the Canadian Pacific Railway made Canada unpopular for Norwegian immigrants. Compared to the readily available farmland in the American Midwest, Norwegian settlers in Canada would have had a great deal of difficulty in obtaining clear title to their land. Land speculators in eastern Canada stood to profit from settlers, and the Canadian government did little to change this situation until the 1890s.

Around the turn of the century, Canadian policies on land settlement began to change, at the same time as land settlement policies became more restrictive in the American west. Farming areas in the United States were no longer able to absorb so many immigrant farmers. Into this vacuum of expectations moved CPR land agents and a vigorous advertising campaign by the Dominion government.

Norwegian settlers in the American Midwest faced mounting debts and few opportunities for expansion. They had acquired experience in prairie farming and the Canadian Prairies offered them a second chance. Hundreds of thousands of settlers moved from the United States to Saskatchewan and Alberta, and a sizable proportion of them were Norwegian. The 1921 census gives an indication of the extent of this indirect migration to Canada. Of the 68,856 listed of Norwegian origin, 32.2 per cent had been born in the United States, 33.6 per cent in Norway and 34.2 per cent in Canada.

The 1971 census lists 179,290 residents of Norwegian origin, an increase from 148,681 in 1961. The greatest concentration of Norwegian Canadians were to be found, in order of size, in British Columbia, Alberta, Saskatchewan, Ontario and Manitoba.

One of the first Norwegian settlers in Canada was Willard Ferdinand Wentzel, an explorer with the Northwest Company at the beginning of the nineteenth century. Norwegians were among the first Red River settlers brought in by Lord Selkirk in the years 1812–15. They established the Norway House trading post on the northern end of Lake Winnipeg in 1815, one of the oldest trading posts in the West and still an active Hudson's Bay Company centre.

Alberta has a long history of Norwegian settlement. The 1971 census listed 51,305 Alberta residents of Norwegian origin. In

1886, several Norwegians settled in Calgary as part of a sawmill crew for the Eau Claire Lumber Company, the first major industry in that community. In the 1890s and the early part of the twentieth century, large numbers of Norwegians moved from the American west to seek homesteading opportunities in Alberta. One group settled in the area of central Alberta now known as the New Norway district, and was soon reinforced by additional settlers from the United States, especially South Dakota.

Other Norwegian settlements established in central Alberta during this period include Crooked Lake, Skandia, St. Joseph, Asker, Edmonton, Camrose (originally Bakken and Oslo), Rosebush, Perry Point, Meeting Creek, Donalda (originally Bethania), Martins, Earling, Round Hill (originally Trondhjem), Bawlf, Bethlehem, Kingman, Ryley, Amish Creek, and communities with such Norwegian names as Viking, Edberg and Bardo. In the Eagle Hills district there were communities with Norwegian names such as Bergen and Sundre.

Norwegian settlement in the Peace River district first began at Grande Prairie in 1908. In 1912, a group of Norwegian pioneers founded the nearby settlement of Valhalla. The black soil in the Peace River district was much richer than that of the Palliser Triangle to the south, and when many Norwegian farmers in Southern Alberta and Saskatchewan suffered crop failures in the 1930s, they moved to the richer soil regions of the Peace River district.

The 1971 census listed 36,160 persons of Norwegian descent living in Saskatchewan. Until the 1961 census, the Province of Saskatchewan had the largest Norwegian population in Canada. The first Norwegian settlement in Saskatchewan was started at Glen Mary,

about 50 miles (80 km) east of Prince Albert, in 1894.

Hanley, in the Assiniboia district which later became a part of Saskatchewan, first attracted Norwegian settlers in 1903. In the same year, a major Norwegian settlement which attracted large numbers of settlers from the United States was started in the Outlook district. Soon the whole area from Outlook to Hanley had become a Norwegian settlement. Communities in Saskatchewan that were founded prior to the First World War by Norwegian pioneers, or had many Norwegians among their first settlers, are Howarden, Strongfield, Loreburn, Elbow, Macrorie, Ardath, Conquest, Bounty, Swanson, Delisle, Pike Lake, Birch Hills, Brancepath, Weldon, Kinistno and Melfort. Saskatchewan communities with distinctive Norwegian names include Gruenfeld, Hagen, Gronlid, Stenen, Erickson, Engen, Nelson and Norland.

Although Norwegians had been active in establishing Norway House at the beginning of the nineteenth century, permanent settlers of Norwegian origin did not arrive in Manitoba until much later. In 1887 Norwegians founded Numedal, a community near the North Dakota border, but few traces remain of the earlier settlement. The Dominion government set aside some 80,000 acres (32,374 ha) of land north of the original Manitoba boundary to attract Scandinavian settlers, and many Swedes and Norwegians settled in New Scandinavia.

Manitoba never became a centre for Norwegian culture in the same way that it did for Scandinavian groups such as the Icelanders and the Swedes. The most prominent Norwegian-Canadian newspaper, *Norröna*, was published in Winnipeg until 1970, but early Norwegians were more attracted to farmlands in Alberta and Saskatchewan, even before these regions became formal provinces. In 1971, 8,960 Norwegian Canadians lived in Manitoba.

Until the Second World War, Norwegians settled mainly in the Prairie Provinces and were highly concentrated in local farming communities, many of which had been founded by Norwegians. However, in the 1930s, the Depression and the drought and dust storms in many regions of the west caused thousands of homesteads to be abandoned. The topography of many Norwegian settlements located in areas such as the Palliser Triangle was affected by the drought and the winds blowing away the soil, and while many Norwegians moved to other parts of Canada such as the Peace River district and British Columbia, a number of them returned to Norway.

The first Norwegian who became a permanent settler in British Columbia was Hans Helgesen, who arrived in 1860 and settled near Victoria during the gold rush era. He later became a member of the provincial legislature. The first Norwegian settlement was organized near Matsqui in 1884 by John L. Broe.

After 1893, Norwegians settled in British Columbia because of the activity of the land companies and the offer of assistance to new settlers by the provincial government. Norwegians also came to British Columbia from Minnesota and other parts of the United States. In 1894, Pastor C. Saugstad of the Lutheran Free Church in Minnesota negotiated with the provincial government to settle the valley at Bella Coola. The colony drew up a constitution while still in Minnesota and arrived in Vancouver in October, 1894. The colony was small but it prospered, and many of the descendants of these pioneers live in Bella Coola today. A similar colony of Norwegian settlers was established at Quatsino at the upper end of Vancouver Island and came to be known as the Scandia settlement. The colony failed, however, for lack of reserves.

During the Depression, the Norwegian population in British Columbia more than doubled as many migrated from the Prairies to the West Coast. In the 1940s, industries in British Columbia were a particular attraction for Norwegians living on the Prairies.

Today, people of Norwegian descent are most numerous in New Westminster, Vancouver and Prince Rupert as well as in most communities along the coast. In the 1971 census, British Columbia had 53,245 Norwegian Canadians, the highest figure for any province in Canada. Vancouver has become the centre for Norwegian culture in this country. An indication of this is the fact that 7,075 of the 16,350 Norwegian-born in Canada in 1971 lived in British Columbia.

Ontario has gradually attracted more Norwegian Canadians. In 1971, 20,590 Norwegian Canadians lived in Ontario. Many are the descendants of early western pioneers who left the Prairies to seek careers in Toronto and Ottawa. Others left Norway after the Second World War, and were attracted to the industries of Ontario.

Official relations between Canada and Norway were very close during the Second World War. In November, 1940, the "Little Norway" camp north of Toronto was opened to train Norwegian air force pilots. This camp, built and maintained by funds provided by the Government of Norway in London, England, was the first foreign air force training camp on Canadian soil. In September, 1976, Crown Prince Harald of Norway unveiled a plaque commemorating this co-operation between the two countries.

In 1971, there were 3,820 Norwegian Canadians living in Quebec, mainly in the

Greater Montreal area. There were also substantial concentrations of Norwegians in Nova Scotia (about 2,000, mainly in Halifax) and in New Brunswick.

Since the Second World War, migration of Norwegians to Canada has been small, about 13,000 all together. These immigrants were mainly from professional and clerical backgrounds and gravitated towards the cities of Ontario and British Columbia. The economy of Norway is very stable today, especially with the discovery of the North Sea oil, and there are few economic motives for Norwegians to leave their homeland.

As ever-increasing numbers of Norwegians arrived in Canada, there developed a need on the part of these settlers for their own cultural and social institutions. Many immigrants had difficulty coping with the English language. As a large number of Norwegians settled in rural farming areas, there were fewer English-language influences and a greater reliance on social activities in the Norwegian language. Since so many Norwegian settlers had come from the United States, Norwegian-American organizations tended to extend their activities into Canada.

With the Lutheran Church as the state church of their homeland, it was natural that most Norwegian immigrants would turn to some form of Lutheranism in Canada. The 1941 census showed that of those of Norwegian birth in Canada, 84.7 per cent were at least nominally of the Lutheran faith, while the United Church had the second largest number of Norwegian-born, with 5.4 per cent.

The Haugean revivalist movement of the early nineteenth century had its effect on what form of Lutheranism the Norwegian immigrants would adopt. Many felt no need to perpetuate the outward forms of the Norwegian state church in North America. Although there was some disagreement on how much of the accustomed liturgy should be preserved, most Norwegians living in North America recognized an increased role for laymen in the church including a need for lay preachers.

Many of the early Norwegian settlers in western Canada had belonged to various synods of the Norwegian Lutheran Church in the United States, and these church bodies felt a responsiblity to organize churches in Canada. The early churches became organized by three different Norwegian-Lutheran organizations: The Hague Synod (founded in 1846), the Norwegian Synod (1853), and the United Norwegian Lutheran Church (1890). In 1917, these three merged to form the Norwegian Lutheran Church which changed its name to the Evangelical Lutheran Church in 1946.

In 1960, this North American Norwegian Lutheran body merged with the United Danish Church and the American Lutheran Church of German background to form the American Lutheran Church. In 1967, the Canadian section of this North American church body became the Evangelical Lutheran of Canada.

Norwegian Lutherans, by themselves or in co-operation with other Lutheran organizations, opened a number of colleges and seminaries. The oldest is Camrose Lutheran College, which opened in 1911 as a Norwegian Lutheran Academy. It eventually became affiliated with the University of Alberta. Outlook College opened in 1915 at Outlook, Saskatchewan. It closed in 1936 because of the Depression, but reopened in 1939 as the Saskatchewan Bible Institute, later renamed the Lutheran Collegiate Bible Institute, and became a more general Lutheran body.

Norwegian Lutherans co-operated with Lutherans of other ethnocultural backgrounds to found the Canadian Lutheran Bible Institute in 1932 at Camrose as a Christian leadership school and the Luther Theological Seminary in Saskatoon in 1939, which is affiliated with the University of Saskatchewan.

An important factor that influenced the retention of Norwegian customs was the readiness of Norwegians to intermarry with members of other ethnocultural groups. Another factor was the considerable internal migration within Canada caused by the Depression and the search for jobs in Canadian industry during and after the Second World War.

*Norröna*, founded in Winnipeg in 1910, is the longest-established Norwegian-language newspaper in Canada, and is the only Norwegian-language newspaper today. The *Canada Skandinaven* was founded in 1911 in Vancouver and continued to 1940. There have been short-lived local Norwegian newspapers printed in Canada at Norden, Saskatchewan, and in Vancouver, but competition from larger, American-based papers proved to be too strong. *Hyrden (Shepherd)* was a periodical published as an organ of the Norwegian Lutheran Church in Canada. When it began publication in 1924 it was written mainly in the Norwegian language, but by 1949 it was entirely in English.

The readership for Norwegian-language periodicals is continually declining as fewer Canadian-born Norwegians can read their ancestral language. In the 1971 census, 27,405 persons claimed Norwegian as their mother tongue. A more revealing statistic points out that only 2,160 of the 179,290 Canadians of Norwegian ethnic origin listed in the Canadian census reported Norwegian as the language they commonly used at home.

The only Norwegian cultural body with a widespread organization is the Sons of Norway, which was founded in 1895 at Minneapolis as a mutual aid and fraternal society. It is the largest Norwegian organization in North America with a membership of over 80,000. Over the years, the Sons of Norway has become a more universal body with a fraternal and social organization. English has become the working language. The central organization publishes a monthly magazine, *The Viking*, with news of both American and Canadian lodges.

There are Sons of Norway lodges in Alberta (Calgary, Claresholm, Camrose, Edmonton, and Grande Prairie) and British Columbia (Vancouver, Burnaby, Surrey, Campbell River, Chilliwak, Dawson Creek, Duncan, Fort St. John, Kamloops, Kinnaird, Nanaimo, Penticton, Port Alberni, Powell River, Prince George, Prince Rupert, Squamish and Victoria.) In Victoria, the Sons of Norway social centre is named "Little Norway."

Other Norwegian cultural organizations in British Columbia include the Norsemen's Federation in North Vancouver, the Norwegian Club in Delta, and the Northland Society "Midnight Sun" in New Westminster. There are also distinctive Norwegian organizations in Montreal and Halifax.

Norwegians also promote their cultural heritage in co-operation with other Scandinavian groups, the most notable organizations being the Scandinavian Centre Association in Edmonton (in which the Sons of Norway lodge plays a role) and the Scandinavian Centre in Calgary. Both are incorporated as co-operatives, and promote social activities, language instruction, folk dancing, and commemorative national days of the respective countries.

In Saskatchewan, Norwegians work with other Nordic groups to support Scandinavian clubs in Saskatoon, Moose Jaw and Birch

Hills. There are Scandinavian clubs in Montreal, Toronto and Oshawa, and a Nordic society in Ottawa.

There have been some distinctive contributions by Norwegians in Canada, but in general Norwegians have adapted so readily to Canadian society that their achievements have not usually been regarded as the contributions of a distinct ethnocultural group.

One of the most notable achievements by a Norwegian-born citizen in Canada was Henry A. Larsen's exploration of the Arctic. As a member of the RCMP, Larsen traversed the Northwest Passage in his ship, the *St. Roch*.

Norwegian Canadians have been very active in sports, particularly in skiing, where names such as Anne Heggtviet and Karen Magnusson in figure skating have gained international prominence. Norwegians have also joined and have taken active leadership roles in western populist organizations that were community based, such as the CCF in Saskatchewan and the Social Credit in Alberta.

As Norwegians settled in Canada and their children enjoyed the full benefits of the Canadian educational system, more and more second and third generation Norwegians made contributions in the professions. The Norwegians were the first to explore what is now Canada, and now, nearly a thousand years later, are still playing vital roles in the growth and development of the country.

# Pakistanis

ALTHOUGH SOME PAKISTANIS came to Canada as early as the eighteenth century, it was not until 1951 that they came in any significant numbers, and the latest immigration figures indicate that 9,709 Pakistanis immigrated to Canada in the period 1946–73. With the rise in the numbers of immigrants in the past few years, however, the total is estimated to be over 18,000 today.

A quota system for immigrants from the East was introduced by the Canadian government in 1951, allowing for the immigration of 100 Pakistanis a year. There was no significant immigration, however, before 1967, and the quota was rarely filled. The introduction of a new immigration act resulted in a marked increase in immigration from Pakistan. From 1967 to 1975, according to immigration statistics, 13,811 persons were recorded as immigrants of Pakistani origin.

The Pakistanis are distributed throughout Canada, with the largest percentage settling in Ontario, followed by Quebec, Alberta, British Columbia, Manitoba and Saskatchewan. The large urban centres are the most popular areas for settlement, but Pakistanis do not concentrate in any particular areas of the cities.

Pakistani immigrants tend to be young, married, and accompanied by their families; they have a good command of the English language; there are few with less than minimal education; and their occupational level is high. The vast majority of Pakistani immigrants have made a successful adjustment to Canadian life, and are likely to take out Canadian citizenship when qualified.

The Pakistani culture is predominantly Muslim, and the Pakistani immigrants belong to the Muslim community at large in Canada. The Muslims, including groups from the Arab states, India, Turkey and other places, have organized parochial centres and numerous mosques and congregations in almost every locality where they have settled in substantial numbers. The Islamic centres were formed in an attempt to preserve Islam as a separate religious institution in Canada, and offer classes in Islamic studies and religious education for Muslim children on a weekly basis.

Most of the centres at this time, however, are facing difficulties. Since the Islamic community is very small in Canada and the member families are scattered over wide areas of a city, it is difficult to bring the Muslim children together frequently enough for religious education.

In addition to life centred on mosques or Islamic centres, there are secular activities associated with such organizations as the Pakistan-Canada Association and the Pakistani Student Association on various university campuses. The Pakistan-Canada Association of Toronto, founded in the early 1960s, has a membership of 3,000. Both this association and the student associations meet regularly, with special gatherings on August 14 to celebrate Pakistan's independence.

There are at least two Pakistani-language newspapers (Urdu-English) in Toronto, *Crescent* and *Hal-E-Pakistan*, both published fortnightly. Both have recently begun publishing as news outlets for Pakistani immigrants. They are largely devoted to articles on Pakistan and bulletins of social activities in Toronto.

The Pakistani group living in Canada is as yet newly established and is beginning its cultural contribution to this country. Its members are concerned at this time with integrating into Canadian society while retaining their traditional cultural heritage, especially their religious beliefs.

# Poles

AT THE CLOSE OF THE MIDDLE AGES, Poland in union with Lithuania constituted one of the powers of Central Europe. The state began to disintegrate in the mid-seventeenth century as a result of internal weakness and the expansion of Russia, Austria and Prussia. By the late eighteenth century, Poland was unable to resist the combined might of these three powers, and a series of partitions eliminated the country as a political entity. This was the signal for the beginning of emigration from Poland.

Canada attracted few of these early immigrants, but those that it did were usually well educated and politically active. The history of a developed community life among Polish Canadians really begins with the first wave of settlement in the Madawaska River Valley in 1858. Families from the Kaszuby region of northwestern Poland, geographically similar to the Madawaska area, came there after experiencing Prussian repression in their homeland, and other Kashubs soon followed. By the 1890s there were more than one thousand Kashubs in the Renfrew County area.

This was the first of an ever-increasing stream of Polish immigration to Canada. Poles from the Prussian-occupied areas of Poland settled in Waterloo County around 1860, while some Poles who had originally emigrated to the northern United States were attracted to Canada in the 1850s and 1860s by expanding opportunities in construction, particularly in the railways. For others, the incentive to immigrate came from the Dominion Lands Act of

1872 which facilitated the acquisition of homesteads on the Prairies.

At the turn of the century, further growth in Polish immigration was promoted by the vigorous policies of Sir Clifford Sifton, Minister of the Interior in Laurier's government. A recruiting campaign was initiated in Central and Eastern Europe, and as a result some 115,000 Polish settlers came to Canada between 1896 and 1918, most of them from the Austrian-dominated province of Galicia. A large number of these people followed their Ukrainian (Ruthenian) neighbours to western Canada, with Winnipeg becoming a major centre for the Polish as well as the Ukrainian settlers.

The First World War temporarily disrupted the flow of Poles to Canada, and in 1919, after the Polish republic had been established, a consulate was opened in Montreal, and another a year later in Winnipeg. Polish immigration to Canada became more orderly as farmers and farm workers became the dominant group to settle in Canada from Poland. In 1921 there were 53,404 Canadians of Polish origin.

The Depression considerably slowed the movement of Poles into Canada, with the annual number of immigrants in the period 1931–39 dropping from about 7,000 to a low of about 500. The outbreak of the Second World War further inhibited Polish immigration, and in the period 1940–45 only about 800 Poles came to Canada, including 500 who worked as skilled engineers and technicians for the Canadian armaments industry. While there were 145,503 Polish Canadians in 1931 (an increase of almost 200 per cent from 1921), there were only 167,485 in 1941, and most of the growth can be attributed to natural increase.

With the end of the Second World War, the influx of Poles from Western Europe quickly resumed. About 4,500 Polish ex-servicemen who had served with the Allies entered Canada on the strength of two-year contracts as farm labourers under a special order-in-council, while 36,500 Polish displaced persons were admitted and another 14,000 Poles either immigrated under normal circumstances or came as temporary visitors and remained as landed immigrants.

The later groups of Polish immigrants were from all social classes, but contained a particularly high component of professional people. Some even had a working knowledge of Canada's official languages, but despite these advantages, they, like many of the Polish immigrants, experienced considerable hardships. They all experienced the residue of prejudice against Central European immigrants that persisted from an earlier period. Those whose professional training had a specifically Polish orientation could not immediately practise their professions in Canada, and had to accept menial employment until they could requalify. It should be noted, however, that engineers, mechanics, scientists and tradesmen adjusted quickly.

After 1953, Polish immigration abated, with only about 3,000 immigrants entering Canada annually. Between 1953 and 1971, the number of Polish immigrants totalled about 55,000. Poland was the fifth leading source country for immigration to Canada in 1951, and the Polish-Canadian population rose to 219,845 in that year. Significant Polish immigration was sustained by large numbers of Poles in the United Kingdom and Western Europe who were to come to Canada, but after this group had arrived the immigration figures for Poland declined. Direct immigration from Poland to Canada was reduced drastically with the Communist takeover in that country in 1945 although the advent of a new government in 1956 did alleviate this situation some-what, as sponsored relatives were allowed to visit their families abroad once written invitations were obtained. Many such visitors chose to remain in Canada as landed immigrants. Between 1951 and 1957, 18,773 Polish immigrants entered Canada, those figures dropping off to 12,422 for the period 1958–62, 8,549 for 1963–67 and 6,388 for 1968–73. Currently, an average of about 1,200 new immigrants from Poland arrive each year.

One feature of the Polish group in Canada is its continual geographic redistribution. In 1931, about 60 per cent of the total Polish-Canadian population lived on the Prairies, with only about 30 per cent residing in Ontario. By 1971 this proportion had shifted, with 45 per cent in Ontario and 36 per cent on the Prairies. Over 50 per cent of Polish postwar immigrants settled in Ontario, contributing strongly to a general population shift from Winnipeg to Toronto. New opportunities in eastern Canada also contributed to this trend.

According to the 1971 census figures, there were 316,425 Canadians of Polish descent, 114,115 of whom lived in Ontario. 42,705 were to be found in Manitoba, 44,325 in Alberta, 29,545 in British Columbia, and 23,970 in Quebec, with the remainder residing in smaller numbers in the other provinces. The Polish-Canadian population actually declined between 1961 and 1971, with 316,425 listed in the 1971 census compared to 323,517 in 1961. Of the 1971 total, 51,180 Polish Canadians resided in Toronto, with 25,915 in Winnipeg, 20,410 in Montreal, 16,945 in Edmonton, 15,070 in Hamilton and 14,985 in Vancouver.

Polish immigrants arriving between 1858 and 1914 represented, for the most part, the economically poorest classes of Polish society, those for whom immigration was the only way to improve their lot. With a very different life-style from the Canadian norm and unable to speak either of the dominant languages, they were exposed to ridicule and active discrimination, despite the arduous physical labour which they contributed to the development of Canada's wilderness.

To deal with discrimination and loneliness, these early settlers organized themselves around the church. The first Polish priest known to have worked in Canada was the Jesuit missionary Gaspar Matoga, and the oldest Polish parish in Canada was established by the Kashub community at Wilno, Ontario, in 1872. The Oblate Fathers established churches for the Polish immigrants in western Canada, and the first Catholic church in the west, the Holy Ghost parish in Winnipeg, was founded in 1898.

Although over 70 per cent of Polish Canadians are Roman Catholic, the presence of other religious groups should also be noted, including a significant number of Polish Anglicans, Lutherans, and members of the United Church. There is a separate Polish Catholic National Church, not affiliated with the Roman Catholic Church, which has parishes in Montreal, Brandon, Winnipeg, Oshawa, Hamilton and Toronto.

After taking care of their spiritual needs, Polish immigrants began to form various secular organizations to meet their growing social, cultural and economic needs. The first objective of many groups was to raise sufficient funds for the purchase or construction of a community hall. This was done by levies on the membership, dances, picnics and competitions. Between the two world wars, at least one such hall was built or bought in every large centre of Polish population. To provide for the economic security of the members of the associations, most of the older associations established insurance policies with sickness and death benefits. In addition, credit unions quickly sprang up across the country, the first organized by the Polish community of Toronto in 1945 with the help of the pastor, Father A. Puchniak. Named the St. Stanislaus Credit Union, it initially had capital assets of only a few hundred dollars, but its popularity was such that it has grown to over 13,000 members and capital assets of over 30 million dollars. It is the largest financial institution of its kind in North America, and there are another 20 Polish credit unions operating across Canada, providing financial assistance to immigrants during the initial difficult period of adjustment. Offering their services in the Polish language, these credit unions facilitate the purchase of homes and the establishment of businesses.

One of the most important secondary functions of the Polish parish organizations became the maintenance of the Polish language among the children of immigrants. The parish schools taught the Polish language, history, folksongs and customs, and national dances, as well as giving religious instruction. Subsequently, secular organizations undertook educational programs, with the result that a network of part-time, Polish-language schools came into existence. Classes were held after regular school hours either in parish or community halls, and occasionally even in private homes.

At the present time, most Polish schools in Canada are affiliated with the Polish Teachers' Association, an organization which coordinates the efforts of over 160 teachers in almost 70 schools across the country. Altogether, there are about 3,600 students served by this system of Polish-language education.

Scouting is probably the largest and most influential Polish community organization aimed at youth. Scouting was established in Poland in 1910, and although there were numerous Scout troops organized by Poles in Canada between 1930 and 1939, the movement did not really become established in this country until 1950 with the postwar influx of Polish immigration. Today there are some 2,000 Polish-background Boy Scouts, 1,500 Girl Guides, 700 Senior Scouts and 1,000 Friends of Scouting.

There are numerous other youth organizations within the Polish community. Each parish has a youth group, and most adult organizations have special youth sections designed to bring the younger members of the community into contact with their activities. Polish student clubs operate at several universities, while specialized groups devote themselves to folklore, theatre and sports.

After the initial period of settlement, during which church-affiliated organizations constituted the main form of community association, the Poles in Canada began to found secular fraternal and social organizations. One of the first recorded was the Mutual Aid Society, founded in 1872 in what is today Kitchener, Ontario. In Toronto, the Association of Polish Citizens was organized in the 1890s. It merged with several smaller organizations and adopted the name Polish Alliance Friendly Society in Canada. It quickly grew into one of the largest and most active Polish organizations in Ontario, and its original affiliation with the Catholic church was dropped. In 1933 it founded its own newspaper, the *Zwiazkowiec (Alliancer)*, which is currently a semi-weekly.

In conjunction with the Polish Veterans' Mutual Aid Society, the Polish Youth Club and the Polish Political Front, the Polish National Union was formed in 1937, with its head office in Toronto. In July, 1950, it began publishing a weekly, *Glos Polski (Polish Voice)*.

Numerous other Polish organizations exist in various parts of Canada. The first Polish organization in Montreal, the Sons of Poland, was founded in 1902. In 1934, the Polish Mutual Aid Society of Montreal was established. It now has six branches in Quebec.

The first non-parochial association in Winnipeg was started in 1904 under the name of the Sokol Gymnastic Association, and in British Columbia, the oldest and most influential association has been the Zgoda Association of Vancouver, established in 1926. All of the Polish associations have similar aims in preserving Polish language and identity in Canada through the maintenance of language schools, publications, theatre, dance groups, sports activities, libraries, choirs and art exhibits.

Because of the large numbers of Polish ex-servicemen who immigrated to Canada after both world wars, Polish veterans' associations have become an important element of the community structure. Veterans of the First World War formed the Polish Army Veterans' Association, with headquarters originally in New York, but in 1930 became more international with a branch being established in Toronto, and shortly thereafter in Windsor, Hamilton, Kitchener and Oshawa.

After the Second World War, the Polish Combatants Association was formed in Canada to promote the welfare of Polish veterans. It grew rapidly until about twenty branches were established across the country, with most branches acquiring halls for their social and cultural activities, and various auxiliaries were established as affiliates. There are also Polish branches of the Royal Canadian Legion, and numerous other veterans' organizations such as the Polish Air Force organization, cadets and Underground Army associations.

Traditionally, women have taken an active part in the life of the Polish community through the women's auxiliaries of the major organizations. These auxiliaries served specialized functions relating to charitable programs and education. With the new waves of Polish immigration in the 1950s, the arrival of female Polish immigrants with higher education led to the establishment of numerous women's organizations. In 1950 the Federation of Polish Women in Canada established branches across the country, eventually affiliating itself with the Canadian Council of Women. Unlike an auxiliary, the Federation is an independent organization with its own by-laws. At present it has about four hundred members across the country, with headquarters in Toronto. The Marie Curie Women's Club, whose membership is primarily composed of women holding university degrees or who are the wives of Polish professional men, is limited to the Toronto region but is not affiliated with any parent organization. It collaborates with the Adam Mickiewicz Foundation in providing educational grants to Polish students.

A successful fund-raising venture was the Polish Millenium Foundation, incorporated in 1964 in preparation for the celebration of 1,000 years of Christianity in Poland in 1966. A foundation named in honour of the Polish novelist Wladyslaw Reymont was established by the Polish Alliance Friendly Society in 1969.

There are a number of publications appearing in Canada which are directed at the Polish community. In addition to those previously mentioned in connection with various organizations, the weekly *Czas (Times)* is published in Winnipeg; *Kurier Polsko-Kanadyjeki (Polish-Canadian Messenger)* and the left-wing *Kronika Tygodniowa (Weekly Chronicle)*, both weeklies.

Polish businessmen's associations were established in the 1930s in Toronto, Winnipeg and Hamilton to promote business skills and education. Similarly, the Association of Polish Engineers in Canada was established with branches in Toronto, Montreal, Ottawa and Sarnia. This association publishes its own periodical, the *Bulletin*.

Formed in 1944, the Canadian Polish Congress is a federation of most Polish organizations and associations operating in Canada. With its headquarters in Toronto, it co-ordinates the activities of Poles across the country in dealing with various levels of government and Canadian society at large. It is particularly concerned with issues involving immigration policy, minority rights and problems of language and culture.

The present Canadian Polish Congress grew out of the earlier Federation of Polish Societies in Canada, which had been established in 1931 and reconstituted as the Congress in 1944. At present, some 190 organizations belong to the Congress, and general meetings are held every two years in different regions of Canada.

The Polish community has contributed its full share to the enrichment of the cultural heritage of Canada, initially through the toil and sacrifice of the many who laboured to clear land and establish communities in the wilderness, and later through the efforts of those working in fields such as education, medicine, law, the arts and technology.

# Portuguese

UNDER PRINCE HENRY the Navigator, Portugal entered a period of colonial and maritime expansion which at its height saw Portuguese colonies around the world, and it was at this time that Portuguese explorers made their first contacts with Canada.

Portuguese emigration to Canada has been a major phenomenon only for the past three decades, but Portugal's long-standing association with Canada dates back as far as the early sixteenth century. Gaspar Corte-Real, for example, is known to have crossed the entrance to Davis Strait in 1501, and explored either Hamilton Inlet on the coast of Labrador or the eastern coast of Newfoundland.

After this exploration, the Portuguese began to utilize the cod fisheries on the Grand Banks off the coast of Newfoundland. For many years Portuguese and Spanish fishermen annually sailed to Newfoundland to pull in rich harvests of fish. Numerous Portuguese place names along the Atlantic coast today bear witness to the early explorations made by Portuguese fishermen, including Trinity Bay and Conception Bay in Newfoundland, which are Anglicized versions of Portuguese names. On the other hand, Terra Nova, a name which has been given to a river, a village and a national park in Newfoundland, is the original Portuguese for "new land." Numerous Portuguese place names are also evident in Labrador, including the name of the territory, which was taken from the Portuguese word used to describe the original explorer, a Portuguese "lavrador", a "farmer" or "small landowner".

The majority of Portuguese Canadians (some 60 per cent or more) come from the Azores, an archipelago located 800 miles (2,625 km) from the coast of Portugal. Primarily islands of farming communities, the Azores suffer from overpopulation and lack of suitable land, coupled with a lack of industrialization, all of which give rise to emigration.

Canada's second largest group of Portuguese immigrants, approximately 38 per cent, comes from the Portuguese mainland, traditionally an agricultural country. Most of the immigrants come from the small towns and villages in the central and northern districts of the country. Others come from the ancient city of Lisbon, the country's capital.

A few Portuguese immigrants to Canada come from Madeira, an island of volcanic origin located some 360 miles (580 km) southwest of Lisbon off the African coast. Many immigrants from Madeira were formerly employed in the tourism industry there.

The Portuguese, like other immigrants, have left their homeland for many reasons. Some have come to Canada because they were underemployed, some for political reasons; however, most have been motivated by an overriding desire to improve their economic position.

The first significant Portuguese immigration to this country resulted from initiatives taken by the Canadian and Portuguese governments which, for different reasons, wanted Portuguese to settle in Canada; Portugal sought suitable destinations for emigrants from the Azores, and Canada wanted more agricultural labourers. As a result of this the first large Portuguese group migration to Canada took place in 1952. Twenty persons from the island of Terçeira in the Azores arrived in that pilot group. A year later, in May 1953, 110 men, most of whom were married with families that would join them later, landed at Halifax.

Portuguese government initiative also played a role in later group migrations. In 1959 and 1960, for instance, Canada received an influx of Portuguese from the Azorean islands of Faial and Pico after authorities there requested that families left homeless by volcanic eruptions be accepted. Since then, government-sponsored programs have brought large numbers of railway workers, agricultural labourers and tradesmen to Canada. By 1973, Portuguese immigration into this country had become so large that Portugal was the fourth leading source country for immigrants to Canada, after having placed ninth in 1968 and sixth in 1960. Whereas only 108 Portuguese had immigrated to Canada in the period 1946–50, the figures jumped to 8,115 persons in the period 1951–57, 16,731 from 1958 to 1962, 32,473 from 1963 to 1967, and 54,199 in the period 1968–73, for a total of 111,626 from 1946 to 1973.

The original Portuguese settlers of the early 1950s were scattered far and wide across the farms of the nation or posted to isolated northern regions as railway section hands. Since then, however, the vast majority of Portuguese immigrants have settled in southern Ontario and Quebec, and to a lesser extent in British Columbia. At the time of the 1971 census, there were 75,197 persons of Portuguese origin in Ontario, 18,799 in Quebec, 9,952 in British Columbia, 4,423 in Manitoba and 2,000 in other provinces.

Over half of those Portuguese Canadians living in Ontario have made their homes in Metropolitan Toronto (47,500 in 1971), concentrating in the Dundas-Bathurst area and the area around Kensington Market. Some streets in this district, such as Augusta, are almost entirely inhabited by Portuguese

Canadians.

Some Portuguese have moved to suburbs such as Mississauga and Downsview, while others have settled in smaller Ontario cities and towns, including Galt which, with some 9,000 Portuguese Canadians, can claim to have the highest percentage of Portuguese (almost 25 per cent) in its population of any Canadian centre. Other main centres of Portuguese settlement include Ottawa, Kingston, Hamilton, Kitchener, London and Windsor, with smaller centres in Quebec and the West.

In the Province of Quebec, most Portuguese have settled in Montreal, and have concentrated near the city centre. Smaller numbers can also be found in Hull, Quebec City, St. Therese, Sherbrooke and Schefferville.

Portuguese communities in the western provinces, like those in central and eastern Canada, are generally located in the larger centres, such as Vancouver, Calgary, Edmonton and Winnipeg. Some communities, however, have grown up around mining and industrial sites such as Thompson in Manitoba and Kitimat in northern British Columbia. Portuguese families have also settled on fruit farms in the southernmost part of British Columbia's Okanagan Valley.

Because many Portuguese are relatively recent immigrants, they do not necessarily remain in the area where they first settle. In metropolitan areas, for instance, families have already moved from districts with concentrations of Portuguese into the wider Canadian community.

When the first Portuguese immigrants arrived in the 1950s there was no established ethnocultural community to offer support and there were no politically active families to provide advice and guidance. As a result, the newcomers had to become established on their own. Now there are not only well-established Portuguese communities in most of Canada's larger centres, but also a wide range of essential services in Portuguese.

Toronto, for example, has mobilized a range of resources both within and outside of the Portuguese community to help solve some of the problems faced by Portuguese Canadians. Counselling is provided in such areas as legal aid, financial problems and family difficulties. Some government agencies are hiring Portuguese clerks and officials.

The Portuguese Social Services Council has made use of facilities in the Kensington Community School during evening hours to help immigrants find work and deal with immigration regulations and other matters.

In Montreal a group of volunteers, the Canadian-Portuguese Committee, which represents a cross-section of the Portuguese community, has played an important role in helping the Portuguese immigrants adjust to life in Canada. Formed in 1968, it was active in creating greater understanding between Portuguese parents and school authorities and in organizing recreational groups for children and teenagers. The Portuguese Centre of Referral and Social Promotion has been in operation since 1972, and provides a broad range of services to the Portuguese in the Montreal area.

The overwhelming majority of Portuguese are Roman Catholics, and the church tends to form the focal point of their lives. In Toronto, the first Portuguese-language services were held in 1955 at St. Michael's Cathedral by an American Franciscan Father who had worked in Brazil. The first church to become a Portuguese parish, however, was St. Mary's, where masses have been conducted in Portuguese since 1968.

During the first decade of heavy immigration after 1952, Portuguese communities often lacked pastoral care in their own language. The picture changed considerably in the 1960s when there was a dramatic increase in the number of Portuguese priests. They have played an important part in organizing social and recreational activities in centres such as Ottawa, Hamilton, London, Winnipeg, Calgary, Edmonton, Vancouver and Montreal.

Organizations of all sorts play important roles in the lives of Portuguese Canadians. Some organizations exist for a short time, disappear, and are replaced by new ones. Others are more firmly established. The first major Portuguese club formed in Canada was the Associaçaõ Portuguesa do Canadá (Portuguese Association of Canada), founded in Montreal in 1956 to provide Portuguese immigrants with a social centre, to preserve Portuguese culture and to advise on integration into Canadian society. The first Portuguese Club of Toronto is among the largest Portuguese organizations in Canada. In addition to social clubs, some of which recruit their members from a particular region of Portugal (for example, Casa de Algarve or Madeira House in Toronto), there are sporting clubs such as Benfica, named after a famous Portuguese soccer team, political and professional clubs.

The first Portuguese newspaper to be published in Canada was *O Luso-Canadiano* (*The Portuguese Canadian*), which started as a monthly publication of the Associaçaõ Portuguesa Canadá in Montreal. It was published from 1959 to 1971. Present day newspapers include *Voz de Portugal* (*Voice of Portugal*), *A Tribuna* (*The Tribune*), and *O Lusitano* (*The Lusitanian*), published in Montreal, and *O Correio Português* (*Portuguese Post*), *Jornal Português* (*Portuguese Journal*) and *Jornal Açoreano* (*Azorean Journal*), published in Toronto. In western Canada there are *O Mundial* (*The Globe*), published in Winnipeg and *O Mensagerio* (*The Messenger*) and *Sentinala* (*Sentinel*), published in Vancouver.

The Portuguese enjoy the drama, colour and music along with the feeling of community associated with festivities and family celebrations. Community events are often associated with religious festivals, many of which feature processions through the streets of the Portuguese community. A number of these parades mark the appearance of Our Lady of Fatima. Other celebrations commemorate historical events in Portugal such as April 25. The anniversary of the death of Portugal's national poet, Luis de Camoes, in 1580, is commemorated on June 10, Portugal Day. Other festivities mark the arrival of the first Portuguese immigrants to Canada and an annual picnic is held in Madeira Park outside Toronto.

The Portuguese as a group began to come to Canada when the government recognized the contribution they could make to agriculture and actively sought them. Portuguese today are firmly established in the business and professional community, but are still very involved with agriculture and the construction trades, where they are, in effect, helping to build Canada and feed Canadians.

# Roumanians

IN 1878, Roumanian independence from the Ottoman Empire was recognized by the European powers. Many Roumanians, however, were living outside the country, mainly in the provinces of Transylvania and Bukovina, then part of the Austro-Hungarian Empire. These provinces were included in the territory which Roumania received at the peace settlement in 1919. It was from these two provinces, particularly from Bukovina, that the majority of early Roumanian immigrants came to Canada. A feeling of oppression as a result of living under a foreign government, the desire to own land and general economic conditions were the main factors influencing the decision to emigrate. Most of these early emigrants were peasants whose families had lived on the land for generations.

Early settlements were founded at Regina, Limerick, Dysart, Kayville, Flintoft and Canora in Saskatchewan; Inglis in Manitoba; and Boian and Ispas in Alberta. The last two communities were named after villages in Roumania.

Roumanians were also attracted to Quebec, particularly Montreal, early in the century, partly because French has traditionally been the second language in Roumania. By 1908, about eighty Roumanians had established themselves in Montreal, and as their numbers increased, most lived in an area bounded roughly by St. Laurent Blvd. in the west, Iberville St. in the east, Sherbrooke St. in the south and Mount Royal Ave. in the north. After 1929, when there was a gradual shift from the drought-stricken prairies to the cities, the Roumanian population of Montreal increased, and received a further boost with the arrival of a new wave of Roumanian immigrants after the Second World War.

The second wave of Roumanian immigration occurred between 1921 and 1929. Immigrants came to join relatives and friends who were already established in Canada and were in a position to guide and assist them. Consequently, in 1931 there were already 29,056 Canadians of Roumanian origin. Beginning in 1929, however, with droughts in western Canada hindering the settling of newcomers, the Dominion government placed an effective check on immigration. The ensuing economic depression threw many out of work, and some returned to Roumania. As a result, according to the 1941 census the number of Roumanian Canadians dropped to 24,689.

Significant Roumanian immigration did not occur again until the movement of displaced persons after the Second World War. For the most part, these people were educated professionals from the cities of Roumania. They took any form of work available under the circumstances, while at the same time preparing themselves to become established in the fields for which their education and experience had prepared them.

According to the 1971 census, the Roumanian ethnocultural group in Canada consisted of 27,375 persons; 9,255 of them living in Ontario, 5,550 in Saskatchewan, 4,670 in Alberta, 3,765 in British Columbia and 2,320 in Quebec. These numbers, however, are apparently misleading, since according to the 1961 census there were 43,805 Canadians of Roumanian origin, and no considerable number of Roumanians then in Canada left the country. Evidently, the results of the 1971 census reflect rather an intensive process of integration and redefinition of their identity. There are 11,300 persons in Canada who consider the Roumanian language as their mother tongue.

It is estimated that there are at present 45,000 Canadians of Roumanian origin. The largest Roumanian communities are in the area of Regina, with approximately 7,000 persons; Windsor, 6,000; Montreal, 5,000; Toronto, 4,000; and Kitchener, 3,000. Smaller concentrations of Roumanian Canadians are to be found in Edmonton, Winnipeg, Timmins, Calgary and Boian, Alberta.

Roumanians have brought to Canada a wealth of folklore, folksongs and dances, of which they are justifiably proud. When a Roumanian group comes together for a festival or special occasion, almost invariably the program includes a display of singing and dancing in national costume.

One such occasion is Roumanian National Day, observed on May 10, to commemorate the turning point in Roumanian history in 1878 when the country gained its independence from the Ottoman Empire. Roumanian groups often participate with other ethnocultural groups in larger displays such as the annual United Nations Day celebration sponsored by the United Nations Association of Montreal. An earlier event of this kind was the New Canadian Folksong and Folkdance Festival, organized by the Canadian Pacific Railway at Regina in 1929. Nearly one hundred Roumanian dancers and singers took part, wearing colourful costumes which added greatly to the charm of the performance.

Many of the customs kept alive by the Roumanians are of a religious nature. For many Roumanians the church is the social as well as the religious focus of their lives. Most belong to the Roumanian Orthodox Church,

while a small number are Greek Catholics or Baptists. The first Roumanian Orthodox Church in North America is the Church of St. Nicholas in Regina. It was built in 1901, and a few years later St. Mary's, a Roumanian church at Boian, Alberta was completed.

In Montreal, a small chapel in a private house on St. Laurent Blvd. served as a place of worship until the tiny Roumanian community there had sufficient funds to build its own church in 1910. This modest wooden structure was replaced in 1918 by the present Church of the Annunciation or Buna-Vestire (literally, "good news") at the corner of Iberville and Rachel Streets.

In the intervening years the number of Roumanian Orthodox parishes in Canada has grown to more than twenty, over half of which are in the Prairie Provinces. Attached to each Orthodox parish is a women's auxiliary whose functions include decorating the church and attending to the welfare of the parishioners. Many parishes also have a youth group which is a branch of American Roumanian Orthodox Youth. This organization has more than twenty chapters in the United States and Canada. It held its first convention in Canada in 1965 in Regina, where religious activities centred around the old Church of St. Nicholas, host of the convention. Participating groups also took part in large demonstrations of Roumanian folk dancing and singing. Costumes and handicrafts from many districts of Roumania were on display.

Mutual benefit and cultural organizations have sprung up in most communities from time to time. Some have flourished for a number of years before disappearing, while others remain active as centres of Roumanian culture. Many of these local clubs are branches of a large American organization called the Union and League of Roumanian Societies of

America. Founded as a mutual benefit society, one of its main functions is to preserve the culture and traditions of Roumania. Other Roumanian associations which are still functioning are Graiul Romanesc in Windsor, Sosietea Unirea Romanilor in Hamilton, Mihail Eminescu in Regina, and Imparatul Traian in Limerick and Kayville, Saskatchewan.

Two newspapers written in the Roumanian language have appeared in Canada in recent years. *Ecouri Romanesti* (Romanian Echoes), a monthly published in Toronto, and *Curantul Romanesc* (The Romanian Voice), a monthly published in Hamilton, are both characterized by their strong support of the concept of freedom from the Communist influence in Roumania. The Church of the Annunciation in Montreal issues the bulletin *Troita* (Roadside Cross) which describes the activities of the church and the current affairs of the Roumanian community in Montreal. Other widely read publications in the Roumanian language include *American Roumanian News*, published for over fifty years in Cleveland, Ohio; *Solia*, published in Detroit by the Roumanian Orthodox Episcopate of America; and *Cronica Romaneasca*, published by the National Committee for a Free Europe, with headquarters in New York City. Many Roumanian parishes publish their own bulletins in the English and Roumanian languages for local distribution.

The Roumanians have a historic presence in Canada and are still vitally concerned with the retention of their cultural heritage.

# Russians

THE RUSSIANS CONSTITUTE the largest single linguistic group among the Slavic nations of the world, and the largest single national group within the Soviet Union, forming approximately half of the entire population of the U.S.S.R.

Russian settlement in North America began as early as the eighteenth century, when Alaska was colonized by Russian explorers and merchants who penetrated as far south as California. Yet there is no evidence of Russian settlement along the coast of what is now British Columbia. The first Russians to settle in Canada did not arrive until the late 1890s, when members of the pacifist Doukhobor religious sect chose to leave Tsarist Russia rather than serve in the army. In the year 1899 and thereafter, some 7,000 Doukhobors entered Canada in the largest single wave of Russian settlement in this country's history.

The Doukhobors settled in the Prince Albert and Yorkton areas of Saskatchewan, but unfortunately, within a few years were involved in a dispute with the Canadian government over the nature of their land rights, community privileges and citizenship status. The Doukhobors had been granted their land communally and intended to work it in this manner, living in centrally located villages, but the government interpreted the grant to mean that each family would live separately on its own plot of land. Furthermore, the Doukhobors refused to take the traditional oath of allegiance which might involve them in the military service that was contrary to their religious beliefs. As a result, a split developed in the community, and part of the group moved to the Kootenay region of British Columbia in 1907.

Apart from the Doukhobor immigration, the number of Russians entering Canada before the First World War was very small. The exact number is difficult to establish, since immigration statistics of the time listed anyone coming from any part of the Russian empire under the classification of Russian. Canada was not a popular destination for those Russians who emigrated, and most initially went to Western Europe, the United States and South America. Despite this, small Russian communities developed in Montreal, Toronto, Windsor, Sydney, Timmins, Winnipeg, Vancouver and Victoria. Most of those who settled in Canada were of peasant background, having left agricultural pursuits in Russia to work in Canadian industry. A few of these early immigrants chose emigration from Russia because of their intense personal convictions and opposition to the Tsarist regime, and with the revolution of 1917 some individuals in Canada returned to Russia, while a few others organized political groups in Canada to assist the new Communist regime in the Soviet Union.

After the First World War, Russian immigration into Canada continued in a very erratic fashion. At least part of the immigration consisted of people fleeing the effects of the revolution, although many intellectuals who left Russia preferred to settle in other European countries. A large part of the wave to Canada was composed of agricultural workers and industrial labourers seeking to improve their economic situation. It is interesting to note that of the substantial number of Russian leftists in Canada in the 1930s, a large number joined the Canadian "Mackenzie-Papineau" Battalion which fought on the Republican side during the Spanish Civil War.

By the 1930s, the Depression had cut into immigration as the government attempted to protect the jobs of workers already in Canada, and restrictions were imposed. Despite this decrease in the flow of Russian immigrants, there were groups of about 2,000 persons in Montreal, 1,500 in Toronto, and several hundred in other Canadian cities.

During the Second World War there was virtually no Russian immigration to Canada, and it was not until the period 1948–53 that Russians began entering Canada again in significant numbers. This group was characterized by higher levels of education and a general tendency towards urban settlement. Two distinct streams can be discerned among these immigrants: the first is a secondary immigration, consisting of Russians who had originally left Russia and settled in various European countries, and a second stream composed of Russians directly from the Soviet Union who found themselves in Germany after the war either because of their opposition to Stalin or because they had been sent there as forced labour. These Russians represented all social classes, but because on the whole they were younger and more aware of their Russian heritage, they added a talented and vocal element to the Russian community in Canada. The postwar immigration was, on the whole, much more representative of Russian society.

After 1953, Russian immigration to Canada declined drastically. For example, in the early part of the 1970s, immigration from all of the Soviet Union had declined to an annual average of about 230 individuals, of which the greater part were probably not Russians, but members of various other national groups.

The census figures for the number of Russians in Canada have fluctuated widely, largely because of the difficulty in establishing which persons are ethnically and linguistically Russian. For example, the 1961 census recorded 119,168 Canadians who claimed a Russian background, but a large part of this number were in fact members of the Jewish, Ukrainian, Byelorussian or other groups. As a result, the 1971 census listed only 64,475 Russians, probably a much more realistic figure. Of this latter number, 31,745 (49.2 per cent) claimed a knowledge of the Russian language.

The province with the largest Russian population is British Columbia, largely as a result of the Doukhobor communities there. At the time of the 1971 census 22,995 Russians were residing in British Columbia with a further 12,580 in Ontario, 10,235 in Alberta and 10,030 in Saskatchewan. Quebec and Manitoba had substantially smaller Russian-Canadian communities with 4,060 and 4,040 individuals respectively, while the number of Russians in Canada's remaining provinces was small.

In contrast to the situation before the war, Canada's Russian community is overwhelmingly urban. According to the 1971 census, the largest concentration of Russians could be found in Vancouver, with some 7,310 individuals, but sizable communities could also be found in Toronto (5,270), Montreal (3,605), Calgary (3,110), Edmonton (2,295), Winnipeg (2,100) and Saskatoon (1,935). Smaller cities such as Hamilton, Ottawa, Kitchener, London, Regina, Windsor, St. Catharines and Victoria have communities of between 500 and 1,000 Russian Canadians each. Further, it must be remembered that many thousands of Doukhobors continue to reside in their communities in Kootenay, Grand Forks and Brilliant, British Columbia.

The religious life of the Russian-Canadian community illustrates its diversity. According to the 1971 census, only some 10,085 Russians claim affiliation with the Russian Orthodox Church. A slightly larger number (10,870) belong to the United Church of Canada. An even larger number (12,670) are listed as belonging to other religious groupings, for example, the Doukhobor sect. A large number (8,505) of Russians are Roman Catholic, while the remainder are associated with various Protestant groups. This statistical data suggests that many of the earlier Russian immigrants have left the Orthodox religious faith and have joined those Protestant groups prominent in Canada.

Despite these statistics, it remains true that many of the vocal and active Russian Canadians continue in their affiliation with the Russian Orthodox Church. At the present time there are some forty Russian Orthodox parishes in Canada, although they represent two different religious currents within the Orthodox movement. Slightly more than half of these parishes belong to the Russian Orthodox Church Abroad. The remainder of the parishes are affiliated with the Orthodox Church in America, which includes in its membership numerous non-Russian churches which also follow the Byzantine rite. Both ecclesiastical organizations are headed by archbishops in Canada, with ruling synods located in the United States.

One of the oldest Russian parishes in Canada is the Church of Sts. Peter and Paul, founded in 1907 in Montreal and a member of the Orthodox Church in America. Another parish, the Church of St. Nicholas, was originally established in Montreal in 1927 and is affiliated with the Russian Orthodox Church Abroad.

In Toronto, the first Russian parish was formed in 1920, and at present there are three Russian Orthodox churches, including the Church of Christ the Saviour, which is affiliated with the Orthodox Church in America, and the Church of the Holy Trinity, which is a member of the Russian Orthodox Church Abroad. A third church was built five years ago. During the early period of immigration, Russian Orthodox churches were established at Sydney and Winnipeg. At present, the Russian churches are not restricted to only those individuals who speak Russian.

Unlike most Eastern European ethnocultural groups in Canada, the Russians do not have a central co-ordinating body to act as an umbrella organization for the whole of Canada. However, during the Canadian centennial celebrations, a Union of Russian Ethnic Organizations was formed in Quebec.

Within the Russian community there is a broad spectrum of political organizations. On the left wing is the Federation of Russian Canadians, with some fifteen branches across the country. There is also the Russian Liberation Movement with about five branches. On the right wing is the Monarchist Union, the activities of which seem to be confined almost entirely to the city of Montreal.

Apart from the political groupings, there are Russian fraternal associations representing common educational or military backgrounds, including the Kadet Association and Russian branches of the Canadian Legion. For the most part, Russian organizations tend to be cultural in their aims, and several such active groups exist across Canada, such as the Gusli group in Montreal.

Toronto has a number of interesting Russian cultural organizations. Perhaps the most active is the Russian Cultural Society, founded in 1950, a small Literary Circle,

founded in 1949, a Drama Circle, and the "Sovremennik" Publishing Association founded in 1960 which publishes the Russian literary journal of the same name. Most of the Toronto groups engage in publishing, with the Russian Cultural Society regularly producing the journal *Russkoe Slovo v Kanade* (*Russian Word in Canada*), while the Literary Circle has occasionally produced collections of verse.

There are other Russian cultural societies in different Canadian cities. The group Votrechi, founded in 1954, is active in London, while a cultural society was founded in Vancouver in 1956. One of the more prestigious and active cultural organizations is the Ottawa Chekhov Society, founded in 1974 and currently producing its own club bulletin.

Most of these Russian cultural societies share a common aim of promoting the best aspects of Russian cultural creativity. Periodical publications in particular are characteristic of most of these groups, and eleven such bulletins appear in Canada at present. In Montreal, two Russian churches produce their own bulletins. In addition to the two Toronto publications previously mentioned, there also appear the left-wing newspaper *Vestnik* (*The Herald*) and a monthly bulletin issued by the Russian Baptist Church. A similar Baptist publication also appears in Windsor, while the Russians of London have a local parish bulletin, a newsletter issued by the Russian Liberation Movement, and a bulletin produced by the Zaria Publishing Company. Another Russian-language publishing house, the Monastery Press of Montreal, is a religious publisher. The *Novoye Russkoye* (*New Russian World*) is a popular American publication which contains a Canadian section.

One important aspect of Russian organizational activities centres around the youth of the community. There are two Russian scouting groups, one in Toronto and one in Montreal, and the Russian Orthodox Church in Montreal is the centre for the Canadian Russian Orthodox Youth Association. A more strictly cultural role has been played by various St. Vladimir Youth Societies. The structure of the society is very informal.

There are several parish schools specializing in instruction in the Russian language, the principles of religion, and occasionally Russian literature, geography and history. There are two such major schools, one in Toronto and one in Montreal. There are about a dozen other schools of this type across Canada.

Because of the specific religious and social practices of the Doukhobor group in Canada, it is necessary to treat them as a separate and distinct entity within the Russian community. Indeed, some Doukhobors disclaim any connection with Russians, rejecting entirely the principle of nationality.

The Doukhobor sect arose in Russia in the eighteenth century. The word *Doukhobor* comes from the Russian *Doukhoborets*, meaning "spirit-wrestler" and refers to the spiritual struggle for goodness which lies at the heart of Doukhobor beliefs. According to this, every man has the capacity to experience the spirit of God which resides in him, and to follow that spirit in conducting his own life. As a result, the Doukhobors have a particular abhorrence of murder, since it violates that innate divine spirit; hence the strict pacifism which lies at the heart of Doukhobor ideology, a pacifism which is opposed to any form of coercion, even by the institutions of the state. Coupled with this is a strict communal mode of existence, stressing co-operation and equality. As a consequence of these beliefs, the Doukhobor community has often found itself in open conflict with state authorities, both before its

emigration in Russia, and in Canada. The threat of conscription into the Russian army led the Doukhobors to emigrate to Canada in 1899, and subsequent disputes over matters such as the oath of allegiance and land tenure led to further difficulties. By 1907, the original settlement in Saskatchewan had broken apart as a result of these disputes, and about 6,000 Doukhobors embarked on a trek to British Columbia, where they purchased their own land and could be more independent of government interference. On the other hand, some 3,000 Doukhobors accepted the conditions of settlement offered them by the government in Saskatchewan, and remained there, causing a fundamental rift in the community.

At present there are over 12,000 Doukhobors in Canada, divided into at least three recognizable sections. The Independent Doukhobors of Saskatchewan, descendants of the original settlers who decided to accept the government conditions, number over 3,200, and seem to have become almost completely integrated into Canadian life. They have no press, and little organizational structure to unite them. The largest group is the Union of Spiritual Communities of Christ, centred on the Grand Forks area of British Columbia. This group publishes the journal *Iskra* (*The Spark*). Also, there is the small radical group known as the Sons of Freedom, located in the region around Krestova and Brilliant, British Columbia. Altogether there are some 9,000 Doukhobors in British Columbia, with perhaps 2,500 Sons of Freedom, and the rest belonging to the Communities of Christ.

Russians have made numerous distinguished contributions to Canadian life. It should be mentioned that the most recent waves of immigration have been the most educated, politically conscious and culturally active, and from their ranks have come scholars, ballet dancers, artists and musicians. An area of particular Russian contribution has been the establishment of ballet in Canada. The early Russian immigrants contributed to the physical development of this country, while those who came later brought with them a rich culture to incorporate into the Canadian society.

# Scots

SCOTS EMIGRATION from Scotland to Canada did not become a recognizable phenomenon until after New France came under British rule in 1760. Prior to that date only a few Scots had settled in what is now Canada, some of whom were probably Roman Catholics who sought a more congenial religious climate in New France. Others were disillusioned Highlanders, many Roman Catholics, who had experienced hardships as a result of the Jacobite Rebellions of 1715 and 1745. Only two organized attempts were made to settle Scots in this country before 1760. The attempts, both failures, were made in 1622 and 1623 by Sir William Alexander.

Between the middle and the end of the eighteenth century, however, a steady stream of Scots set sail for the New World from Scotland. Some of these were small tenant farmers from the Lowlands who had been caught up in the dislocation caused by recent agricultural changes, while others were dispossessed Highland chieftans and their immediate relatives seeking to regroup their fortunes overseas after the crushing of the Stuart uprising in 1746.

In the closing years of the century the stream became a torrent. From then until the end of the nineteenth century it would flow unchecked except for periodic setbacks. Although the Lowlands supplied its share of immigrants, including unemployed artisans and factory workers, agricultural labourers and small tenant farmers, it was the Highlands that were most affected by the emigration. It was here that socio-economic conditions combined to cause great hardship to the crofter. After 1800, and in some cases before the turn of the century, the crofter would be adversely affected by a variety of developments, including excessive population growth, the notorious sheep clearances which forced crofters from their small, rented farms or crofts to make room for sheep, the failure of the kelping industry, successive potato famines, especially the calamitous one of 1845, the deterioration of the fishing industry and agricultural depression.

In the wake of the clearances, three hundred tenants from the estate of Captain John Macdonald of Glenaladale sailed for Prince Edward Island in 1772, the first in the mass movement of Highland Scots to the Atlantic Provinces. A year later the advance guard of the great Highland emigration to Nova Scotia, two hundred Highlanders, arrived at Pictou aboard the *Hector*, the *Mayflower* of Scottish Canadians. Highland reinforcements arrived in 1790 to join the Glenaladale Macdonalds and in 1791 to join the settlers already established at Pictou, which was rapidly becoming an important centre of population. Also in 1791, some Roman Catholic immigrants settled on the western shores of Cape Breton. Soon this part of the world became a Scottish enclave, where the inhabitants spoke only Gaelic and where the fishermen of the western Highlands and islands discovered a country well suited to their way of life.

Large numbers of Scottish United Empire Loyalists also found their way to the old Province of Nova Scotia. Many of these were part of the main movement of Loyalists which left the port of New York in 1783 in a mass exodus arranged by Sir Guy Carleton. Among these Scots were men of the 42nd Highlanders who acquired a group of lots in Parrtown, as Saint John, New Brunswick, was then called.

Scottish United Empire Loyalists also flocked to the part of the old province of Quebec which in 1791 became the province of Upper Canada. Conspicuous among these Loyalist families were the Macdonnells, Roman Catholics from Glengarry in Inverness who had settled on the estate of Sir John Johnston in the Mohawk Valley in New York and later joined the King's Royal Regiment of New York raised by Sir John. When the War of Independence was over the Macdonnells, along with other members of the regiment, colonized the uncleared country on the north bank of the St. Lawrence west of the area settled by the French. The area they chose, now known as Glengarry County, later served as a magnet for other Scottish settlers, including a group who came from Scotland in 1803 after the disbanding of the Glengarry Fencibles, a Roman Catholic regiment organized during the Napoleonic Wars. Their chaplain, Father Alexander Macdonnell, obtained a grant of 200 acres (81 ha) for every emigrating family and then managed to get each one out of Scotland before the British government, worried by the wholesale exodus of Scots to the New World, placed an embargo on emigrant ships.

Other Scots settlements in this period were organized by Lord Selkirk. Concerned about the plight of Scottish crofters, the wealthy philanthropist obtained a grant of land in Prince Edward Island and then sent out colonists to settle it. The first three shiploads, which brought some eight hundred settlers, arrived in August, 1803. Lord Selkirk came to the site of the new colony to supervise the arrival of the settlers, then left in September to return the following year. The settlers adjusted so well to their new surroundings that he sent fresh contingents to join them over the next few years.

In 1804 Selkirk launched a colonization scheme at Baldoon near Lake St. Clair, but this failed. More successful was his Red River settlement. In 1811, after acquiring a substantial interest in the Hudson's Bay Company, he obtained a large land grant in the Winnipeg basin (Assiniboia) on which to found a colony of Highlanders and Irish. The following year two parties of settlers arrived by way of Hudson Bay to lay the foundations of the new colony at the forks of the Red and Assiniboia Rivers. The new arrivals underwent many privations and succeeded in keeping the colony alive only with the aid of additional settlers who arrived in 1814 and 1815.

Further difficulties were encountered with the Northwest Company, which bitterly resented the fact that the settlement sat astride the great fur trading route to the northwest and cut off vital supplies of pemmican from the area. At one point the Nor'Westers even succeeded in completely dispersing the settlers, but a Hudson's Bay Company force helped re-establish them. When more trouble broke out, Lord Selkirk moved west and with the help of mercenaries restored his colony. It gradually grew until by 1820 it was firmly rooted as the first farming settlement in the northwest of British North America.

After the Napoleonic Wars thousands of Scots emigrated not only to Upper Canada, but also to Lower Canada, concentrating in the area now known as the Eastern Townships and the region lying to the west as far as the St. Lawrence River. Alexander Tillock Galt, son of the Scottish novelist John Galt, began his career by arranging for Scottish settlers to establish themselves on the Quebec holdings of the British American Land Company. Although most of their descendants have left the rugged countryside of Megantic, Athabaska and Beauce counties, Scottish names are still numerous in the area.

In postwar Upper Canada, anti-American sentiment paved the way for the Imperial government's first experiment in government-sponsored colonization and an influx of Scottish settlers. Determined to discourage further American migration into the province, the government in 1815 sent out a number of "industrious" Scottish families. In the spring of 1816 these new arrivals joined demobilized British regulars in occupying a range of townships west of the Rideau River. Many of the soldiers, after helping to build settlers' houses, roads and bridges, drifted away from the area, but the Scots around Perth in Lanark County stayed on to found an enduring and a sturdy community. In 1820, Lanark County received nearly 1,200 Scots, many of them unemployed Lowlanders assisted by emigration societies. Others followed in 1821 and 1822, lured by a grant of 100 acres (40.5 ha) to each family and a small amount of cash.

Another centre for Scottish settlement in Upper Canada was MacNab Township in Renfrew County on the Ottawa River. It was named after Archibald MacNab who started a settlement of his own clansmen there after he arrived from Orkney in 1823. He was a colourful character who ruled his tenants in such an autocratic manner that they rebelled. Eventually his power was checked by the Executive Council of the Province of Canada and he left the country.

The most remarkable settlement promoter in Upper Canada's history, however, was Colonel Thomas Talbot. The settlements which he founded on a huge tract of land fronting on Lake Erie attracted thousands of settlers, many of them Scottish Highlanders. His settlements prospered, and by the time he was forced to hand over his colonizing agency to the provincial government in 1837, he had established thousands of colonists in twenty-seven townships.

Between Lakes Erie and Huron Scottish settlement concentrated in Guelph, which was founded in 1827, and was under the control of its founder, the Scottish novelist John Galt. At that time he was closely involved in the work of the Canada Company, which he helped to launch in 1824. The company also founded the towns of Galt and Goderich, other centres of Scottish settlement, before its contract to settle 1,100,000 acres (404,680 ha) of Crown land in the Huron Tract expired in 1843. In the 1840s, Huron and Bruce Counties were settled in part by more Scots.

Scots continued to emigrate to Canada in substantial numbers throughout the remaining years of the nineteenth century, the largest numbers coming between 1851 and 1855, the period when Highland emigration reached its peak. In both 1851 and 1855, for example, over 7,000 Scots are estimated to have left their homeland for British North America.

This great exodus spilled over into the twentieth century, leading to unprecedented numbers of Scottish settlers arriving in Canada in certain key years. In 1910 and 1911, for instance, when the western boom was at its height, an estimated 62,624 people of Scottish origin arrived in this country from overseas, 27,938 in 1910 and 34,686 in 1911. Not until 1957, when 24,533 immigrants of Scottish descent arrived from Scotland and the United

States, would these numbers come close to being equalled.

The first census following Confederation, in 1871, puts the number of people of Scottish origin in the original four provinces at 549,946. This number continued to increase, until by 1921 there were 1,173,635 Scottish Canadians, increasing to 1,346,350 in 1931, 1,403,974 in 1941, 1,547,470 in 1951, and 1,902,302 in 1961. The census of 1971 recorded 1,720,390 Canadians of Scottish origin spread throughout the country. Of these 774,080, by far the largest number, lived in Ontario, while the second largest group, 263,910, resided in British Columbia.

Although the Scots have played a conspicuous role in many aspects of this country's development, their role initially was a military one. Scottish-born General James Murray became military governor of Quebec shortly after the capitulation of Montreal in 1760. At the end of military rule in 1764 he became the first civil governor of the Province of Quebec, in which capacity he played an important role in the shaping of the area's character in the first years of British rule.

Many of the soldiers under Murray's command were Scots, among them the kilted Fraser Highlanders who scaled the heights of Quebec and pointed out the path that led to victory for the British forces under Wolfe. Disbanded in 1764, the regiment was revived in 1775 to become the garrison of Quebec during the American seige in the winter of 1775–76. For their services the officers and men received grants of land in the province, which they used to found soldier settlements.

From these times, a distinctly Scottish tradition has been preserved in many Canadian regiments. The survival of full Highland military dress, Gaelic regimental mottos, the bagpipes and the military balls at which Scottish dances are performed stem from a tradition which originated in the eighteenth century. In both the First and Second World Wars these Canadian Highland regiments attracted many Canadians of Scottish descent.

With the establishment of British rule in Quebec a new figure, the Scottish fur trader, appeared on the scene. Some, in the rush to exploit the profitable fur trade, arrived even before the conclusion of hostilities, Alexander Henry being a notable example. Along with several of his Scottish colleagues he would play an important role in developing fur trade routes to the northwest and in exploring the interior of this continent.

An illustrious colleague of Henry's was Sir Alexander Mackenzie, who while in the service of the Northwest Company travelled by the Slave River, Great Slave Lake and an unexplored river which he called "River of Disappointment", now the Mackenzie, to the Arctic Ocean. In 1793 he crowned his achievement by crossing the Peace River Pass and the divide named after him and arriving at the Pacific. Another famous fur trader-explorer was Simon Fraser, the son of a Loyalist, who in 1808 accomplished one of the most dangerous feats in the history of western exploration when he followed the course of the river that bears his name to the Pacific Ocean.

The most prominent Scottish fur-trading merchant was Simon MacTavish, who moved from Montreal to Albany when the Quebec Act of 1774 annexed the Indian fur-bearing territories in the southwest to Quebec. He was one of the partners in the original agreement on the northwest trade and was instrumental in founding the Northwest Company in 1783.

Scots not only made an important contribution to the geographical knowledge of Canada through their explorations, they also played a leading role in bringing order and unity to the country. One Scot who stands out in this connection is Sir James Douglas. During the Fraser River gold rush of 1858, when he was chief factor of the Hudson's Bay Company and Governor of Vancouver Island, Douglas moved quickly to establish orderly control of the mainland, build roads and bridges and get adequate supplies to the miners. For his actions he was made first governor of the mainland colony of British Columbia in 1858.

When the North West Mounted Police was formed in 1873, many Scots joined its ranks. One of those who came to play a leading role in the force was Colonel James Farquharson Macleod, who led the long land march from Dufferin, Manitoba, across the Prairies to Alberta to establish Fort Macleod and restore law and order at Fort Whoop-Up.

Scots and Canadians of Scottish descent have always played a leading role in Canadian politics. An outstanding figure in the early days was Bishop John Strachan, a native of Aberdeen. Appointed to the Executive Council of Upper Canada in 1818 and to the Legislative Council in 1820, he became a spokesman of the Family Compact, dividing his wide-ranging interests among politics, education and religion.

A bitter foe of the Family Compact was Robert Gourlay, an energetic and officious Scot who had grand ideas for promoting more effective British settlement in Upper Canada. Another foe of the Family Compact was William Lyon Mackenzie, born in Dundee, Scotland. In 1824 he founded the *Colonial Advocate*, which became the leading newspaper in Upper Canada. He was politically outspoken, and became the leader of the radical element in the province. At various times he was a member of the House of Assembly and the first city council of Toronto, which chose

him as mayor. After his abortive attempt at revolution in 1837 he fled to the United States. The Rebellion of 1837 nevertheless led to the granting of responsible government to the Province of Canada in 1841.

Scots also played a predominant role in bringing the various provinces together into Confederation. John A. Macdonald and his great political opponent, the Liberal politician and newspaper publisher and editor George Brown, banished their lifelong differences and worked together after Confederation. At the Confederation conferences they were backed by such influential Scots as Oliver Mowat of Ontario and Samuel Leonard Tilley of New Brunswick.

It was largely through the diplomacy and statesmanship of John A. Macdonald that the British North America Act was framed and Confederation became a reality. At its inception he became Canada's first prime minister, a position he was to relinquish only once before his death in 1891, and then only to another Scot, Sir Alexander Mackenzie, Canada's Liberal prime minister between 1873 and 1878.

In this century, William Lyon Mackenzie King, who dominated Canadian politics for the better part of twenty-seven years, was of Scottish descent, being a grandson of William Lyon Mackenzie. King, who was an ardent admirer of his grandfather, helped to organize the first federal Department of Labour, of which he became the first deputy minister, before becoming a Liberal Member of Parliament in 1908. He became prime minister in 1921, a position he was to hold for most of the period 1921–48.

The Scots have always attached a great deal of importance to education. This is shown by the fact that the early Scottish settlers in this country assigned top priority to both a church and a schoolhouse. Many clergymen founded schools and taught in them. The Rev. Thomas McCullough, who came as a Presbyterian minister to Pictou, Nova Scotia, in 1803, first taught boys in a log cabin, then founded Pictou Academy, the first non-sectarian school for higher education in Nova Scotia. He later became the first principal of Dalhousie University.

In addition to Dalhousie, which was founded by Lord Dalhousie, who was Lieutenant-Governor of Nova Scotia from 1816 to 1820, McGill, the University of Toronto, Queen's, St. Francis Xavier and the University of New Brunswick all owe their foundation to Scots. McGill University, for example, was founded by James McGill, a wealthy Montreal merchant who willed a parcel of land for a university or college and a sum of $10,000 to establish and maintain it. The institution's first principal was the Rev. John Bethune, the son of the first Presbyterian minister in Canada.

Dr. John Strachan, the prominent Family Compact member, was also an outstanding educator who in 1827 secured a charter and a subsidy of 500,000 acres (202,340 ha) to provide income for King's College, Toronto, of which he was president for twenty-one years. When the college was removed from the aegis of the Anglican Church and absorbed into the University of Toronto, he founded the Anglican Trinity College.

The University of New Brunswick was founded largely under the direction of William Dawson, a distinguished Scottish-Canadian principal of McGill, while St. Francis Xavier University, founded in 1852 at Arichat, Nova Scotia, and transferred to Antigonish in 1855 by the Right Rev. D. McKinnon, Bishop of Arichat, had a long succession of Scottish and Scottish-Canadian principals.

In the west, Bishop Robert Machray, a Scot by birth, was the first chancellor of the University of Manitoba. Dr. Walter Murray, of Scottish descent, was president of the University of Saskatchewan for nearly thirty years after its establishment in 1907.

More recently, Scottish studies have gained a place in such Canadian universities as St. Francis Xavier and the University of Guelph. At Guelph there is an interdepartmental committee on Scottish studies which seeks to encourage graduate studies in this area. It also holds colloquia once or twice a year at which papers dealing with Scottish and Scottish-Canadian topics are presented before being published.

Scots and Scottish Canadians have made a distinctive contribution to Canadian literature. Among the leading contributors are the poets Robert W. Service, Duncan Campbell Scott and Wilfred Campbell. Campbell also wrote extensively in prose, one of his notable works being the first volume of *The Scotsman in Canada*, in which he deals with the Scottish settlements of eastern Canada.

Scotsmen in Canada and Canadians of Scottish origin have also played a formidable role in journalism. In addition to George Brown, founder of the *Globe*, and William Lyon Mackenzie, founder and editor of the *Colonial Advocate*, their numbers have included such well-known names as John Neilson, editor of the Quebec *Gazette*, John Dougall, father and son, of the Montreal *Witness* and Lord Atholstan of the *Montreal Daily Star*.

Since Canadians of Scottish origin have been thoroughly integrated into the Canadian population, many of the distinctive features of their way of life have tended to disappear. One feature which has been retained, however, is the Scottish society. There are numerous Scottish societies, including the North British Society of Halifax, founded in 1768 as a charitable as well as a social organization, the St. Andrews Society, which is represented in many Canadian centres, and the Caledonia Society, founded mainly for the promotion of athletics and largely responsible for the continuing popularity of the Highland Games. Among the earliest records of the Games in Canada are those of the Caledonian Club of Prince Edward Island, established in 1838.

The many curling clubs in Canada, while not specifically Scottish societies, owe their existence to the Scots who brought the game of curling to Canada. It is now played in almost every city and town in the country.

There are also a large number of clan societies such as the Clan Donald, Clan MacLeod, Clan Chisholm and Clan MacMillan, which are connected with similar organizations located around the world. They hold their local ceilidh and, in most cases, publish monthly or bi-monthly papers containing not only society information but also historical and other notes.

One of the most important Scottish societies established in recent years is the Conference on Scottish Studies organized at the meeting of the Learned Societies held at York University, Toronto, in 1970. This society, which is composed of professional academics as well as interested laymen, publishes a semi-annual journal, *Scottish Tradition*, which contains articles on Scottish history, culture and literature and their transmission to other parts of the world.

The increased interest in Scottish history and culture has been responsible for the addition of a regular Scottish feature to the program of the Canadian National Exhibition in Toronto, the Scottish World Festival. When it was first introduced in 1972, it featured the chiefs of four clans, Scottish athletes and entertainers as well as a spectacular tattoo.

Much of the folk culture of the early Gaelic-speaking Highlanders, whether it be songs, stories, dances or music, has survived through their descendants. Oral literature in particular has flourished. It owes its healthy state to the work of such individuals as the Gaelic poet John MacLean, family baird to the Laird of Coll, who came to Nova Scotia in 1819. He wrote numerous secular and religious songs, some of which still circulate orally among the people of that province. His grandson, the Rev. A. MacLean Sinclair, also contributed to the survival of Gaelic by editing thirteen small but important volumes of Gaelic poetry.

Newspaper editors and publishers have likewise contributed to the promotion of Gaelic, including the Cape Breton writer and publisher Jonathan G. MacKinnon, who published a weekly Gaelic newspaper *Mac-Talla (Echo)*, from 1892 to 1904 and edited a monthly magazine *Fear Na Ceilich (The Visitor)* from 1928 to 1930.

Its status is now such that Gaelic is recognized by the schools of Nova Scotia as an optional subject. And, on Cape Breton Island, where several thousand people still speak Gaelic as their mother tongue, there is a Gaelic advisor attached to the Division of Adult Education in the schools to train teachers in Gaelic language and literature.

Little more needs to be written about the presence and contributions of Scots in Canada. From their very beginning, their influence has touched all aspects of Canadian life, and it is very difficult today to name some aspect of general Canadian life where the Scottish presence has not had some effect. The numerous Scottish names in Canada attest to their numbers. The Scottish tradition will not be soon forgotten.

# Serbs

As is the case with other national groups which originated in the territories of the present-day Yugoslavia, it is impossible to say how many Serbs have entered Canada during the different migrations, and it is extremely difficult to determine the present population of the Serbian ethnocultural group in Canada. Before 1900, the Serbs were not listed separately in the census, but were classified as Austrians, Hungarians or Turks in accordance with the political status of the immigrants' place of origin. The term "Serbian" appeared for the first time in the census of 1901, although in succeeding years they were again unlisted, but reappeared later in the official statistics as Serbo-Croats and Yugoslavs.

According to the 1971 Canadian census, there were 5,225 Serbs in Canada, 4,490 of whom lived in Ontario. The actual number of Canadians of Serbian origin is higher, however; estimates vary from 10,000 to 15,000. Apparently some Serbs reported their ethnicity in the 1971 census as Yugoslavs, and there may be over 250,000 Yugoslavs of the first, second and third generations in Canada.

In the middle of the nineteenth century Serbs, like many other Europeans, looked forward to new opportunities in the "overseas" countries of Canada and the United States. These Serbs were mainly agricultural workers from the continental area of the Balkans as well as fishermen from the Dalmatian coast. The occupational profile of the immigrants seems to vary according to the migrational period.

There are five easily distinguishable periods of Serbian migration to Canada and to North America in general. The immigration of Serbs to the Province of British Columbia in the 1850s marks the beginning of Serbian settlement in Canada. One of the first Serbian settlers was Spiro Obradovich, who came to the Kootenay River district in 1854. Four years later, after the discovery of gold in the Fraser River, Serbian prospectors settled along the Fraser River in the years 1860–65. Some of these men moved on to the Klondike to continue their search for gold. In 1860 a Serb settlement was established in Vancouver. The majority of Serbs in British Columbia, usually young, single men, were mainly employed in the mining and forest industries, many to be found in the lumber camps around Phoenix, Golden, Prince Rupert and Kamloops.

The second wave of Serbian immigration began around the 1870s. Most of the Serbian immigrants from this period were from the Serbian territories under Austro-Hungarian control. At the turn of the century, Serbs began migrating to the other provinces in Canada. Attracted by the free homesteads offered by the Canadian government, at a time when the situation in Serbia was one of rural overpopulation with developments in the money market aiding the growth of peasant indebtedness, Serbian farmers arrived in Saskatchewan in 1903. The land reminded them of the old homeland, and the Serbian community in Regina is one of the oldest in the country.

Following the recession in the United States, in 1907–08 many Serbs came to Alberta from Montana, Idaho, Washington and Utah. These Serbian pioneers worked in the coal mines around Lethbridge and built roads in McLeod and Cadomin. They also worked on the railway, helping to lay the

Canadian National tracks from Edmonton to Vancouver and then on the Grand Trunk Pacific track from Edmonton to Prince Arthur, British Columbia. The work was exceedingly difficult and the terrain varied from river valleys to high, rocky mountain passes. Their goods were delivered by boats in summer and by sleighs in winter.

In 1903, a small group of Serbs settled in Toronto, and by 1914 this community consisted of approximately two hundred men. The centre of their social and recreational activities was the Belgrad Coffee House, established in 1911. Other Serbian settlements in Ontario before the First World War were in Hamilton and Niagara Falls, where the immigrants worked on the construction of the Ontario Hydro transmitter, and on the Welland Canal.

The years 1912–14 witnessed the beginning of organized community life for Serbian immigrants. In 1912, the Serbian Orthodox Church was established in Regina, and in 1913, St. Nicholas Serbian Orthodox Church was organized in Hamilton, Ontario. In 1914, Serbian Canadians in Toronto opened a night school for the study of the English language.

During the First World War, many Serbs from Canada and the United States returned to their homeland to fight as volunteers. Many also joined the Canadian army. While Serbian immigration was curtailed by the war, it was renewed in 1918.

The migration that occurred between the two world wars is considered as the third phase of Serbian immigration to Canada. Large numbers of Serbians came in the years 1924–29 and 1934–39. The immigrants were primarily single men or married men who left their families at home with plans to bring them over when their financial situation had improved. The Serbs from this group tended to settle in the industrial centres of Ontario and in the mining and mill towns of northern Ontario and British Columbia. In Toronto, the Serbian-Canadian population approached 1,000 persons in 1928. Between the world wars, the social and cultural life of the Serbian immigrants had undergone a rapid development. New churches and Serbian halls were established, and in many communities fraternal lodges, dance and song groups, sports clubs and women's groups were formed, all of which had the goal of preserving Serbian culture, heritage and traditions.

Serbian voluntary associations and organizations were formed to ease the economic hardships of newly arrived immigrants and to facilitate their integration into Canadian society. After the Second World War, however, many Serbians in Canada returned to Yugoslavia. In May 1947, for example, more than 500 Serbians returned, but after a time in Yugoslavia many became disillusioned and re-emigrated to Canada.

The fourth phase of Serbian immigration marked the beginning of a new occupational structure among Serbian newcomers. Up to that time, Serbians who came to Canada were primarily unskilled and semi-skilled workers. The postwar immigrants of the 1947–53 period were of varying occupations. Many highly educated ex-politicians, academics and military personnel found themselves outside Yugoslavia for various reasons and ended up in Canada, where they attempted to put their skills and training to constructive use. In comparison, the last and current group of Serbian immigrants are of a very heterogeneous nature. They may be placed in two categories: independent and sponsored immigrants. The independent immigrants are, as a general rule though not exclusively, better qualified and have either trade diplomas or university degrees, while the sponsored immigrants vary educationally from those with public school education to persons with university degrees. The sponsored immigrants also vary widely in age. In the period 1951–63, one-third of all male Serbian immigrants who entered Canada were between 15 to 34 years of age, while as a group Serbian immigrants range from the very young to the very elderly.

Almost all Serbs belong to the Orthodox church, and have built a half-dozen beautiful churches in Canada since the first church was built in Regina in 1912. Architecturally, the churches in Windsor, Toronto and Niagara Falls are remarkable in design.

Among the largest Serbian organizations in Canada are the Serbian National Shield Society of Canada, with headquarters in Windsor, Ontario, and the Serbian National League of Canada, with headquarters in Hamilton. The membership of the Serbian National Society consists primarily of Serbs who immigrated prior to the Second World War and Canadian-born Serbs, while the members of the Serbian National League are drawn mainly from refugees who immigrated after the Second World War. Other Serbian organizations include the Serbian National Federation, the Serbian Brothers Help of Canada, the Circle of Serbian Sisters, Serbian university clubs and several professional and business associations across the country. In addition to these exclusively Serbian organizations, there are other groups to which Serbians belong, such as those frequently called Canadian Yugoslav Societies. One such organization is Bratstvo-Jedinstvo (Fraternity and Unity), which organizes an annual festival of national songs and dances in Wellandport, Ontario. There are also recently organized Yugoslav clubs in London and Hamilton, Ontario.

A number of cultural organizations exist, such as the Cultural and Historical Society (Njegos). The Society is collecting historical data from the period of the Second World War in an attempt to preserve the Serbian heritage for future historians. A Serbian cultural club was founded in Toronto in 1952. There are also several youth groups, notably folklore organizations which perform Serbian national dances at inter-ethnic festivals. Among the best known are the Gravčanica Choir from Windsor and the Strazhilova Choir of Toronto.

A very successful charitable organization is the Serbian Aid Society, which was founded in 1952, with headquarters in Toronto and branches in other cities. The organization collects funds to help handicapped or needy Serbs throughout the world, and provides assistance to new Serbian immigrants settling in Canada. The Serbian Business and Professional Association, founded in Windsor in 1961, has helped many Canadians of Serbian origin start their own businesses.

The Serbs, like many other immigrant groups, have felt the need to establish newspapers in their own language. The first Serbian newspaper published in Canada was *Kanadski Glasnik* (*Canada Herald*). This newspaper began publication in Welland, Ontario, in 1916, and continued to publish for two years, with a circulation of about 1,750 readers.

There are at present several Serbian newspapers in Canada. The ones which claim the largest number of readers are *Glas Kanadskih Srba* (*Voice of Canadian Serbs*), *Kanadski Srbobran* (*The Canadian Serbian*), *Bratsvo* (*Fraternity*), and *Naŝe Novine* (*Our Newspaper*), formerly *Jedinstvo* (*Unity*). The last newspaper is a joint venture of both Croats and Serbs working together as a "Yugoslav" group. There were also a number of other Serbian newspapers that were published in Canada but have ceased operation.

Serbian customs have been highlighted in Canada for quite some time. The First Serbian Day in Canada was held on June 23, 1946, and song festivals participated in by groups such as the Serbian Singers Federation are featured. There are also annual festivals sponsored by the Serbian League of Canada, the Serbian Shield Society of Canada, and the Diocesan Day of the Eastern America and Canadian Diocese. Serbian war veterans also hold an annual festival, Draža Mihailovich Day, in Winona, Ontario.

There are several Serbian and Yugoslav radio programs available to Serbians, but virtually no Serbian English-language publications to serve the community. In the area of sports, Serbians have shown remarkable success in organizing soccer clubs.

Many Serbs have contributed to Canada in various ways. They have helped in the development of western Canada and have explored undeveloped parts of Canada in an effort to begin anew in this country. Serbs are now prominent in the business community, and are active in the Canadian academic community. There is no question that their presence has added a great deal to the physical and cultural development of this country, and will continue to do so.

# Slovaks

THE FIRST LARGE-SCALE emigration from Slovakia took place in the early 1870s and was directly largely towards the United States. The first Slovaks to come to Canada were from the United States, and came to this country when they could no longer find work there. The first recorded Slovak immigrant to Canada was Joseph Bellon, who arrived in Toronto in 1878. However, Western Canada rather than the urban areas held the greatest attraction for the early Slovak immigrants.

The 1880s marked a period of increased Slovak immigration to Canada, largely from the mining centres of Pennsylvania and Ohio. Of some note in this regard are the activities of Paul Esterhazy, an immigration agent who organized the settlement of the various "Austro-Hungarian" families in Hun's Valley, Manitoba. Among the families which Esterhazy brought with him in 1885 from Pennsylvania were a number of Slovaks. The same year saw Slovak miners settling in Lethbridge, Alberta, from the mines of Shelby, Montana, and Lethbridge quickly became an important Slovak centre in Canada, with its own church and community organizations. To this day, several hundred Slovaks reside in and about the community. Similarly, Slovaks from Ohio settled in British Columbia, and one of them, Andrew Shutty, was commemorated by the name of Shutty County as a tribute to his work on behalf of the Slovak community in establishing a Slovak church in Kaslo, British Columbia.

With the coming to power of the Laurier government in 1896, aggressive new immigration policies were developed by Sir Clifford Sifton, and this resulted in further Slovak immigration. For example, several hundred Slovak miners from Pennsylvania moved to British Columbia, while smaller groups settled in Alberta and Manitoba. Crow's Nest Pass attracted a large number of these settlers, and several hundred Slovak Canadians still live there.

The first Slovak-Canadian publication

appeared at Blairmore, Alberta, in 1910, along with one of the first Canadian Slovak fraternal organizations independent of American Slovak organizations. Numerous other Slovak groups settled throughout the Canadian West, but because of the imprecision of immigration record-keeping at the time, it is impossible to give an exact number, since Slovaks appeared in census figures under Hungarian, Slav, Austrian and other groupings.

Although this initial immigration of Slovaks to Canada had come from the United States, in the years immediately preceding the First World War, increasing numbers of immigrants came directly from Slovakia, most to join friends and relatives already settled in Canada. During the war the Slovaks, along with other East European peoples, suffered from hostility and suspicion because they came from a state with which Canada was officially at war. Many Slovaks in Canada suffered internment as enemy aliens and were released only after representations by the Slovak League of America.

The end of the First World War and the founding of the Czechoslovak state brought many changes to the Slovak people, but immigration to Canada continued. It has been estimated that between 1921 and 1939, some 34,000 Slovaks entered this country as part of a massive exodus of some 217,000 Slovaks from their native land, an exodus which constituted almost 10 per cent of the total population of Slovakia. Most of these immigrants had a much higher level of education than the previous wave of Slovak immigrants, and most of them had several years of military service behind them, a trade, and political experience gained from national and social struggles in Slovakia. Many of these political attitudes were imported into Canada, and were reflected in the types of organizations which

sprang up here.

Unlike the first wave of settlers, which tended to move to western Canada, the inter-war wave was attracted by the possibilities open to them in the mining and smelting areas of Quebec and Ontario, especially in Timmins, Sudbury, Noranda and Arvida. Furthermore, many of these immigrants chose larger Canadian centres for their homes rather than farm settlements or small mining towns. In these urban centres, the Slovaks tended to establish themselves as contractors, carpenters and bricklayers. By 1951, more than one-third of Canadian Slovaks were urban dwellers.

An important centre of Slovak settlement was Winnipeg, where the first Canada-wide Slovak organization, the Canadian Slovak League, was founded in 1932. This appeared to be an indication of further Slovak immigration, but immigration to Canada ceased during the Second World War, and the subsequent establishment of Communist rule in Slovakia further inhibited immigration. An important wave of immigration, however, resulted from the Soviet invasion of Czechoslovakia in 1968, and the immigrants in this wave tended to be highly trained and educated.

The 1971 census of Canada records 24,030 Canadians of Slovak origin, of whom 17,370 or 72.3 per cent claim familiarity with the Slovak language. By far the largest concentration of Slovak Canadians is in Ontario, where 15,005 or 62.4 per cent of the group resides. Smaller groups can be found in Alberta (2,650 or 11.0 per cent), Quebec (2,305 or 9.6 per cent) and British Columbia (2,070 or 8.6 per cent). The most important urban centres of Slovak population in Canada are Toronto, with 4,490 Slovak Canadians, Montreal (2,065), Thunder Bay (1,645), Windsor, Ontario (1,380), St. Catharines (1,330) and Hamilton (1,225), with smaller concentrations in other cities.

According to the census, well over 70 per cent of the Canadian Slovak population lives in the major urban centres of Canada.

Immigration to Canada declined dramatically after 1968. In 1970, some 1,411 Czechoslovak citizens entered Canada, but by 1974 that number had shrunk to 148.

The nature of initial Slovak immigration to Canada, based as it was on a large number of mobile miners seeking work wherever they could get it, meant that a settled community life centred around the church would be difficult to realize. Furthermore, the lack of clergy speaking the Slovak language further complicated the process of setting up a religious structure in the community.

Within the Canadian Slovak population, three religious affiliations are prominent, reflecting the religious composition of the Slovaks themselves. The most numerous are the Roman Catholic Slovaks, but Greek Catholics and Lutherans constitute highly prominent religious groupings as well.

The first church associated with the Slovak community was erected in 1886 in Hun's Valley, Manitoba. Although the church was originally intended for Paul Esterhazy's "Hungarian" settlers, it soon became evident that most of the worshippers were Slovaks and Poles, each group sitting on its own side of the church and singing hymns in its own language. A Slovak church was built in Coleman, Alberta, in 1905, and another at Fort William, Ontario, in 1907, where a large Slovak–Canadian community existed to support it. Unlike the first two churches, the latter has survived to the present day as a Slovak religious centre, while Fort William became an important centre of Slovak cultural and community life.

Among Slovak Roman Catholics, parochial organizations were founded in Montreal in 1927, Toronto (1927) and Windsor (1929). Initially, the parishes used the church facilities of other Roman Catholic groups, notably those of the Poles, whose language is comprehensible to Slovaks, but ultimately, with the help of American Slovak organizations, these parishes were able to acquire or build their own churches by the early 1940s. After the Second World War, the establishment of a Communist government in Czechoslovakia led to the expulsion of many Slovak priests, and those who immigrated to Canada strengthened Slovak Roman Catholic organizations here. As a result, Slovak Roman Catholic parishes were established in Hamilton, Sarnia, Winnipeg and New Westminster, British Columbia, while a Jesuit missionary centre was established in Galt, Ontario and a minor seminary in Sarnia. Furthermore, Slovaks were also associated with the foundation of churches in Welland, Ontario, in 1958 and in Rosewood, Manitoba, in 1966.

Before the Second World War, the Slovak Greek Catholics in Canada were represented by only one parish, in Lethbridge, Alberta, founded in 1921. In other centres, Slovak Greek Catholics tended to use the facilities of Ukrainian Greek Catholics wherever possible. Several Slovak Greek Catholic priests came to Canada after the Communist takeover in Czechoslovakia and encouraged the formation of a more stable religious structure in the community. In the 1950s and 1960s, nine Slovak Greek Catholic parishes were founded in Canada, in Toronto, Hamilton, Montreal, Windsor, Oshawa, Welland, Sudbury and Delhi.

The Slovak Lutheran community has also suffered from a lack of Slovak clergy, and therefore sought help from German Lutherans in Canada and from the American-based Synod of Slovak Lutheran Evangelical

Churches, founded in 1902. The first Slovak Lutheran congregation was founded in Fort William in 1927, and a church was finally constructed there in 1947. Other Slovak Lutheran congregations were also founded in Montreal, Toronto, Windsor, Chatham, Ontario, Timmins, Bradford and Smithville.

Because Slovak immigration to Canada initially came by way of the United States, many of the first Slovak organizations in this country were branches of American-based groups. Among these were the first Catholic Slovak Union, founded in Cleveland in 1890, the National Slovak Society, founded in Pittsburgh in 1890, the Slovak Roman and Greek Catholic Union, the Slovak Evangelical Union founded in 1893 by Lutheran Slovaks, and the Slovak Catholic Sokol, founded in 1905. Most of these organizations were founded with a definite religious affiliation in mind, but they were also mutual assistance associations, providing financial benefits, insurance and loans to their membership, as well as a cultural milieu for the preservation of Slovak national identity. All of them developed branch organizations in various centres across Canada. Most of these American-based groups continue their activities in Canada, and have numerous adult and youth branches across the country, with a membership of several thousand persons. The most important American Slovak organization was the Slovak League of America, founded in Cleveland in 1907, but it disbanded its branches in Canada when the Canadian Slovak League was founded in Winnipeg in 1932.

It has been estimated that there were 78 branches of American Slovak organizations operating in Canada in the 1930s. After the First World War, with a greater influx of Slovaks into Canada, the need for autonomous Canadian Slovak groups was discerned. In 1928 the first Slovak Benefit Society was organized in western Canada with branches in Regina and Estevan, Saskatchewan, Blairmore, Alberta, and in New Westminster and Crow's Nest Pass in British Columbia. In 1933, Slovaks in the mining camps of eastern Canada had organized the National Slovak Benefit Society. Ultimately, these two benefit organizations were united in 1946 to form the Canadian Slovak Benefit Society. With members of many religions, this organization tends to concentrate on the immediate needs of its members, providing them with a wide variety of financial and cultural services.

The Canadian Slovak League, founded in Winnipeg in 1932 as the autonomous successor to the Slovak League of America, has been much more concerned with political issues, particularly those affecting the status of Slovakia. It has consistently advocated independence for Slovakia, and continues to speak out on matters of concern to the Slovak nation. At present, it has over fifty branches across Canada, the majority of which are in Ontario, where most Slovaks reside. The Canadian Slovak League is the largest Slovak organization in Canada. Its headquarters are in Montreal, and it unites several thousand members across Canada. Particularly important among its activities is the promotion of its youth section, especially seven Slovak dance groups.

After the Second World War, several new Slovak organizations were formed with a strong political interest resulting from the large number of Slovak refugees who entered the country. These organizations include the Slovak National Council Abroad, the Slovak Liberation Committee, both of which merged to form the Slovak Liberation Council, two veterans' organizations called the Slovak Legion and the Union of Slovak Combatants, and the professional and businessmen's associations founded in Toronto and Montreal, in 1961 and 1962 respectively.

Undoubtedly the most important single centre of Slovak life in Canada is Toronto. Not only do a number of Slovak organizations have their headquarters there, but the large Slovak population of the city makes the publication of three newspapers possible, the *Kanadsky Slovak* (*Canadian Slovak*), the official organ of the Canadian Slovak League, *Slovensky Hlas* (*Slovak Voice*), and the *Ludove Zvesti* (*People's News*), a publication of the Slovak Benefit Society.

The Slovak World Congress, a federation of most Slovak organizations in Canada and other countries, met in Toronto in June, 1971, bringing together almost 1,500 delegates, observers and guests from Slovak communities in seventeen countries from around the world. This is an indication that Slovak organizational life is paralleling the emergence of the Slovak presence in Canada, especially strong since the Second World War. With a concern for their own cultural retention, their homeland and their adopted country, the Slovaks are making many positive contributions, individually as members of the Canadian labour force and collectively through their various organizations, towards the development of this country and the best interests of their former homeland.

# Slovenes

UNTIL THE 1971 CENSUS Canadian statistics did not list Slovenes as a separate ethnocultural group. They were included among Hungarians, Italians, Yugoslavs or Austrians; in the 1960s some Slovenes who had settled in France

as miners came to Canada and were listed as French. According to the 1971 census, there were 7,305 Slovenes in Canada, 5,635 of whom were in Ontario, predominantly in Toronto, 470 in British Columbia, 425 in Quebec and the remainder spread out across the rest of Canada. The actual number of Slovenes in Canada is likely somewhat higher, one estimate being as high as 20,000 persons.

One of the first known contacts between Slovenes and Canada came during the first half of the nineteenth century. A Slovenian missionary, Reverend Frederick Baraga, came in 1830 to work among the Indians of the Lake Superior area. He learned the language of the Ottawa and Chippewa Indians, publishing a *Theoretical and Practical Grammar of the Otchipwe Language*, which earned him the title "Father of Indian Literature." This was followed by a dictionary of the Otchipwe language in 1853 defining 30,000 words, which is regarded even today as a standard work. He also published prayer books and hymnals for Indians, and sermons for missionaries which are still in use. He published subsequent books, and a biography of him has recently been written. Some of the present Slovene organizations in Canada bear his name.

Large numbers of Slovenes began to immigrate to North America in the last quarter of the nineteenth century. This was due partly to the missionary reports of Reverend Baraga, which attracted other priests who made substantial contributions to Native religious life, and made North America better known among Slovenes.

The majority of Slovene immigrants went to the United States, but some came to Canada and took part in many pioneering enterprises such as the development of Canadian mines, road construction and farming. When the United States government placed restrictions on European immigration after the First World War, more Slovenes came to Canada. Two large communities, Timmins and Kirkland Lake, were established in northern Ontario, and in time many Slovenes purchased farms on the Niagara peninsula, where they now operate fruit farms between Hamilton and St. Catharines. At Beamsville they established a Slovenian Farmers' Co-operative and built a Slovenian Farmers' Home, a centre of their economic and cultural activities.

Sizable groups settled in other centres, including Nanaimo, Fernie, Port Alberni, Ladysmith, South Wellington, Vancouver, Grand Forks, Rossland, Trail, Cassidy, Osoyoos and Penticton in British Columbia; at Canmore, Bankhead, Coleman, Banff, Botha and Evergreen in Alberta; at Frenchman Butte and Quill Lake in Saskatchewan; at New Waterford and Caledonia Mines in Nova Scotia; and in Montreal.

According to Yugoslav statistics, 4,281 Slovenes emigrated to Canada during the period 1921–36. These and earlier arrivals came mainly for economic reasons, but following the Second World War a larger influx, starting in 1948, was caused by the establishment of the Communist regime in Yugoslavia. After spending some years in displaced persons' camps in Europe, many of the Slovene political refugees were accepted as non-sponsored immigrants to Canada. They started life anew, working in forests, on farms and on railroads. A large proportion settled in Metropolitan Toronto. As time passed, the differences between earlier and later groups of immigrants diminished and both have been successful in their integration into the Canadian way of life. Many are well-established as businessmen, especially in the construction industry.

In the years 1956–58, some Slovenians took advantage of the opportunity provided by the Hungarian uprising and emigrated to Canada. The Slovenes, in particular those who came to Canada as political refugees, show strong interest and profound concern for the political development of their country of origin, especially when their relatives and friends have remained behind. Many of the Slovenes have brought with them their political affiliations and continue to debate Slovenian political issues. Others attempt to draw all of these political elements into one concerted effort to work for a non-Communist Slovenia. On the other hand, some Slovenes have chosen a complete integration into Canadian society.

The Slovenes are predominantly Roman Catholics, and their churches and parishes constitute major centres of religious, social, cultural and recreational activities. In Toronto, two Slovenian parishes were formed after 1950.

The older of the two parishes, Our Lady Help of Christians, was established in 1953 while the newer one, Our Lady of the Miraculous Medal, was formed in New Toronto in 1960. Although both churches occupy key positions in the lives of the Slovenes as religious and cultural centres, their geographic locations and the circumstances surrounding their inception account for slight differences in the composition of their membership. Our Lady Help of Christians was established after many Slovenes had settled in Toronto and, consequently, membership is not restricted to a particular geographic location. New immigrants to Toronto, especially those who are single or who are temporarily without their families, also gravitate towards this parish. Membership at present is estimated to be approximately 6,000 individuals.

The New Toronto parish, on the other

hand, tends to serve a fairly localized Slovenian community, although members are also drawn from Mimico, Islington, Port Credit and Cooksville. Established in 1960 by families who had originally attended the older parish and then moved out to build homes in New Toronto, this parish grew from an original 82 families to a present membership of about 450 families. Numbers would seem to be increased by the arrival of relatives of parishioners and families moving out from the city to establish themselves in the suburbs.

The parishes offer a variety of services and activities, including Slovenian-language classes for children from Grades 2–8, English-language classes for adults, social and cultural clubs for teenagers and participation in organizations such as Boy Scouts, Girl Guides, and the Council of Christian Men, among others. A folklore group and dance group are also attached to Our Lady Help of Christians Church, and Slovenes from all over participate in these groups. In Toronto, a religious monthly, *Božja Beseda (God's Word)*, is published.

Other parishes are located in Hamilton, Montreal and Winnipeg. Priests stationed in the Slovenian parishes make periodic visits to look after the spiritual needs of Slovenes in many other rural and urban centres of Canada. Most of the parishes have also purchased farms near larger cities. They serve as pleasant places to hold family picnics, and in the summer religious services are held there.

The Slovenian National Federation of Canada, founded in 1952, is an organization devoted to the promotion of the idea of a non-Communist and democratic Slovenia, and to the development of the cultural and social life of Slovenes in Canada. It publishes the monthly *Slovenska Država (Slovenian State)* in Toronto. A number of Slovene credit unions and sports associations exist among Slovenes in Toronto and in other cities in Ontario. Worth mentioning are the cultural associations Večerni Zvon and Simon Gregorčič, the Slovenian theatre in Toronto, a folklore group and an association of Slovene students. Very active in Slovene life in Toronto is the Slovenian Home, which sponsors the Bishop Baraga organization, sport club and hunters' club.

The Slovenes coming from various European locations, do not allow their interest in their homeland to wane. They form close associations in the land of their choice, maintaining the best of their Old World culture, to help build a stronger and better Canada.

# Spanish

EVEN THOUGH SPANISH emigration to Canada has become a recognizable phenomenon only in the last twenty to thirty years, Spain's association with this country is a longstanding one, dating back several centuries to the voyages of the Basque fishermen to Canada's Atlantic coastal waters and Spanish exploration of the Pacific Coast.

Spain had long been known for her explorers, both native born and those sponsored by the Spanish monarchs, the most famous of whom was Christopher Columbus. He sailed in the Golden Age of Spanish exploration, at a time when Spain laid claim to nearly half of the known world. Basques, along with Portuguese, Bretons and others, probably reached the rich fishing grounds off Newfoundland as early as the first quarter of the sixteenth century. Place names such as Port aux Basques and Ile aux Basques recall the expeditions made by Basque fishermen to Newfoundland waters.

On the Pacific coast, at least fourteen Spanish expeditions carried out explorations between 1542 and 1792, in the process discovering and charting many straits, islands and bays. Today places such as Alberni, Laredo Strait, Carmelo Strait, Mazarredo Sound, Mount Bodega, Quadra Rocks and Narvaez Bay testify to the early Spanish presence in this part of the world. Vancouver Island even had a Spanish name at one time. It was called Quadra and Vancouver Island to commemorate the friendship between the Spanish navigator Bodega y Quadra and Captain George Vancouver.

For the next hundred years there was little contact between Spain and Canada, because when large-scale emigration began from Europe in the nineteenth century, the majority of Spaniards who left their country went to South America. The subject of Spanish and Italian immigration to Canada's northwest was broached in 1886, but the Department of Agriculture, which then handled immigration, let it be known that it could not make special colonization arrangements for Spanish and Italian immigrants. Not until the opening years of this century did a very modest Spanish emigration to Canada get underway, with the arrival of about 2,000 Spaniards in the years 1913 and 1914.

It was reported in the 1971 census that there were 27,515 people of Spanish origin in Canada. More than 11,000 immigrants with Spanish citizenship arrived in Canada between 1956 and 1967; between 1946 and 1955 just over 1,000 had arrived to join the tiny Spanish community that had existed since the turn of the century. Since Canada's Centennial year, approximately 700 have emigrated each year, most to settle in Ontario and Quebec. The 1971 census figures reveal that 10,825 Canadians of Spanish descent live in Ontario and 10,330 in Quebec, out of a total of 27,515.

Spanish-speaking people have come to Canada from Spain and several South American countries. The standard language of Spain is Spanish, with Catalan being widely spoken in the northeast and Basque in the north. Galician is also spoken in the northwestern provinces. Spain has traditionally been an agricultural country, its main products being vegetables, cereals and fruits, chiefly citrus. In recent years, however, it has been a semi-industrial state thanks to a program of industrialization and financial reforms introduced in 1959 by the government. After years of stagnation the economy began to improve dramatically in the 1960s, which caused immigration to fall steadily from a high of 20,045 in 1969 to approximately 4,500 in 1974.

The Spanish, like other emigrants, left their homeland for a number of reasons. Some undoubtedly emigrated because they were underemployed in their homeland, some because of the political climate, and others because they were seeking both adventure and escape from an authoritarian dictatorship. The majority, though, were probably motivated by an overriding desire to improve their economic status.

Many Spanish immigrants are skilled workers, including technicians, welders, electricians and mechanics, and business and professional men and women who have been attracted to Canada's urban centres. Others are farmers who emigrated to Canada in 1957 under a special arrangement concluded between the Spanish and Canadian governments. A number are labourers who have found work in the mines and forests of Ontario and Quebec.

In 1960, another scheme devised by the Spanish and Canadian governments resulted in fifty young Spanish women coming to this country to work for a year as domestic servants. This group included women from many different walks of life in Spain.

Recreational and social organizations have been founded in the larger areas of Spanish concentration to help immigrants find jobs and to provide counselling as well as a variety of other services such as language instruction. Active organizations include Asociación Hispano de Vancouver, which was founded in 1971 and which publishes a monthly bulletin called Hispanos Boletín; Club Hispano in Toronto; a Spanish association in Montreal which supports a soccer team; and a Circulo Hispano Americano in Winnipeg. Alberta, which had 1,305 residents of Spanish origin in 1971, boasts four Spanish organizations—the Community of Spanish Language and Culture, the Organization of Hispanic Cultures, the Spanish Canadian Club and the Don Quixote Club.

There are at least three other Spanish voluntary associations which currently exist in Montreal, including Centro Gallego, Centro Social Español and Club Español de Quebec. The programs of these organizations reflect the music, language, literature and customs of Canadians of Spanish origin.

In 1976 there were at least five Spanish periodicals published in Canada: *Correo Hispano-Americano*, a weekly which was founded in Toronto in 1969; *Mundo Ilustrado*, founded in 1975 and published bi-monthly in Toronto; *El Popular*, which was founded in 1970 in Toronto and is issued twice a week; *Quincenario Hispano*, published twice a month in Vancouver, and *Correo Español de Quebec*, which is published several times a year by La Federación de Asociaciones Españolas de Quebec. A local radio station in Vancouver also has a Spanish hour.

Several Spanish-speaking Canadians have made notable contributions to the Canadian art scene, while others have made their marks as designers in Canadian television and film studios. Spanish Canadians have also introduced songs and dances, an integral part of Spain's rich cultural heritage, to the Canadian scene. In a number of cities, schools which provide instruction in Spanish dancing have been founded. In Toronto, for instance, a Spanish dance group has been connected with the Folk Arts Council. A number of Spanish business organizations have been started. Spanish priests are attached to various parishes in the country. All of these factors indicate that the Spanish are interested in giving of their heritage to this country while establishing themselves as citizens.

# Sri Lankans

THE PEOPLE OF SRI LANKA, formerly known as Ceylonese, come from an island about 20 miles (32 km) off the southeast coast of the Indian subcontinent. Ceylon became an independent state of the Commonwealth when independence was achieved from Britain in 1948. In May 1972 it became the Republic of Sri Lanka, remaining a member of the Commonwealth.

There has always been much unemployment and underemployment in Sri Lanka, especially among the educated youth. Each year thousands of young Sri Lankans leave the country for the United States, Canada, Australia, New Zealand, Great Britain, and other European countries.

As an identifiable group, Sri Lankans are among the newest arrivals in Canada, most of them having come in the 1960s and 1970s. Few have been here as long as fifteen years. The recency of Sri Lankan immigration to Canada is documented in Canadian immigration statistics which showed that between 1955 and 1966 only 630 Sri Lankans and former Ceylonese entered Canada. For the period 1946–73, 1,998 Sri Lankans are reported as having emigrated to Canada. The Sri Lankan community in Canada currently numbers approximately 10,000 persons.

Again according to immigration statistics, places of residence chosen by Sri Lankans have almost always been the biggest urban centres in Canada, including Toronto, Montreal, Vancouver, Ottawa and Calgary. There are more than 3,000 Sri Lankans in Toronto today.

Most Sri Lankans emigrated for economic or political reasons. They came to Canada to obtain job satisfaction, career mobility, education and a better future for their children. Some have also come in reaction against the political and economic systems in their homeland. Because the majority of them are well-educated, they tend to integrate well into Canadian life. Most Sri Lankan immigrants come with the intention of making Canada their permanent home, and thus they generally have a very positive attitude towards Canadian culture, education and lifestyle.

The majority of Sri Lankans are Buddhist Sinhalese and form one community based on their identity as Sri Lankan nationals. They wish to be known as a Sri Lankan community, and are now in the process of being organized. Sri Lankan immigrants in some communities have formed such organizations as the Ceylon Club or Sri Lanka-Canada associations, one of which was formed in Toronto a few years ago and now has about three hundred members and publishes its own newsletter.

Since the Sri Lankan community is very small and scattered, the core of activities among Sri Lankans centres around family and kin. For most of the Sri Lankans in Canada, the interpersonal ties, private and intimate ones formed by the family and friendship groups, seem to be much more important than the associations or clubs in maintaining a group identity. And even though they are resolved to remain Canadians, they are still Sri Lankan in many ways, and wish to remain that way and share their heritage with other Canadians.

# Swedish

SWEDEN WAS ONE OF the earliest European countries to begin a permanent settlement in North America. From 1638 to 1655, a group of Swedish and Finnish settlers initiated the New Sweden colony on the banks of the Delaware. The Colony was short-lived and was quickly integrated into the American colonial mainstream.

The first Swedish immigrants to North America generally arrived on an individual basis. A large proportion of these early immigrants were seamen. Until 1845, most of the other Swedes who left for the United States were persons of a higher social and educational background who wanted a more progressive political climate and greater personal and religious freedom than their native country had been able to provide.

From 1846 to 1850, several thousand Swedish immigrants arrived in the United States. Most of them travelled in groups based on strong leadership or at least on family ties and common roots in certain regions of Sweden. Many immigrants sought land in the American Midwest, although some were skilled craftsmen and settled in towns. These early Swedish settlements in the American Midwest became important bases for the growing migration from Sweden.

From 1868 to 1914, more than one million Swedes immigrated to the United States and Canada. A large proportion of emigrants had been landless labourers and the sons and daughters of small farmers who stood no chance of inheriting a title to the family land. A series of crop failures from 1866 to 1868 brought starvation and economic hardship to many parts of Sweden and provided an added impetus to emigrate. As Swedish society became more mobile, a broader spectrum of society left for America. The Lutheran Church actively encouraged destitutes to emigrate. Labour organizers, economically emancipated women, and whole families emigrated. The entire movement of emigrants was encouraged by emigration promoters and by the fact that fares fell low enough to make emigration a reality.

Swedish immigration to Canada began on a small scale in the early 1870s as part of the mass migration of Swedes to this continent. Until 1914, most Swedish immigrants arrived in Canada by way of the United States, primarily from Minnesota and North Dakota. As an indication of this pattern, from 1901 to 1920 about 6,000 persons left Sweden directly for Canada, while during this same period the total of Swedish-born immigrants in Canada exceeded 20,000.

When the United States introduced a quota on immigrants in 1923, Canada became the main destination for Swedish immigrants. Between 1921 and 1930, over 20,000 of them arrived in Canada. The 1931 census listed 81,306 residents of Swedish origin and 34,415 Swedish-born.

The great majority of early Swedish immigrants to Canada, whether from Sweden or the United States, were farmers or farmhands. Around the turn of the century, industrial workers, unable to fulfill their ambitions in the urban areas of Sweden, began arriving in greater numbers. By the 1920s, a large proportion of the Swedish immigrants were industrial labourers, and many sought opportunities in Canadian cities and industrial areas.

During the Depression, Canadian immigration restrictions limited Swedish immigration, while several thousand Swedes returned to Sweden from Canada. However, in the postwar period from 1944 to 1960, some 7,000 immigrants of Swedish origin arrived in Canada. Many of these newcomers were engineers, businessmen, and representatives of Swedish export industries. Some of these immigrants were originally of Finnish or Estonian origin and had first migrated to Sweden before leaving for Canada. Since the Second World War most Swedish immigrants have been attracted by job opportunities in the major Canadian cities.

The 1971 Canadian census listed 101,870 Canadians of Swedish origin compared to 121,757 in 1961. Of these, 21,680 were born in Sweden compared to 32,632 in 1961. While Canadians of Swedish origin can be found in all provinces of Canada, about 80 per cent live in the provinces of Manitoba, Saskatchewan, Alberta and British Columbia.

The first definite evidence of Swedish settlers in Canada is found in the Red River

Valley of Manitoba. Two Swedish names appeared among Lord Selkirk's group of settlers. Few of the early Swedish settlers went to the Maritimes. Some settled around Toronto and Montreal, but by far the largest number found their way to the Prairie Provinces and British Columbia.

The first Swedes of the mass migration leaving for North America began arriving in Canada in the early 1870s. Many came to Canada along the Red River by boat from Minnesota and stepped ashore in Winnipeg.

Most of the Swedish newcomers settled on the Canadian Prairies, which were virtually uninhabited at this time. With the completion of the Canadian Pacific Railway in 1885, the western regions of Canada had direct communication with the East, and became open for rapid settlement. The policies of the Canadian government encouraged settlement in the West, and the first Swedes who arrived from the United States came to take advantage of free land being offered.

Winnipeg became the centre for immigrants from Sweden. The first Swedish-language newspaper was founded in Winnipeg in 1886, the first Swedish church three years later. All national Swedish organizations that were established in Canada began their activities in Winnipeg. For several decades Winnipeg retained its position as the leading Swedish centre in Canada. Yet in 1971, only 8,955 Swedish Canadians (about 9 per cent of the national total) lived in Manitoba.

Many Swedish immigrants would first arrive in Winnipeg, then move elsewhere in search of free land. Many of these homesteaders, having little or no money, sought employment in the bush or with the railways during the winter. In 1887, Emmanual Öhlan moved from Winnipeg to found the community of Stockholm in the fertile Qu'Appelle valley of Saskatchewan, then part of the Northwest Territories. This community was for many years one of the most active Swedish communities in Canada, with several Swedish congregations and churches. Dubuc, a nearby community, also had a substantial Swedish population. This district took a leading role in promoting Swedish culture. The Swedish-Canadian League, with lodges in many Swedish centres, was organized in the 1920s. Swedes from central Canada used to gather at Round Lake for their *tings* at midsummer, but with the passing of the first generation, these gatherings have ceased.

Saskatchewan has long been attractive for Swedish immigrants. According to the 1931 census, Saskatchewan recorded the largest number of Swedish inhabitants, with one out of every four Swedes in Canada living in that province. In 1971, 14,635 Swedish Canadians (14 per cent of the national total) lived in Saskatchewan. Other communities in Saskatchewan that have attracted sizable numbers of Swedish settlers include Broadview, Buchanan, Canwood, Elfros, Hendon, Kipling, Percival, Prince Albert, Melfort, Wadena and Beaty.

Many Swedish pioneers settled in Alberta long before it became a province, and subsequently in the cities of Calgary and Edmonton. The area between these two cities has a greater concentration of Swedes than any other rural district in Canada. Many of its communities were founded by Swedish immigrants or include an important element of such settlers among their first inhabitants. These communities include Wetaskiwin, New Sweden, Calmar, Falun, Malmo, Thorsby and Westerose.

With the completion of the CPR, many Swedes made their way to British Columbia. Revelstoke had a relatively large Swedish population in the 1890s. Other communities with a Swedish population include Campbell River, Cranbrook, Greenwood, Kimberley, Malakwa, Matsqui, Nelson, Port Alberni, Prince George, Prince Rupert, Rossland, Silverhill, Smithers and Trail.

With the outbreak of the Second World War, great changes took place in the settlement patterns of Swedish Canadians. Many Swedes went to the Pacific Coast for the milder climate and the opportunities offered by the war industries. Vancouver soon replaced Winnipeg as the capital of Swedish culture in Canada. In 1971, 31,930 Swedish Canadians lived in British Columbia.

Ontario has proven increasingly attractive to Canadians of Swedish origin. Historically, the most popular area for Swedish immigrants has been the Kenora district in northwestern Ontario. Swedes first settled on the northern shore of Lake of the Woods in the 1890s. Many Swedes became farmers in the Kenora district while others played an important part in the commercial development of the community. In the postwar period, a number of Swedish immigrants have settled in Toronto.

Few Swedes were initially attracted to eastern Canada. There were some 2,000 Swedes living in Quebec in 1971, most of whom lived in and around Montreal. There is a Swedish cultural society in that city, the only one east of Ontario. There were approximately 1,500 Swedish Canadians living in the Maritimes in 1971.

Much of the life of the early Swedish communities in Canada was centred around the church. The Mission Covenant Church was the first Swedish church in Canada, founded in Winnipeg in 1885. The first Swedish Lutheran church was also organized in Winnipeg in 1890. Today, almost all Swedish churches conduct their services in the English language, but for many years they were a bastion of the Swedish language and culture in this country, providing a cultural link between the Swedish immigrant and his Canadian-born children.

The Lutheran Church is still the largest denomination among Scandinavians, although in 1971 only one in three claimed to be of the Lutheran denomination, whereas the 1931 census listed 62.3 per cent of Swedish Canadians as being of the Lutheran denomination. As well as the Baptist and Mission Covenant churches, the United Church has also gained many members among Swedish immigrants, and most notably among their Canadian-born children. In 1931, 15 per cent of Swedish Canadians were members of the United Church; by 1971, 28 per cent of all Scandinavians in Canada (there was no breakdown for individual Scandinavian groups) were members of the United Church.

Most Swedish immigrants, while they could master enough English to meet their daily needs, relied almost exclusively upon Swedish in their family and social life, especially in the West. Since there were no English-language classes available until after the Second World War, there was a cultural and linguistic need for periodicals in the Swedish language.

*Canada-Tidningen*, until it amalgamated with the *Swedish American Tribune* of Chicago in July 1970, was the longest running and most influential Swedish-language newspaper in Canada. This newspaper was established as a weekly in Winnipeg in 1892. Although there are conflicting opinions, it is believed that *Den Skandinaviske Canadiensaren* was an earlier version of the aforementioned paper. The latter, the first Swedish-language periodical in Canada, had been established as a monthly in Winnipeg in 1886.

There have been a number of other Swedish-language periodicals published in Winnipeg over the years. *Canada Posten* (*The Canada Post*) was established in 1904 by the Swedish Mission Covenant Church. *Forum* was a semi-radical monthly magazine supported by several Forum clubs. *Idog* was a periodical published by the Swedish Good Templar Lodge in Winnipeg. During the Depression, *Frihet* (*Liberty*) was a radical monthly founded by unemployed Swedes which supported the cause of the unemployed and advocated socialism.

In Vancouver, *Nya Svenska Pressen* (*The Swedish Press*) was founded in 1937, although several predecessors existed dating back to 1913. In late 1976, this newspaper experimented with a short term amalgamation with *Svenska Posten* (*The Swedish Post*) of Seattle, Washington, but financial problems forced this experiment to be postponed.

Since 1961 there has been a Swedish-language newspaper to serve Swedes living in eastern Canada, particularly the many Swedish immigrants who have settled in Toronto since the Second World War. *Canada-Svenska* (*The Swedish Canadian*) is a semi-monthly published in Toronto.

By 1971, only 21,680 persons in Canada claimed Swedish as their mother tongue, the largest number of whom, over 7,000, lived in British Columbia, Alberta and Ontario. The number of Swedish-born had declined to 14,110 in 1971 versus 19,338 in 1961. Over 5,000 of the Swedish-born lived in British Columbia, with another 3,000 in Ontario.

In addition to the churches and the Swedish-language newspapers, there developed a desire for social organizations directed to the needs of the Swedish community and controlled by members of that community. The only Swedish organization that has a national structure is the Vasa Order of America, which has lodges throughout Canada and the United States. The Vasa Order was founded in 1896 in Connecticut as a mutual benefit society. The original aims of the Order were to give material and moral help to members and their families who were sick or injured; to help pay funeral expenses; and to establish senior citizens' homes. The Order gradually became a more social and cultural organization to promote an awareness of Swedish culture among its members. The Strindberg Lodge in Winnipeg is the oldest Vasa Order Lodge in Canada, having been founded in 1913.

In the 1890s two temperance societies were founded in Winnipeg, one of which, the lodge Framtidens Hopp (Hope of the Future) lasted well into the 1930s and became a part of the Scandinavian Grand Lodge of the International Order of Good Templars in Canada.

In 1901, the Norden Society was organized as a sick benefit society. It is still active in Winnipeg. The Swedish Male Choir (Svenska Sängarbröderna) was formed in 1911 and offers annual concerts featuring Swedish, Icelandic, Norwegian and English songs. It is affiliated with the American Union of Swedish singers. The Viking Club is another Swedish group active in Winnipeg. Swedes also work in co-operation with other Scandinavian groups in Winnipeg to support the Scandinavian Centre.

In the 1940s, many Swedes left the Prairies and moved to British Columbia. There were existing Swedish clubs in the Vancouver area, but the influx of thousands of new Swedish settlers brought about a revival and expansion of activities. Among the clubs active today are the Swedish-Canadian Club, established in 1931; the Swedish Cultural Society, formed in 1951; the Harjedal Society; and the Bellman

Male Chorus. All of these clubs have their activities in the Swedish Community Hall in Vancouver, as does the Lodge Norman of the Vasa Order. There is a Swedish Park in Vancouver. The Swedish-Canadian Rest Home Association, first established in 1946, built a rest home in North Vancouver in 1946 and another in Burnaby in 1957.

The Swedish Co-ordinating Committee in Vancouver, a joint council of delegates from the various Swedish organizations, initiates co-operation within the Swedish community and with other ethnocultural groups. There is a similar organization, the United Swedish Societies, for Swedish Canadians in Winnipeg.

In addition to the lodges of the Vasa Order in Alberta, Swedes have promoted their culture mainly through co-operation with other Scandinavian groups. The most notable are the Scandinavian Centre Association in Edmonton, which was built by all the Scandinavian groups in that city and incorporated as a co-operative, and the Scandinavian Centre in Calgary. In Saskatchewan, Swedes work with other Scandinavian groups to support Scandinavian clubs in Saskatoon, Moose Jaw and Birch Hills. Swedish clubs in eastern Canada can be found in Montreal and Mossley, Ontario. There are Scandinavian clubs in Montreal, Toronto and Oshawa, and a Nordic Society in Ottawa.

The Swedes of western Canada adapted quite readily to their surroundings. Aside from their social and cultural organizations, most Swedish Canadians were participants in community activities such as co-operatives, credit unions and wheat pools. Swedish Canadians provided a strong base for populist movements such as the CCF in Saskatchewan and the Social Credit in Alberta. Many Swedish farmers also made outstanding contributions to agriculture in the west.

# Swiss

IT MAY SEEM PARADOXICAL that the first Swiss settlers in this country were often military men, but this can be easily explained even though the Swiss have the reputation of being a neutral country. From the beginning of the sixteenth to the middle of the nineteenth centuries, the Swiss cantons, having renounced any idea of military conquest for their own benefit, signed "capitulations" with other European countries, by which it was agreed to let those countries levy regiments among the Swiss, then highly regarded for their military skills, discipline and bravery.

Thus, as far back as 1604, reference can be found to the military quarters of Swiss soldiers on St. Croix Island in Acadia. These soldiers were followed in 1643 by five young Swiss who took up service under the Lieutenant-General of Acadia and, between 1721 and 1745, by a small contingent of the Karrer Regiment in the service of France which reinforced the garrison at Louisbourg.

One of the first Swiss known to settle in Canada, however, was Pierre Miville (1602–69), who came to this country some time prior to October 28, 1649, the date on which he and his son François (1630–1711) received lands in the seignury of Lauzon on the south shore of the St. Lawrence River across from the Plains of Abraham. Records also show that Pierre Miville, François Miville, Jacques Miville and four other Swiss were granted lands in 1665 at la Grande Anse, now La Pocatière, by Alexandre de Prouville, chevalier de Tracy. Envisaging, no doubt, a flourishing Swiss colony in the area, de Tracy named the tract "Canton des Suisses fribourgeois." The district is still popularly known as "Le canton des Suisses," although only Francois Miville and his brother Jacques settled at La Pocatière, and then only outside the canton and long after they had received their grants.

Undoubtedly the best-known Swiss to emigrate to Canada in the seventeenth century was Jacques Bizard (1642–92), a soldier who accompanied Count Frontenac to New France in 1672. Bizard rose to be a major of the governor's guard and eventually town-major of Montreal. Finally, in 1678, he was made seigneur of L'Ile de Bonaventure, now known as Île Bizard. In the early 1760s, Lawrence Ermatinger, the ancestor of all the Canadian Ermatingers, a well-known family of Swiss origin, arrived in Canada. He entered the fur trade and later became involved in the founding of the Northwest Company. The 1760s also saw the arrival in this country of a group of Swiss officers who had served in the British forces during the Seven Years' War. They settled in Hopewell Township, in what is now New Brunswick, after hearing enticing reports on the area.

Several French-speaking Swiss achieved positions of importance during the first decades of the English administration in Quebec, including Conrad Gugy (c. 1734–86), who became a member of the Legislative Council and a pioneer in Canada's mining industry. The one name which stands above others in this era was Sir Frederick Haldimand. The first person of Swiss birth to figure prominently in Canada's history, he entered the British military service in 1754, and became Governor General of Quebec in 1778. Another Governor General of Canada of Swiss origin was Sir George Prevost (1767–1816), a military man born in the United States.

In their valiant defence of Canada during the War of 1812, Prevost's armies included the two Swiss regiments de Watteville and de Meuron. The de Watteville regiment had arrived in Montreal on June 12, 1813, and eventually took part in the battles of Oswego and Fort Erie (Niagara). The de Meuron's most prominent battle was fought at Plattsburgh in September, 1814. Both Swiss mercenary regiments served in Canada under the British flag.

There is no question that many of the approximately 2,000 German-speaking Mennonites who emigrated to Upper Canada from Pennsylvania between 1786 and 1820 were of Swiss origin. One group settled in the Niagara district in the present counties of Haldimand, Lincoln and Welland, another in York County at Whitchurch and the third, the most important, along the Grand River. This latter settlement became the nucleus of the large German-speaking community of Waterloo County.

After the War of 1812 and the disbanding of the de Watteville and de Meuron regiments, a small number of Swiss officers and men established themselves in the military colony at Perth, Ontario, and in the military settlement located near Drummondville, in Lower Canada. Another thirty or so Swiss from these regiments joined expeditionary forces with Lord Selkirk, who was organizing a relief for the Red River settlement, at that time being harassed by the Northwest Company. This expedition was halted by news of the massacre at Seven Oaks, but later a small contingent of thirty soldiers took Fort La Fourche (Fort Douglas) at the Red River on January 10, 1817, and soon re-established order in the colony.

In 1821 they were joined by a party of 200 Swiss who had been recruited in Switzerland by one of Lord Selkirk's agents. The new immigrants had been influenced in their decision to emigrate by the enthusiastic description of the "Eldorado of the North" and by the prevailing economic climate of Switzerland, where they were suffering from the effects of the famine of 1813–17 and from the general recession in Europe following the Napoleonic Wars. Unfortunately, the Red River was not the land of milk and honey described by the immigration agents, and the Swiss gradually migrated to the United States.

Another pioneer of Swiss birth, Sebastian Fryfogel (1791–1873) is credited with opening the Huron Tract east of Lake Huron, a vast territory developed under a clever scheme by the Canada Company. Later in that century and during the opening decades of the twentieth, other centres were founded and settled by Swiss immigrants. These included Blumenau, in Alberta, and Zurich, a colony of Bernese farmers established near Nipissing, Ontario. The Blumenau colony was founded by Carl Stettler, who later founded Stettler, Alberta.

Swiss not only took up land on the Prairies during the time of Clifford Sifton, but they also settled in the far west. At the instigation of the Canadian Pacific Railway, which was then opening up the Rockies to mountain climbing, a small group of Swiss alpinists came to British Columbia and Alberta to serve as guides. At first, most of them returned to Switzerland each year at the end of the tourist season, but in 1912 some of them arrived accompanied by their families and settled in the village of Edelweiss near Golden, British Columbia. Later, other guides settled in the Jasper area.

The census of 1871 showed 2,962 persons of Swiss origin in Canada; in 1881, 4,588 such persons, steadily increasing until the census of 1961, which showed 11,381 Swiss Canadians. Yet figures also show a total for the years 1946–73 of 37,661 Swiss who emigrated to Canada. The discrepancy in the figures is likely the result of the fact that significant numbers of Swiss returned to Switzerland. For instance, from 1960 to 1974, 8,871 Swiss returned to their homeland from Canada.

The 1971 census showed that Ontario had the largest number of Swiss-born residents with 4,840, followed by Quebec with 3,970 and British Columbia with 2,875, for a total of 13,895. Yet in spite of their comparatively small numbers, the Swiss boast a large number of associations and clubs in this country. In Toronto and Montreal, the founding of Swiss clubs preceded even the establishment of Swiss consulates: the Swiss National Society of Montreal, the oldest Swiss association in Canada, came into being in 1874 and the Toronto Swiss Society, no longer in existence, in 1905. In addition to Canada's oldest Swiss association, Montreal's Swiss population also supports the Swiss Women's Club Edelweiss (founded 1922), the Matterhorn Young Swiss Club (1953), an association of young Swiss men and women who seek to keep alive Swiss traditions and give assistance to newly arrived Swiss, La Société Suisse-Romande (1954), which brings together French-speaking Swiss mainly for social activities, the Swiss Alpine Rifle Club and the Swiss Carnival Society. The Swiss Club in Toronto, founded in 1918, is now the principal Swiss association in that city.

Swiss associations are also found in Quebec City, Ottawa, Calgary, Edmonton, Vancouver, various small British Columbia centres and in Winnipeg and other centres in Manitoba.

The *Swiss Canadian News* is a bulletin published monthly in English by the Swiss Club in Toronto. On the west coast, the *Swiss Herald* is published, a periodical put out by the

Swiss Society of Vancouver. Another quarterly, the *Swiss Canadian Review—Revue Suisse-Canada*, is aimed at all Swiss in Canada.

Swiss-born Canadians have made outstanding contributions in many fields. Many have made reputations in the hotel and restaurant business, and others have become progressive dairy farmers and cheese experts. Canadian industry and outdoor sports have also benefited from the Swiss presence. Music, the arts and education also contain numerous Swiss names. The Swiss came early to Canada and have been contributing to the country ever since in a wide variety of areas.

# Syrians

THE MIGRATION of Syrians to Canada falls into four distinct periods. The first, between 1901 and 1925, saw 803 Syrian immigrants come to Canada. This group, like subsequent groups up to the 1955 period, comprised both Syrians and Lebanese, for they were not separated for statistical purposes. The second period of migration falls between 1926 and 1945, when 78 immigrants came to Canada, and the third between 1946 and 1954, when 118 immigrants arrived. The period of greatest migration was the fourth, between 1955 and 1975, when 2,732 Syrian immigrants came to Canada. From this calculation it can be concluded that between 1901 and 1975, a total of 3,731 Syrians were admitted to Canada. This is only an estimate, however, since the statistics prior to 1955 comprised both the Syrian and Lebanese groups. The Syrian consulate in Montreal, however, places the total number of Syrians in Canada at around 3,000 persons.

There were a number of reasons for emigration, mainly the desire for a better economic life and the various conflicts raging in and around the country. Upon arrival in Canada, the greatest number of Syrians (52.3 per cent for the period 1956–76) reported Quebec as their destination, while 38.2 per cent reported Ontario and the remainder went to the rest of Canada. The greatest concentration of Syrian Canadians is in Montreal, while those in Ontario tend to be more dispersed.

The early Syrian immigrants expected to return home after a short period in Canada, but the later immigrants have come with the idea of settling permanently, and since many of them are well educated they integrate easily into Canadian society. They have in general shown a high degree of adaptability and have applied themselves successfully to many types of employment, including the professions.

The Syrian population is served by the *Arab World Review*, which is published in English, French and Arabic. The Syrians in Canada are divided equally in religion between Muslims and Christians of various denominations. The Muslim Syrians are served by the Muslim mosques built by other Arab groups in Canada. While they participate in the clubs and organizations of other Arab groups, since they have no national organization of their own, the Syrian group in Montreal is at present seeking to establish a youth group to embrace social and cultural advancement.

Although many Syrian immigrants long for their homeland initially, they continue to make a valuable contribution to Canadian society as they settle and integrate into the mainstream of Canadian life. They are vitally concerned with events in their homeland and with passing down their heritage to their children, but also with accepting the Canadian lifestyle and becoming a part of it.

# Tibetans

IN 1965, the independent Kingdom of Tibet became an Autonomous Region of the People's Republic of China. A region of unique physical, cultural and geographic characteristics, it is situated on a high plateau and surrounded by mountain masses. The country was invaded by China in 1950 and in 1959 the Dalai Lama, the Tibetan spiritual leader, fled to India. About 100,000 Tibetans followed him or migrated to other countries.

The first Tibetans to emigrate to Canada were 228 refugees who arrived in 1971 and 1972 under a special arrangement between the Canadian government and the Dalai Lama. While many had settled in Buddhist areas of Nepal, Sikkim and Bhutan, others were relocated to refugee camps in India, and from there the first Tibetans were invited to Canada. The largest group of 98 arrived in March, 1971, and the others followed during that year and in 1972. Since 1972, however, Tibetan immigration to Canada has been almost nil, with the possible exception of a few immigrants who have been sponsored or nominated by relatives already settled here.

For such a small group, approximately 300 persons, the Tibetans settled widely across Canada, mainly in Ontario, Quebec and the Prairies. Although many of them had occupations in their homeland and in the refugee camps, most went to work on farms in the regions that they settled. Unaccustomed to Canadian society and climate, they nevertheless worked hard. By 1973, four families of the 70 refugees sent to the Taber area of Alberta had migrated to British Columbia in search of better working conditions.

Although concerned with problems of basic survival in a different culture, Tibetans are anxious to participate in Canadian activities and to share their heritage with Canadians. Tibetans are now working in factories, grocery stores, and in the construction industry. Some have migrated to live in the larger cities. In Toronto there are about ten Tibetan families and in Montreal there are approximately fifteen families. In Toronto, they have joined forces with the Asian community. They established their own Tibetan Cultural Society and in May 1972 participated in an Asian Community Conference sponsored by the International Institute of Metropolitan Toronto. The Society began publishing a newsletter called *Sunflower* in 1973, with news in both Tibetan and English. With a grant from the Local Initiatives Program, the Society was able to promote Tibetan culture and heritage through the newsletter, lecture trips, and visits to other Tibetan communities. In Montreal the Tibetan community has formed the Tibetan Cultural and Community Centre.

Tibetans are taking advantage of opportunities to educate their children and are encouraging them to learn both English and French. Several adults attended language classes and for several months after their arrival took classes which would help them integrate more fully into Canadian society.

# Trinidad and Tobago

*See also West Indians*

THE INHABITANTS of the Caribbean islands of Trinidad and Tobago are a unique product of many cultures, and their claim to racial diversity is certainly justified. Spain ruled the islands for over three centuries, and the British presence began at the end of the eighteenth century. While the British have left their stamp on the political and many of the social institutions of the islands, the other groups have borrowed customs from one another and have adapted many of their own to the Trinidadian milieu. Regardless of race or origin, Trinidadians abroad tend to view themselves as Trinidadians, at least among the first generation of immigrants to Canada.

Many of the West Indians studying at Canadian universities during the early 1960s were Trinidadians. In later years the pattern of immigration and the levels of occupation and skill which the immigrants possessed approached the general West Indian pattern. During the peak years of immigration from Trinidad (1973–74), over 600 managers and professionals came to Canada, along with more than 1,500 clerks and over 2,000 skilled and semi-skilled workers. Between 1946 and the first quarter of 1976, immigration statistics estimate that a total of 40,174 people from Trinidad and Tobago immigrated into Canada. As with the other West Indian islands, the main wave of immigration to Canada has taken place within the past fifteen years.

Within the past twenty years, Trinidadian society has undergone fundamental changes. These changes have been hastened by the spread of western values as well as the physical presence of American military bases during the 1940s. These influences have tended to override the traditional values of urban Trinidadians no matter what their racial background. Yet there remains an awareness of a unique identity that is unquestionably Trinidadian. And it is from the "grass roots" of this group that much of what is known today as Trinidadian popular culture originates.

The Roman Catholic Church is very influential in Trinidad, and the two most important schools in the capital are under its auspices. This has no doubt influenced the choice of religion for many who have passed through their doors, some of whom now reside in Canada.

There are many unique cultural and festive activities which are particularly Trinidadian. These include the calypso, the art form for which the Caribbean has become famous and which is native to Trinidad. While the calypso is already familiar in Canada, many of the old "patois" folk songs which deal with themes Trinidadian are being revived and included in the repertoires of West Indian folksinging groups in Canada. In addition, the pre-Lenten Carnival or Mardi Gras which is held in Trinidad each year has been celebrated in Canada since the mid-1960s in centres such as Toronto and Montreal.

Steelbands and limbo dancing are also common in Canada. Several steelbands exist in Toronto, and provide entertainment for West Indian and other social events. Limbo dancing is of Trinidadian origin, and has been a major item in the repertoire of many variety nightclub acts.

Because Trinidadians place so much emphasis on gathering together for a "fete" or party, they have tended to form very few formal organizations. There are a few recreational clubs with a high Trinidadian membership, but on the whole, those who wish to join organizations usually join one of the other organizations which serve other West Indians or the Black community. From time to time, however, attempts are made by some Trinidadians to form specific national organizations.

Trinidadians in Canada on the whole value the goal of integration into Canadian society, but without the loss of their identity. In Trinidad, for many, race was important in that it provided a common focus for interacting with other groups. In Canada, however, they attempt to succeed as individuals and as recent immigrants this is their major preoccupation.

# Turks

THE FIRST TURKISH immigrants are believed to have arrived in Canada in the 1880s, but they were few in number, and it is not known if they stayed permanently. More Turks came to Canada in the 1890s and a total of 156 Turks arrived between 1900 and 1904.

Turkish immigration increased after that, when a total of 3,922 Turks arrived in Canada during the period 1906–14, only 262 in the long interlude between 1915 and 1955, and a further 5,710 in the years between 1956 and 1975. Most came as a result of uncertain political and economic conditions in Turkey, and the state of the world economy in general. The

new migration, in particular, included a large number of professional people.

Of a total number of 5,910 Turkish immigrants to Canada between 1946 and 1975, 2,539 (or 43 per cent) chose Quebec as their destination, 2,571 (43.5 per cent) chose Ontario, and the remainder were divided among the rest of the provinces. Quebec and Ontario together accounted for 86.5 per cent of Turkish Canadians during the past 30 years, and the Turkish-Canadian population today is estimated at between 10,000 and 12,000 persons.

The recency of the new Turkish settlement in Canada has not allowed for the establishment of an umbrella organization, and the few associations or clubs in existence, including those of Montreal, Toronto, Windsor and Vancouver, are limited in their attempts to fill the gaps that exist in this area. The Turkish community is aware of the vital role that associations and organizations play in the life of any community, and there is an urge to increase the number of such organizations. The Turkish Cultural Association of Montreal, founded in 1964, is trying to fill part of this need through folk dancing, sports, social evenings, conferences, and a Turkish-language Sunday school, as well as through a women's branch. Other Turkish clubs in Canada include the Association Turque de Montreal, the Turkish Canadian Cultural Association (Ottawa) founded in 1971, the Turkish Cultural and Folklore Society of Canada (Toronto) founded in 1973 and the Turkish Canadian Friendship Association of Toronto. A youth organization has also been formed in Montreal for Turkish university students.

Almost all Turks follow the Islamic faith, celebrate the Islamic religious holidays, and although they do not have a mosque of their own in Canada, they share those established by other Muslim groups. The Christian Turks are also served spiritually by the various churches of their choice.

The Turks in Canada celebrate National Day on October 29, anniversary of declaration of the Turkish Republic. They are served, in addition to various organizational news bulletins, by *Sesimiz* (*The Voice*), a publication which appears six or seven times yearly. Since 1977, the Turks residing in Ottawa have been served by a weekly, hour-long cable-TV program.

Many Turkish immigrants have proved their ability to integrate into Canadian society and to reach a high level of success in cultural and professional circles, adding a further dimension to Canadian society. The increasing number of professionals and skilled tradesmen in their ranks is another indication of their ready desire to contribute to Canadian society and business.

# Ugandan Asians

PRACTICALLY ALL UGANDAN ASIANS are of Indian or Pakistani origin, although a few are Goans. They do not really constitute a distinct ethnocultural group, nor is their culture basically different from that of their ancestors from the Indian subcontinent. Asians had emigrated to the East African coast as traders long before the arrival of the British, but the principal wave of Asian immigration occurred in the eighteenth century when people were needed to work on the railway. Other labourers and professionals came in the nineteenth century, and soldiers were sent out from the Indian subcontinent in the twentieth. Many stayed after their contracts had expired. In 1972, in a

wholesale attempt to Africanize the country, the Ugandan government ordered the expulsion of 50,000 Ugandan Asians. Approximately 30,000 went to the United Kingdom, and the Canadian government invited 6,000 to settle in Canada. In 1972, the Ugandan Asians formed Canada's newest community.

Stripped of their possessions by the Ugandan government, many of the immigrants arrived in Canada virtually penniless. Between September and November, 1972, a total of 4,426 Ugandan Asians arrived on 31 flights chartered by the Canadian government to bring them to their new home without delay. By mid-1973, an additional 1,215 had come on scheduled flights from Uganda, the United Kingdom and other countries in which they had been stranded after their expulsion.

Most of the refugees entering the country through Montreal went to special immigration facilities in that city, and from there spread out to other parts of Canada. Over 1,200 went to British Columbia, most of them going to Vancouver, where there was a large Asian community. Ontario received 1,847, more than 40 per cent of whom went to Toronto. Other settlements included Quebec (625), Manitoba (200), Alberta (211), Nova Scotia (139), Saskatchewan (73), New Brunswick (67), Newfoundland (10) and Prince Edward Island (15).

Eleven committees were established, including federal, provincial and municipal representatives as well as Canadian volunteers, to assist the Ugandan Asians in the first few months after their arrival. Through the work of these committees, most Ugandan Asians were able to find accommodation and work.

The Ugandan Asians brought a variety of skills and professional attainments, but many turned to other occupations initially while obtaining Canadian qualifications. Others went into business for themselves or took Manpower Training Programs.

Several religious communities can be identified among Ugandan Asians, including Hindus, Sikhs, Muslims and a few Christians, the latter group mainly Goans.

While there is as yet no Ugandan Asian umbrella organization in Canada, there are local associations in Montreal, Toronto, London, Windsor, Edmonton and Vancouver. The Ugandan Asian community has been joined by the Asians from other East African countries who are also attempting to establish themselves in this country.

# Ukrainians

THE 47-MILLION Ukrainian people constitute, after the Russians, the second largest Slavic nation in Europe. Occupying the fertile lands north of the Black Sea, the Ukrainian people developed as a distinct linguistic and ethnocultural entity among the eastern Slavs.

The political, social and economic conditions prevailing in the Ukrainian lands during the nineteenth and early twentieth centuries encouraged emigration. While the Tsarist government effectively blocked Ukrainian emigration to the West and instead actively encouraged Ukrainians of agricultural backgrounds to migrate to Siberia and other parts of Asia, conditions in Austria-Hungary were more favourable for Ukrainian emigration to North and South America. Although the year 1891 has traditionally been accepted as the beginning of mass Ukrainian immigration into Canada, it is clear that Ukrainians had settled in small numbers in this country long before

then. There were apparently soldiers of Ukrainian origin in the de Meuron and de Watteville regiments which fought for Canada in the War of 1812, and were later with Lord Selkirk. Furthermore, individual Ukrainians had entered Canada from the United States prior to 1891 and had settled in Manitoba.

On September 7, 1891, two Ukrainian pioneers, Vasyl Elyniak and Ivan Pylypiw disembarked in Montreal in what was the beginning of massive Ukrainian emigration to Canada. These first two settlers sent encouraging reports back to the western Ukraine about the possibility of settlement in Canada, and were followed by Dr. Joseph Oleskiw, who toured Canada in 1895 and wrote glowing reports about the possibilities of settlement in the country. The initial trickle of a few hundred individuals, mainly from Galicia, turned into a stream of thousands, and it is estimated that, between 1891 and 1914, Canada admitted from 170,000 to 200,000 Ukrainians. Approximately 97 per cent of these came from the Austrian provinces of Galicia and Bukovyna.

The first wave of Ukrainian immigrants to Canada consisted of peasant farmers fleeing the oppressive social and economic conditions prevalent in Galicia. Their initial aim was to continue their traditional agricultural pursuits in this new and uninhabited environment, and their earliest settlements were characterized by white-washed thatched huts like those they had left behind. With increased education and prosperity, these early homesteads yielded to frame houses, modern machinery, and advanced agricultural techniques.

Strains of Ukrainian wheat preceded the Ukrainian farmers to Canada, and the "first Ukrainian immigrant" was a hardy variety of wheat brought to Canada by Scots in 1843. This strain, 'Red Fife', was particularly well-suited to Canadian conditions since it matured ten days faster than other kinds of wheat. 'Red Fife' was followed by 'Alberta Red Winter Wheat,' imported from Ukraine in 1902. (Many Ukrainians believe it unnecessary to use "the Ukraine" and prefer to say simply "Ukraine".)

The advent of the First World War had two effects on the Ukrainian community in Canada. First, immigration from Galicia virtually ceased and was not resumed in any large numbers until the latter part of the 1920s. Second, considerable friction developed between the Ukrainian community and the Canadian government, which considered the Ukrainians as enemy aliens. Yet some 10,000 Ukrainians enlisted in the armed forces, often anglicizing their names to avoid discriminatory treatment.

The First World War brought a profound change in Ukraine. As the occupying powers went down to defeat, it seemed as if independence could be achieved, and Ukrainian Canadians were quick to support Ukrainian national aspirations. A Ukrainian Canadian Citizens' Committee was formed in Winnipeg in 1918 and later sent delegates to the Paris Peace Conference to make representations in favour of recognizing the independence of Ukraine. An independent Ukrainian National Republic was proclaimed on January 22, 1918, but lasted only until the country was incorporated into the Soviet Union in 1922, while substantial segments of the population came under Polish, Czechoslovakian and Roumanian rule.

The turbulent events in Ukraine temporarily interrupted the flow of immigrants to Canada. Between 1918 and 1939, however, some 70,000 Ukrainian immigrants entered Canada, the vast majority in the second half of the 1920s.

The immigrants making up this second wave were of a different type from those who had come earlier. War veterans, intellectuals fleeing persecution, and professionally trained workers entered the country and found an organized Ukrainian community structure ready to receive them. Churches, schools, newspapers, organizations and community centres had appeared with rapidity during the pre-1914 period, and the second wave of immigrants could take advantage of their existence in facilitating settlement in Canada.

The outbreak of the Second World War had fundamental consequences not only for Ukraine, but also for Ukrainian immigration to Canada and for Ukrainian-Canadian organized life. Once more, Ukrainian volunteers joined the Canadian Armed Forces, with at least 40,000 ultimately serving in all branches. At the same time, realizing the implications of the war for both Canada and their homeland, Ukrainian-Canadian organizations united to speak with a unified voice on Ukrainian matters. In 1940, the Ukrainian Canadian Committee was established in Winnipeg, uniting the five nationwide Ukrainian-Canadian groups, the Ukrainian Catholic Brotherhood, the Ukrainian Self-Reliance League, the Ukrainian National Federation, United Hetman Organization and the Ukrainian Workers' League.

Following the Nazi-Soviet pact of August 1939, and the German aggression against Poland, the U.S.S.R. invaded Poland and annexed western Ukraine, and in 1940 annexed northern Bukovyna from Roumania.

During the war, both the Nazis and Soviets occupied Ukraine. With the end of the war came large groups of displaced persons and political refugees to Western Europe. The western Ukrainians were granted refugee status, but many eastern Ukrainians were forcibly repatriated. This was stopped by 1947, however, and the remaining eastern Ukrainian refugees were allowed to stay in the West. As a result, the postwar Ukrainian emigration once again was derived primarily from western Ukrainian lands.

With the co-operation of the Canadian government, some 32,000 Ukrainians entered the country between 1947 and 1952. As these displaced persons gradually found homes, immigration tapered off, and between 1953 and 1960 only 4,500 Ukrainian immigrants entered Canada. The Soviet Union's restrictive emigration policies have cut off all further emigration from Ukraine, and since 1960 no more than 200 Ukrainians have entered the country annually. Many of this third wave have been professionals, politically active and strongly anti-Communist.

By 1971, there were 580,660 Canadians of Ukrainian origin, over 80 per cent of them Canadian-born with the majority residing in the three Prairie Provinces. Over the past three decades, however, a gradual shift of population from the farms to the cities and from the west to the east has been taking place. Most members of the third wave of immigration, for example, settled in the cities of eastern Canada. In 1971, the largest concentration of Ukrainian Canadians was still in Winnipeg, where over 64,000 resided, followed by Edmonton with 62,650 and Toronto with nearly 61,000. Other major centres of Ukrainian population in Canada are Vancouver, Montreal, Calgary, Saskatoon, Hamilton, Thunder Bay, Regina and the St. Catharines-Niagara area.

The earliest community life of Ukrainian immigrants centred around religious institutions. Among Ukrainians, however, there is not a great deal of religious homogeneity now, since two major traditional churches have lost some ground to other religious affiliations. The most important religious institutions are the Ukrainian Catholic (or Uniate) Church and the Ukrainian Greek Orthodox Church, although there are a substantial number of Roman Catholics and members of various Protestant denominations.

The Ukrainian Catholic Church observes the traditional Eastern rite, but constitutes part of the Catholic Church and owes its allegiance to the Pope. It is the largest religious grouping in the Ukrainian-Canadian community, since about 30 per cent of all Ukrainian Canadians adhered to it in 1971. The first Ukrainian Catholic Mass was celebrated in Canada on April 12, 1897, and the first Ukrainian Catholic Church was erected in 1898 at Star, Alberta. From these beginnings the church has grown into a major organization with five episcopal sees. Its organization is so extensive that in 1956 the Pope designated Winnipeg as a Metropolitan See.

The Ukrainian Greek Orthodox Church emerged from a church council held in July, 1918, when those dissatisfied with the influence of the Russian Orthodox and Roman Catholic churches on Ukrainian religious life decided to create an autocephalous Orthodox church with its own bishops chosen by a general convention of priests and laymen elected by their congregations. The Ukrainian Greek Orthodox Church has grown into an imposing body, commanding the adherence of about one-fourth of the Ukrainian-Canadian population. Its episcopal organization parallels that of the Ukrainian Catholic Church, with a Metropolitan See in Winnipeg and episcopasees in Toronto, Edmonton and Saskatoon. It also maintains St. Andrew's College at the University of Manitoba.

Other religious groupings embracing Ukrainian Canadians include the Ukrainian

Orthodox churches based in the United States, Roman Catholics, and Protestants. About 60 per cent of the more than 10,000 Ukrainian Protestants belong to the United Church, and there are also sizable Anglican (20 per cent), Lutheran (6 per cent) and Baptist (6 per cent) memberships.

The first Ukrainian-Canadian cultural organization was the Prosvita (Enlightenment) Society, founded in 1898 at Edna-Star, Alberta. In time, hundreds of different political, religious, women's and youth organizations came into being. In 1905 the Ukrainian Mutual Benefit Association was founded in affiliation with the St. Nicholas Ukrainian Catholic Church in Winnipeg. The idea of church-affiliated lay organizations developed with the creation of the Ukrainian Greek Orthodox Church, the Ukrainian Self-Reliance League and its auxiliary women's and youth organizations drawn from the Greek Orthodox membership. Similar organizations were established among Ukrainian Catholics in 1932 under the name Ukrainian Catholic Brotherhood, with its own women's and youth auxiliaries.

In response to the political events taking place in Ukraine, two essentially political organizations emerged between the world wars, the United Hetman Organization and the Ukrainian National Federation. The former emerged in 1934 from the Ukrainian Sporting Sitch Association of Canada. It was monarchist in orientation, favouring the establishment of a hetmanate form of government in Ukraine. The Ukrainian National Federation, on the other hand, emerged in 1932 from the Ukrainian War Veterans' Association, which had been formed in Canada in 1928. It promoted a patriotic, nationalist ideology, quickly expanding its activities to include women's and youth auxiliaries.

The Ukrainian Workers' League emerged from the Ukrainian Labour and Farmers' Temple Association in 1936. The Ukrainian Self-Reliance League, the Ukrainian Catholic Brotherhood, the Ukrainian National Federation, the United Hetman Organization and the Ukrainian Workers' League joined in 1940 to create the Ukrainian Canadian Committee, a representative co-ordinating body in which each of the participating organizations retains its autonomy, yet all participate to advance common aspirations.

Today the Ukrainian Canadian Committee has expanded to include over thirty national Ukrainian organizations, among which are the Ukrainian Canadian Veterans' Association, the Canadian League for Ukraine's Liberation, the Ukrainian Professional and Business Federation, and the Ukrainian Canadian University Students' Union. The Ukrainian Canadian Committee has its headquarters in Winnipeg, where a Congress is held every three years.

Outside the Ukrainian Canadian Committee there are left-wing Ukrainians whose activities can be traced back to the old Ukrainian Labour and Farmers' Temple Association. In 1948 this organization constituted itself as the Association of United Ukrainian Canadians.

Many of the organizations mentioned above have women's auxiliaries, youth clubs, drama societies, dance groups and choirs, and many publish newspapers or periodicals.

Of the seven national Ukrainian youth organizations, the Ukrainian Canadian University Students' Union is undoubtedly the most active. The Ukrainian Catholic Youth, the Ukrainian National Youth Federation, and the Canadian Ukrainian Youth Association are affiliated with their adult parent organizations: the Brotherhood of Ukrainian

Catholics, the Ukrainian National Federation, and the Ukrainian Self-Reliance League respectively. The Ukrainian Youth Association of Canada is associated ideologically with the Canadian League for Ukraine's Liberation, and the Ukrainian Democratic Youth Association with the Association of Ukrainian Victims of Russian Occupation. Finally, the entirely independent Ukrainian Youth Association called Plast follows the principles of the world Boy Scout and Girl Guide movements.

From the arrival of the first Ukrainian immigrants, the struggle to maintain and develop the Ukrainian language and culture has been at the heart of the community's efforts. An early medium of culture and enlightenment was provided by the Prosvita (Enlightenment) Society. A training school for Ukrainian teachers was established in Winnipeg by the Manitoba government in 1905. Ukrainian language and literature programs were established after the Second World War at the universities of Saskatchewan, Manitoba, Montreal, Toronto, Ottawa and a number of other Canadian institutions of higher learning. Ukrainian was also introduced at the high school level as an optional credit course in the provinces of Saskatchewan (1952), Alberta (1958), and Manitoba (1961).

In addition, the Ukrainian community as a whole prepares younger students for these courses by operating Ukrainian-language schools for students before they enter high school. Most of the large Ukrainian organizations operate networks of such schools, and it has been estimated that approximately 10,000 students benefit from these facilities.

In addition to the language schools, numerous other Ukrainian educational institutions, foundations and "national homes" have been established. Several *bursas* or boarding schools were established to further the education of Ukrainian students from rural areas. A number of cultural foundations were also established to promote and finance Ukrainian cultural activities. Of the dozen or so in existence, the most important is the Taras Shevchenko Foundation.

Ukrainian-Canadian scholars working in the areas of higher education and research in Ukrainian studies have been active in Canada. The Canadian Association of Slavists established a Conference on Ukrainian Studies in 1974. Earlier, the Ukrainian Free Academy of Sciences was founded in 1949, and the Canadian branch of the Shevchenko Scientific Society was established in Canada in the late 1940s.

Most of the large Ukrainian newspapers are organs of the national Ukrainian associations or churches. The earliest Ukrainian-Canadian newspaper, *Kanadyisky Farmer (Canadian Farmer)*, appeared in 1903 in Winnipeg and still publishes. The two main centres of Ukrainian periodical publishing are Winnipeg and Toronto. *Novyi Shliakh (New Pathway)*, the Catholic newspaper *Postup (Progress)*, *Ukrainsky Holos (Ukrainian Voice)*, the Protestant *Evenhelsky Ranok (Evangelical Morning)* and the Ukrainian Canadian Committee *Bulletin* are printed in Winnipeg. Toronto publications are *Vilne Slovo (Free Word)*, the Catholic *Nasha Meta (Our Aim)*, *Homin Ukrainy (Ukrainian Echo)* and *Batkivshchyna (Fatherland)*, the latter associated with the United Hetman Organization. Organs of the left-wing Association of United Ukrainian Canadians are the weekly *Ukrainian Life and Word*, and the bi-monthly *Ukrainian Canadian*. Approximately 80 per cent of all publications are in the Ukrainian language. The circulation of individual periodicals ranges from 2,000 to 10,000, while bulletins reach from 500 to 1,000 readers.

The Ukrainian community has made numerous cultural contributions to Canadian life. A Ukrainian travelling theatre appeared in the West as early as 1915, and in 1926 a school of Ukrainian folk dancing was established. To co-ordinate cultural activities, the Ukrainian Association of Creative Artists of Canada was established in Toronto in 1955. The Ukrainian Cultural Workers' Association of North America was also created in that city. Ukrainian cultural achievements also include contributions in the visual arts and architecture.

Urban labourers of Ukrainian origin formed fraternal organizations and mutual benefit associations to deal with their new circumstances early in their initial period of immigration. Out of these associations came the Ukrainian credit union movement which began in 1939 with The New Community Savings and Credit Union, founded in Saskatoon. By the end of the 1960s there were some sixty Ukrainian credit unions across Canada with an estimated membership of approximately 50,000 and collective assets of over sixty million dollars.

In recent years, the Ukrainian community of Canada has developed links with Ukrainians around the world. The first World Congress of Free Ukrainians was held in New York in November 1967, and at the second, held in Toronto in 1973, some one thousand delegates from twenty countries participated.

One of the more significant events in the Ukrainian community was the establishment in July 1976 of the Canadian Institute of Ukrainian Studies at the University of Alberta, in Edmonton, to develop, promote and maintain all aspects of Ukrainian-Canadian and Ukrainian university studies and research. The Institute became the main project of the executive of the Ukrainian

Canadian Professional and Business Federation in Edmonton. A Canadian Institute of Ukrainian Studies Foundation was established by the Federation in May 1975, along with a national board of directors and an executive in Toronto, and has important connections with the Shevchenko Society in Europe. In March 1979, a Chair of Ukrainian Studies was founded at the University of Toronto.

The Ukrainians in Canada have fully integrated into the mainstream of Canadian society while retaining a strong attachment to their ethnocultural heritage, and as a group are one of the main proponents of multiculturalism in Canada.

# Uruguayans

ONE OF THE LAST REGIONS in South America to be colonized by the Spanish, Uruguay was formally established as an independent country in 1828. The official language of Uruguay is Spanish, and the predominant religion is Roman Catholicism.

Since 1973, Uruguayans have been coming to Canada at the rate of about 600 yearly, while just over 1,000 Uruguayans had entered Canada in the three previous years. Although economic and social welfare are important factors contributing to Uruguayan immigration to Canada, political considerations also play a large part, and a certain number of Uruguayans are political refugees. A recent agreement entered into by the Canadian government for the acceptance of 1,000 Latin American refugees now in Argentina, although primarily intended to apply to Chileans, is expected to swell the Uruguayan numbers as well.

Although Uruguayans have formed some sporting and social organizations in Canada, they are not yet sufficiently numerous to make any real impact as a distinct national group. They would appear, however, to be strongly supportive of developments originating in the Latin American community as a whole. Uruguayan Canadians have tended to settle mainly in the major centres such as Toronto or Montreal, although there are also small communities in cities such as Sudbury. Because of the difficulties in adjusting to a new situation and working in a new language, the majority of Uruguayans work initially as manual labour and factory labour.

In Canada, Uruguayans have been forced to cope with all of the common difficulties faced by immigrants. These have been compounded by the fact that Latin Americans in general are among the most recent arrivals. On various local levels, considerable effort has been made to find some solutions to the problems involved. Significantly, although each Latin American country is a distinct entity with its own heritage and traditions, the major developments involve Latin American Canadians as a whole rather than as individual territorial groupings. Thus, in Toronto, Uruguayans have, for example, co-operated with immigrants from throughout Latin America to organize day care centres, folk groups and a Latin American choir, and to assist in the work and development of the Centro Para Gente de Habla Hispana, the Centre for Spanish-speaking Peoples. The centre has been in existence since 1973 and affords information, counselling and orientation in all areas where misunderstandings could arise. It also offers English and Spanish classes. In Montreal, the Latin Association de Sud-Americanos has been formed as a result of similar joint community effort and concern.

While the Uruguayans are not yet a numerically large segment of the Canadian population, they are working together with other Latin American Canadians for the betterment of the community as a whole.

# Vietnamese

BEFORE 1975, the Vietnamese community in Canada was very small, numbering a few thousand at most. The largest community was the one formed in Montreal, with between 800 and 1,000 residents, in addition to a few in Quebec City and Toronto. Most of the residents were students, the rest being engaged in some professional career.

The fall of Saigon in May 1975 turned more than 150,000 Vietnamese nationals out of their country. About 6,500 had arrived in Canada by the end of the year, boosting the total Vietnamese population in Canada to over 8,000. The great majority of refugees, most of whom had facility in the French language, settled in Quebec. In Montreal alone, approximately 4,000 people made their first homes in Canada. Others scattered throughout the country, with about 500 Vietnamese settling in Toronto.

Wherever they have settled, the Vietnamese tend to be widely dispersed, seeking low-rental housing wherever it can be found. In Montreal, about four thousand Vietnamese newcomers have tended to be concentrated in a twenty-block area of apartment buildings near the University of Montreal.

The federal government, through Canada Manpower, ensured that the refugees had a minimum income while looking for jobs or, in some cases, while taking language training. However, underemployment remains one of their major problems, since many were professionals in their homeland, and find that their level of fluency in the two official languages is inadequate in technical terms.

The Vietnamese community has quickly organized in Montreal, Toronto, Quebec City and Ottawa. The Vietnamese Fraternal Association of Toronto, formed in 1972 by a small group, expanded its membership and reorganized its aims to help in the resettlement of the refugees.

In Montreal, besides the community-wide Vietnamese Association, smaller groups such as the Vietnamese Students' Club and the Anti-Communists' Club have been active, and they publish their own newsletters. The Vietnamese fraternal associations in both Toronto and Montreal tend to be non-political, while the Union of Vietnamese in Canada is more politically inclined.

The majority of Vietnamese are Buddhists or are from a Buddhist background. They practise Buddhist or Confucianist rites on such occasions as marriages and deaths. A group of Buddhists in Montreal are in the process of forming a Buddhist association, while some Catholics tend to form their own associations.

The adjustment to a new life has been far from easy or comfortable for the refugees, particularly older Vietnamese. The Vietnamese in Canada realize that it will likely take more than one generation to integrate into the Canadian society, but the fact that they are overcoming language and cultural barriers offers hope for the future.

# Welsh

CANADIANS OF WELSH ORIGIN have found that their distinct language and identity usually disappears within a couple of generations of their arrival in Canada, but most do manage to nurture and keep alive cherished ancestral traditions.

The first known Welshman to come to Canada was Sir Thomas Button, a naval officer who commanded an expedition in search of the Northwest Passage in 1612. Sailing in the *Resolution*, which was accompanied by Henry Hudson's ship the *Discovery*, he passed through the Hudson Strait to the west shore of Hudson Bay. Not finding a westward passage, he returned home the following year to London, where his backers had interpreted his long absence to mean that he had reached Asia.

The next Welshman to be recorded was Major Gwillim of the 50th Foot, who served under General Wolfe at the Battle of the Plains of Abraham. He was the father of the diarist and artist Elizabeth Posthuma Gwillim, wife of Colonel John Graves Simcoe, the first Lieutenant Governor of Upper Canada. The American colonies supplied many United Empire Loyalists of Welsh origin. In the 1880s and '90s, Welsh immigrants arrived from both Wales and the United States, in particular the coal mining regions of Pennsylvania.

A large number of Welsh dissenters entered Canada before Confederation at various times. Those who entered Upper and Lower Canada were staunch Presbyterians who were the driving force behind the establishment of the early Protestant churches, and often came into conflict with Roman Catholic authorities here.

In the nineteenth and early twentieth centuries, Welsh immigration received its chief impetus from the large-scale unemployment resulting from economic depression in Wales. In 1906, for example, over 5,000 Welsh emigrated to Canada, establishing a twentieth-century record for Welsh immigration into this country. Not until the close of the 1920s would the number of Welsh entering Canada again reach comparable levels, with 3,316 in 1928 and 3,586 in 1929. Another peak year for Welsh immigration was 1957, the year following the Suez Crisis, when 2,629 Welsh entered the country. It is difficult to gain entirely accurate figures on Welsh immigration, however, as they have traditionally been grouped with the English for statistical purposes.

Early in the nineteenth century a number of families from the Pennsylvania Welsh Tract, a settlement founded by seven companies of the Welsh Society of Friends in 1682, journeyed to Upper Canada and established the Quaker settlement of York County. They were thoroughly Americanized, however, since their ancestors had left Wales more than a century previously.

There was a Welsh military presence in Canada during the American Revolution and the War of 1812. Three Welsh regiments, the 23rd, 24th and 41st, served in Canada, and all played a major role in the American Revolution, the War of 1812 and the Rebellion of 1837. When demobilized, some Welsh decided to remain in Canada, and a number settled near Kingston and London, and in the Niagara peninsula. In recent years the Toronto Welsh Society has provided mascots to Fort Henry in Kingston in recognition of the Welsh military achievement.

One of the earliest attempts to encourage Welsh emigration to Canada was made by Colonel John Graves Simcoe, who supported an application for land made by Colonel Thomas Talbot. In a letter to the British Colonial Office, dated February 11, 1803, Simcoe states that Talbot planned to persuade a large group of Welsh and Scottish families who had emigrated to New York in 1801 to resettle in Yarmouth Township. The application went unheeded, but in the years that followed Talbot did succeed in locating thousands of settlers, some of whom were Welsh, on the Talbot Settlement, a huge tract of land fronting on Lake Erie.

In 1815 another attempt was made to promote a Welsh settlement in Upper Canada, this time by Major David Byron Davies of the 100th regiment, then stationed at Niagara. Support for this scheme came from the lieutenant governor of the province, General Sir Gordon Drummond, who presented Davies's proposal to the British government. After this proposition was turned down, no further attempt was made to bring Welsh settlers into Upper Canada until 1821, when John Mathews, a native of Llansamlet, Wales, received permission to establish his relatives in the province. He finally succeeded in establishing a Welsh community, four years after obtaining his own grant from Colonel Talbot in Southwold Township, situated northwest of the present city of London. When his thirty-four relatives were located on lots 25 miles (40 km) from his homestead, the so-called "Welsh Settlement" came into being.

In 1831, Mathews retired from his farm and went to live in the village of Stamford near Queenston. Here he came into contact with many other Welsh immigrants, some of whom he persuaded to take up land beside his settlers in the adjoining townships. As it grew, the Welsh Settlement became well known throughout Upper Canada, with the result that Welsh immigrants arriving in Montreal and Toronto often heard of it and chose to make it their home. Before 1850, a total of 385 Welsh settlers had located in the area. By this time, however, all of the available land in the settlement had been occupied. Consequently, young people growing up in the 1860s had to look elsewhere for land. By the end of the century, many young Welsh were going to the west, which had recently been opened to settlement.

The Welsh Settlement, which had become one of the most prosperous farming communities in Canada by the opening of the twentieth century, managed to retain its identity for more than a half century thanks to the role played by the church in the community. As long as the church was the centre of activity and Welshmen occupied its pulpit, the Welsh characteristics of the settlement persisted. These were rapidly lost, however, following the retirement in 1875 of the last Welsh minister. Since then the Settlement has been completely integrated into the fabric of Canadian life.

The second recorded group migration of Welsh to Canada was triggered by the discovery of gold in British Columbia's Cariboo country in 1858. Welshmen in both Wales and the United States caught the fever and emigrated to the province. Some from Aberdare, Wales, for instance, even auctioned their possessions to make the trip. A handbook on British Columbia was put on the market and Liverpool emigration agents, who catered to the Welsh, offered passage to the emigrants. So contagious was the fever that by 1862 one in three of the working population of Rhymney, Wales, was said to be keen on emigrating.

The true gold rush to the Cariboo region was short lived, however, because surface mining was soon superseded by deep diggings for which large capital expenditures were necessary. And, as in all gold rushes, more were ruined than rewarded for their efforts. Still, many of those Welshmen who sought gold and failed stayed on to form the nucleus of a permanent settlement. Some, because of the skills they had acquired in the mines back home, even went to work for the mining companies that replaced the casual, independent prospectors.

The third group immigration of Welsh to Canada occurred in 1902 when 234 Welsh, who had been living in Patagonia, a region in Argentina, South America, journeyed to Bangor, Saskatchewan. Patagonia had been incorporated into Argentina in 1881 and the settlers were obliged to become Argentinian citizens. The Welsh now had to pay taxes and submit to compulsory military service. When this situation was aggravated by the damage inflicted by a series of floods on the local economy, many decided to seek a new home elsewhere. The choice of the site in Saskatchewan was doubtless prompted by the fact that a Welshman, Evan Jenkins, who had formerly lived in Patagonia, had taken up residence in the Bangor area.

At the time of the 1971 census, there were 74,415 people of Welsh origin in Canada, considerably fewer than the 143,942 people of Welsh origin recorded in the 1961 census. Obviously, significant numbers of persons reported in the Welsh category in 1961 must have been reported as English in 1971. That same year the largest number of people of Welsh origin were shown as living in Ontario (29,070). British Columbia had the second largest number (17,300), followed by Alberta (10,625), Manitoba (4,680), Saskatchewan (4,130), Quebec (2,820), and fewer than 6,000 in the Atlantic Provinces combined. Those in

Quebec live mainly in the immediate vicinity of Montreal, while those in Ontario are mainly in the southwestern part of the province and in Toronto.

One of the cherished traditional Welsh festivals is the *Gymanfa Ganu*, a song festival which is staged at the local, provincial, national and international levels. Another festival participated in by the Canadian Welsh is the *eisteddfod*, a festival of music and poetry. Churches, often named after St. David, the patron saint of Wales, play an important part in preserving the Welsh culture. A good example of this is the Dewi Sant United Church on Melrose Ave. in Toronto, which has a Welsh-speaking minister, conducts Welsh-language classes, and forms one of the strongest bastions of Welsh culture in Canada today. The St. David's Society, a Welsh cultural club located in centres across Canada, is also instrumental in preserving the Welsh culture. In addition, there are Welsh societies in Toronto, Ottawa and Montreal, which also have Welsh choirs.

The Welsh are an old group in Canada, and they helped to settle the country in the early years of our land. They are currently faced with the problem of loss of identity due to their cultural closeness to the English. They are, however, managing to keep the culture alive, and on St. David's Day, March 1, Canadians of Welsh origin celebrate their heritage.

# West Indians (Caribbeans)

*See also: Barbadians, Haitians, Jamaicans, Trinidad and Tobago*

CANADIANS OF WEST INDIAN, or Caribbean, origin come largely from the former British West Indies, which comprised those islands of the Antilles in the Caribbean Sea whose major colonizers were the British. Guyana (formerly British Guiana) on the mainland of South America has a cultural tradition similar to that of the former British West Indies. All the islands in the English-speaking archipelago, including Antigua, Grenada, Barbados, Jamaica, Trinidad and Tobago, Montserrat, St. Lucia, St. Kitts-Nevis, and St. Vincent are members of the British Commonwealth, although not all have maintained the British sovereign as head of state. In addition to sharing a similar history and political, economic and social institutions, they also have a similar climate and vegetation. Consequently, the cultural characteristics and experiences of their racially diverse people are more or less the same throughout. Although the name "West Indian" has historically been used to describe this community, today many "West Indians" refer to themselves as "Caribbeans".

The recorded history of the British West Indies and Guyana began with the arrival of Columbus in 1492. This is not to ignore the existence of an indigenous sedentary agricultural people, the Caribs and the Arawak Indians, who were the original natives of the islands. These people, kin of the North American Indian, were almost totally eliminated as a group under the harsh system of forced labour imposed on them by Spanish colonizers. Generally, Spanish culture and influence was relatively marginal, even though Spain ruled Jamaica for over 150 years and Trinidad for three centuries. Once the British established their ascendancy over the Spaniards, the islands began to develop as agricultural colonies.

The largest group of people in the West Indies, the Africans, were brought as slave labour to work on the sugar plantations. This was started by the Spaniards, and between 1680 and 1786 over two million slaves were imported into the area. It is at this time that the Jamaican dialect began to evolve and many of the typical Jamaican dishes became a major item of diet. The dialect of the smaller islands is a mixture of French, Spanish and English. While Barbados and Jamaica were firmly under British influence for most of the colonial period, Dominica, Grenada, St. Lucia and St. Vincent were gained from France and Trinidad from Spain during the second half of the eighteenth century.

The Chinese and East Indian presence dates from the abolition of slavery in 1838. Trinidad and Guyana were the first colonies to which the British imported significant numbers of indentured labour from India and China, to work the sugar plantations abandoned by the newly freed slaves. This importation continued for eighty years, in time completely changing the structure and composition of the population in Guyana and Trinidad. Today, the population structure of Trinidad is almost equally divided between Blacks and East Indians. In Guyana, there are more East Indians than Blacks in the popula-

tion. After the East Indians had completed their periods of indenture they were given land to cultivate, allowing for the development of a class of small landholders cultivating sugar cane. In other islands, Blacks who were small landholders specialized in producing a variety of cash crops for the local markets.

The Chinese left the land immediately after their indentureship was served and began to set up small businesses. They soon emerged as the successful trading class throughout the larger islands of the West Indies. In Guyana, the population was further diversified by the immigration of a few thousand Portuguese from Madeira. Many descendants of these people are now living in Canada.

The British remained the group of dominant influence even though many of them retired to England and administered their plantations through managers. They set the pattern for all to emulate. Racial origin was also important in determining social status, although the ramifications of this varied from one island to the next. Although there was no legal discrimination against the large majority of the people of African descent, there was a bias built into the social structure of the societies of the British West Indies in favour of the planters and the colonial administrators, and this worked against the aspirations of the people of African descent.

West Indians are accustomed to striving for better standards of living. The educational system through which most of the West Indian immigrants now living in Canada passed was similar to that of the average English child in Britain and all the school leaving examinations at the secondary school level were set and marked by British examination boards. Most immigrants, therefore, were predisposed favourably towards Britain, Canada and the United States, and there was very little trauma accompanying the decision to emigrate. The only possible exceptions to this generalization were perhaps those who left Guyana and Jamaica, because of the fundamental changes in the political and economic life of these countries.

Prior to 1966, there were many West Indians studying in Canada, especially students from Trinidad. Many of them applied for landed immigrant status after graduation. During the peak years of emigration, St. Vincent and Grenada lost 884 and 751 emigrants to Canada respectively. There were few professionals among these emigrants; the majority were confined to the service and recreation categories as well as clerical and skilled groups.

Over 130,660 West Indians have emigrated to Canada since 1946. This is a conservative estimate, for it does not include those West Indians who have come to Canada from other parts of the world outside the Caribbean. Most of these immigrants have arrived within the past twenty years. At least 85 per cent have settled in Ontario, and the large majority of these in an urban environment, especially Toronto.

Since 1970 there have been small areas of concentrated West Indian settlement in Toronto, but on the whole settlement patterns have been influenced by income, and consequently the majority are scattered across the city.

West Indians, like many recent immigrants, gather with their compatriots for social occasions. In each city where there has been a significant West Indian community, a variety of island-centred organizations have sprung up to cope with settlement problems and to meet a variety of socio-cultural needs. These clubs also help to overcome the sense of isolation which many West Indians feel when entering a society which is different from the one to which they have been accustomed. There are a number of organizations which serve both Canadians of West Indian descent and other Black Canadians. The National Black Coalition attempts to be an umbrella organization tying together the various Black organizations across Canada and presenting a national focus and concern.

Of a more particular nature are the various organizations established to meet the specific needs of the Caribbean group in Canada. These organizations originally appeared on the university campuses. A conference on West Indian affairs was held for the first time in October, 1965, on the campus of Sir George Williams University in Montreal. Listed among its sponsors were the West Indian Societies of Sir George Williams University, McGill University, Macdonald College, Acadia University, the University of Toronto and Queen's University, as well as the Jamaica Association of Montreal, the Negro Citizenship Association of Montreal, the Trinidad and Tobago Association, the Jamaica-Canadian Association of Toronto, the Ibo, Toronto, and the Inter-Caribbean Association of Toronto.

The Jamaica Association of Montreal, the Trinidad and Tobago Association of Montreal and the Jamaica-Canadian Association of Toronto direct their energies towards alleviating the daily problems of West Indian immigrants in Toronto. The declared purpose of the Jamaica Association of Montreal is to create a better understanding among Jamaicans in that city, to protect and promote the common interests of its members, and to take an active interest in the affairs of Quebec. The Jamaica-Canadian Association of Toronto has as its aims to ease the adjustments of settlement for its members and to acquaint Canadians with

Jamaica's culture and way of life. The Trinidad and Tobago Association is more concerned with promoting Caribbean culture in Canada.

Prior to 1969, Caribbeans abroad relied on the overseas editions of the various West Indian newspapers for information about each other and about the home country. *Contrast* and *The Islander*, now amalgamated, were two weekly newspapers published in Canada. While *Contrast* concentrated on the general Black community in Canada, *The Islander* combined reporting on the social and political developments in the home country with local news. *Spear, Caribbean Dialogue* and *Talking Drums* were other publications which emanated from the Black community and which had a wide circulation among Caribbeans.

While West Indians have been present in Canada for many generations, the largest number of them have come as students, studying at Canadian universities. Their contributions to the culture of Canada, adding their rich heritage and customs to the Canadian social scene, and the Caribbean presence in the professions, have combined to make this group a very active one in Canadian life.

# Bibliography

Alberta Department of Education. *A Bibliography of Materials for and About Native People*. Edmonton, 1970.

Allen, G.P. *Days to Remember: Observances of significance in our multicultural society*. Multicultural Development Branch, Ontario Ministry of Culture and Recreation, Toronto, 1977.

Anderson, Grace M. and David Higgs. *A Future to Inherit: Portuguese Communities in Canada*. Toronto: McClelland and Stewart, 1976.

Bailey, Leuba, ed. *The Immigrant Experience*. Toronto, Macmillan, 1975.

Blizzard, F.H. *West Indians in Canada: A Selective Annotated Bibliography*. Guelph, University of Guelph Library, Bibliographic Series, No. 1, 1970.

British Columbia Centennial Committee. *Ethnic Groups in British Columbia*. A selected bibliography. Victoria, 1957.

Burnet, Jean R. *Ethnic Groups in Upper Canada*. Ontario Historical Society Research Publication No. 1, 1972.

Canada. Citizenship Branch. *The Canadian Family Tree*. Ottawa, Queen's Printer, 1967.

————.Department of Citizenship and Immigration. *Citizenship, Immigration and Ethnic Groups in Canada*. A Bibliography of Research. 3 vols. Ottawa, 1959–68.

————.Department of Citizenship and Immigration. *Notes on the Canadian Family Tree*. Ottawa, Queen's Printer, 1960.

————.Department of Indian Affairs and Northern Development. *The Canadian Indian*. Ottawa, Queen's Printer, 1966.

————.Department of Manpower and Immigration. *Canadian Immigration and Population Study*. "Green Paper", 4 vols. Ottawa, Information Canada, 1974.

————.Secretary of State Library. *Canadian Ethnic Groups Bibliography*. Ottawa, 1974.

*Canadian Ethnic Studies/Etudes Ethniques au Canada*, II (1), June, 1970. The University of Calgary. Bulletin of the Research Centre for Canadian Ethnic Studies.

*Communiqué: Canadian Studies*. Association of Canadian Community Colleges. "Multiculturalism". Vol. III, October 1, 1976.

Dawson, Carl. A. *Group Settlement: Ethnic Communities in Western Canada*. Toronto, Macmillan, 1936.

Dawson, Carl A. and E.R. Young. *Pioneering in the Prairie Provinces: The Social Side of the Settlement Process*. Toronto, Macmillan, 1940.

Dyck, Ruth. "Ethnic Folklore in Canada: A Preliminary Survey", in *Canadian Ethnic Studies*, VII (2), 90–101.

England, Robert. *The Central European Immigrant in Canada*. Toronto, Macmillan, 1929.

Gibbon, John Murray. *Canadian Mosaic.* Toronto, n.p., 1938.

Gregorovich, Andrew. *Canadian Ethnic Groups Bibliography.* Toronto, Department of the Provincial Secretary and Citizenship, 1972.

Harney R. and H. Troper. *Immigrants—A Portrait of the Urban Experience, 1890–1930.* Toronto, Van Nostrand, 1975.

Hawkins, Freda. *Canada and Immigration.* Montreal, McGill-Queen's University Press, 1972.

Kerri, James N. *American Indians: A Bibliography of Contemporary Studies and Urban Research.* Ottawa, Canadian Citizenship Branch, Department of the Secretary of State. 1972.

McLeod, Keith A. *Resource List of Multi-Media Materials and Multiculturalism.* Toronto, Faculty of Education, University of Toronto, 1974.

Minorités Ethniques à Québec. Association Inuksiutut Katimajiit (Université Laval) Québec, 1977.

Morton, A.S. *A History of Prairie Settlement.* Toronto, Macmillan, 1938.

Norris, John. *Strangers Entertained: A History of the Ethnic Groups of British Columbia.* Vancouver, Evergreen Press, 1971.

Palmer, Howard. *Immigration and the Rise of Multiculturalism.* Toronto, Copp Clark, 1975.

Patterson, E.P. II. *The Canadian Indian: A History Since 1500*, Don Mills, Collier-MacMillan, 1972.

Radecki, Henry and Benedykt Heydenkorn. *A Member of a Distinguished Family: The Polish Group in Canada.* Toronto, McClelland and Stewart, 1976.

Reid, Stanford, ed. *The Scottish Tradition in Canada.* Toronto, McClelland and Stewart, 1976.

Symons, T.H.B. *To Know Ourselves: The Report of the Commission on Canadian Studies.* Vol. I, II. Ottawa, Association of Universities and Colleges of Canada, 1975.

Troper, H. *Only Farmers Need Apply: Official Canadian Government Encouragement of Immigration from the United States.* Toronto, Griffin House, 1972.

Winks, Robin W. *The Blacks in Canada.* Montreal, McGill-Queen's University Press, 1971.

Woodsworth, J.S. *Strangers within our Gates.* Toronto, Missionary Society for the Methodist Church, Canada, 1909.

# Index

Hamilton (continued)
148, 149; Lithuanians in, 154, 155;
Macedonians in, 157; Maltese in 160;
Poles in, 177, 179, 180; Slovaks in, 202;
Ukrainians in, 225
Hamilton Inlet, 180
Hanley (Saskatchewan), 49, 170
Hansen, Niels M., 59
Hart, Aaron Philip, 140
Hart, Ezekiel, 141
Hart, Samuel, 141
Hearne, Samuel, 71
Heggtviet, Anne, 174
Helgesen, Hans, 171
Heller, Captain, 57
Henday, Anthony, 71
Henry, Alexander, 194
Hillsborough Township (New Brunswick),
90
Hindus, Indian, 114; Indo-Fijian, 79;
Malaysian, 158; Ugandan Asian, 223
Holland, 29, 30, 33, 62
Holland Marsh (Ontario), 63, 66
Hong Kong, 45, 112
Hudson, Henry, 71
Hudson's Bay Company, 91-92, 162, 163,
169, 192, 195
Hungary, 25, 52, 102, 143. *See also*
Austria-Hungary
Hungarian Canadian Cultural Centre,
105
Hungarian Historical Museum of
Toronto, 105
Hungarian Presbyterian Church of
Canada, 103
Hungarian School Board, 103-04
Hungarian Revolution, 143, 206
Hun's Valley (Manitoba), 201, 203
Huntley Township (Ontario), 125
Huré, Pierre, 29
Huron County (Ontario), 91, 193
Hus, Jan, 52
Hutterites, 10, 92, 93

Iceland, 106, 168
Idaho, 11
Igloolik, 121
Ile Royale, 86
Ile Saint-Jean, 86
Illinois, 61
Illyrians, 8
Immigration policies and legislation:
Chinese Immigration Act (1923), 44,
45; "continuous voyage" regulation,
112; Dominion Land Act (1872), 91; to
eliminate discrimination, 99;
"Favoured Nation" status, 92;
favouring European immigrants, 134;
free land incentive, 11, 25, 30, 58, 61-62,
75, 81, 142; to populate Prairies, 58;

post-Depression restrictions, 81;
post-First World War restrictions, 143;
in Quebec, 87; restricting Chinese
immigration, 44, 45; restricting East
Asian immigration, 174; restricting
German immigration, 92-93; of Sir
Clifford Sifton, 12, 26, 91, 116, 201, 217;
for war brides, 63
India, 78, 111, 112, 113, 219, 234
Indian Act, 14, 15, 18, 161
Indian Affairs and Northern
Development, Department of, 15-16
Indo-Fijians, 78-79
Indonesia, 63, 115
Insinger, Robert, 66
International Institute of Toronto, 182,
219
Inuit Cultural Institute, 121
Inuit Development Corporation, 121
Inverness (Cape Breton Island), 32
Iowa, 61, 62
Iran, 122
Iraq, 19, 22
Ireland, 123, 124
Iroquois, 86, 128
Islamic Centre of Quebec, 69
Islamic centres, 175; in Montreal, 20, 69;
in Ottawa, 20; in Toronto, 69; in
Vancouver, 20, 69
Island of St. John, 72
Israel, 127
Italy, 8, 9, 39, 129, 130

Jamaica, 34, 133, 134, 233, 234, 235
James, Thomas, 71
James Bay project, 18, 165
Japan, 135-136, 146
Japanese Canadian Cultural Centre, 140
Jenkins, Evan, 232
Johnston, Sir John, 192
Joliette (Quebec), 153
Jonasson, Sigtryggur, 106-107
Jordan, 19
Journals. *See* Newspapers and journals
Junkins (Alberta), 35

Kandahar (Saskatchewan), 108
Kaslo (British Columbia), 138
Kastrioti, Gjerj, 8
Keewatin, District of, 107, 117, 120
Kelsey, Henry, 71
Kenaston (Saskatchewan), 49
Kenora (Ontario), 53, 213
Kent County (Ontario), 31
King, William Lyon Mackenzie, 195
**Kingston** (Ontario), Austrians in, 27, 28;
Blacks in, 34; Byelorussian conference
in, 41; Czechs in, 52; Welsh in, 231
Kinmount (Ontario), 107
Kirke, Sir David, 72

Kirkland Lake (Ontario), 82, 83, 85, 103,
206
**Kitchener** (Ontario), Belgians in, 31;
Czechs in, 55; Germans in, 91;
Hungarians in, 102, 105; Poles in, 178,
179; Roumanians in, 185
Kootenay (British Columbia), 188
Korea, 145, 146
Korean Catholic Community Centre, 147
Korean Human Rights Council, 147
Korean United Church, 146, 147
Korean War, 145-46
Kossuth House, 105
Krieghoff, Cornelius, 66
Kuomintang, 45
Kurikka, Matti, 84
Kuwait, 19

Labelle, Curé, 31
Labelle County (Quebec), 32
Labourers International Union, 131
Labrador, 71, 106; Inuit in, 116, 117, 118,
120
Lac-du-Bonnet (Manitoba), 148
Ladner (British Columbia), 49
Ladysmith (British Columbia), 83
Laestadius, Lars, 83
Lanark County (Ontario), 193
Lancaster (Ontario), 141
La Ronge Industries, 17
Larsen, Henry A., 174
Latvia, 38, 143, 147-148
Leask (Saskatchewan), 49
Lebanon, 22, 151, 152
Lemon Creek (British Columbia), 138
Lethbridge (Alberta), 52, 75, 130, 198, 201
Lettonia (Manitoba), 148
Libau (Manitoba), 148
Linda River, 75
Lisbon, 181
Lithuania, 38, 143, 153, 175
Lithuania House, 155
Lloydminster (Saskatchewan), 143
Local Initiatives Program, 219
Loch Lomond (New Brunswick), 34
**London** (Ontario), Arabs in, 20; Blacks in,
34; Danes in, 57; Greeks in, 95;
Hungarians in, 102, 103, 104, 105;
Koreans in, 146; Lebanese in, 152;
Lithuanians in, 154; Maltese in, 160;
Welsh in, 231
Long Lake (Ontario), 82
Lower Canada, 11, 72, 74; French in, 87;
Germans in, 90; Loyalists in, 72; Scots
in, 192; Welsh in, 230
Louisbourg, 29, 71-72, 86, 89, 215
Louisiana, 86
Loyalists, 15, 33, 61, 72-73, 74, 90, 95, 125,
192, 230
Lundar (Manitoba), 109

Renfrew County (Ontario), 91, 175
Reserve Mines (Nova Scotia), 50
Revelstoke (British Columbia), 212
Reymont, Wladyslaw, 179
Rhode Island, 140
Richelieu River, 90, 128
Richelieu Valley (Quebec), 32
Richmond (British Columbia), 83, 114
Rideau Canal, 125
Riel, Louis, 163-164
Riel Rebellion (1884), 164
Riverton, (Manitoba), 107
Robinson, John Beverley, 125
Robinson, Peter, 125
Roman Catholics, Albanian, 8, 9; Armenian, 22; Byelorussian, 40; Chilean, 42; Croatian, 50-51; Czech, 54; Dutch, 65; Egyptian, 69; Filipino, 80; French, 30; German, 89, 90, 93; Hungarian, 102, 103; Irish, 124, 126; Korean, 146; Latvian, 148; Lithuanian, 154, 155, 156; Maltese, 159; Métis, 162; Polish, 177; Portuguese, 182-83; Roumanian, 185; Russian, 189; Scottish, 191; Slovak, 203, 204, Slovene, 206-207; Syrian, 69; Trinidadian, 220; from Tobago, 220; Ukrainian, 225, 226 Uruguayan, 228; Walloon, 29, 30
Rosseau (Ontario), 107
Roumania, 25, 92, 95, 142, 143, 224
Roumanian Orthodox Church, 185
Round Lake (Saskatchewan), 212
Rouyn-Noranda (Quebec), 55
Royal Canadian Legion, 56, 179, 189
Rupert's Land, 71, 72, 163
Russia, 38, 88, 142, 147, 145
Russian Orthodox Church, 188-89, 225
Russian Revolution, 39
Ruthenians, 26

Saigon, 229
St. Boniface (Manitoba), 31, 86
**St. Catharines** (Ontario), 75; Armenians in, 22, 23; Blacks in, 34; Georgians in, 89; Hungarians in, 102; Italians in, 130; Lithuanians in, 154; Maltese in, 159; Slovaks in, 202; Ukrainians in, 225
St. Jerome (Quebec), 152
Saint John (New Brunswick), 152
St. Kitts-Nevis, 233
St. Lucia, 233, 234
St. Thomas (Ontario), 125, 160
St. Vincent, 233, 234, 235
Salteaux, 162
Sanden (British Columbia), 138
San Francisco, 46
**Saskatchewan,** Amerindians in, 17; Austrians in, 27; Blacks in, 35; Byelorussians in, 40; Chileans in, 42;

Croatians in, 49; Czechs in, 54; Danes in, 58, 59; Doukhobors in, 185-87, 190; Dutch in, 64; Estonians in, 75; Germans in, 92; Greeks in, 95; Métis in, 163, 164, 165, 166; Norwegians in, 169, 170; Roumanians in, 184; Serbians in, 198, 199, 200; Slovenes in, 206; Swedes in, 211; Ukrainians in, 225, 227; Welsh in, 20, 232
Saskatchewan Bible Institute, 172
Saskatoon, 95, 188, 225, 227
Saudi Arabia, 19
Saugstad, Pastor C., 171
Sault Ste. Marie (Ontario), 49, 50, 83, 129, 130
Schikluna, Lewis, 159
Schumacher (Ontario), 49, 50
Scotland, 153
Scott, Duncan Campbell, 196
Second World War, 26; effect upon Belgian immigration, 31; effect upon Byelorussian immigration, 39; effect upon Canadian economy, 12; Chinese immigrants in, 45; Czech immigrants in, 55; effect upon Dutch immigration, 63; effect upon Italian immigration, 129-130; effect upon Latvian immigration, 148; effect upon Ukrainian immigration, 224
Selkirk (Manitoba), 107, 109, 110
Selkirk, Lord, 169, 192, 216, 223
Semple, Robert, 163
Sept Iles (Quebec), 130
Serbia, 48, 156
Serbian Orthodox Church, 200
Service, Robert W., 196
Seven Oaks Massacre, 163, 216
Shanghai, 46, 112
Shelburne (Nova Scotia), 34, 36
Sherbrooke (Quebec), 152
Shoal Lake (Manitoba), 107
Siberia, 116, 223
Sierra Leone, 33, 34
Sifton (Saskatchewan), 25
Sifton, Sir Clifford, 12, 26, 91, 176, 201, 207
Sikhs, Indian, 111-112, 113-114; Ugandan Asian, 223
Silesia, 52
Simays, E., 29
Simcoe, John Graves, 34, 90, 230, 231
Simon Gregorcic Theatre, 207
Sinclair, A. MacLean, 197
Singapore, 46, 158
Sino-Japanese War, 45
Sioux, 18
Six Nation Indians, 18
Slocan (British Columbia), 138
Slovakia, 202
Slovak Lutheran Evangelical Church, 203

Slovenia, 48
"Slutsak" resort (Ontario), 41
Social Credit Party, 174, 215
Societies. *See* Associations
Society of Canada, 140
Sointula community, 83, 84, 85
Sokol movement, 55
Sorel (Quebec), 90
South Africa, 113
South America, 20, 129, 146
South Dakota, 170
Soviet Union, 21, 39, 75-76, 84, 89, 148, 154, 186, 224, 225
Spain, 20, 99, 234
Spanish Civil War, 81, 187
Special Chilean Movement, 42, 70
Sri Lanka, 209, 210
Stamford (Ontario), 231-232
Standing Buffalo reserve (Saskatchewan), 18
Stankovic, Peter, 51
Stettler (Alberta), 75
Stockholm (Saskatchewan), 212
Stony Indians, 19
Stormont County (Ontario), 90
Strachan, Bishop John, 195, 196
**Sudbury** (Ontario), Arabs in, 20; Argentinians in, 20; Byelorussians in, 40; Chileans in, 42; Ecuadorians in, 66; Finns in, 82, 83, 84, 85; Italians in, 130; Lithuanians in, 154; Uruguayans in, 229
Suez Crisis, 74, 143, 231
Surrey (British Columbia), 83
Swan Lake (Manitoba), 31, 107
Sweden, 75, 76, 77, 153
Swedish Mission Covenant Church, 214
Sydney (Nova Scotia), 50, 152
Sydney Mines (Nova Scotia), 153
Sylvan Lake district, 83
Syria, 19, 22
Syrian Orthodox Church, 152

Tahme (British Columbia), 138
Taipei, 46
Talbot, Colonel Thomas, 125, 193, 231
Taqramiut Nipingit, Inc., 121
Tartu College, 77
Television programming, Italian, 132; Maltese, 160
Texas, 13
Thayendanegea, Chief, 15
Theaford marsh (Ontario), 66
Thirteen Colonies, 10, 29, 33, 72, 90
Thorlaksson, the Reverend Pall, 108
**Thunder Bay** (Ontario), Finns in, 82, 83, 84, 85; Italians in, 131; Slovaks in, 202; Ukrainians in, 225. *See also* Fort William
Tibet, 219